Species Domain

スピーシーズドメイン

Presented by
SHUNSUKE NORO

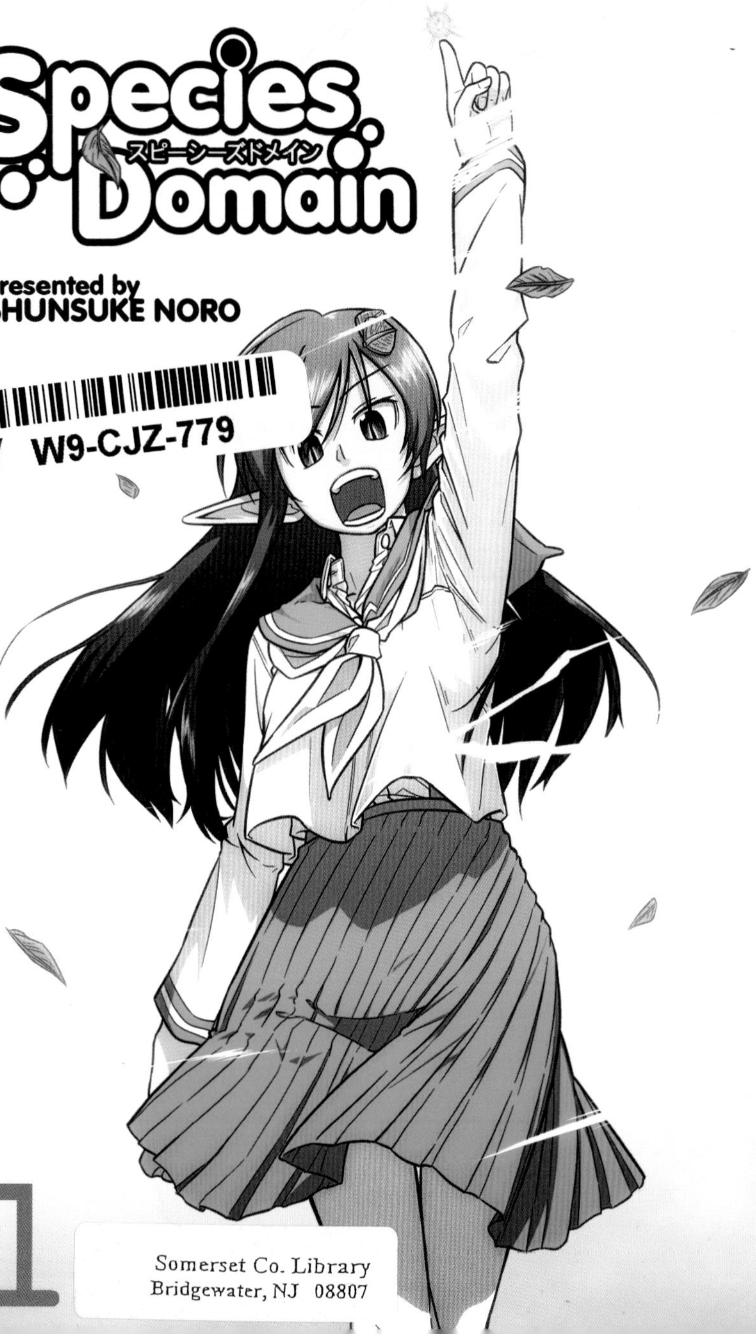

1

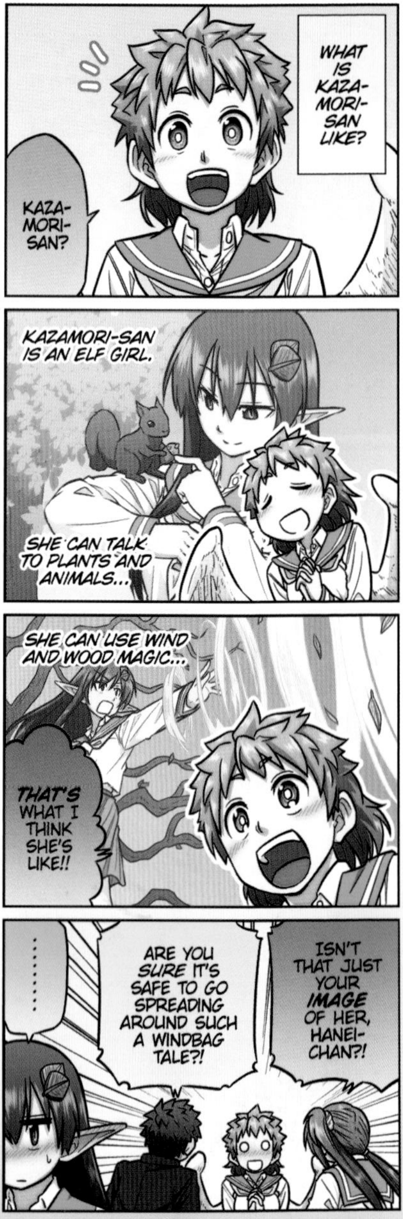
WHAT IS KAZAMORI-SAN LIKE?
KAZAMORI-SAN?
KAZAMORI-SAN IS AN ELF GIRL.
SHE CAN TALK TO PLANTS AND ANIMALS...
SHE CAN USE WIND AND WOOD MAGIC...
THAT'S WHAT I THINK SHE'S LIKE!!
ISN'T THAT JUST YOUR IMAGE OF HER, HANEI-CHAN?!
ARE YOU SURE IT'S SAFE TO GO SPREADING AROUND SUCH A WINDBAG TALE?!
....

"Windbag Tale": a bit like "Wind Legend," maybe?

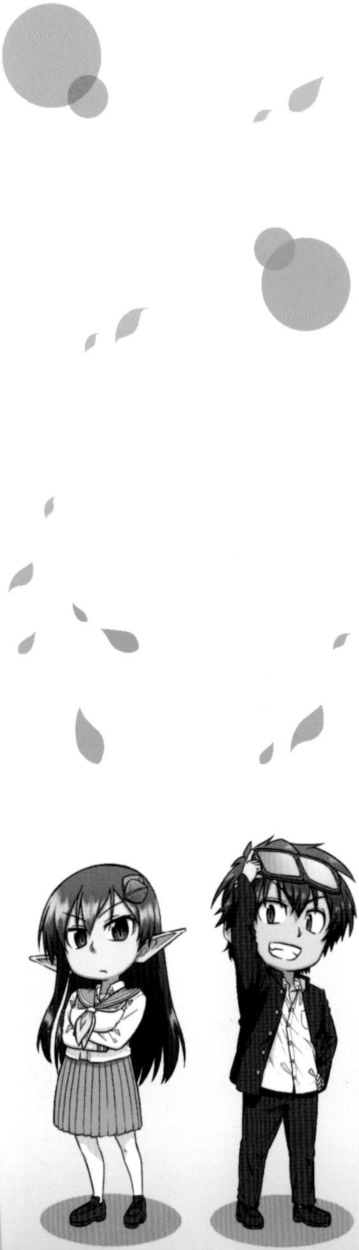

Chapter 1: Kazamori-san the Elf

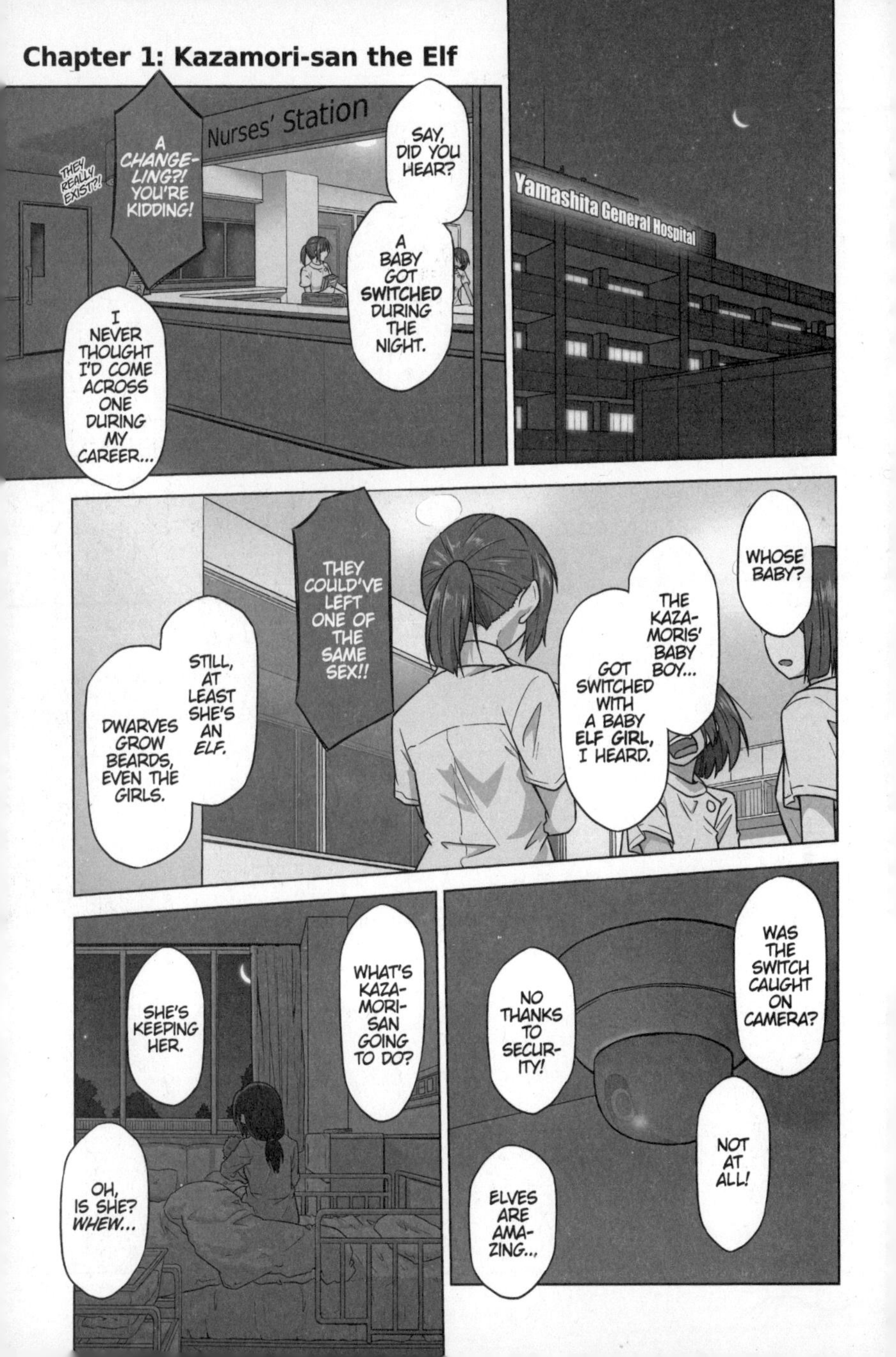
Yamashita General Hospital
Nurses' Station
SAY, DID YOU HEAR?
A BABY GOT SWITCHED DURING THE NIGHT.
A CHANGELING?! YOU'RE KIDDING!
THEY REALLY EXIST?!
I NEVER THOUGHT I'D COME ACROSS ONE DURING MY CAREER...
WHOSE BABY?
THE KAZAMORIS' BABY BOY...
GOT SWITCHED WITH A BABY ELF GIRL, I HEARD.
THEY COULD'VE LEFT ONE OF THE SAME SEX!!
STILL, AT LEAST SHE'S AN ELF.
DWARVES GROW BEARDS, EVEN THE GIRLS.
WAS THE SWITCH CAUGHT ON CAMERA?
NO THANKS TO SECURITY!
NOT AT ALL!
ELVES ARE AMAZING...
WHAT'S KAZAMORI-SAN GOING TO DO?
SHE'S KEEPING HER.
OH, IS SHE? WHEW...

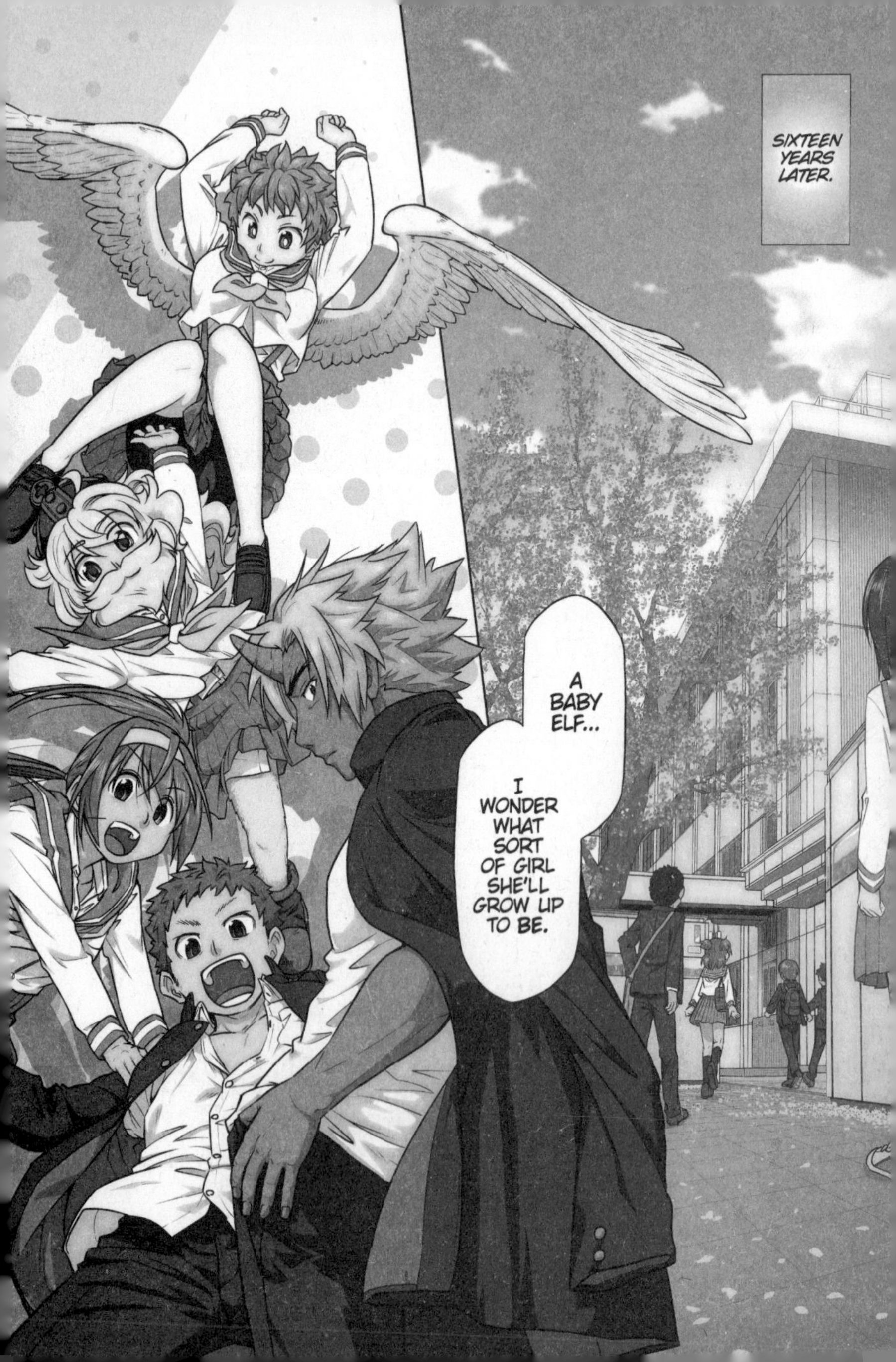
SIXTEEN YEARS LATER.
A BABY ELF...
I WONDER WHAT SORT OF GIRL SHE'LL GROW UP TO BE.

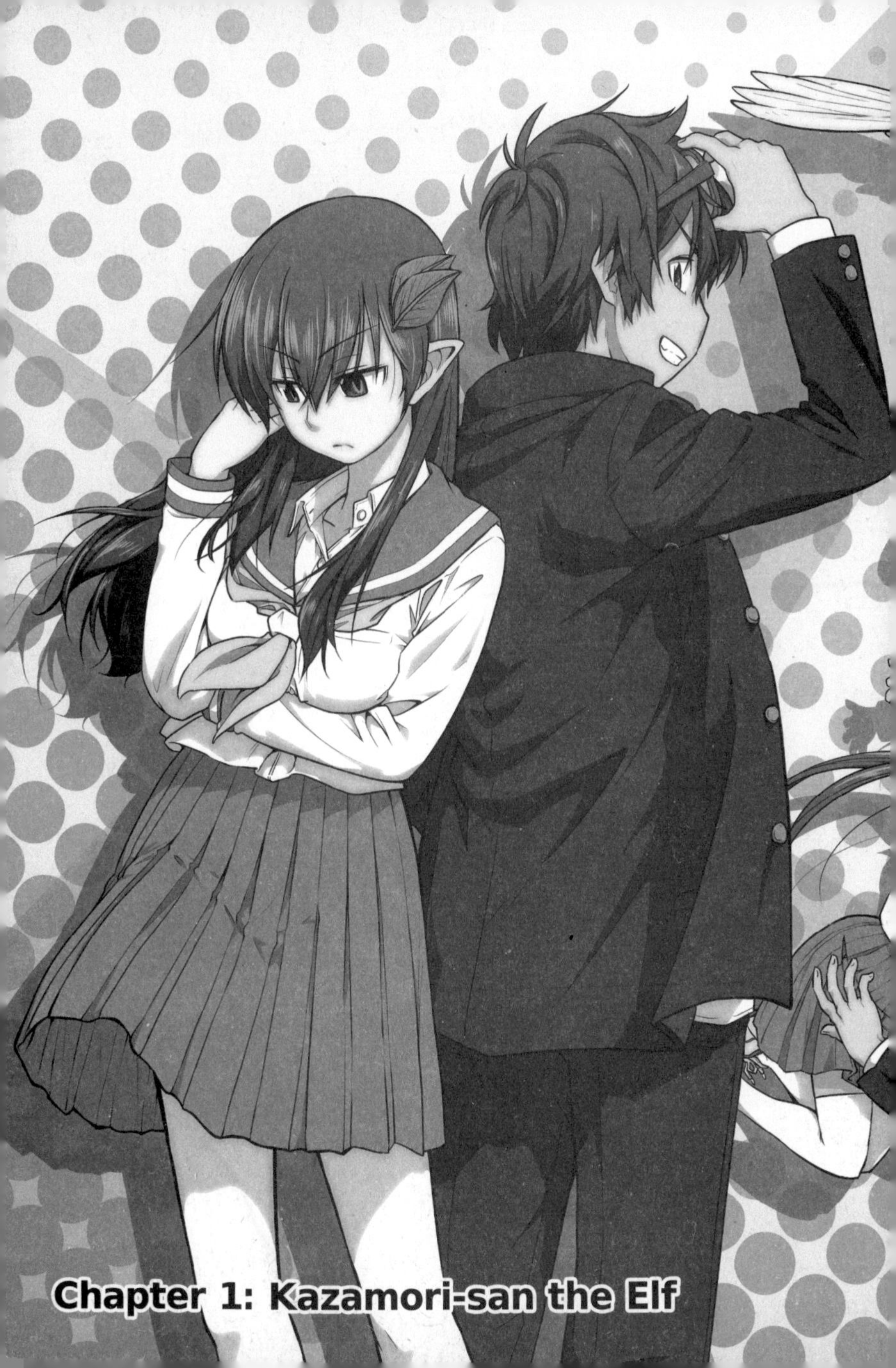

Chapter 1: Kazamori-san the Elf

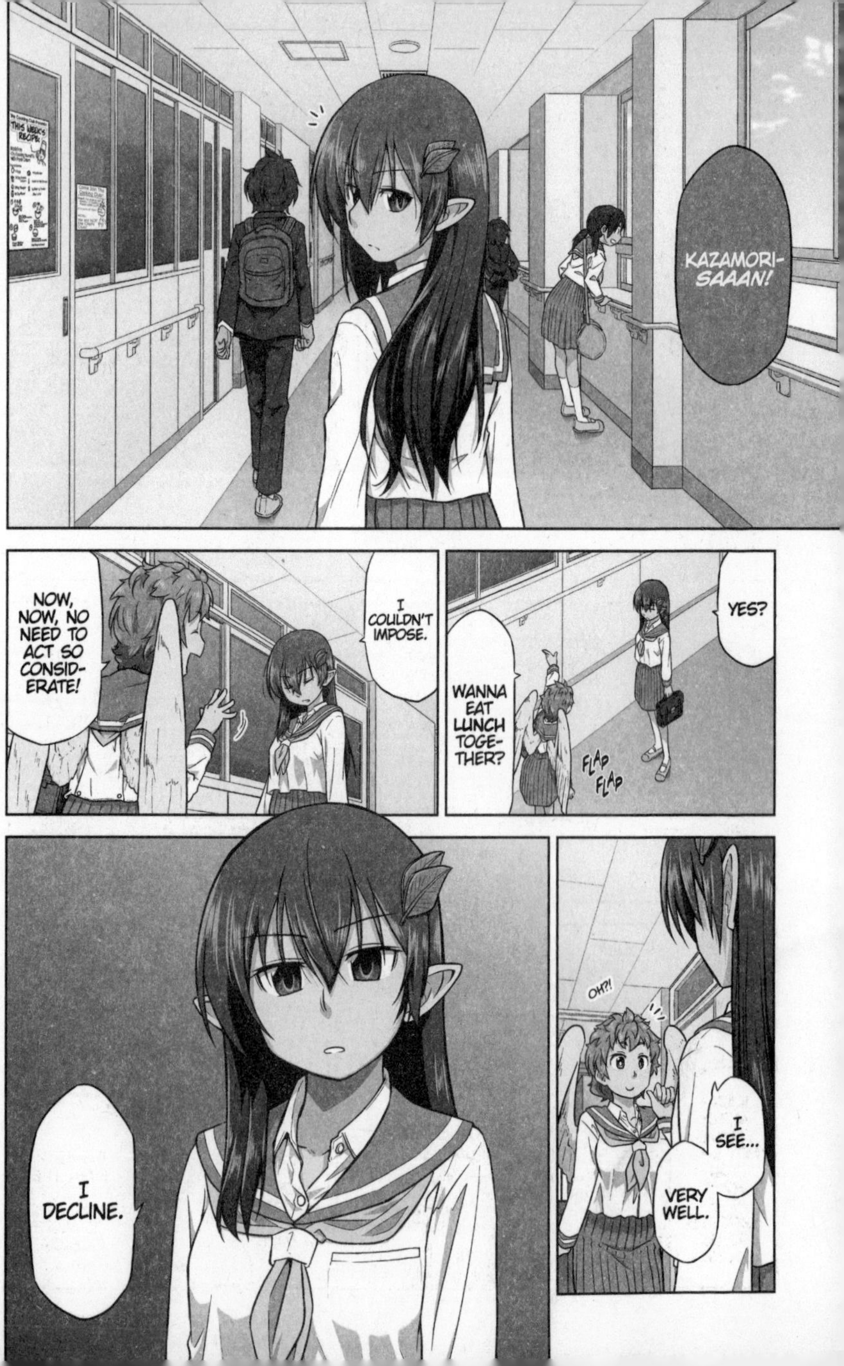
KAZAMORI-SAAAN!
THIS WEEK'S RECIPE:
YES?
WANNA EAT LUNCH TOGETHER?
FLAP FLAP
I COULDN'T IMPOSE.
NOW, NOW, NO NEED TO ACT SO CONSIDERATE!
OH?!
I SEE...
VERY WELL.
I DECLINE.

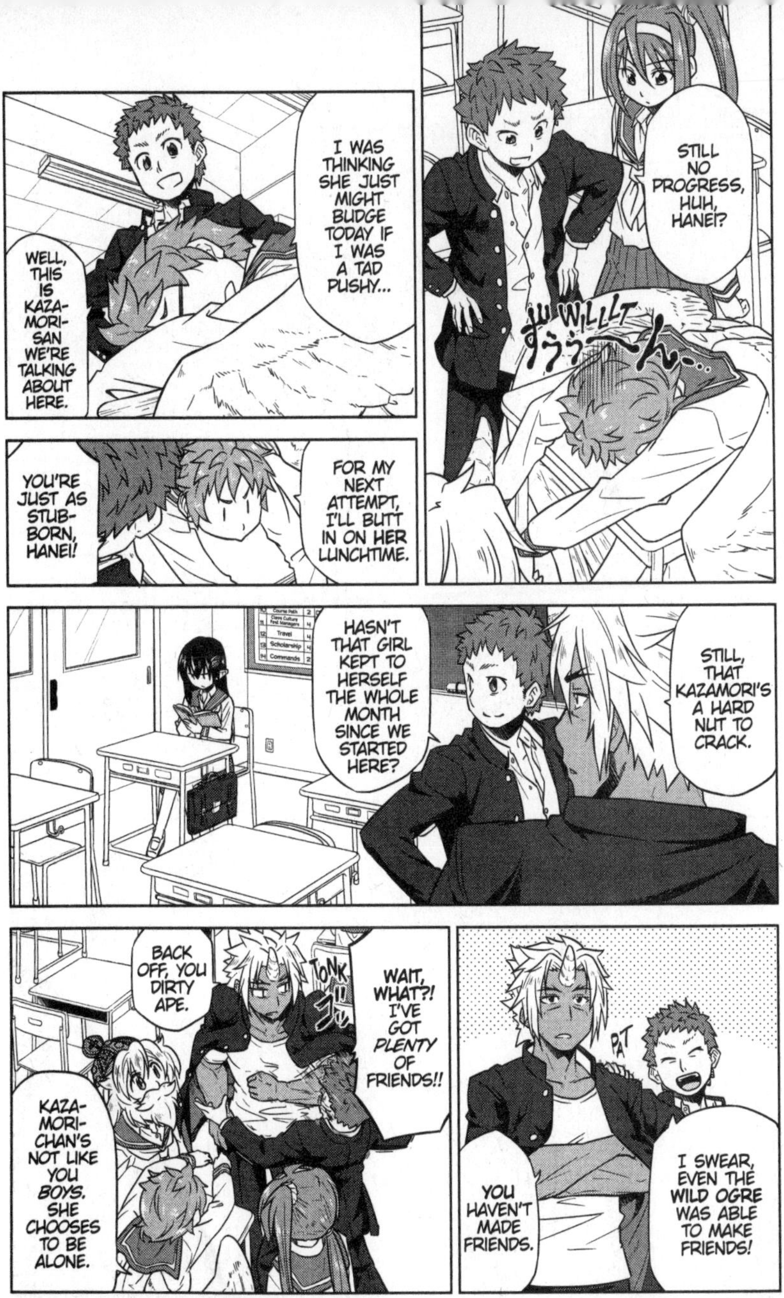
STILL NO PROGRESS, HUH, HANEI?
WILLLT
すぅぅ～ん…
I WAS THINKING SHE JUST MIGHT BUDGE TODAY IF I WAS A TAD PUSHY...
WELL, THIS IS KAZAMORI-SAN WE'RE TALKING ABOUT HERE.
FOR MY NEXT ATTEMPT, I'LL BUTT IN ON HER LUNCHTIME.
YOU'RE JUST AS STUBBORN, HANEI!
STILL, THAT KAZAMORI'S A HARD NUT TO CRACK.
HASN'T THAT GIRL KEPT TO HERSELF THE WHOLE MONTH SINCE WE STARTED HERE?
Course Path
Class Culture Fest Managers
Travel
Scholarship
Commands
I SWEAR, EVEN THE WILD OGRE WAS ABLE TO MAKE FRIENDS!
PAT
YOU HAVEN'T MADE FRIENDS.
WAIT, WHAT?! I'VE GOT PLENTY OF FRIENDS!!
TONK
BACK OFF, YOU DIRTY APE.
KAZAMORI-CHAN'S NOT LIKE YOU BOYS. SHE CHOOSES TO BE ALONE.

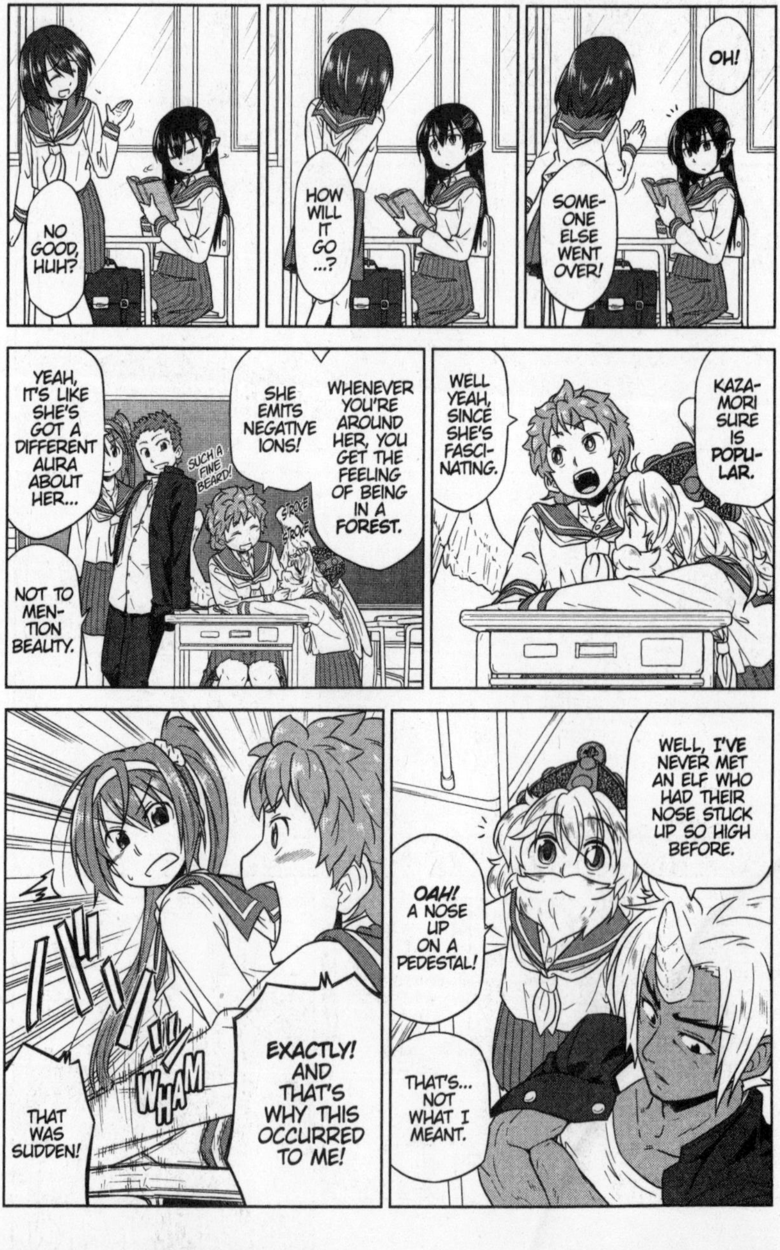
OH!
SOMEONE ELSE WENT OVER!
HOW WILL IT GO ...?
NO GOOD, HUH?
KAZAMORI SURE IS POPULAR.
WELL YEAH, SINCE SHE'S FASCINATING.
WHENEVER YOU'RE AROUND HER, YOU GET THE FEELING OF BEING IN A FOREST.
SHE EMITS NEGATIVE IONS!
YEAH, IT'S LIKE SHE'S GOT A DIFFERENT AURA ABOUT HER...
SUCH A FINE BEARD!
STROKE
STROKE
NOT TO MENTION BEAUTY.
WELL, I'VE NEVER MET AN ELF WHO HAD THEIR NOSE STUCK UP SO HIGH BEFORE.
OAH! A NOSE UP ON A PEDESTAL!
THAT'S... NOT WHAT I MEANT.
EXACTLY! AND THAT'S WHY THIS OCCURRED TO ME!
WHAM
THAT WAS SUDDEN!

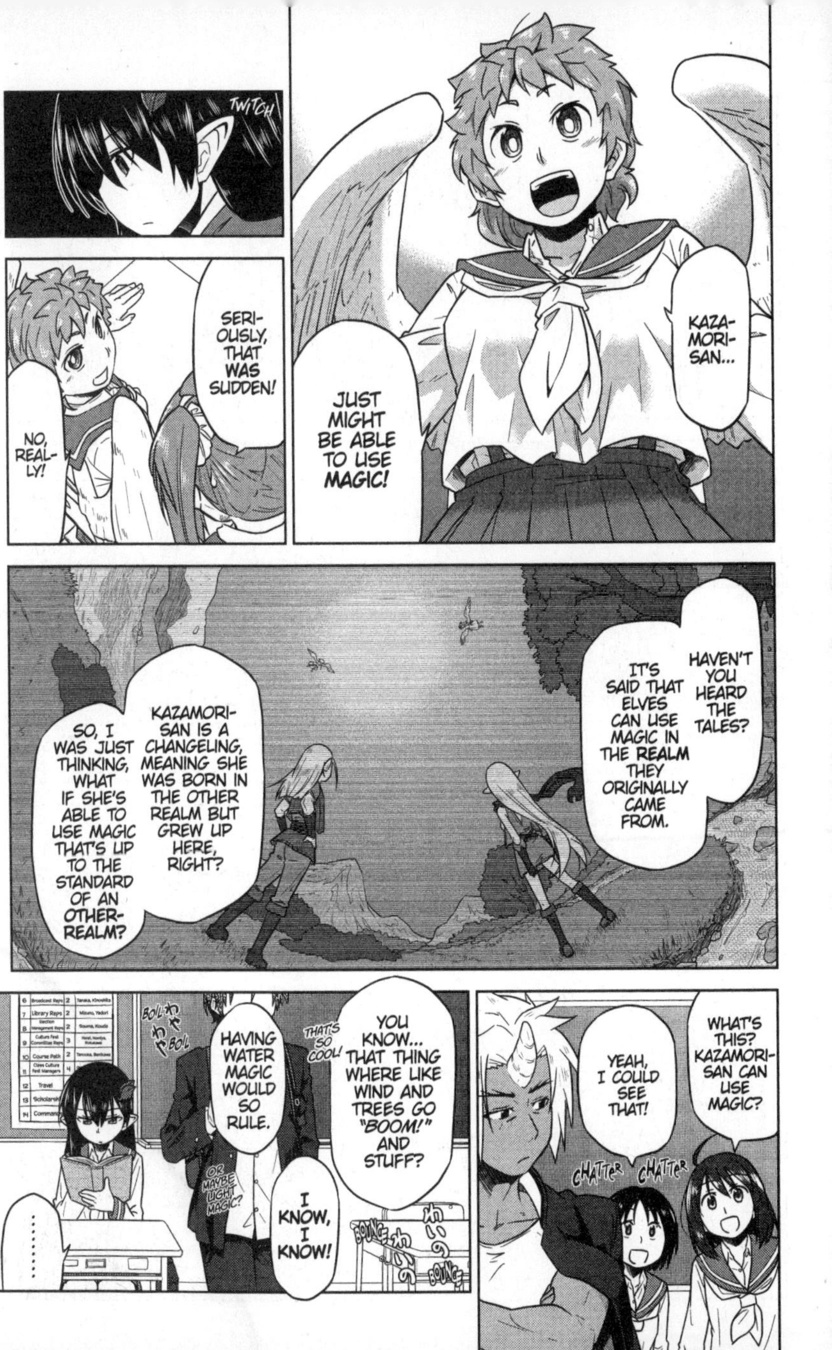
KAZAMORI-SAN...
JUST MIGHT BE ABLE TO USE MAGIC!
TWITCH
SERIOUSLY, THAT WAS SUDDEN!
NO, REALLY!
HAVEN'T YOU HEARD THE TALES?
IT'S SAID THAT ELVES CAN USE MAGIC IN THE REALM THEY ORIGINALLY CAME FROM.
KAZAMORI-SAN IS A CHANGELING, MEANING SHE WAS BORN IN THE OTHER REALM BUT GREW UP HERE, RIGHT?
SO, I WAS JUST THINKING, WHAT IF SHE'S ABLE TO USE MAGIC THAT'S UP TO THE STANDARD OF AN OTHER-REALM?
WHAT'S THIS? KAZAMORI-SAN CAN USE MAGIC?
YEAH, I COULD SEE THAT!
CHATTER CHATTER
YOU KNOW... THAT THING WHERE LIKE WIND AND TREES GO "BOOM!" AND STUFF?
THAT'S SO COOL!
HAVING WATER MAGIC WOULD SO RULE.
BOIL BOIL
OR MAYBE LIGHT MAGIC?
I KNOW, I KNOW!
BOING BOING
......

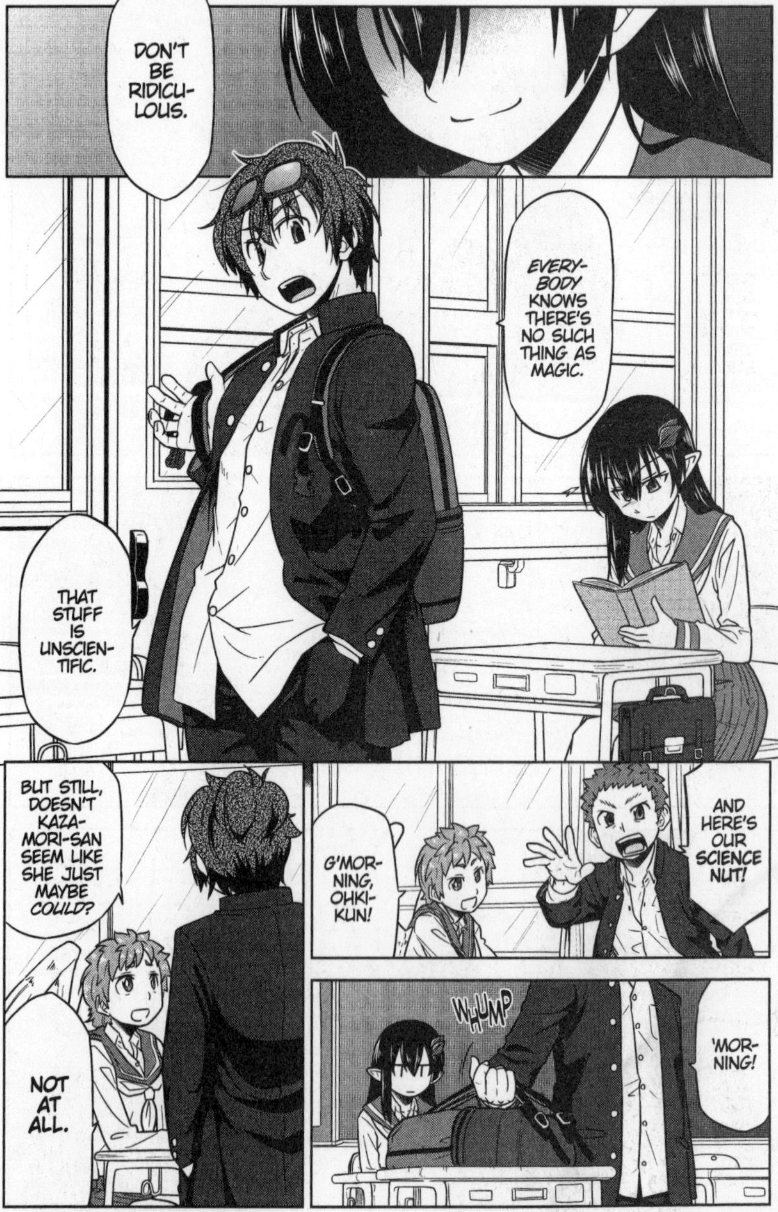
DON'T BE RIDICULOUS.
EVERYBODY KNOWS THERE'S NO SUCH THING AS MAGIC.
THAT STUFF IS UNSCIENTIFIC.
AND HERE'S OUR SCIENCE NUT!
G'MORNING, OHKI-KUN!
WHUMP
'MORNING!
BUT STILL, DOESN'T KAZAMORI-SAN SEEM LIKE SHE JUST MAYBE COULD?
NOT AT ALL.

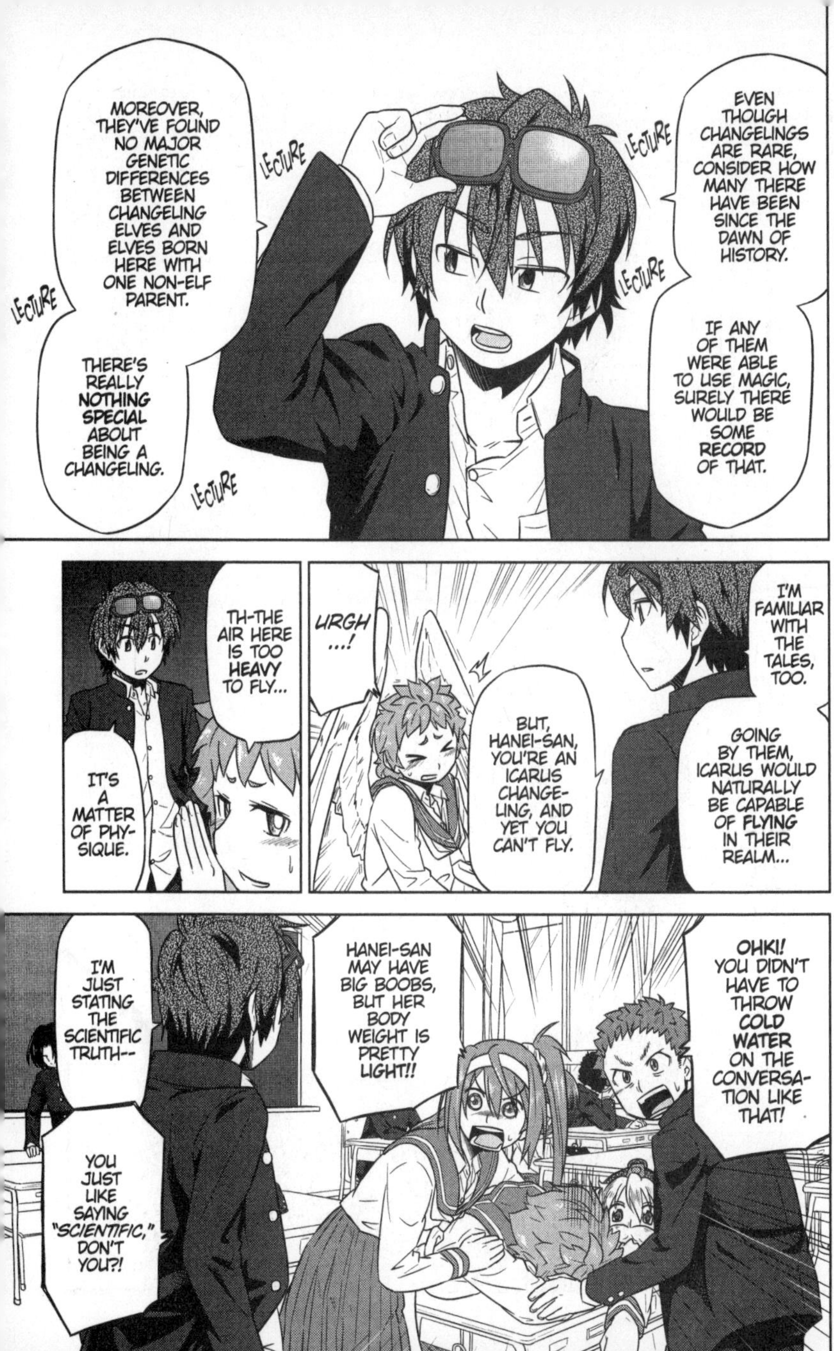
EVEN THOUGH CHANGELINGS ARE RARE, CONSIDER HOW MANY THERE HAVE BEEN SINCE THE DAWN OF HISTORY.
LECTURE
LECTURE
IF ANY OF THEM WERE ABLE TO USE MAGIC, SURELY THERE WOULD BE SOME RECORD OF THAT.
MOREOVER, THEY'VE FOUND NO MAJOR GENETIC DIFFERENCES BETWEEN CHANGELING ELVES AND ELVES BORN HERE WITH ONE NON-ELF PARENT.
LECTURE
LECTURE
THERE'S REALLY NOTHING SPECIAL ABOUT BEING A CHANGELING.
LECTURE
I'M FAMILIAR WITH THE TALES, TOO.
GOING BY THEM, ICARUS WOULD NATURALLY BE CAPABLE OF FLYING IN THEIR REALM...
BUT, HANEI-SAN, YOU'RE AN ICARUS CHANGE-LING, AND YET YOU CAN'T FLY.
URGH ...!
TH-THE AIR HERE IS TOO HEAVY TO FLY...
IT'S A MATTER OF PHY-SIQUE.
OHKI! YOU DIDN'T HAVE TO THROW COLD WATER ON THE CONVERSA-TION LIKE THAT!
HANEI-SAN MAY HAVE BIG BOOBS, BUT HER BODY WEIGHT IS PRETTY LIGHT!!
I'M JUST STATING THE SCIENTIFIC TRUTH--
YOU JUST LIKE SAYING "SCIENTIFIC," DON'T YOU?!

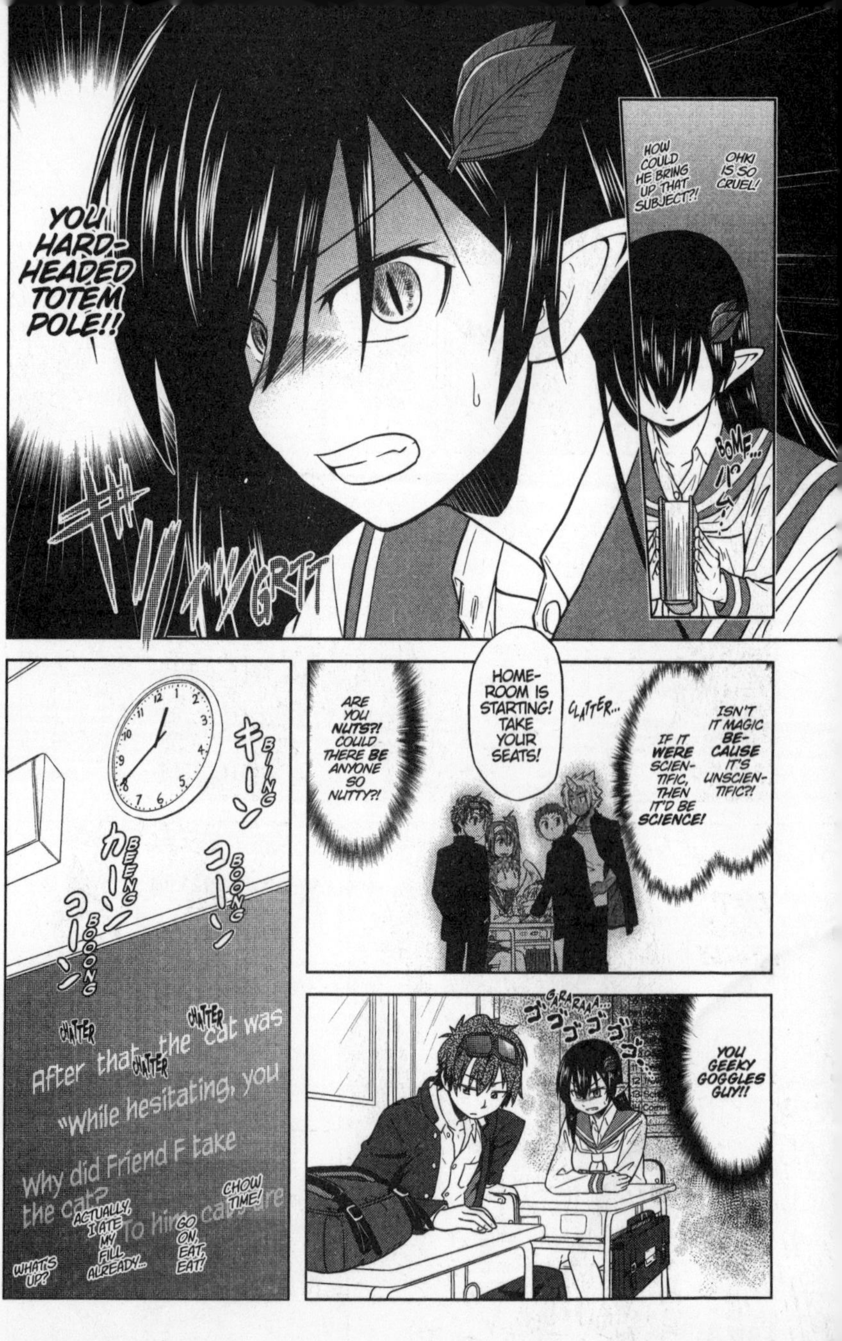
OHKI IS SO CRUEL!
HOW COULD HE BRING UP THAT SUBJECT?!
BOMF...
YOU HARD-HEADED TOTEM POLE!!
GRTT
ISN'T IT MAGIC BE-CAUSE IT'S UNSCIEN-TIFIC?!
IF IT WERE SCIEN-TIFIC, THEN IT'D BE SCIENCE!
CLATTER...
HOME-ROOM IS STARTING! TAKE YOUR SEATS!
ARE YOU NUTS?! COULD THERE BE ANYONE SO NUTTY?!
GARARAAA...
YOU GEEKY GOGGLES GUY!!
BIING
BOONG
BEENG
BOOONG
CHATTER
CHATTER
CHATTER
After that the cat was
"While hesitating, you
Why did Friend F take
the cat? To him cats are
CHOW TIME!
GO ON, EAT, EAT!
ACTUALLY, I ATE MY FILL ALREADY...
WHAT'S UP?

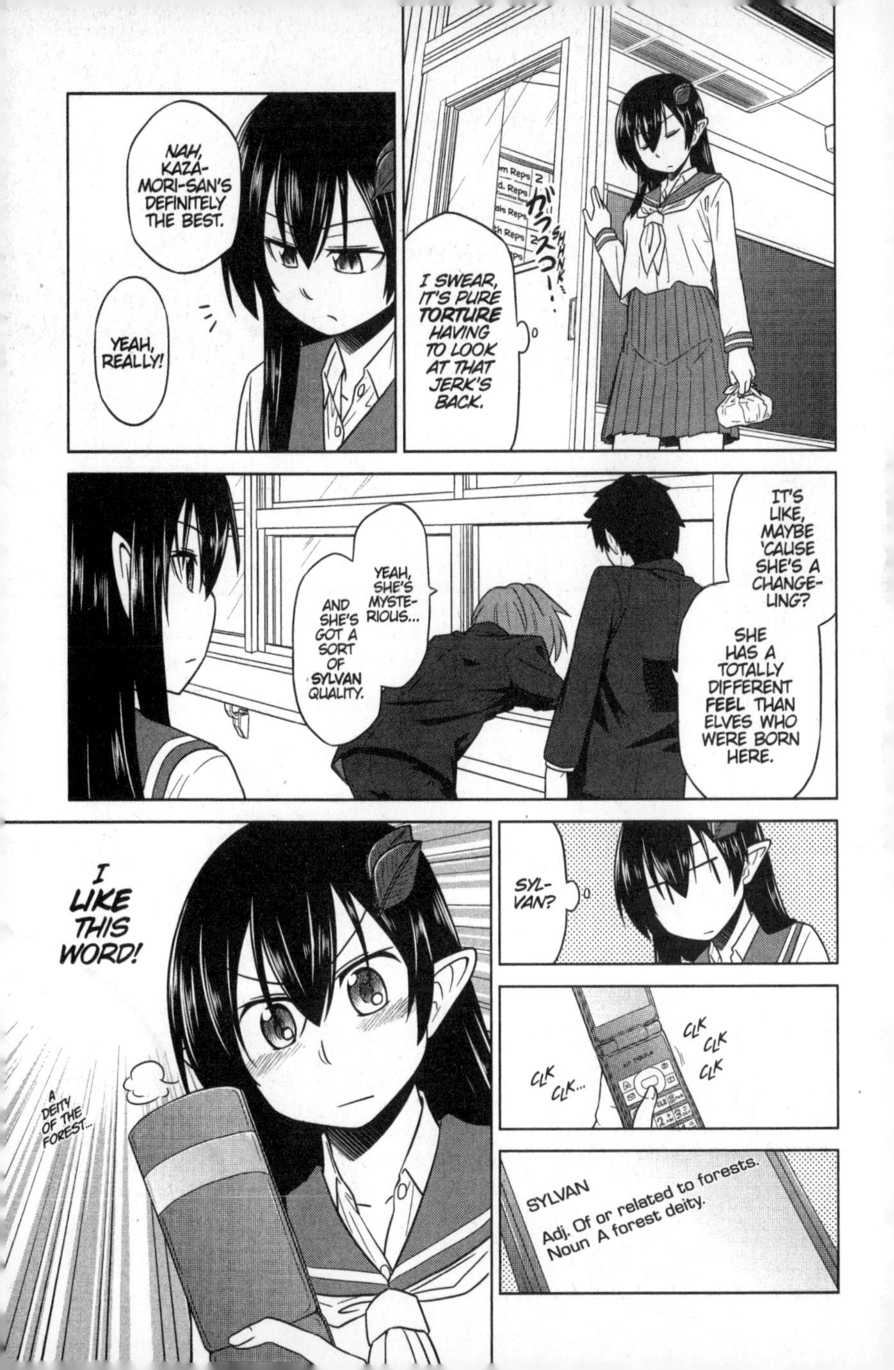
I SWEAR, IT'S PURE TORTURE HAVING TO LOOK AT THAT JERK'S BACK.
SHHHNK...
NAH, KAZAMORI-SAN'S DEFINITELY THE BEST.
YEAH, REALLY!
IT'S LIKE, MAYBE 'CAUSE SHE'S A CHANGELING?
SHE HAS A TOTALLY DIFFERENT FEEL THAN ELVES WHO WERE BORN HERE.
YEAH, SHE'S MYSTERIOUS...
AND SHE'S GOT A SORT OF SYLVAN QUALITY.
SYLVAN?
CLK CLK CLK
CLK CLK...
SYLVAN
Adj. Of or related to forests.
Noun A forest deity.
I LIKE THIS WORD!
A DEITY OF THE FOREST...

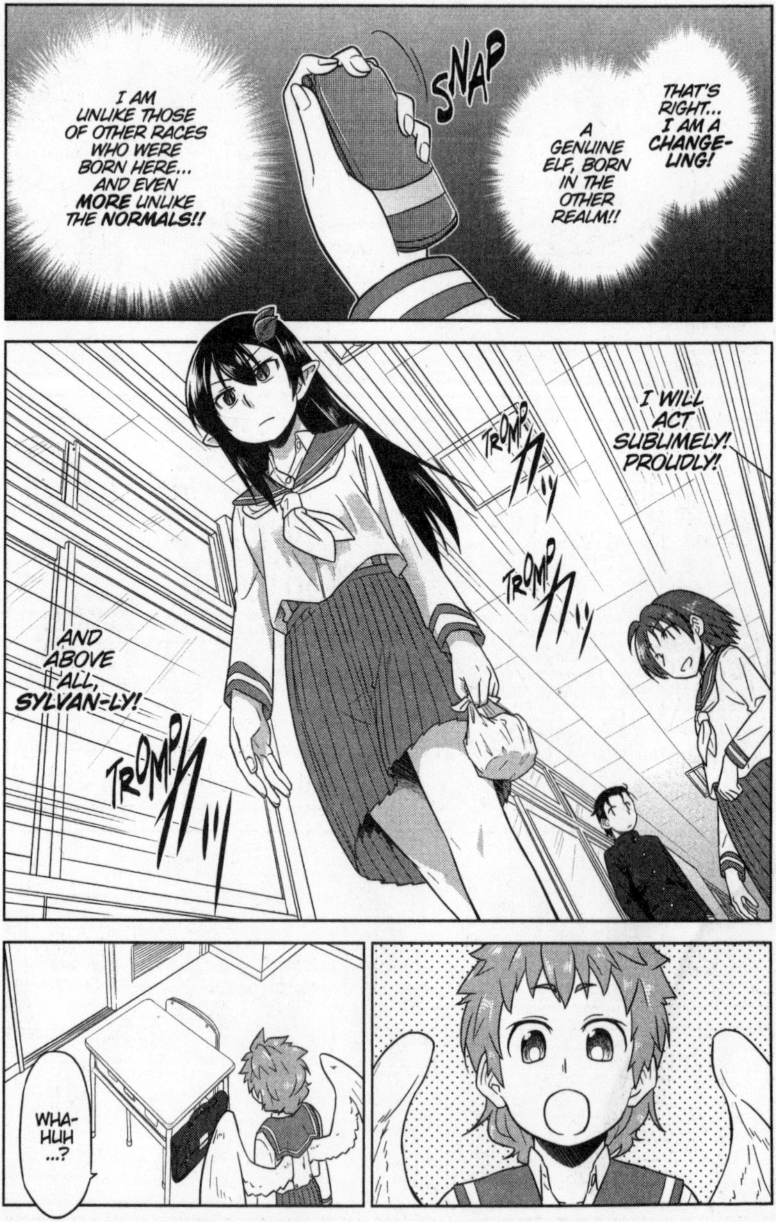
THAT'S RIGHT... I AM A CHANGE-LING!
A GENUINE ELF, BORN IN THE OTHER REALM!!
SNAP
I AM UNLIKE THOSE OF OTHER RACES WHO WERE BORN HERE... AND EVEN **MORE** UNLIKE THE **NORMALS!!**
I WILL ACT SUBLIMELY! PROUDLY!
TROMP
TROMP
AND ABOVE ALL, SYLVAN-LY!
TROMP
WHA-HUH ...?

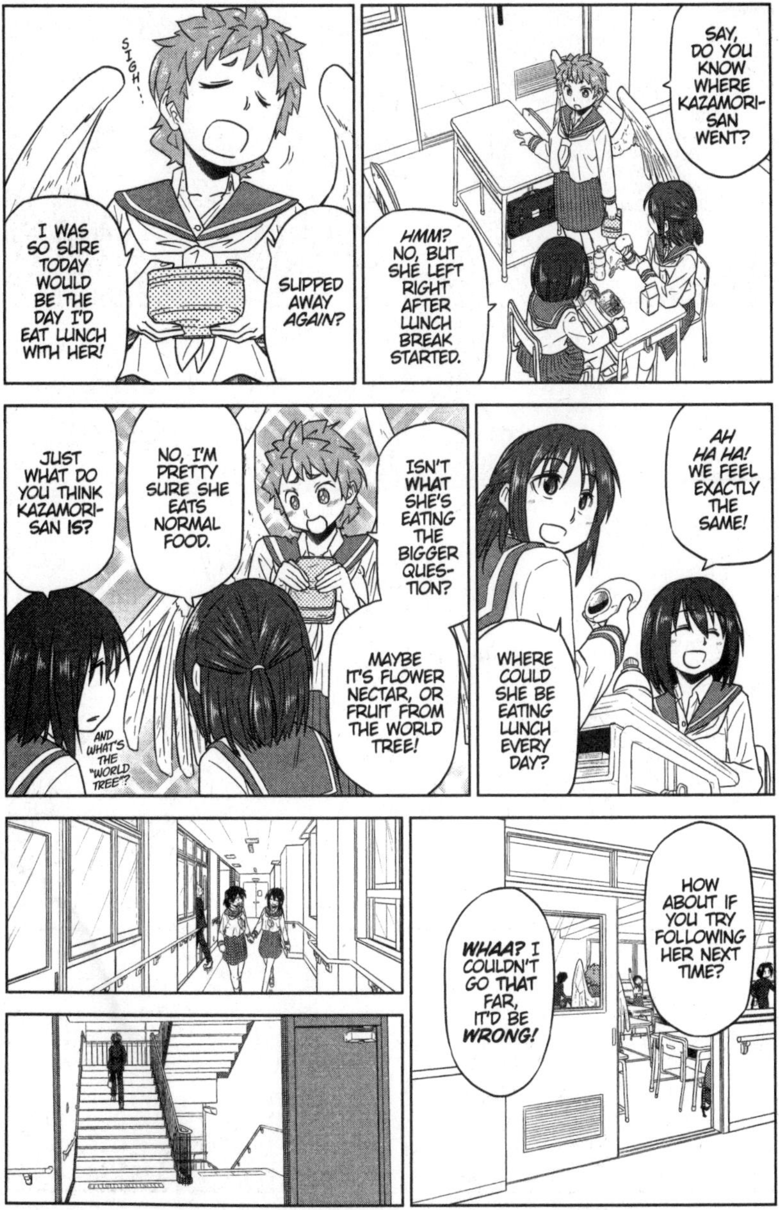
SAY, DO YOU KNOW WHERE KAZAMORI-SAN WENT?
HMM? NO, BUT SHE LEFT RIGHT AFTER LUNCH BREAK STARTED.
SIGH...
SLIPPED AWAY *AGAIN?*
I WAS SO SURE TODAY WOULD BE THE DAY I'D EAT LUNCH WITH HER!
AH HA HA! WE FEEL EXACTLY THE SAME!
WHERE COULD SHE BE EATING LUNCH EVERY DAY?
ISN'T WHAT SHE'S EATING THE BIGGER QUESTION?
MAYBE IT'S FLOWER NECTAR, OR FRUIT FROM THE WORLD TREE!
NO, I'M PRETTY SURE SHE EATS NORMAL FOOD.
JUST WHAT DO YOU THINK KAZAMORI-SAN IS?
AND WHAT'S THE "WORLD TREE"?
HOW ABOUT IF YOU TRY FOLLOWING HER NEXT TIME?
WHAA? I COULDN'T GO THAT FAR, IT'D BE ***WRONG!***

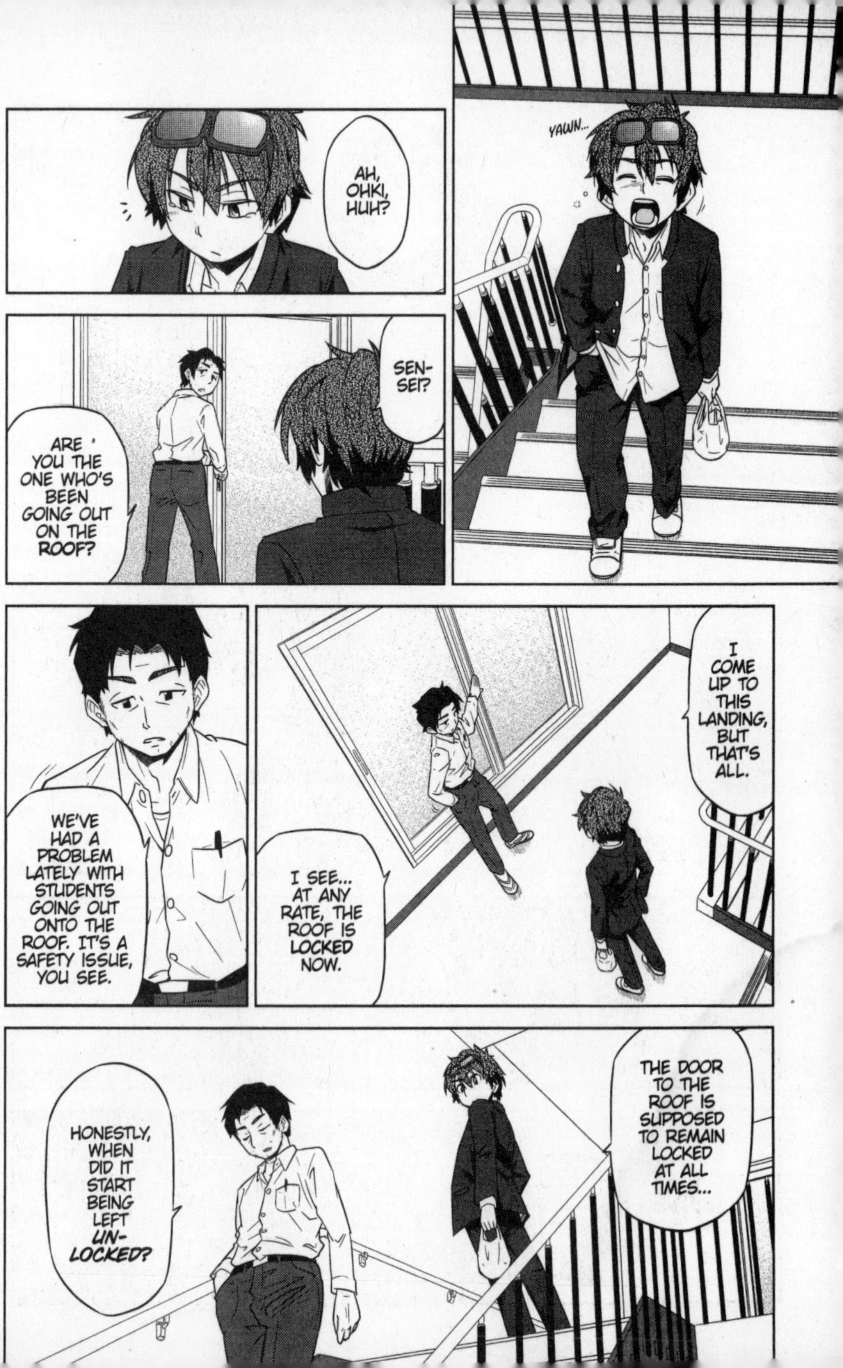
YAWN...
AH, OHKI, HUH?
SEN-SEI?
ARE YOU THE ONE WHO'S BEEN GOING OUT ON THE ROOF?
I COME UP TO THIS LANDING, BUT THAT'S ALL.
I SEE... AT ANY RATE, THE ROOF IS LOCKED NOW.
WE'VE HAD A PROBLEM LATELY WITH STUDENTS GOING OUT ONTO THE ROOF. IT'S A SAFETY ISSUE, YOU SEE.
THE DOOR TO THE ROOF IS SUPPOSED TO REMAIN LOCKED AT ALL TIMES...
HONESTLY, WHEN DID IT START BEING LEFT *UN-LOCKED?*

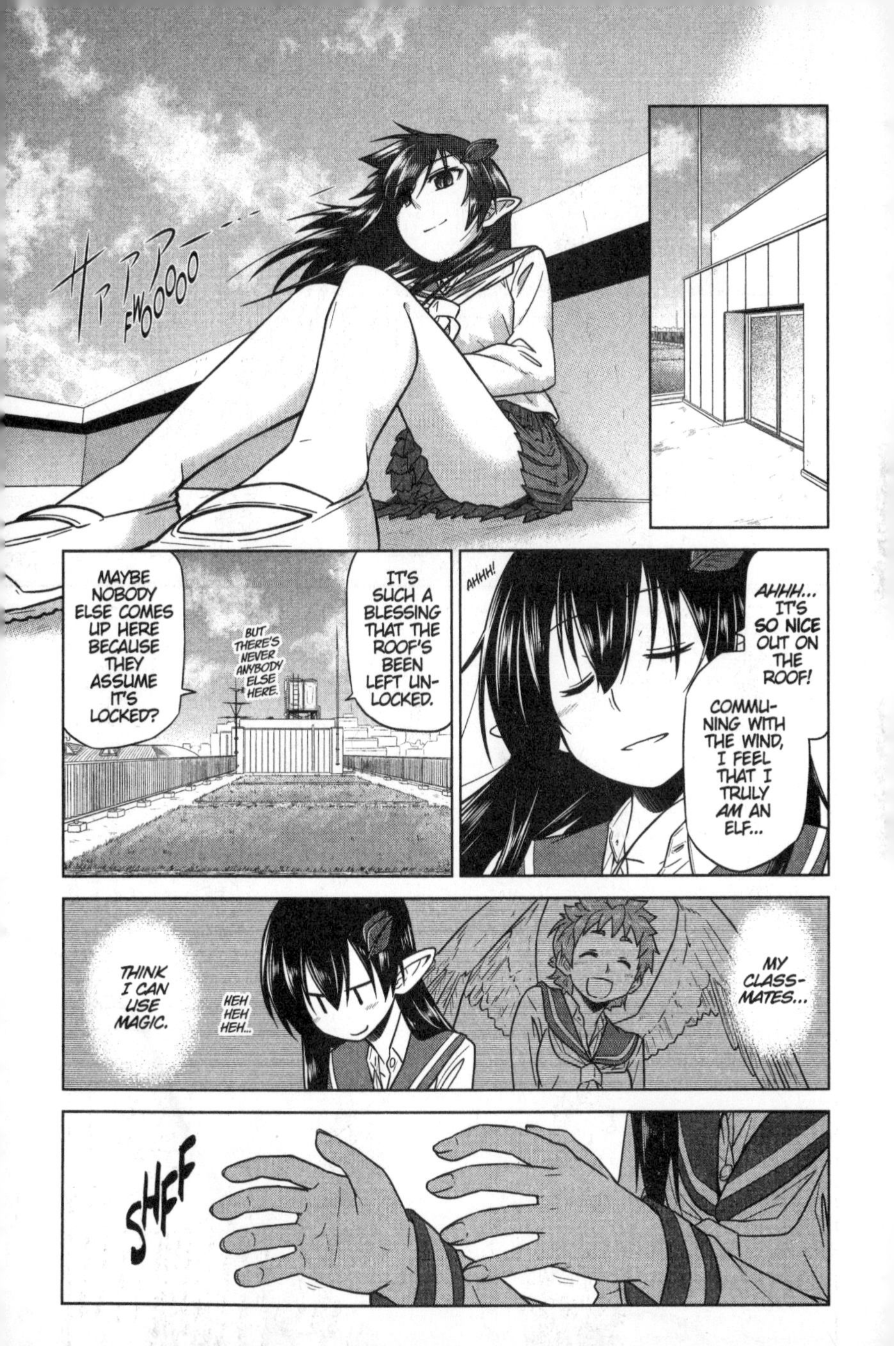

サァァアー
FWOOOOO
AHHH!
AHHH... IT'S SO NICE OUT ON THE ROOF!
COMMUNING WITH THE WIND, I FEEL THAT I TRULY AM AN ELF...
IT'S SUCH A BLESSING THAT THE ROOF'S BEEN LEFT UN-LOCKED.
BUT THERE'S NEVER ANYBODY ELSE HERE.
MAYBE NOBODY ELSE COMES UP HERE BECAUSE THEY ASSUME IT'S LOCKED?
MY CLASS-MATES...
HEH HEH HEH...
THINK I CAN USE MAGIC.
SHFF

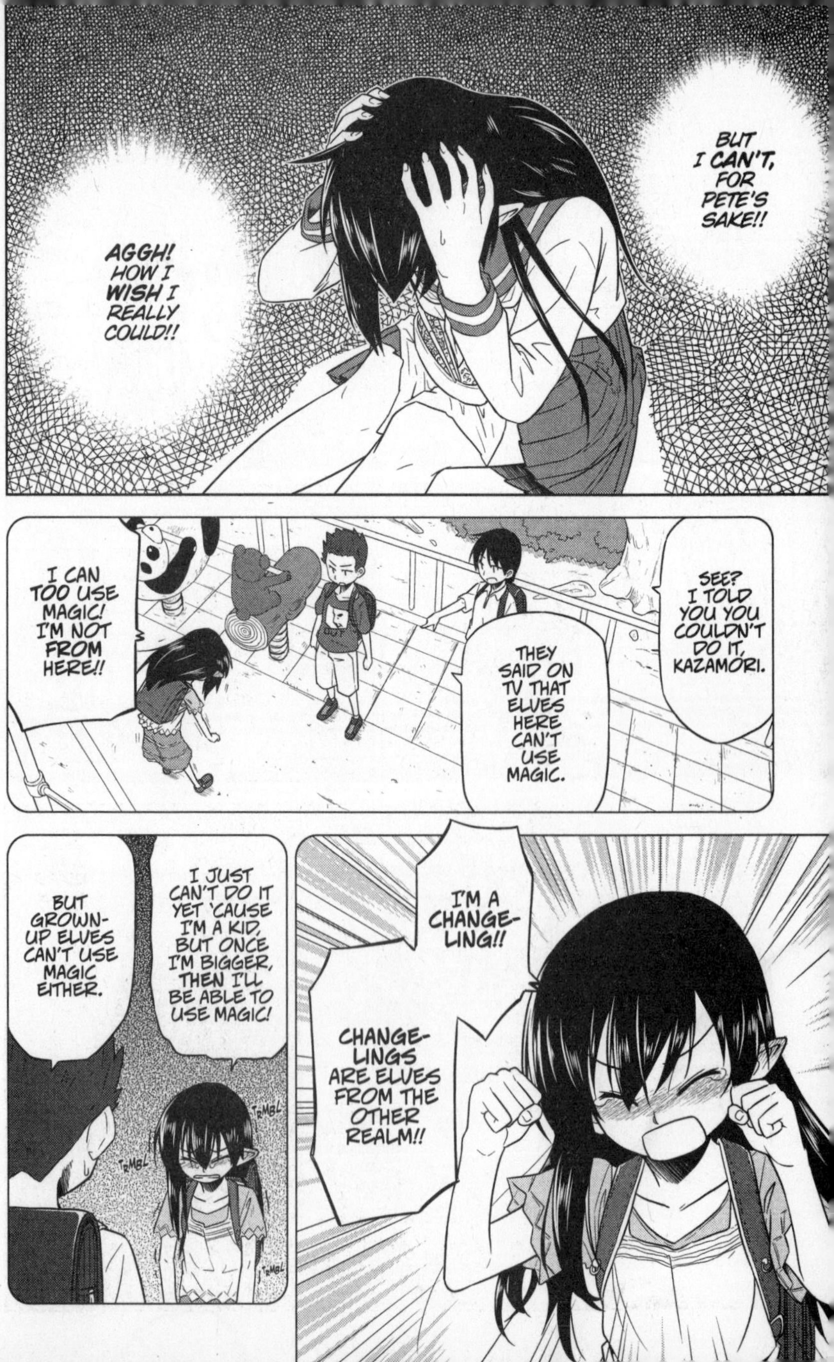
BUT I CAN'T, FOR PETE'S SAKE!!
AGGH! HOW I WISH I REALLY COULD!!
SEE? I TOLD YOU YOU COULDN'T DO IT, KAZAMORI.
THEY SAID ON TV THAT ELVES HERE CAN'T USE MAGIC.
I CAN TOO USE MAGIC! I'M NOT FROM HERE!!
I'M A CHANGELING!!
CHANGELINGS ARE ELVES FROM THE OTHER REALM!!
I JUST CAN'T DO IT YET 'CAUSE I'M A KID, BUT ONCE I'M BIGGER, THEN I'LL BE ABLE TO USE MAGIC!
BUT GROWN-UP ELVES CAN'T USE MAGIC EITHER.
TRMBL
TRMBL
TRMBL

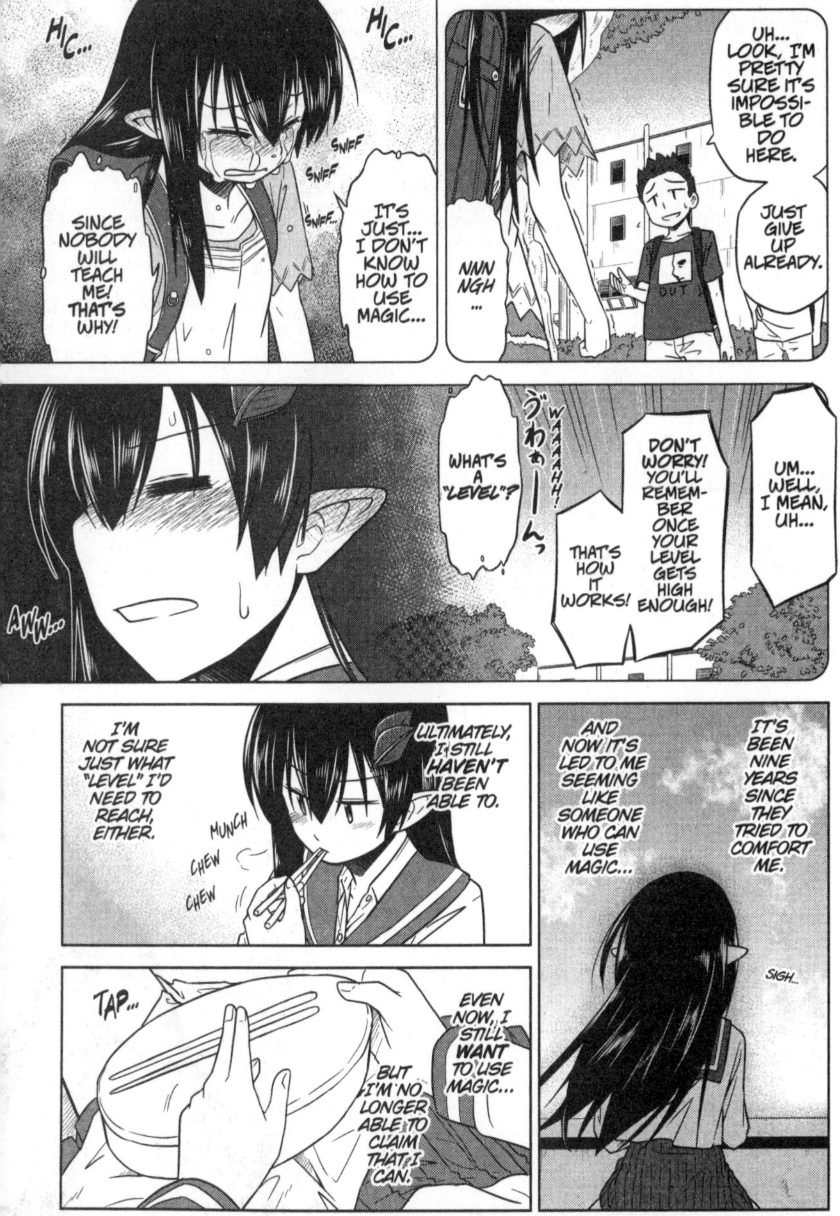
UH... LOOK, I'M PRETTY SURE IT'S IMPOSSIBLE TO DO HERE.
JUST GIVE UP ALREADY.
NNNNGH...
IT'S JUST... I DON'T KNOW HOW TO USE MAGIC...
SNIFF
SNIFF
SNIFF...
HIC...
HIC...
SINCE NOBODY WILL TEACH ME! THAT'S WHY!
UM... WELL, I MEAN, UH...
DON'T WORRY! YOU'LL REMEMBER ONCE YOUR LEVEL GETS HIGH ENOUGH!
THAT'S HOW IT WORKS!
うわぁーーん
WAAAAHH!
WHAT'S A "LEVEL"?
AWW...
IT'S BEEN NINE YEARS SINCE THEY TRIED TO COMFORT ME.
AND NOW IT'S LED TO ME SEEMING LIKE SOMEONE WHO CAN USE MAGIC...
SIGH...
ULTIMATELY, I STILL HAVEN'T BEEN ABLE TO.
I'M NOT SURE JUST WHAT "LEVEL" I'D NEED TO REACH, EITHER.
MUNCH
CHEW
CHEW
EVEN NOW, I STILL WANT TO USE MAGIC...
BUT I'M NO LONGER ABLE TO CLAIM THAT I CAN.
TAP...

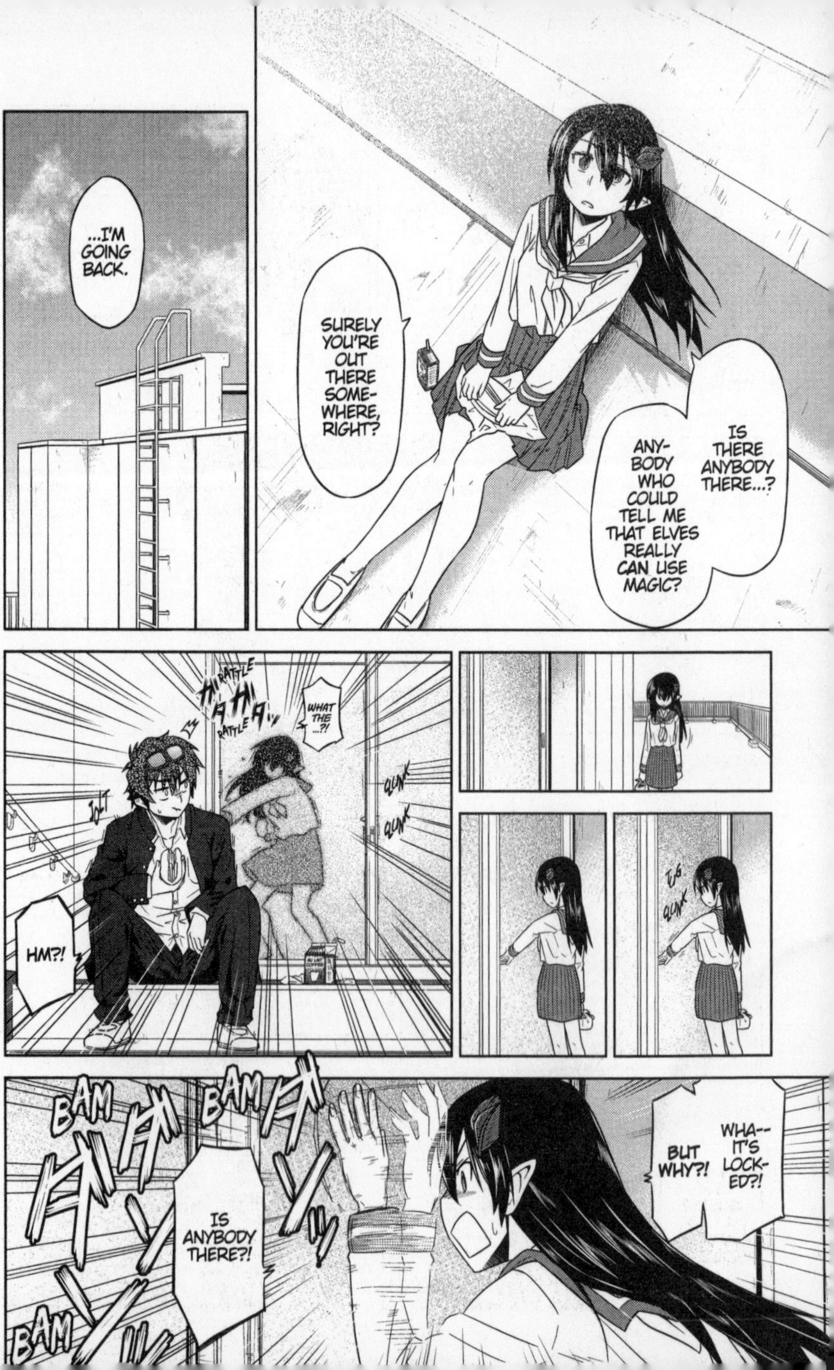
IS THERE ANYBODY THERE...?
ANYBODY WHO COULD TELL ME THAT ELVES REALLY CAN USE MAGIC?
SURELY YOU'RE OUT THERE SOMEWHERE, RIGHT?
...I'M GOING BACK.
TUG
CLUNK
RATTLE
RATTLE
WHAT THE ...?!
CLUNK
CLUNK
JOLT
HM?!
WHA-- IT'S LOCKED?!
BUT WHY?!
BAM
BAM
IS ANYBODY THERE?!
BAM

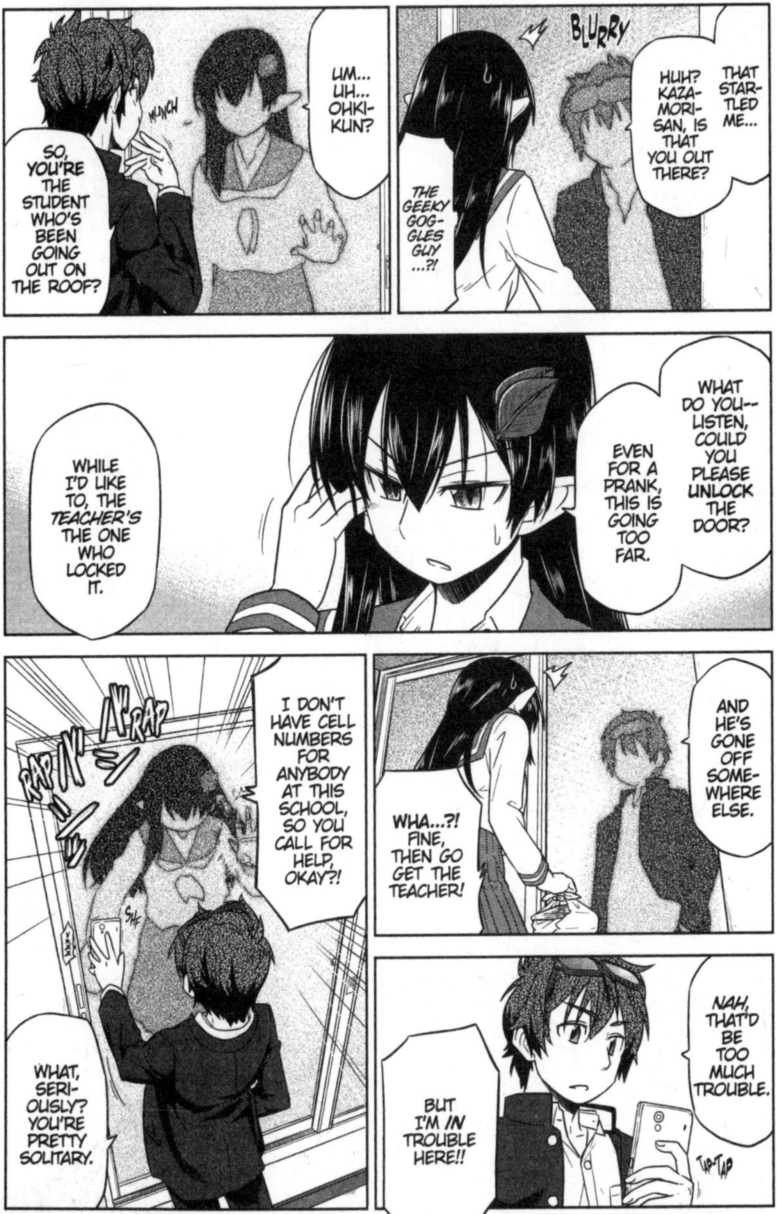
THAT STARTLED ME...
HUH? KAZAMORI-SAN, IS THAT YOU OUT THERE?
BLURRY
THE GEEKY GOGGLES GUY ...?!
UM... UH... OHKI-KUN?
MUNCH
SO, YOU'RE THE STUDENT WHO'S BEEN GOING OUT ON THE ROOF?
WHAT DO YOU-- LISTEN, COULD YOU PLEASE UNLOCK THE DOOR?
EVEN FOR A PRANK, THIS IS GOING TOO FAR.
WHILE I'D LIKE TO, THE *TEACHER'S* THE ONE WHO LOCKED IT.
AND HE'S GONE OFF SOMEWHERE ELSE.
WHA...?! FINE, THEN GO GET THE TEACHER!
NAH, THAT'D BE TOO MUCH TROUBLE.
BUT I'M *IN* TROUBLE HERE!!
TAP TAP
I DON'T HAVE CELL NUMBERS FOR ANYBODY AT THIS SCHOOL, SO YOU CALL FOR HELP, OKAY?!
RAP RAP RAP
WHAT, SERIOUSLY? YOU'RE PRETTY SOLITARY.

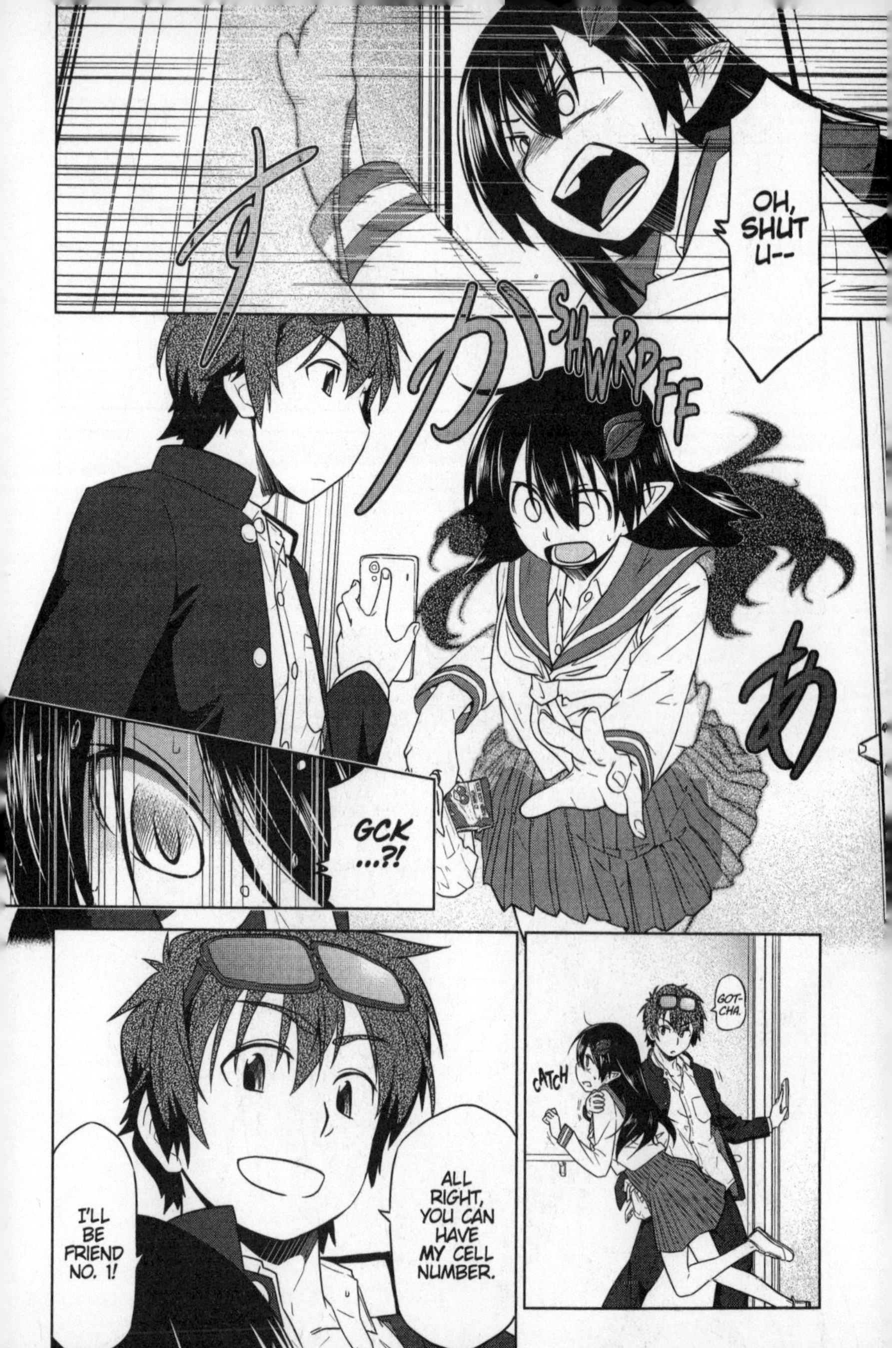
OH, SHUT U--
すか
SHWRPFF
あ
GCK ...?!
GOT-CHA.
CATCH
ALL RIGHT, YOU CAN HAVE MY CELL NUMBER.
I'LL BE FRIEND NO. 1!

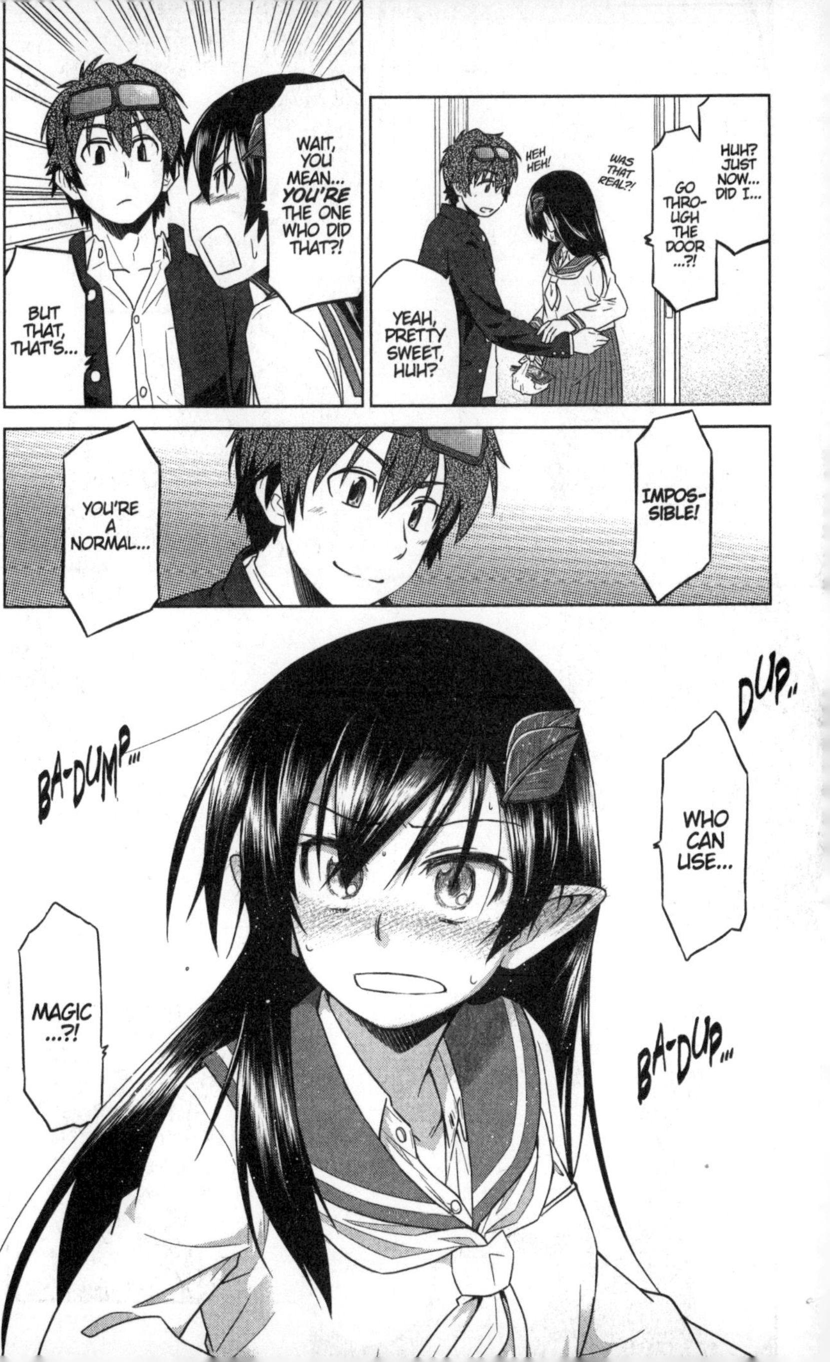
HUH? JUST NOW... DID I...
GO THROUGH THE DOOR ...?!
WAS THAT REAL?!
HEH HEH!
YEAH, PRETTY SWEET, HUH?
WAIT, YOU MEAN... YOU'RE THE ONE WHO DID THAT?!
BUT THAT, THAT'S...
IMPOSSIBLE!
YOU'RE A NORMAL...
DUP..
WHO CAN USE...
BA-DUMP...
MAGIC ...?!
BA-DUP...

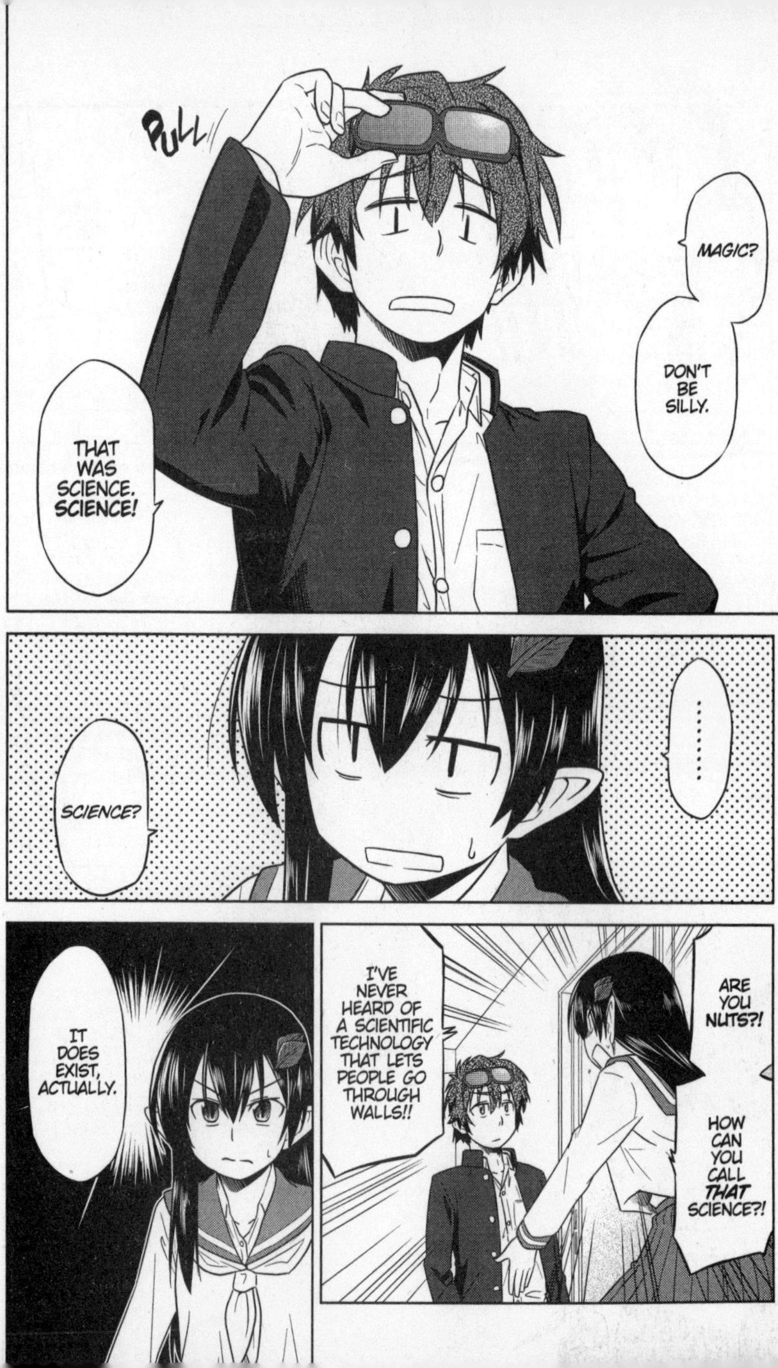
MAGIC?
DON'T BE SILLY.
PULL
THAT WAS SCIENCE. SCIENCE!
……
SCIENCE?
ARE YOU NUTS?!
HOW CAN YOU CALL *THAT* SCIENCE?!
I'VE NEVER HEARD OF A SCIENTIFIC TECHNOLOGY THAT LETS PEOPLE GO THROUGH WALLS!!
IT DOES EXIST, ACTUALLY.

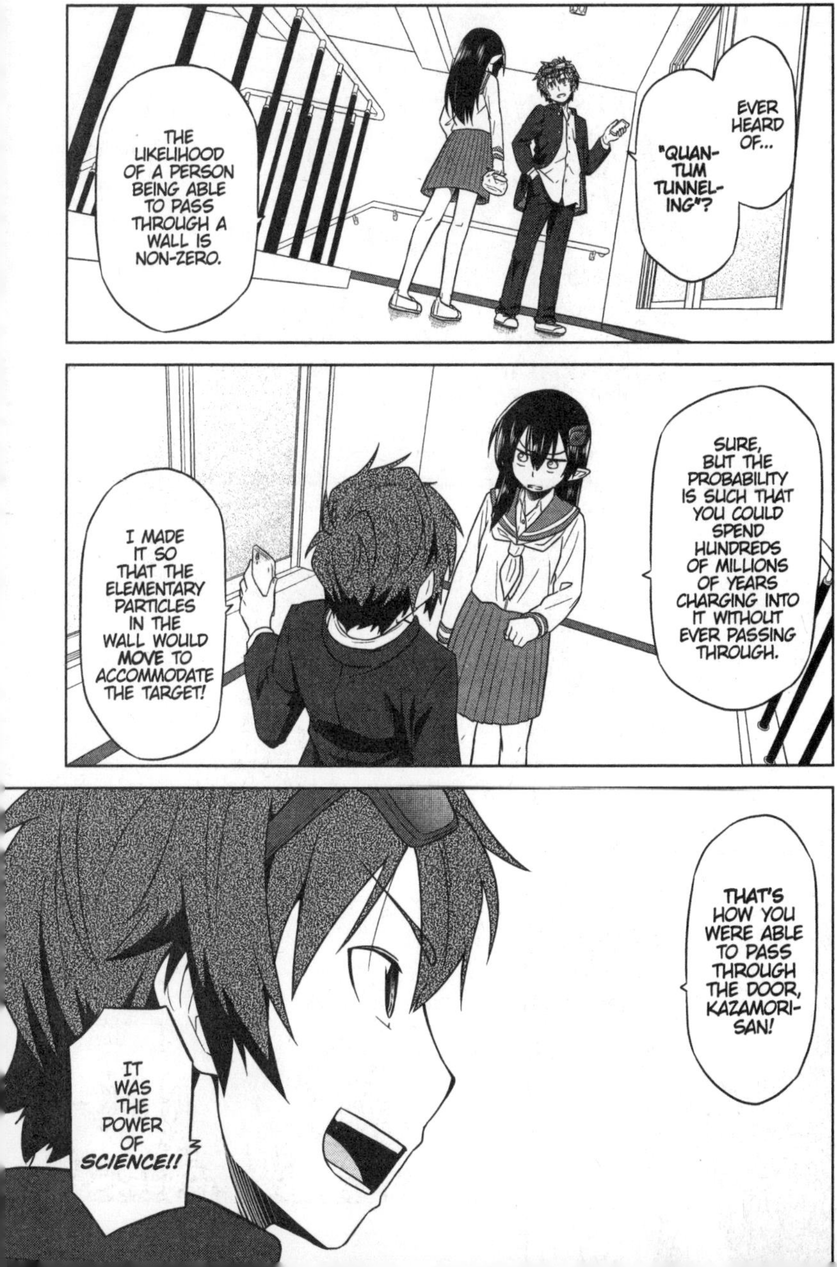
EVER HEARD OF... "QUANTUM TUNNELING"?
THE LIKELIHOOD OF A PERSON BEING ABLE TO PASS THROUGH A WALL IS NON-ZERO.
SURE, BUT THE PROBABILITY IS SUCH THAT YOU COULD SPEND HUNDREDS OF MILLIONS OF YEARS CHARGING INTO IT WITHOUT EVER PASSING THROUGH.
I MADE IT SO THAT THE ELEMENTARY PARTICLES IN THE WALL WOULD MOVE TO ACCOMMODATE THE TARGET!
THAT'S HOW YOU WERE ABLE TO PASS THROUGH THE DOOR, KAZAMORI-SAN!
IT WAS THE POWER OF SCIENCE!!

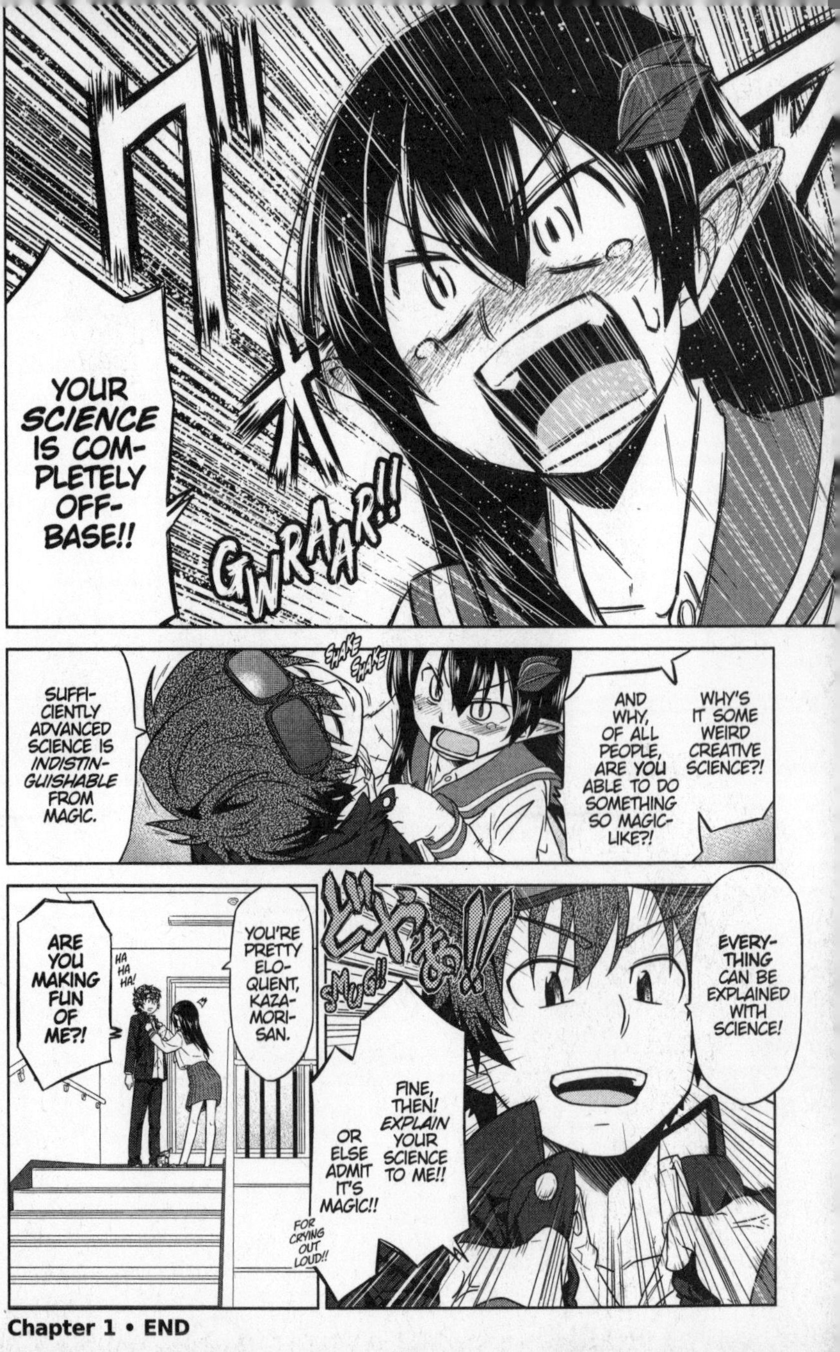
YOUR SCIENCE IS COMPLETELY OFF-BASE!!
GWRAAAR!!
WHY'S IT SOME WEIRD CREATIVE SCIENCE?!
AND WHY, OF ALL PEOPLE, ARE YOU ABLE TO DO SOMETHING SO MAGIC-LIKE?!
SHAKE SHAKE
SUFFICIENTLY ADVANCED SCIENCE IS INDISTINGUISHABLE FROM MAGIC.
EVERYTHING CAN BE EXPLAINED WITH SCIENCE!
SMUG!!
FINE, THEN! EXPLAIN YOUR SCIENCE TO ME!!
OR ELSE ADMIT IT'S MAGIC!!
FOR CRYING OUT LOUD!!
YOU'RE PRETTY ELOQUENT, KAZAMORI-SAN.
HA HA HA!
ARE YOU MAKING FUN OF ME?!

Chapter 1 • END

Chapter 2: Kazamori-san Wants to Use Magic

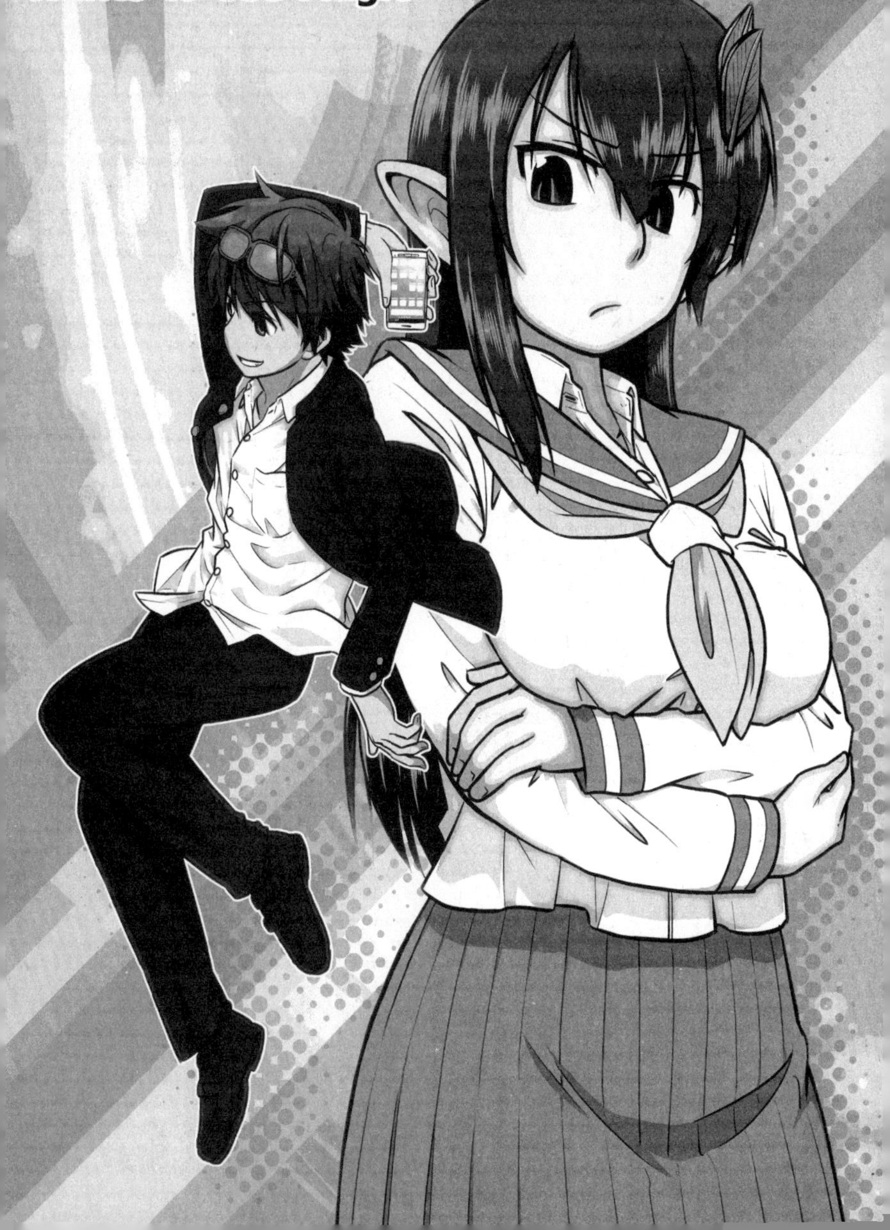

WE KNOW ABOUT ELVES AND ICARUS.
SO THEN, WHAT ARE OGRES AND DWARVES LIKE OVER THERE?
LET'S SEE... WHAT WAS IT...?
I RECALL HEARING SOMETHING...
OGRES SEEM LIKE THEY'D SHOOT OUT FIRE OR LIGHTNING.
LET'S ASSIGN WIND TO THE ELVES.
ALSO OUTIE NAVELS!
I'LL SLUG YOU.
THEN, WHAT ARE DWARVES LIKE?
EXTRA HAIRY?
SCRUFF!
SCRUFF!
WHAT ARE THEY, *YETIS?!*

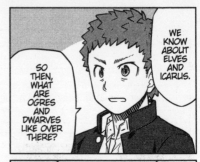

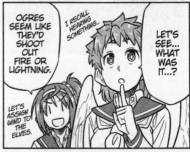

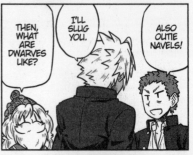

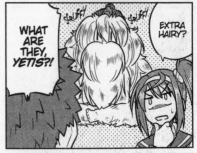

Perhaps Yorkshire terriers?

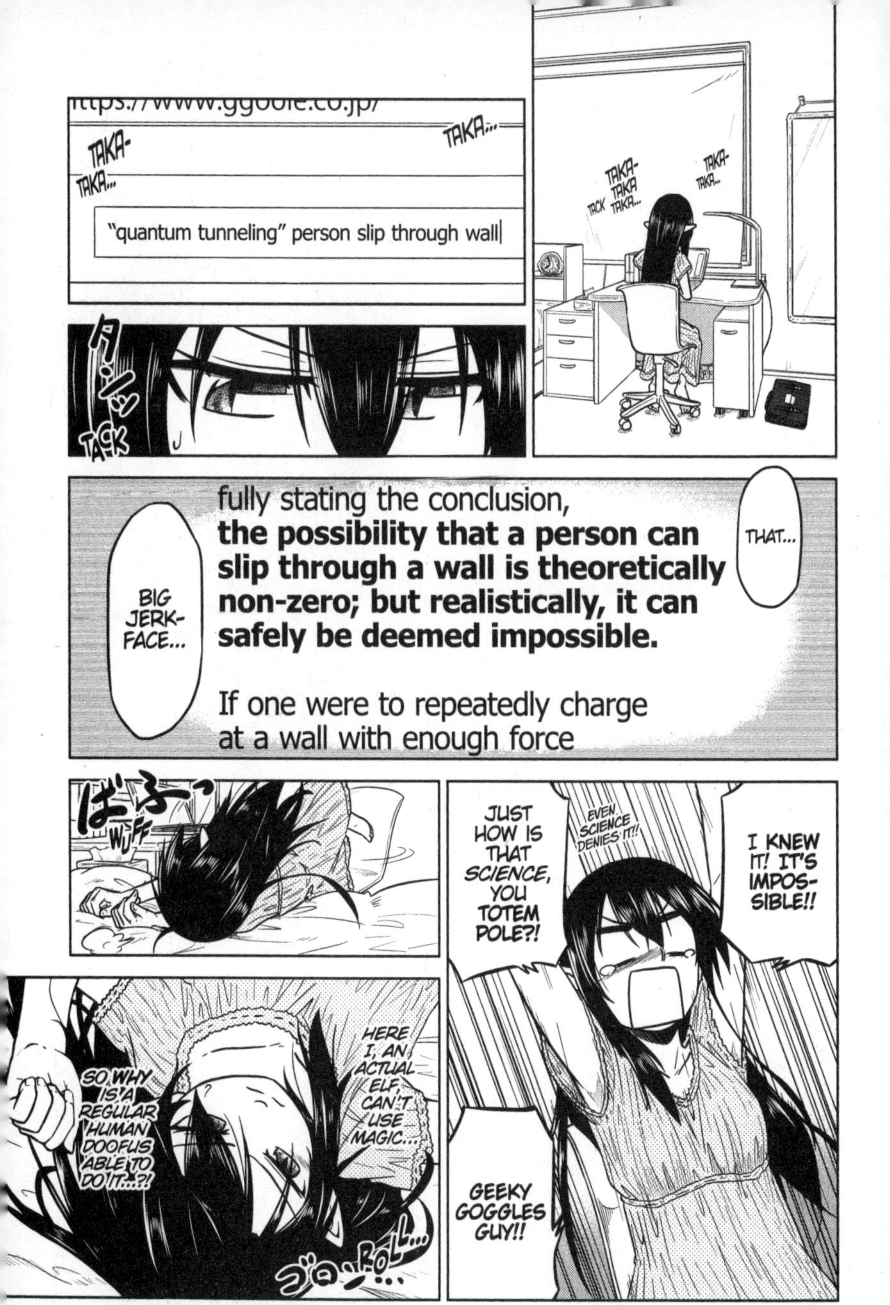

TAKA-TAKA-TAKA...
TACK
TAKA-TAKA...
ttps://www.ggoole.co.jp/
TAKA...
TAKA-TAKA...
"quantum tunneling" person slip through wall
TACK
THAT...
fully stating the conclusion,
the possibility that a person can slip through a wall is theoretically non-zero; but realistically, it can safely be deemed impossible.
If one were to repeatedly charge at a wall with enough force
BIG JERK-FACE...
I KNEW IT! IT'S IMPOSSIBLE!!
EVEN SCIENCE DENIES IT!!
JUST HOW IS THAT SCIENCE, YOU TOTEM POLE?!
GEEKY GOGGLES GUY!!
ばふっ
WUFF
HERE I, AN ACTUAL ELF, CAN'T USE MAGIC...
SO WHY IS A REGULAR HUMAN DOOFUS ABLE TO DO IT...?!
ゴロ…
ROLL...

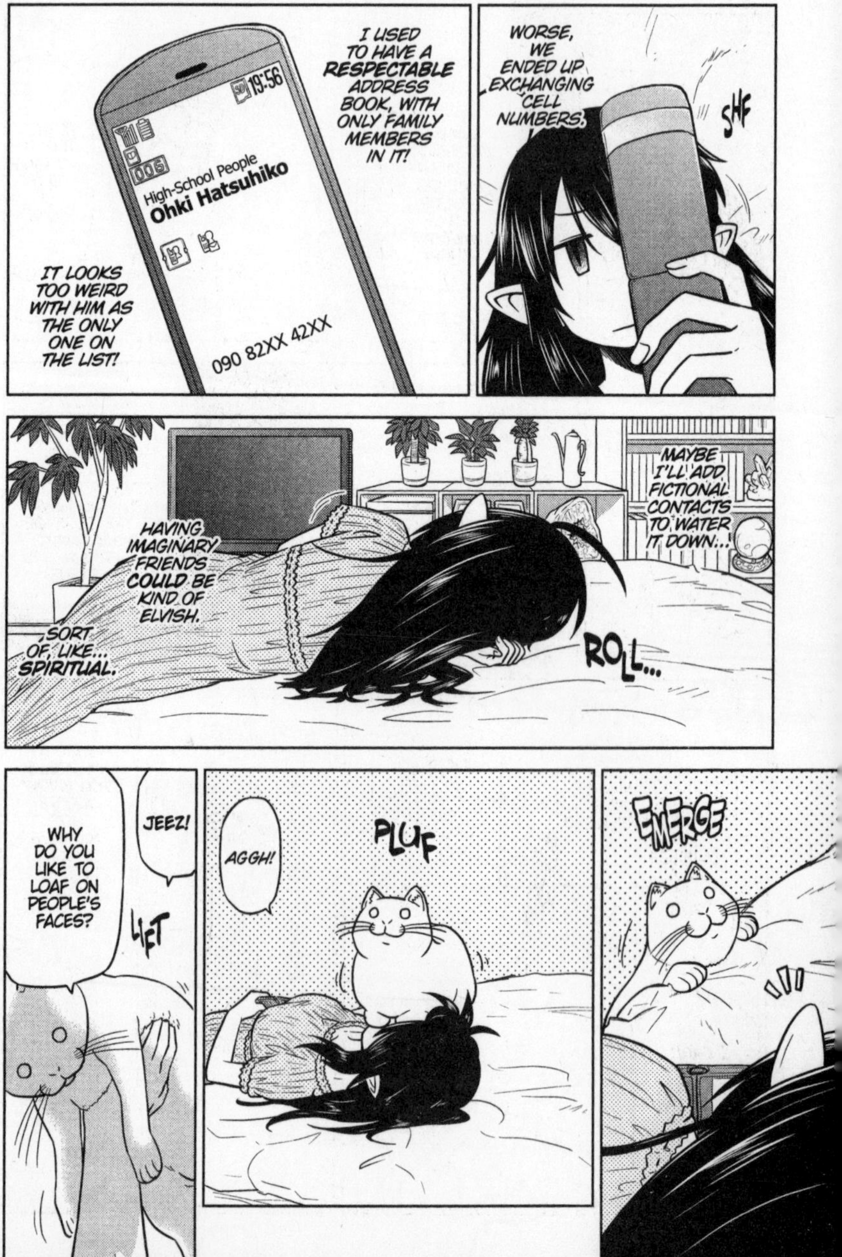
WORSE, WE ENDED UP EXCHANGING CELL NUMBERS.
SHF
I USED TO HAVE A RESPECTABLE ADDRESS BOOK, WITH ONLY FAMILY MEMBERS IN IT!
19:56
006
High-School People
Ohki Hatsuhiko
090 82XX 42XX
IT LOOKS TOO WEIRD WITH HIM AS THE ONLY ONE ON THE LIST!
MAYBE I'LL ADD FICTIONAL CONTACTS TO WATER IT DOWN...!
ROLL...
HAVING IMAGINARY FRIENDS COULD BE KIND OF ELVISH.
SORT OF, LIKE... SPIRITUAL.
EMERGE
!!!
PLUF
AGGH!
JEEZ!
WHY DO YOU LIKE TO LOAF ON PEOPLE'S FACES?
LIFT

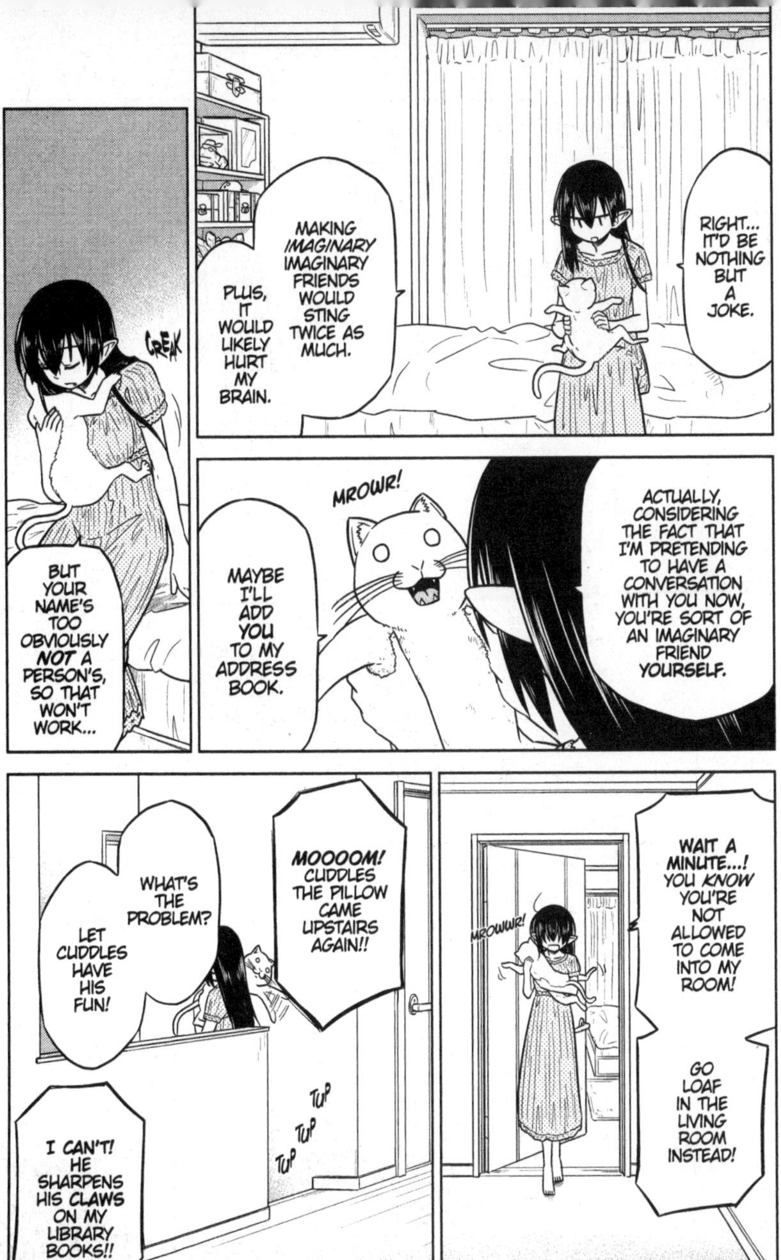
RIGHT... IT'D BE NOTHING BUT A JOKE.
MAKING *IMAGINARY* IMAGINARY FRIENDS WOULD STING TWICE AS MUCH.
PLUS, IT WOULD LIKELY HURT MY BRAIN.
ACTUALLY, CONSIDERING THE FACT THAT I'M PRETENDING TO HAVE A CONVERSATION WITH YOU NOW, YOU'RE SORT OF AN IMAGINARY FRIEND **YOURSELF.**
MROWR!
MAYBE I'LL ADD **YOU** TO MY ADDRESS BOOK.
CREAK
BUT YOUR NAME'S TOO OBVIOUSLY ***NOT*** A PERSON'S, SO THAT WON'T WORK...
WAIT A MINUTE...! YOU *KNOW* YOU'RE NOT ALLOWED TO COME INTO MY ROOM!
MROWWR!
GO LOAF IN THE LIVING ROOM INSTEAD!
MOOOOM! CUDDLES THE PILLOW CAME UPSTAIRS AGAIN!!
WHAT'S THE PROBLEM?
LET CUDDLES HAVE HIS FUN!
I CAN'T! HE SHARPENS HIS **CLAWS** ON MY LIBRARY BOOKS!!
TUP TUP TUP

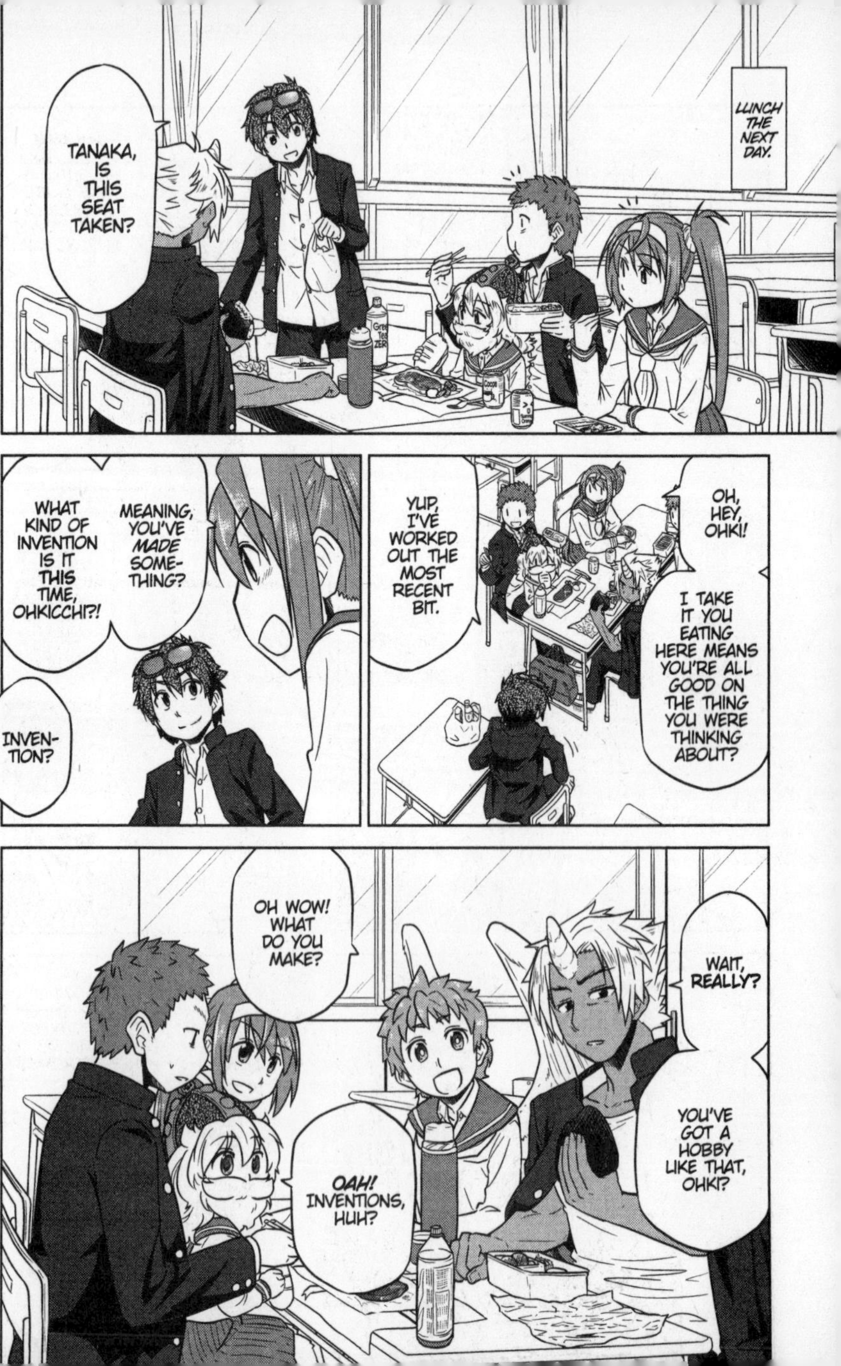
LUNCH THE NEXT DAY.
TANAKA, IS THIS SEAT TAKEN?
OH, HEY, OHKI!
I TAKE IT YOU EATING HERE MEANS YOU'RE ALL GOOD ON THE THING YOU WERE THINKING ABOUT?
YUP, I'VE WORKED OUT THE MOST RECENT BIT.
MEANING, YOU'VE *MADE* SOMETHING?
WHAT KIND OF INVENTION IS IT THIS TIME, OHKICCHI?!
INVENTION?
WAIT, REALLY?
YOU'VE GOT A HOBBY LIKE THAT, OHKI?
OH WOW! WHAT DO YOU MAKE?
OAH! INVENTIONS, HUH?

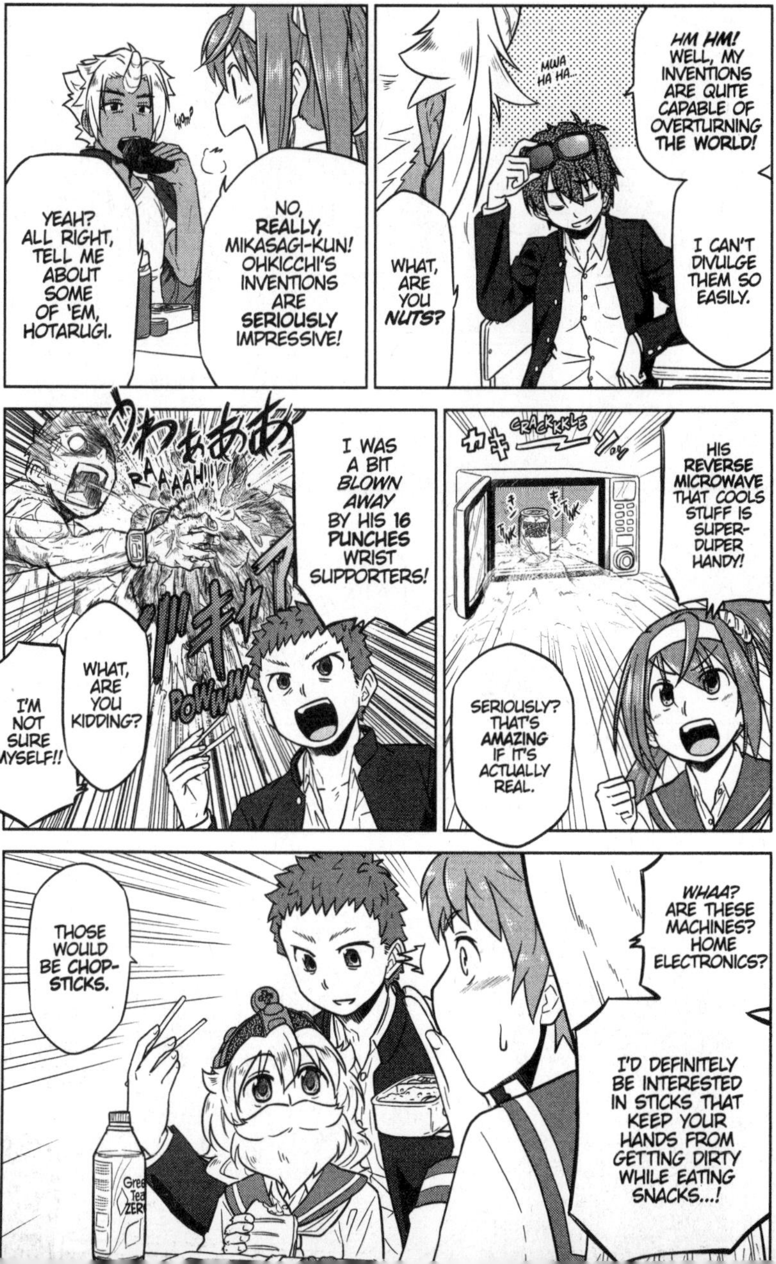
HM HM! WELL, MY INVENTIONS ARE QUITE CAPABLE OF OVERTURNING THE WORLD!
MWA HA HA...
I CAN'T DIVULGE THEM SO EASILY.
WHAT, ARE YOU NUTS?
NO, REALLY, MIKASAGI-KUN! OHKICCHI'S INVENTIONS ARE SERIOUSLY IMPRESSIVE!
YEAH? ALL RIGHT, TELL ME ABOUT SOME OF 'EM, HOTARUGI.
HIS REVERSE MICROWAVE THAT COOLS STUFF IS SUPER-DUPER HANDY!
CRACKKKLE
TINK
TINK
SERIOUSLY? THAT'S AMAZING IF IT'S ACTUALLY REAL.
I WAS A BIT BLOWN AWAY BY HIS 16 PUNCHES WRIST SUPPORTERS!
RAAAAH!!
POWWW
WHAT, ARE YOU KIDDING?
I'M NOT SURE MYSELF!!
WHAA? ARE THESE MACHINES? HOME ELECTRONICS?
I'D DEFINITELY BE INTERESTED IN STICKS THAT KEEP YOUR HANDS FROM GETTING DIRTY WHILE EATING SNACKS...!
THOSE WOULD BE CHOP-STICKS.

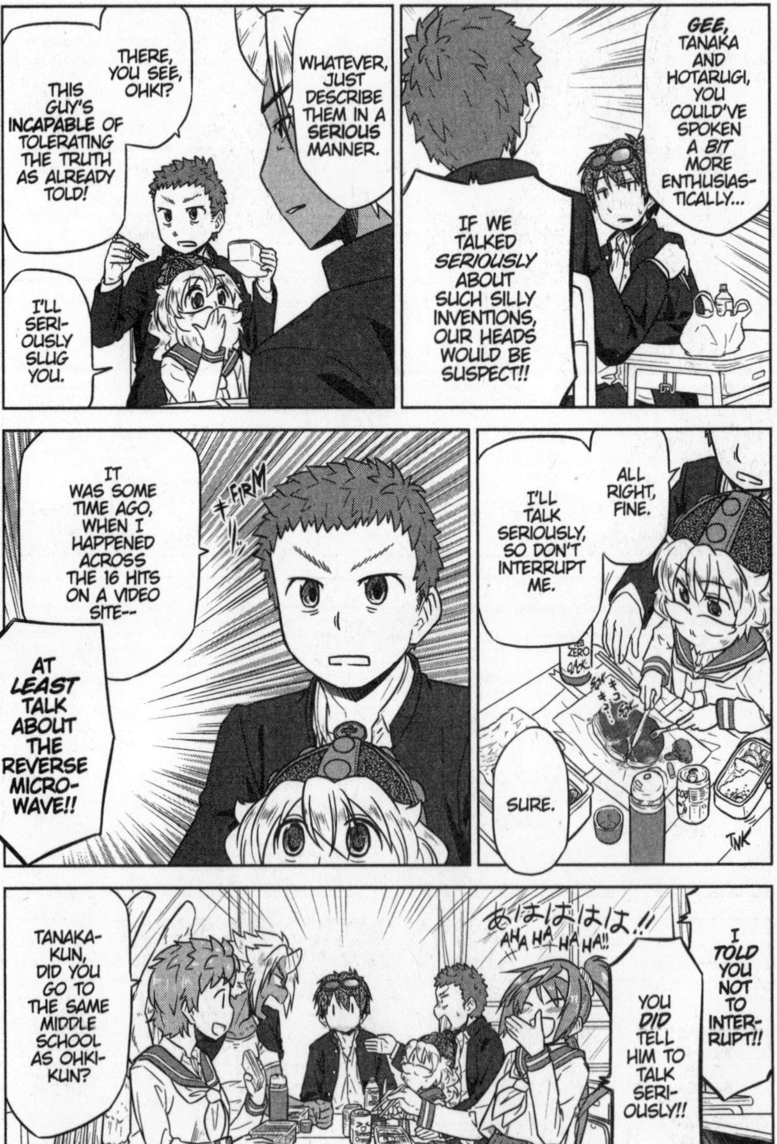
GEE, TANAKA AND HOTARUGI, YOU COULD'VE SPOKEN A BIT MORE ENTHUSIASTICALLY...
IF WE TALKED SERIOUSLY ABOUT SUCH SILLY INVENTIONS, OUR HEADS WOULD BE SUSPECT!!
WHATEVER, JUST DESCRIBE THEM IN A SERIOUS MANNER.
THERE, YOU SEE, OHKI?
THIS GUY'S INCAPABLE OF TOLERATING THE TRUTH AS ALREADY TOLD!
I'LL SERIOUSLY SLUG YOU.
ALL RIGHT, FINE.
I'LL TALK SERIOUSLY, SO DON'T INTERRUPT ME.
SURE.
TNK
FIRM
IT WAS SOME TIME AGO, WHEN I HAPPENED ACROSS THE 16 HITS ON A VIDEO SITE--
AT LEAST TALK ABOUT THE REVERSE MICROWAVE!!
I TOLD YOU NOT TO INTERRUPT!!
YOU DID TELL HIM TO TALK SERIOUSLY!!
あはははは!!
AHAHAHAHA!!
TANAKA-KUN, DID YOU GO TO THE SAME MIDDLE SCHOOL AS OHKI-KUN?

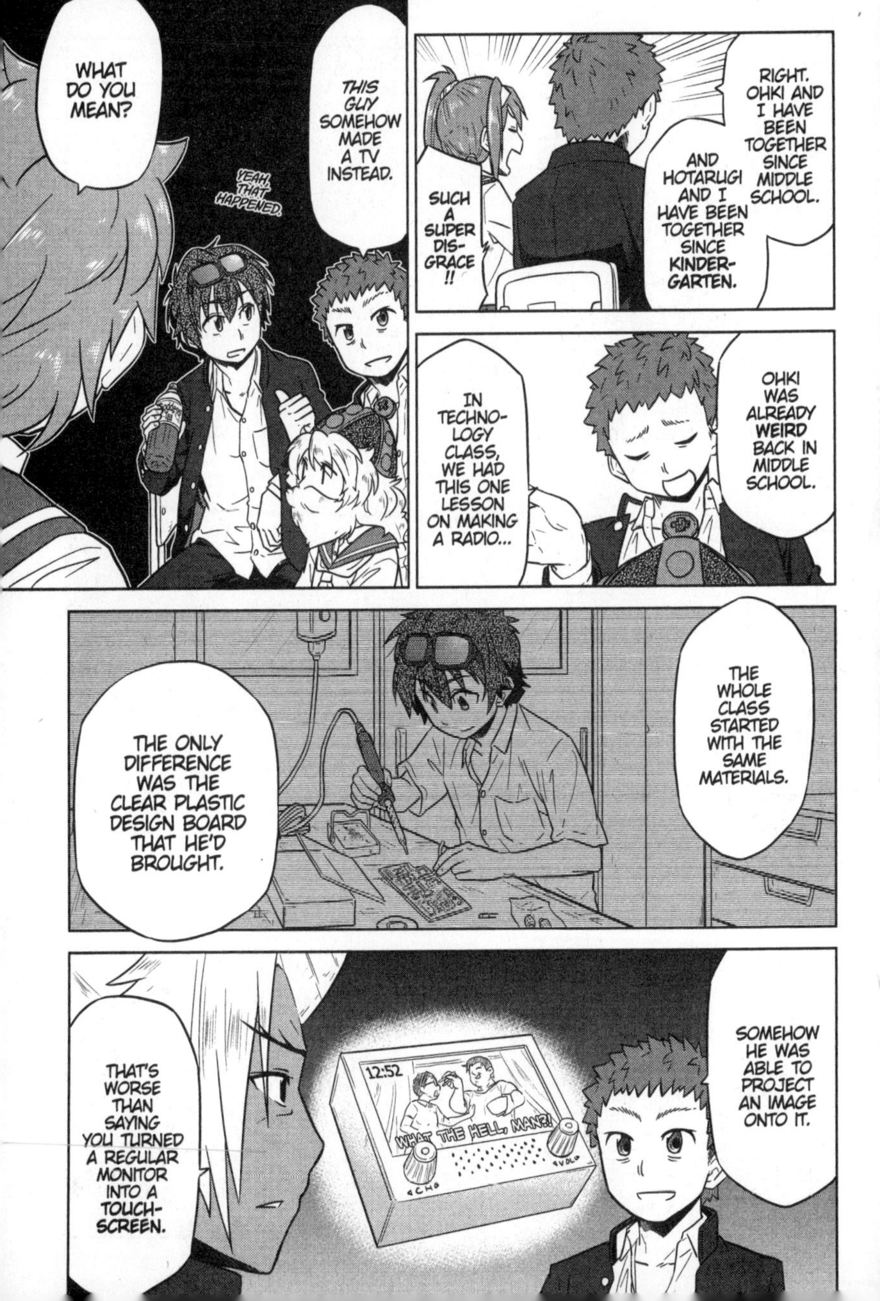
RIGHT. OHKI AND I HAVE BEEN TOGETHER SINCE MIDDLE SCHOOL.
AND HOTARUGI AND I HAVE BEEN TOGETHER SINCE KINDER-GARTEN.
SUCH A SUPER DIS-GRACE!!
OHKI WAS ALREADY **WEIRD** BACK IN MIDDLE SCHOOL.
IN TECHNO-LOGY CLASS, WE HAD THIS ONE LESSON ON MAKING A RADIO...
THIS GUY SOMEHOW MADE A TV INSTEAD.
YEAH, THAT HAPPENED.
WHAT DO YOU MEAN?
THE WHOLE CLASS STARTED WITH THE SAME MATERIALS.
THE ONLY DIFFERENCE WAS THE CLEAR PLASTIC DESIGN BOARD THAT HE'D BROUGHT.
SOMEHOW HE WAS ABLE TO PROJECT AN IMAGE ONTO IT.
12:52
WHAT THE HELL, MAN?!
THAT'S WORSE THAN SAYING YOU TURNED A REGULAR MONITOR INTO A TOUCH-SCREEN.

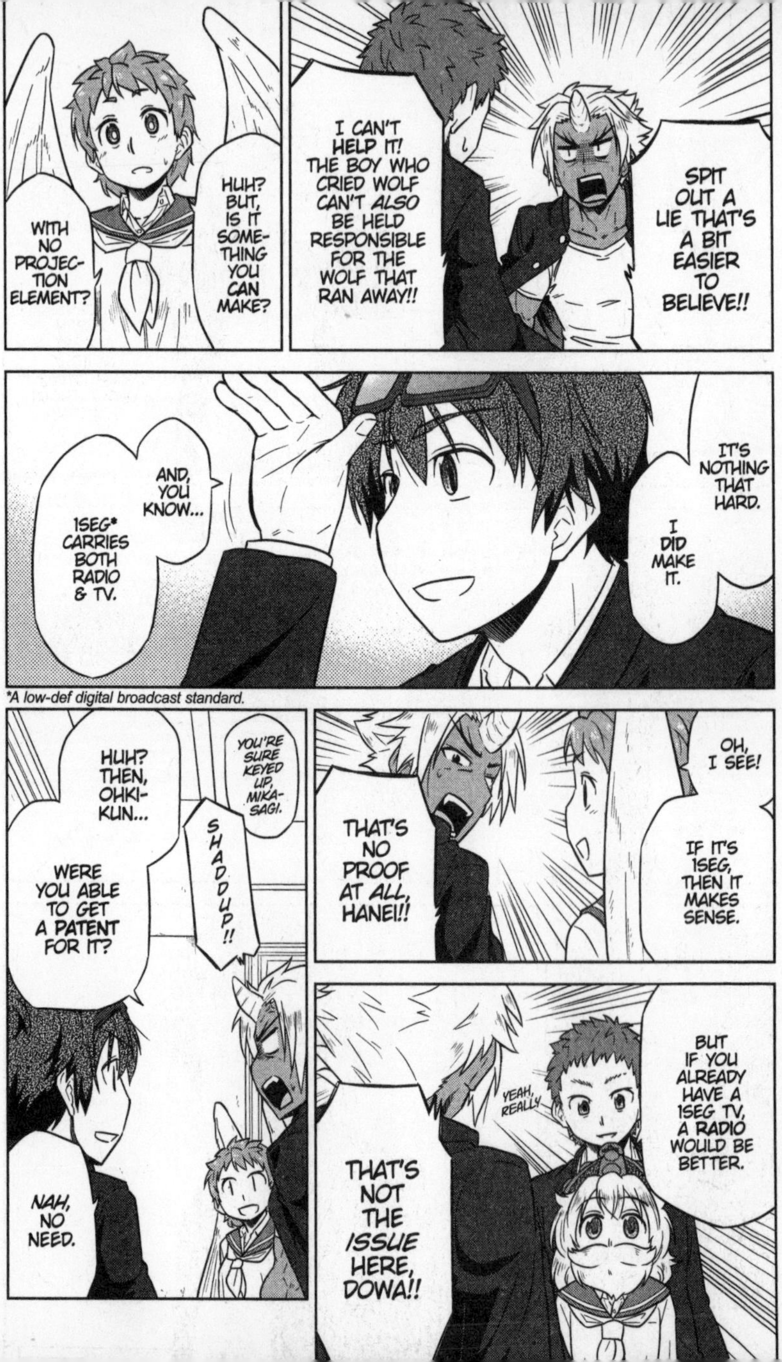
SPIT OUT A LIE THAT'S A BIT EASIER TO BELIEVE!!
I CAN'T HELP IT! THE BOY WHO CRIED WOLF CAN'T *ALSO* BE HELD RESPONSIBLE FOR THE WOLF THAT RAN AWAY!!
HUH? BUT, IS IT SOMETHING YOU CAN MAKE?
WITH NO PROJECTION ELEMENT?
IT'S NOTHING THAT HARD.
I DID MAKE IT.
AND, YOU KNOW...
ISEG* CARRIES BOTH RADIO & TV.
OH, I SEE!
IF IT'S ISEG, THEN IT MAKES SENSE.
THAT'S NO PROOF AT *ALL*, HANEI!!
BUT IF YOU ALREADY HAVE A ISEG TV, A RADIO WOULD BE BETTER.
YEAH, REALLY
THAT'S NOT THE *ISSUE* HERE, DOWA!!
YOU'RE SURE KEYED UP, MIKASAGI.
HUH? THEN, OHKI-KUN...
SHADDUP!!
WERE YOU ABLE TO GET A PATENT FOR IT?
NAH, NO NEED.

*A low-def digital broadcast standard.

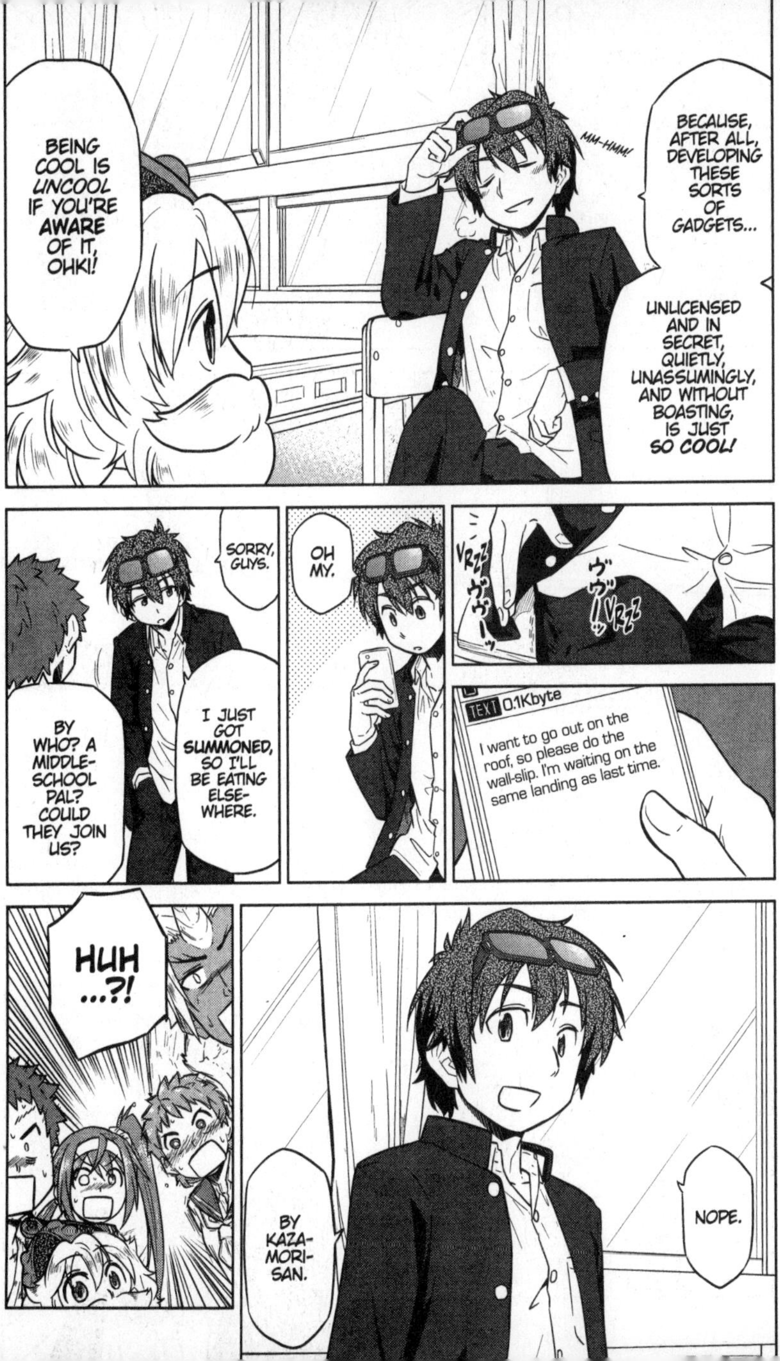

BECAUSE, AFTER ALL, DEVELOPING THESE SORTS OF GADGETS...
MM-HMM!
UNLICENSED AND IN SECRET, QUIETLY, UNASSUMINGLY, AND WITHOUT BOASTING, IS JUST SO COOL!
BEING COOL IS UNCOOL IF YOU'RE AWARE OF IT, OHKI!
VRZZ
ヴヴーッ
VRZZ
TEXT 0.1Kbyte
I want to go out on the roof, so please do the wall-slip. I'm waiting on the same landing as last time.
OH MY.
SORRY, GUYS.
I JUST GOT SUMMONED, SO I'LL BE EATING ELSE-WHERE.
BY WHO? A MIDDLE-SCHOOL PAL? COULD THEY JOIN US?
NOPE.
BY KAZA-MORI-SAN.
HUH ...?!

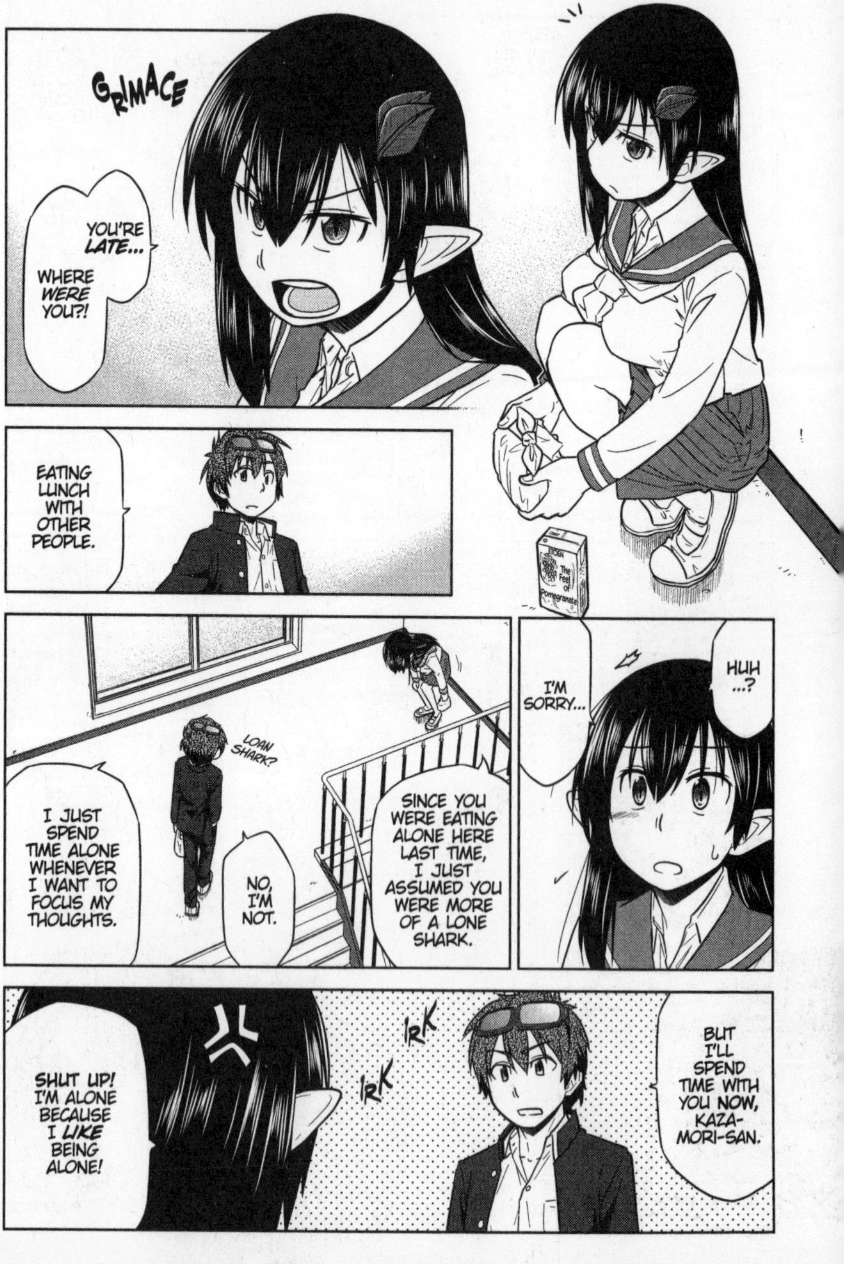
The Feel of Pomegranate
GRIMACE
YOU'RE *LATE*...
WHERE *WERE* YOU?!
EATING LUNCH WITH OTHER PEOPLE.
HUH ...?
I'M SORRY...
SINCE YOU WERE EATING ALONE HERE LAST TIME, I JUST ASSUMED YOU WERE MORE OF A LONE SHARK.
LOAN SHARK?
NO, I'M NOT.
I JUST SPEND TIME ALONE WHENEVER I WANT TO FOCUS MY THOUGHTS.
BUT I'LL SPEND TIME WITH YOU NOW, KAZA-MORI-SAN.
IRK
IRK
SHUT UP! I'M ALONE BECAUSE I *LIKE* BEING ALONE!

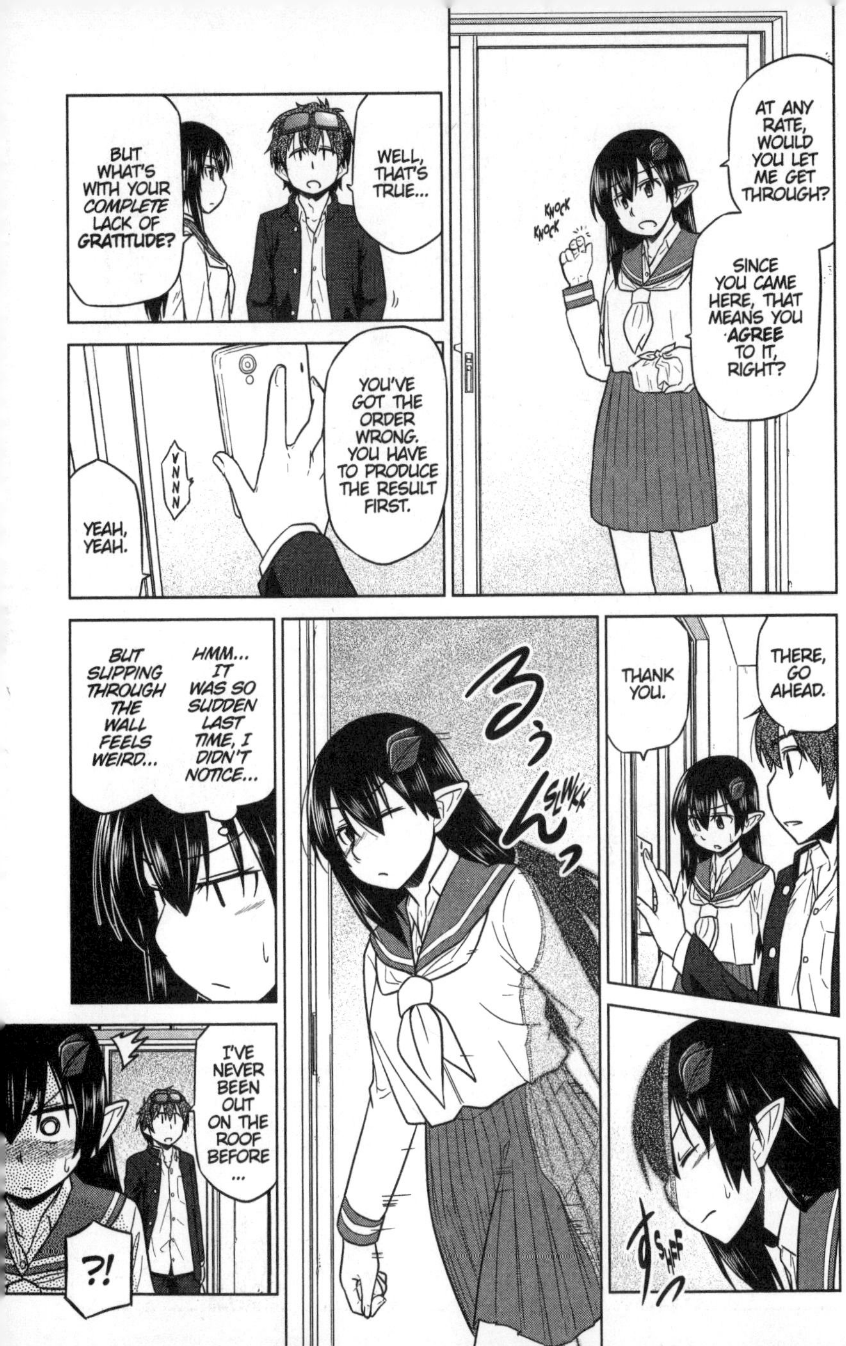
KNOCK KNOCK
AT ANY RATE, WOULD YOU LET ME GET THROUGH?
SINCE YOU CAME HERE, THAT MEANS YOU AGREE TO IT, RIGHT?
WELL, THAT'S TRUE...
BUT WHAT'S WITH YOUR COMPLETE LACK OF GRATITUDE?
YOU'VE GOT THE ORDER WRONG. YOU HAVE TO PRODUCE THE RESULT FIRST.
VNNN
YEAH, YEAH.
THERE, GO AHEAD.
THANK YOU.
SUFF
SLINKK
HMM... IT WAS SO SUDDEN LAST TIME, I DIDN'T NOTICE...
BUT SLIPPING THROUGH THE WALL FEELS WEIRD...
I'VE NEVER BEEN OUT ON THE ROOF BEFORE...
?!

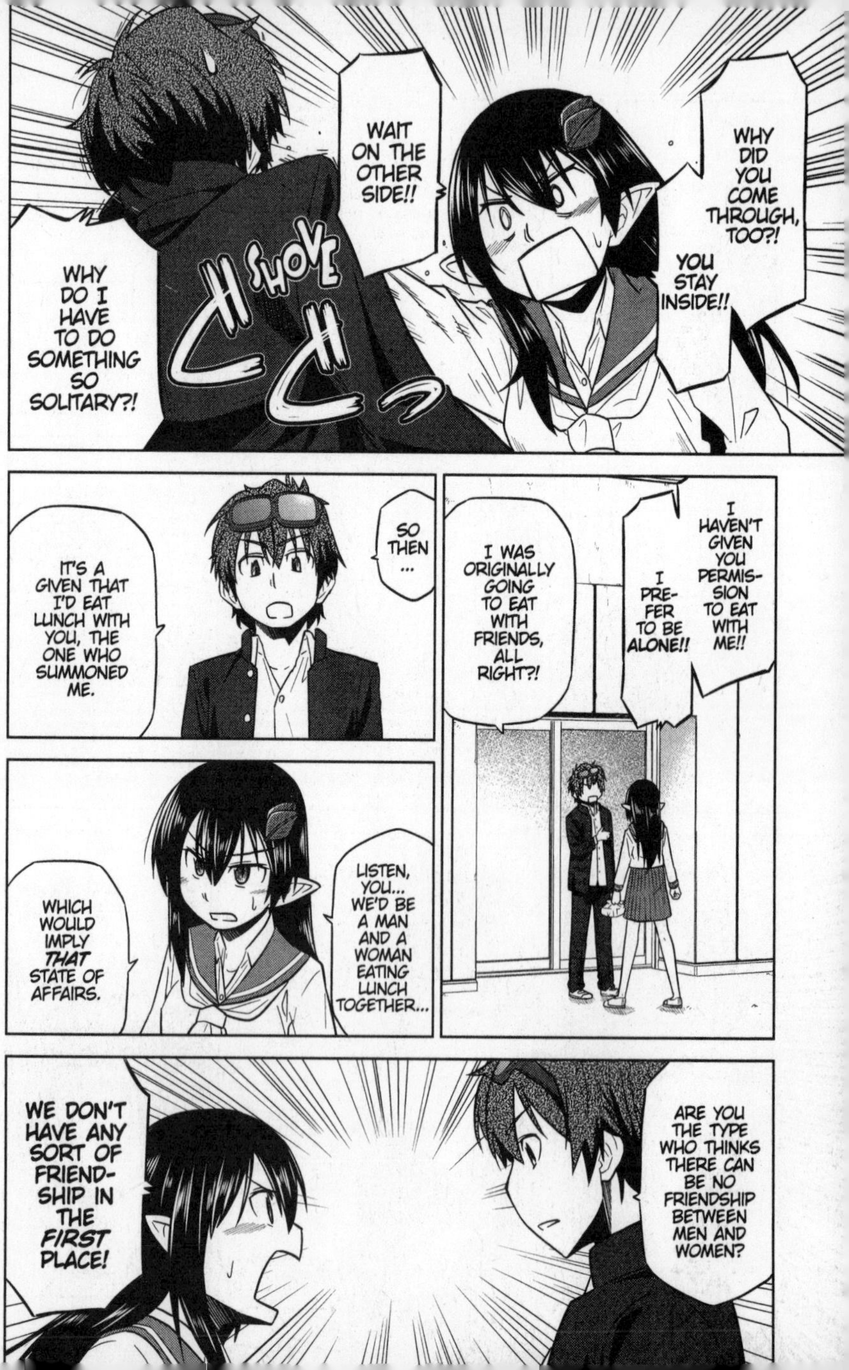
WHY DID YOU COME THROUGH, TOO?!
YOU STAY INSIDE!!
WAIT ON THE OTHER SIDE!!
SHOVE
WHY DO I HAVE TO DO SOMETHING SO SOLITARY?!
I HAVEN'T GIVEN YOU PERMIS-SION TO EAT WITH ME!!
I PRE-FER TO BE ALONE!!
I WAS ORIGINALLY GOING TO EAT WITH FRIENDS, ALL RIGHT?!
SO THEN ...
IT'S A GIVEN THAT I'D EAT LUNCH WITH YOU, THE ONE WHO SUMMONED ME.
LISTEN, YOU... WE'D BE A MAN AND A WOMAN EATING LUNCH TOGETHER...
WHICH WOULD IMPLY *THAT* STATE OF AFFAIRS.
ARE YOU THE TYPE WHO THINKS THERE CAN BE NO FRIENDSHIP BETWEEN MEN AND WOMEN?
WE DON'T HAVE ANY SORT OF FRIEND-SHIP IN THE *FIRST* PLACE!

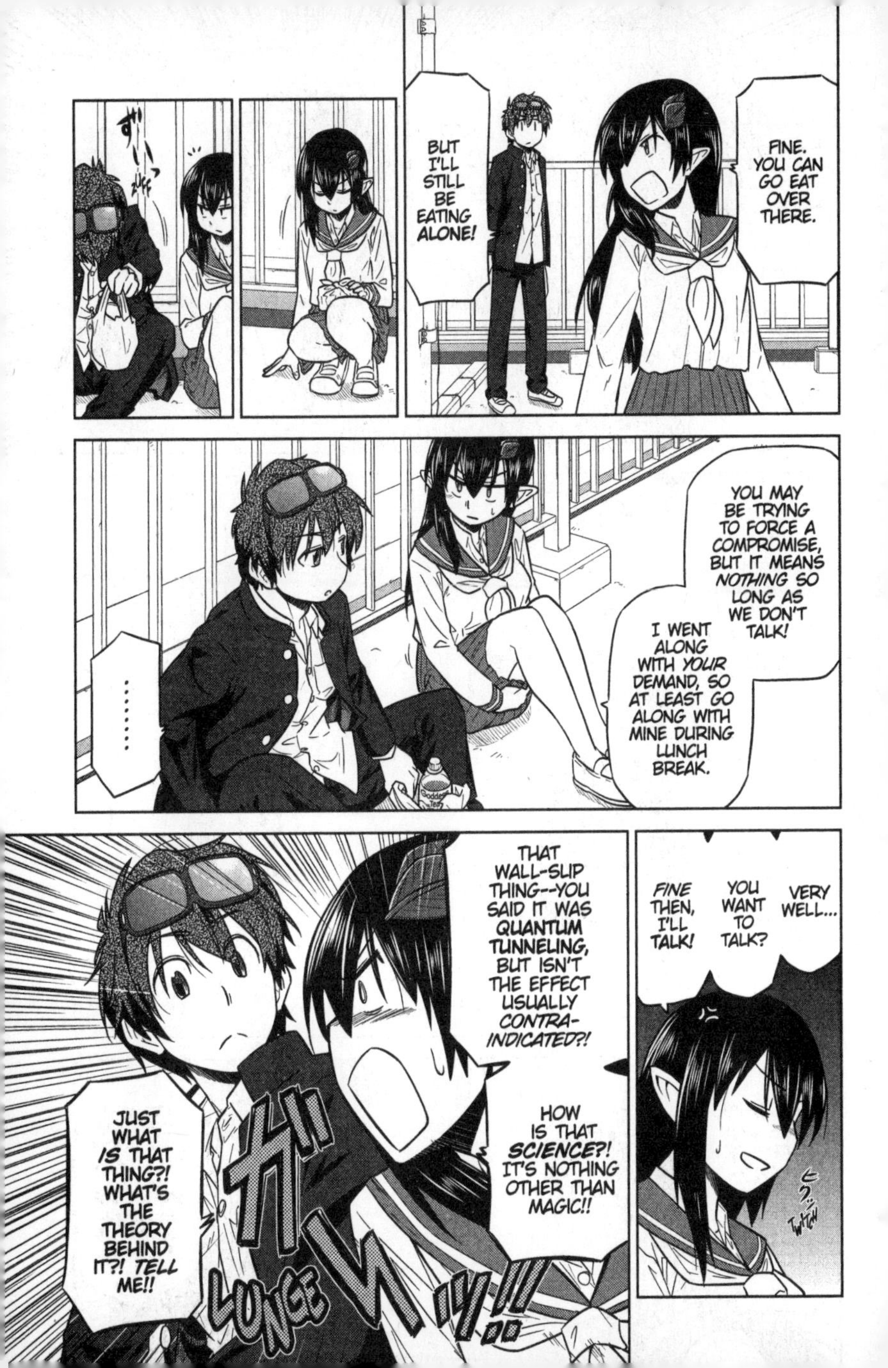
FINE. YOU CAN GO EAT OVER THERE.
BUT I'LL STILL BE EATING ALONE!
ZUFF
YOU MAY BE TRYING TO FORCE A COMPROMISE, BUT IT MEANS NOTHING SO LONG AS WE DON'T TALK!
I WENT ALONG WITH YOUR DEMAND, SO AT LEAST GO ALONG WITH MINE DURING LUNCH BREAK.
......
VERY WELL...
YOU WANT TO TALK?
FINE THEN, I'LL TALK!
TWITCH
THAT WALL-SLIP THING--YOU SAID IT WAS QUANTUM TUNNELING, BUT ISN'T THE EFFECT USUALLY CONTRA-INDICATED?!
HOW IS THAT SCIENCE?! IT'S NOTHING OTHER THAN MAGIC!!
JUST WHAT IS THAT THING?! WHAT'S THE THEORY BEHIND IT?! TELL ME!!
LUNGE

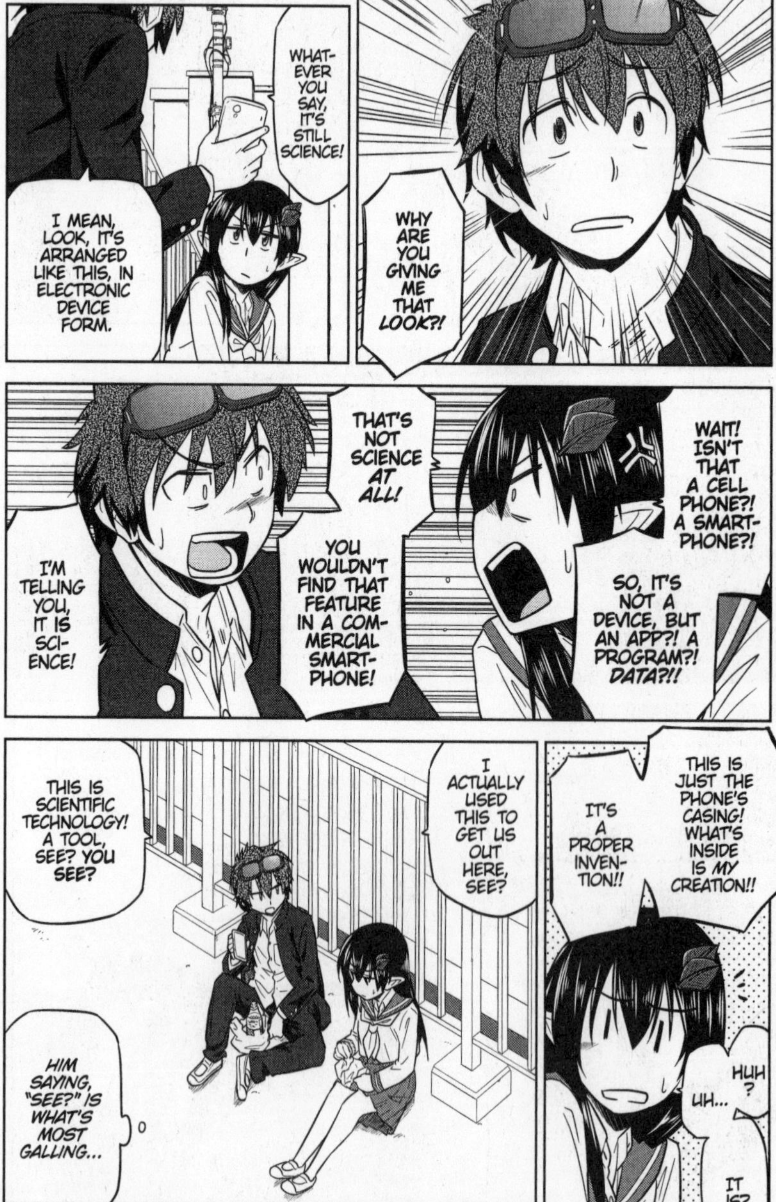
WHY ARE YOU GIVING ME THAT *LOOK?!*
WHATEVER YOU SAY, IT'S STILL SCIENCE!
I MEAN, LOOK, IT'S ARRANGED LIKE THIS, IN ELECTRONIC DEVICE FORM.
WAIT! ISN'T THAT A CELL PHONE?! A SMARTPHONE?!
SO, IT'S NOT A DEVICE, BUT AN APP?! A PROGRAM?! *DATA?!!*
THAT'S NOT SCIENCE *AT ALL!*
YOU WOULDN'T FIND THAT FEATURE IN A COMMERCIAL SMARTPHONE!
I'M TELLING YOU, IT IS SCIENCE!
THIS IS JUST THE PHONE'S CASING! WHAT'S INSIDE IS *MY* CREATION!!
IT'S A PROPER INVENTION!!
HUH? UH...
IT IS?
I ACTUALLY USED THIS TO GET US OUT HERE, SEE?
THIS IS SCIENTIFIC TECHNOLOGY! A TOOL, SEE? YOU SEE?
HIM SAYING, "SEE?" IS WHAT'S MOST GALLING...

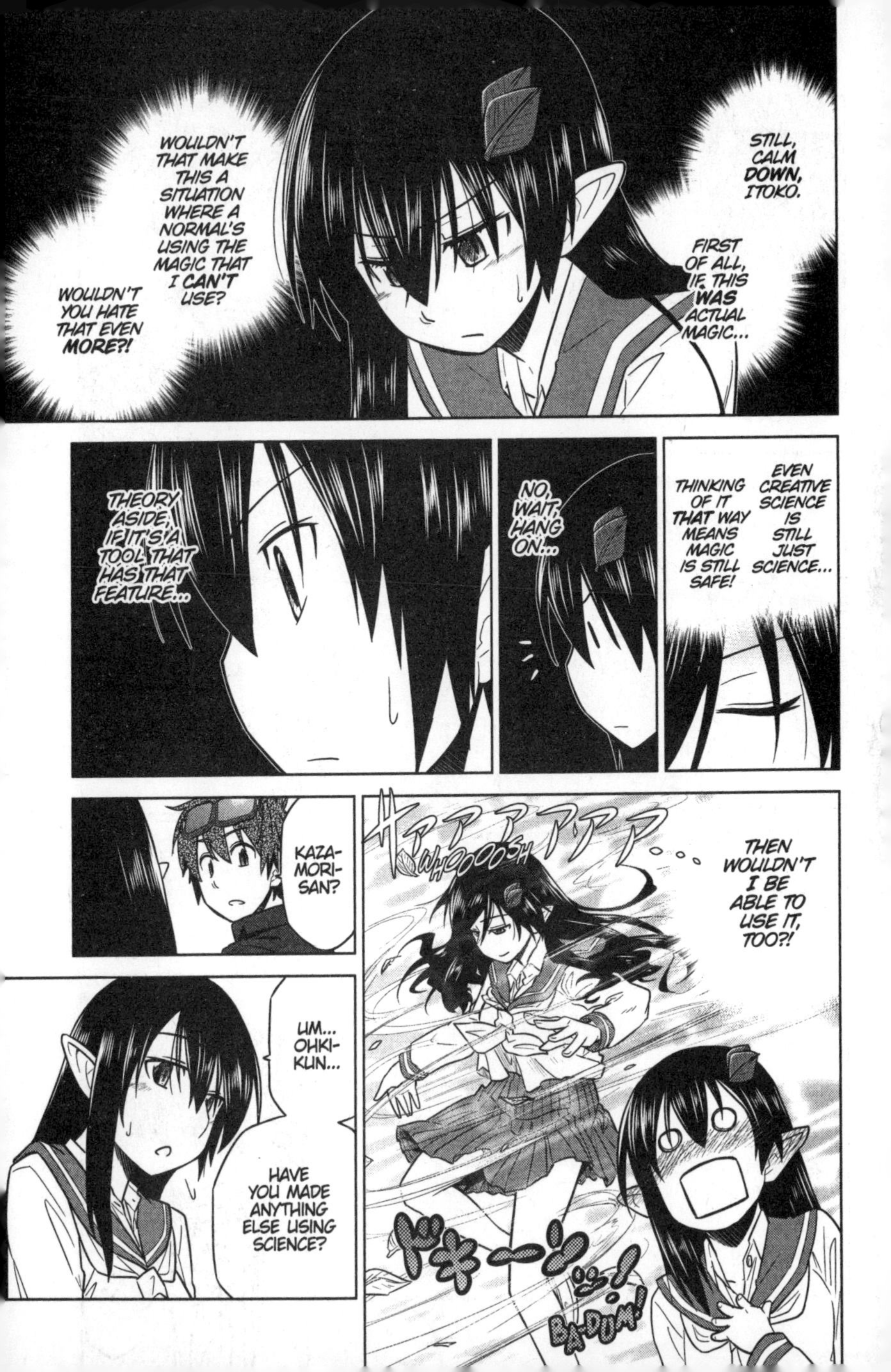
STILL, CALM DOWN, ITOKO.
FIRST OF ALL, IF THIS WAS ACTUAL MAGIC...
WOULDN'T THAT MAKE THIS A SITUATION WHERE A NORMAL'S USING THE MAGIC THAT I CAN'T USE?
WOULDN'T YOU HATE THAT EVEN MORE?!
EVEN CREATIVE SCIENCE IS STILL JUST SCIENCE...
THINKING OF IT THAT WAY MEANS MAGIC IS STILL SAFE!
NO, WAIT, HANG ON...
THEORY ASIDE, IF IT'S A TOOL THAT HAS THAT FEATURE...
WHOOOOSH
THEN WOULDN'T I BE ABLE TO USE IT, TOO?!
BA-DUM!
KAZAMORI-SAN?
UM... OHKI-KUN...
HAVE YOU MADE ANYTHING ELSE USING SCIENCE?

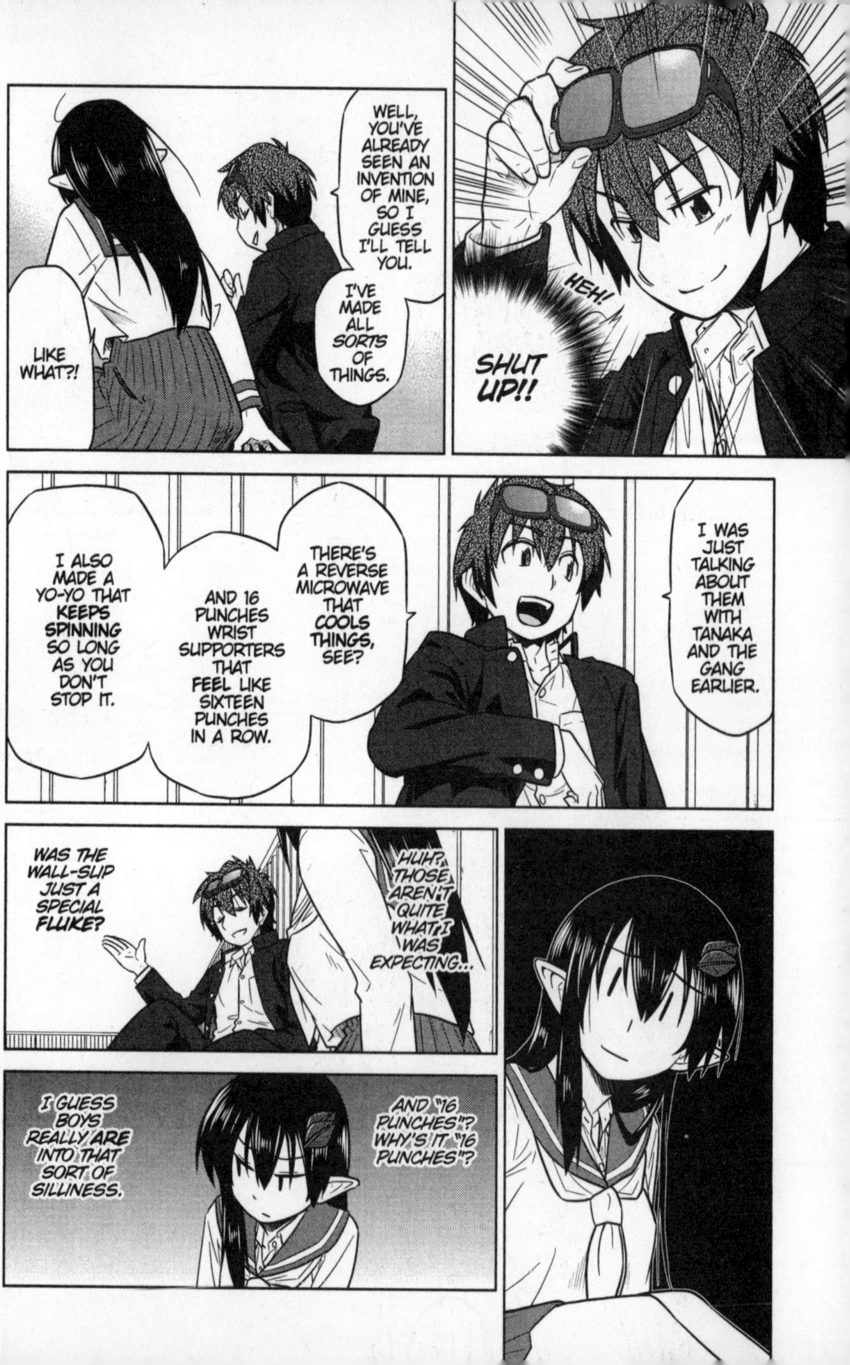

HEH!
SHUT UP!!
WELL, YOU'VE ALREADY SEEN AN INVENTION OF MINE, SO I GUESS I'LL TELL YOU.
I'VE MADE ALL SORTS OF THINGS.
LIKE WHAT?!
I WAS JUST TALKING ABOUT THEM WITH TANAKA AND THE GANG EARLIER.
THERE'S A REVERSE MICROWAVE THAT COOLS THINGS, SEE?
AND 16 PUNCHES WRIST SUPPORTERS THAT FEEL LIKE SIXTEEN PUNCHES IN A ROW.
I ALSO MADE A YO-YO THAT KEEPS SPINNING SO LONG AS YOU DON'T STOP IT.
HUH? THOSE AREN'T QUITE WHAT I WAS EXPECTING...
WAS THE WALL-SLIP JUST A SPECIAL FLUKE?
AND "16 PUNCHES"? WHY'S IT "16 PUNCHES"?
I GUESS BOYS REALLY ARE INTO THAT SORT OF SILLINESS.

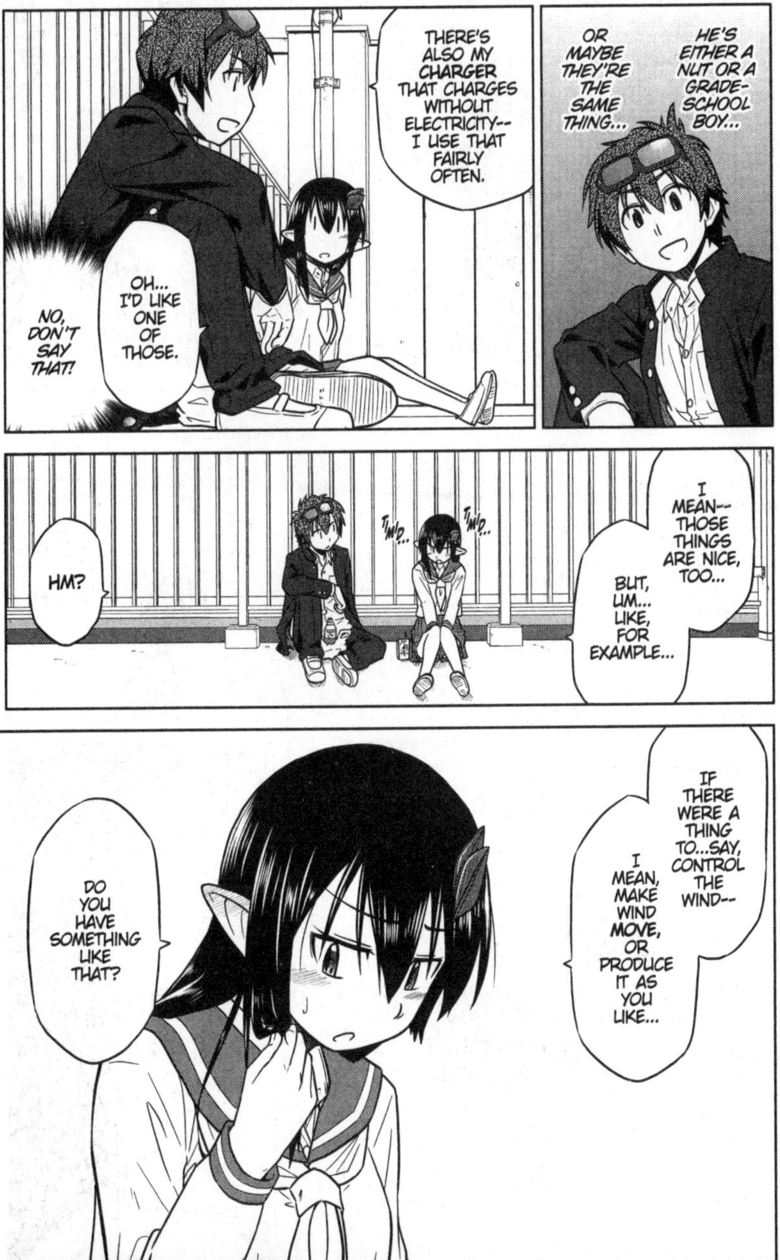
HE'S EITHER A NUT OR A GRADE-SCHOOL BOY...
OR MAYBE THEY'RE THE SAME THING...
THERE'S ALSO MY CHARGER THAT CHARGES WITHOUT ELECTRICITY-- I USE THAT FAIRLY OFTEN.
OH... I'D LIKE ONE OF THOSE.
NO, DON'T SAY THAT!
I MEAN-- THOSE THINGS ARE NICE, TOO...
BUT, UM... LIKE, FOR EXAMPLE...
TIMID...
TIMID...
HM?
IF THERE WERE A THING TO...SAY, CONTROL THE WIND--
I MEAN, MAKE WIND MOVE, OR PRODUCE IT AS YOU LIKE...
DO YOU HAVE SOMETHING LIKE THAT?

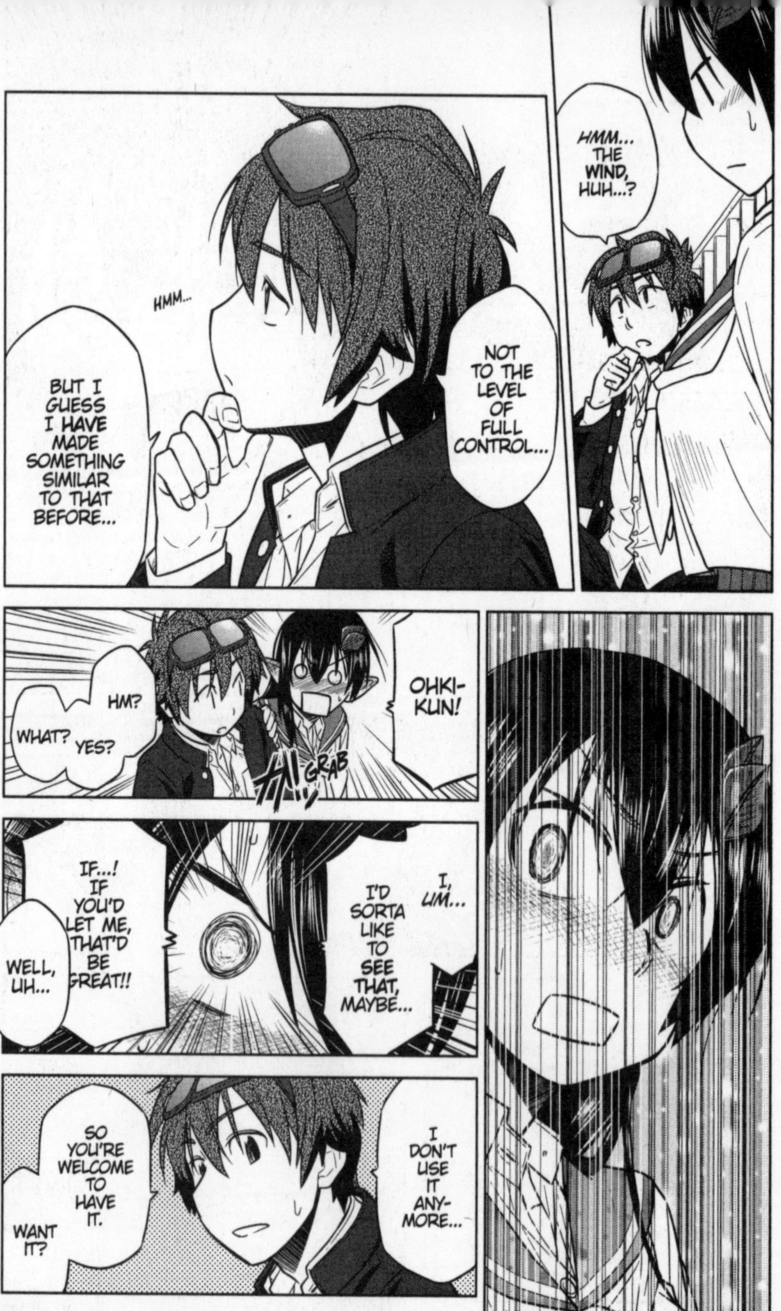
HMM... THE WIND, HUH...?
NOT TO THE LEVEL OF FULL CONTROL...
HMM...
BUT I GUESS I HAVE MADE SOMETHING SIMILAR TO THAT BEFORE...
OHKI-KUN!
GRAB
HM?
WHAT? YES?
I, UM...
I'D SORTA LIKE TO SEE THAT, MAYBE...
IF...! IF YOU'D LET ME, THAT'D BE GREAT!!
WELL, UH...
I DON'T USE IT ANYMORE...
SO YOU'RE WELCOME TO HAVE IT.
WANT IT?

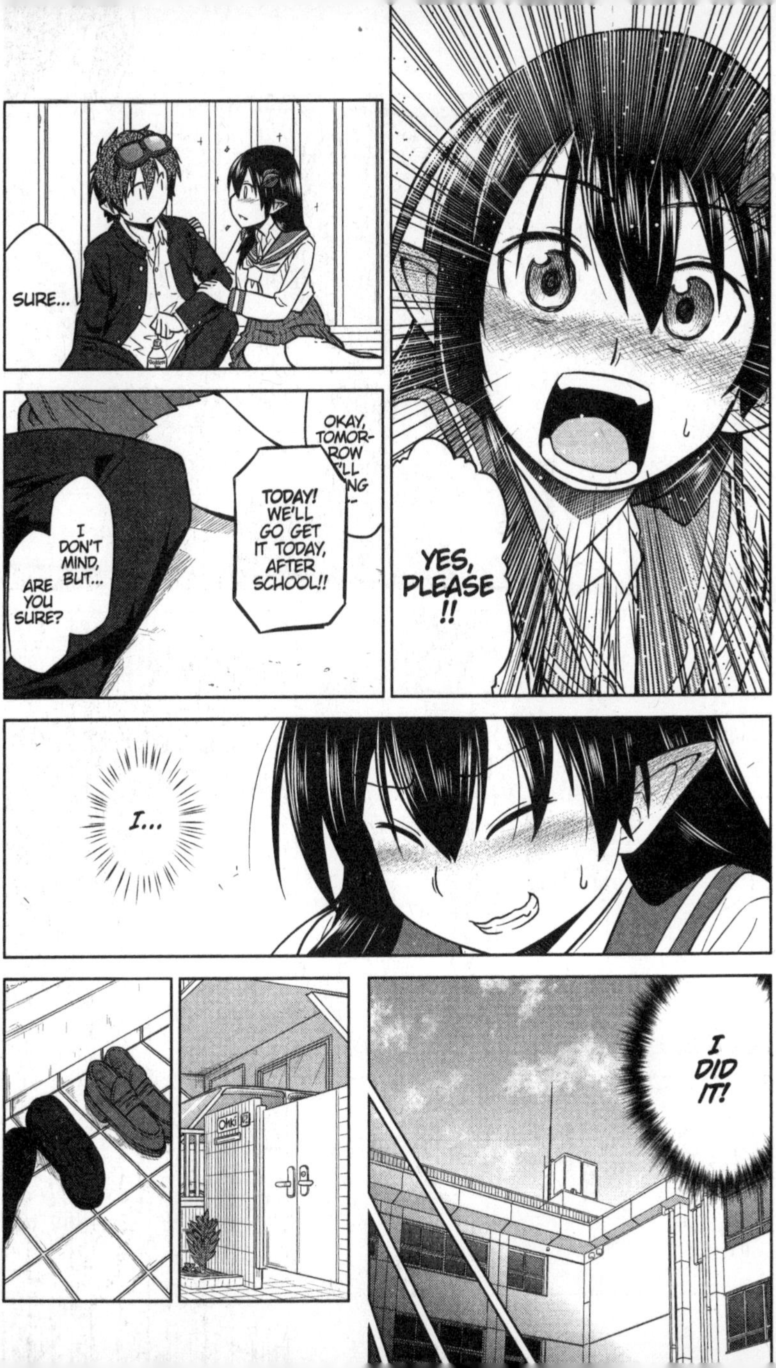
YES, PLEASE!!
SURE...
OKAY, TOMOR-ROW
TODAY! WE'LL GO GET IT TODAY, AFTER SCHOOL!!
I DON'T MIND, BUT...
ARE YOU SURE?
I...
I DID IT!

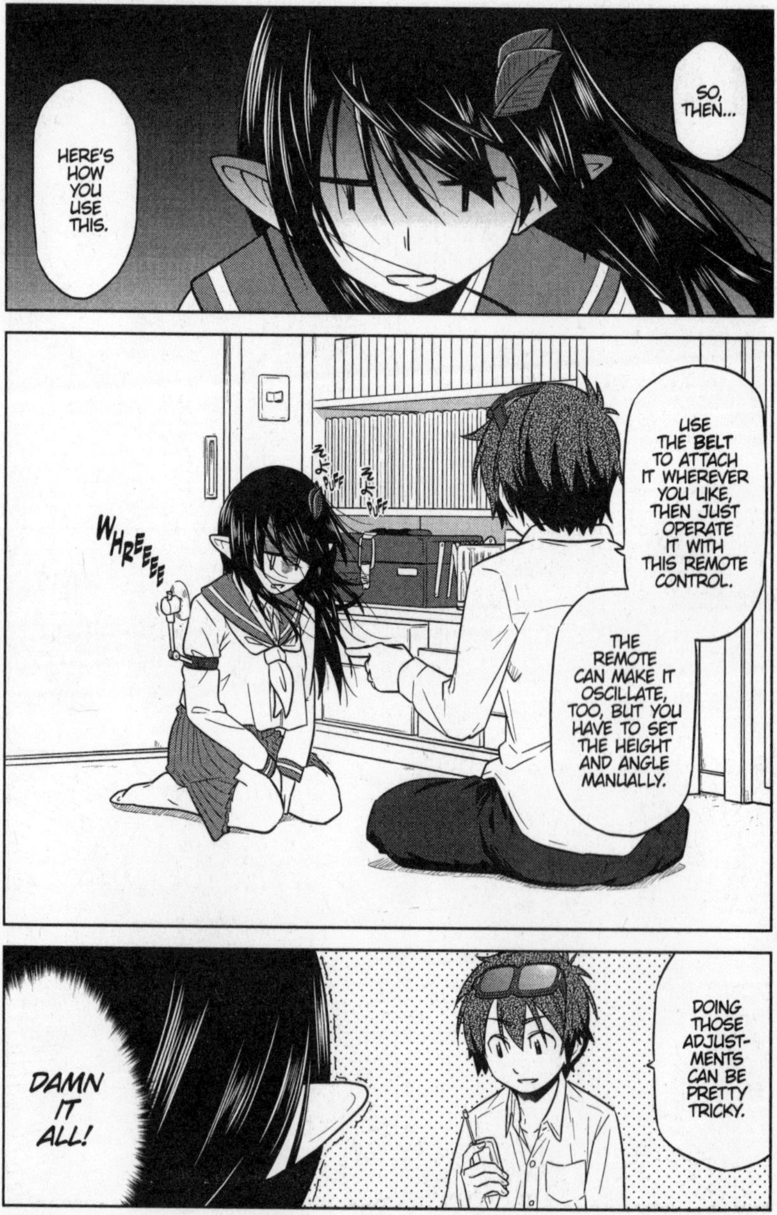
SO, THEN...
HERE'S HOW YOU USE THIS.
USE THE BELT TO ATTACH IT WHEREVER YOU LIKE, THEN JUST OPERATE IT WITH THIS REMOTE CONTROL.
THE REMOTE CAN MAKE IT OSCILLATE, TOO, BUT YOU HAVE TO SET THE HEIGHT AND ANGLE MANUALLY.
PUFF
PUFF
WHREEEEE
DOING THOSE ADJUST-MENTS CAN BE PRETTY TRICKY.
DAMN IT ALL!

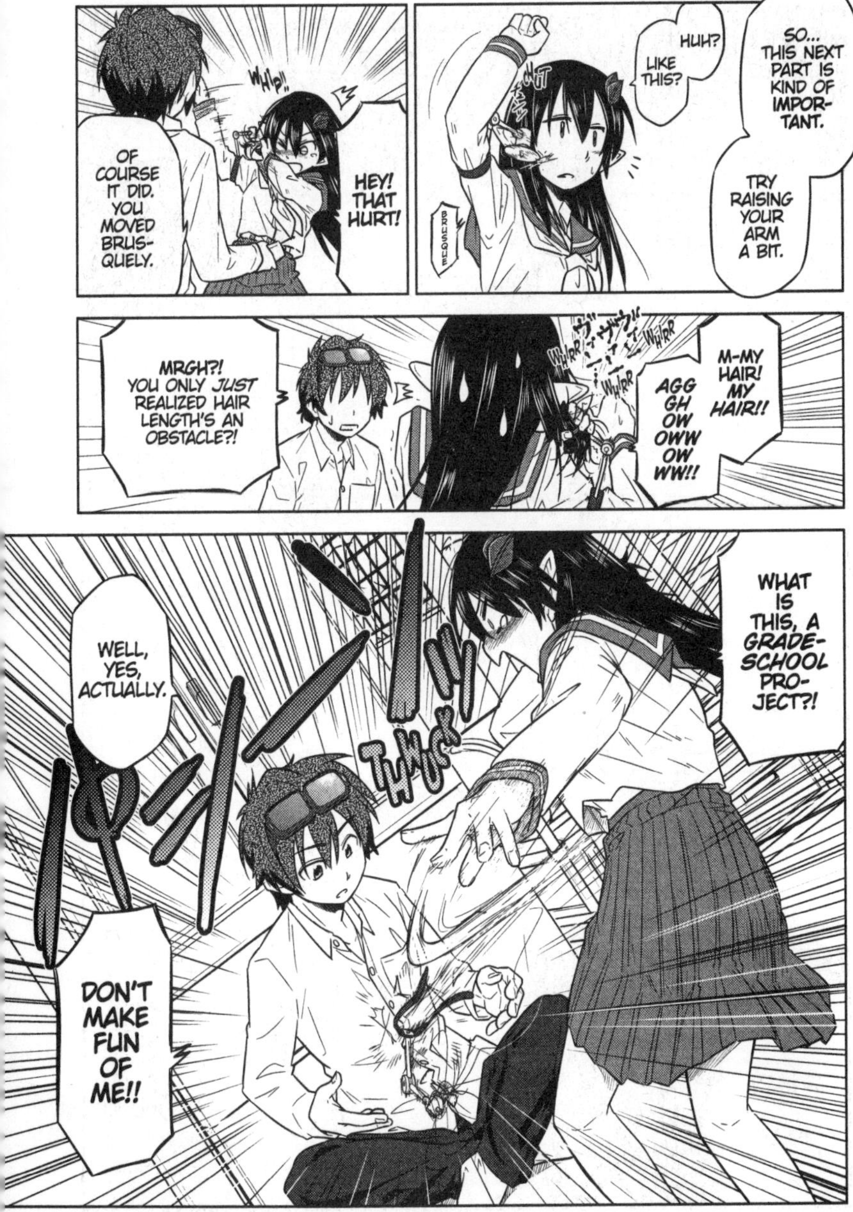
SO... THIS NEXT PART IS KIND OF IMPOR-TANT.
TRY RAISING YOUR ARM A BIT.
HUH?
LIKE THIS?
BRUSQUE
WHIP!!
HEY! THAT HURT!
OF COURSE IT DID. YOU MOVED BRUS-QUELY.
M-MY HAIR! MY HAIR!!
AGG GH OW OWW OW WW!!
WHIRR
WHIRR
WHIRR
MRGH?! YOU ONLY JUST REALIZED HAIR LENGTH'S AN OBSTACLE?!
WHAT IS THIS, A GRADE-SCHOOL PRO-JECT?!
WELL, YES, ACTUALLY.
THWACK
DON'T MAKE FUN OF ME!!

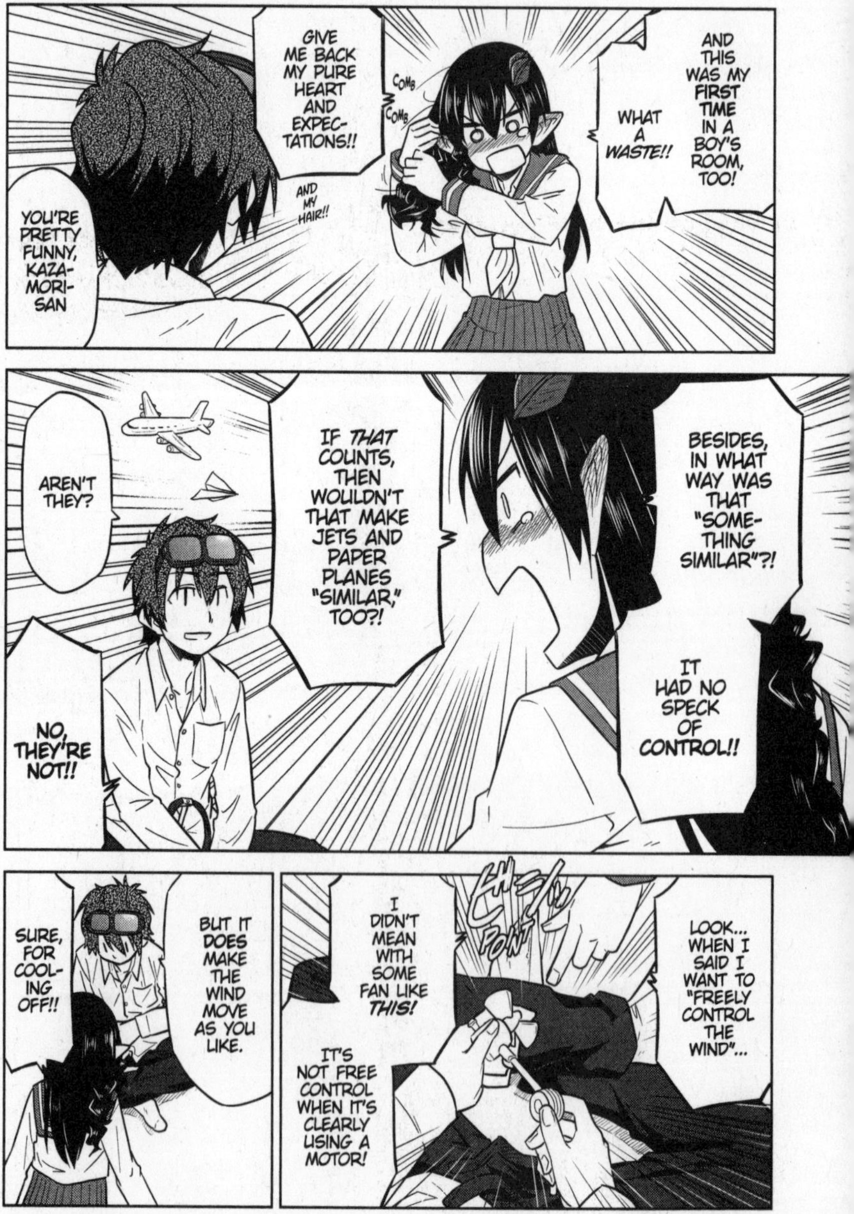
AND THIS WAS MY FIRST TIME IN A BOY'S ROOM, TOO!
WHAT A *WASTE*!!
COMB COMB
GIVE ME BACK MY PURE HEART AND EXPECTATIONS!!
AND MY HAIR!!
YOU'RE PRETTY FUNNY, KAZAMORI-SAN
BESIDES, IN WHAT WAY WAS THAT "SOMETHING SIMILAR"?!
IT HAD NO SPECK OF CONTROL!!
IF *THAT* COUNTS, THEN WOULDN'T THAT MAKE JETS AND PAPER PLANES "SIMILAR," TOO?!
AREN'T THEY?
NO, THEY'RE NOT!!
LOOK... WHEN I SAID I WANT TO "FREELY CONTROL THE WIND"...
PON
I DIDN'T MEAN WITH SOME FAN LIKE *THIS!*
IT'S NOT FREE CONTROL WHEN IT'S CLEARLY USING A MOTOR!
BUT IT DOES MAKE THE WIND MOVE AS YOU LIKE.
SURE, FOR COOLING OFF!!

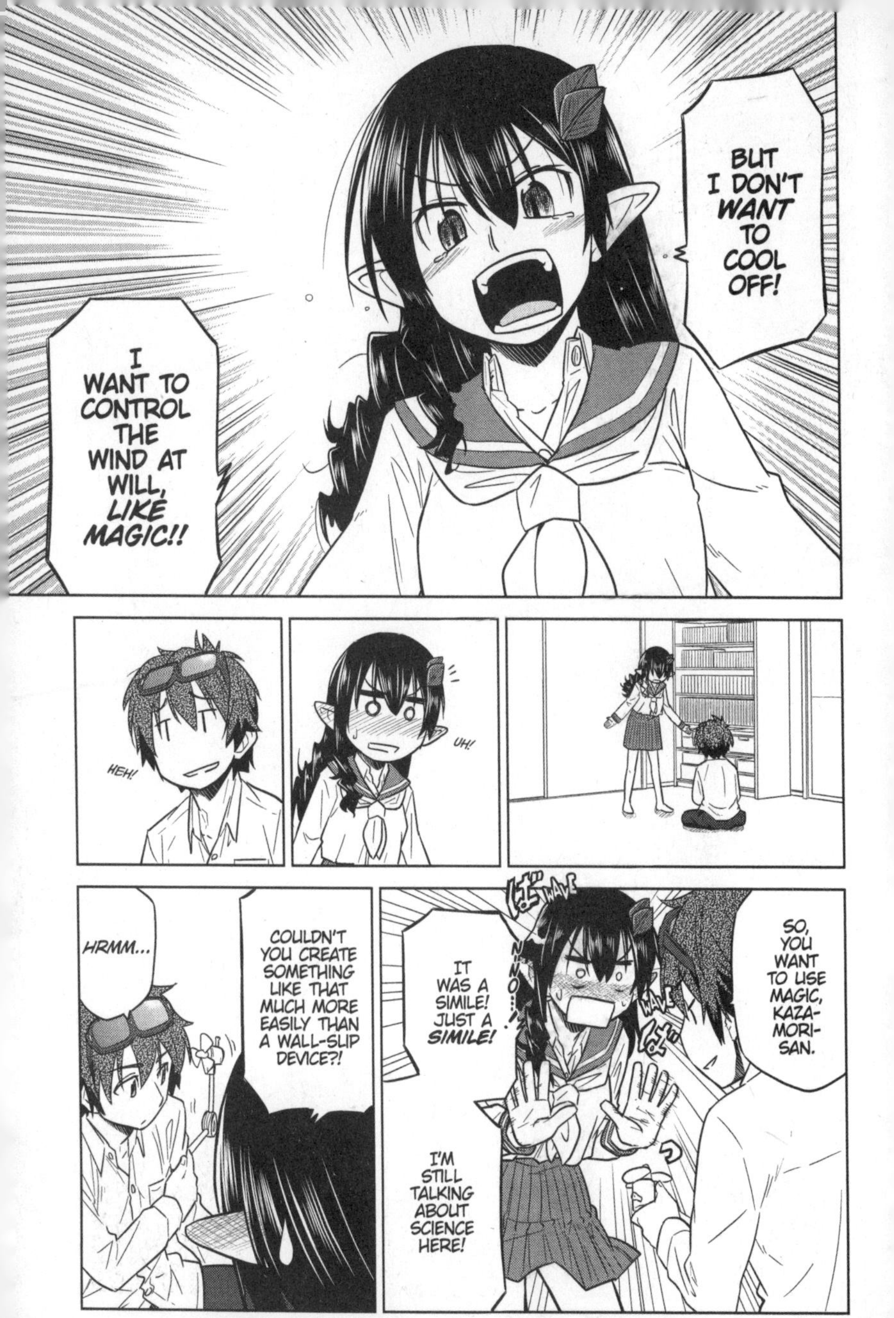
BUT I DON'T *WANT* TO COOL OFF!
I WANT TO CONTROL THE WIND AT WILL, *LIKE MAGIC!!*
UH!
HEH!
SO, YOU WANT TO USE MAGIC, KAZAMORI-SAN.
WAVE
WAVE
N-NO...!
IT WAS A SIMILE! JUST A *SIMILE!*
I'M STILL TALKING ABOUT SCIENCE HERE!
COULDN'T YOU CREATE SOMETHING LIKE THAT MUCH MORE EASILY THAN A WALL-SLIP DEVICE?!
HRMM...

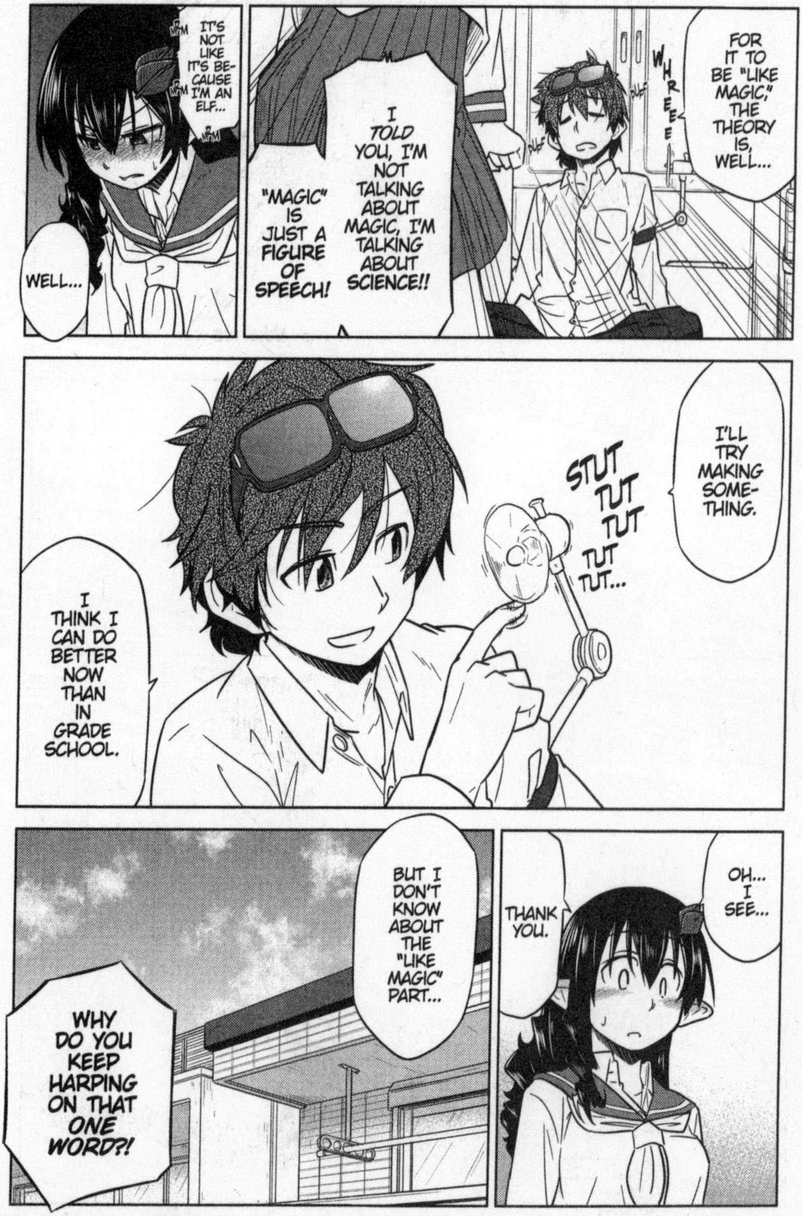
FOR IT TO BE "LIKE MAGIC," THE THEORY IS, WELL...
WHREEE
I TOLD YOU, I'M NOT TALKING ABOUT MAGIC, I'M TALKING ABOUT SCIENCE!!
"MAGIC" IS JUST A FIGURE OF SPEECH!
IT'S NOT LIKE IT'S BECAUSE I'M AN ELF...
WELL...
I'LL TRY MAKING SOMETHING.
STUT TUT TUT TUT TUT...
I THINK I CAN DO BETTER NOW THAN IN GRADE SCHOOL.
OH... I SEE...
THANK YOU.
BUT I DON'T KNOW ABOUT THE "LIKE MAGIC" PART...
WHY DO YOU KEEP HARPING ON THAT *ONE WORD*?!

Chapter 2 • END

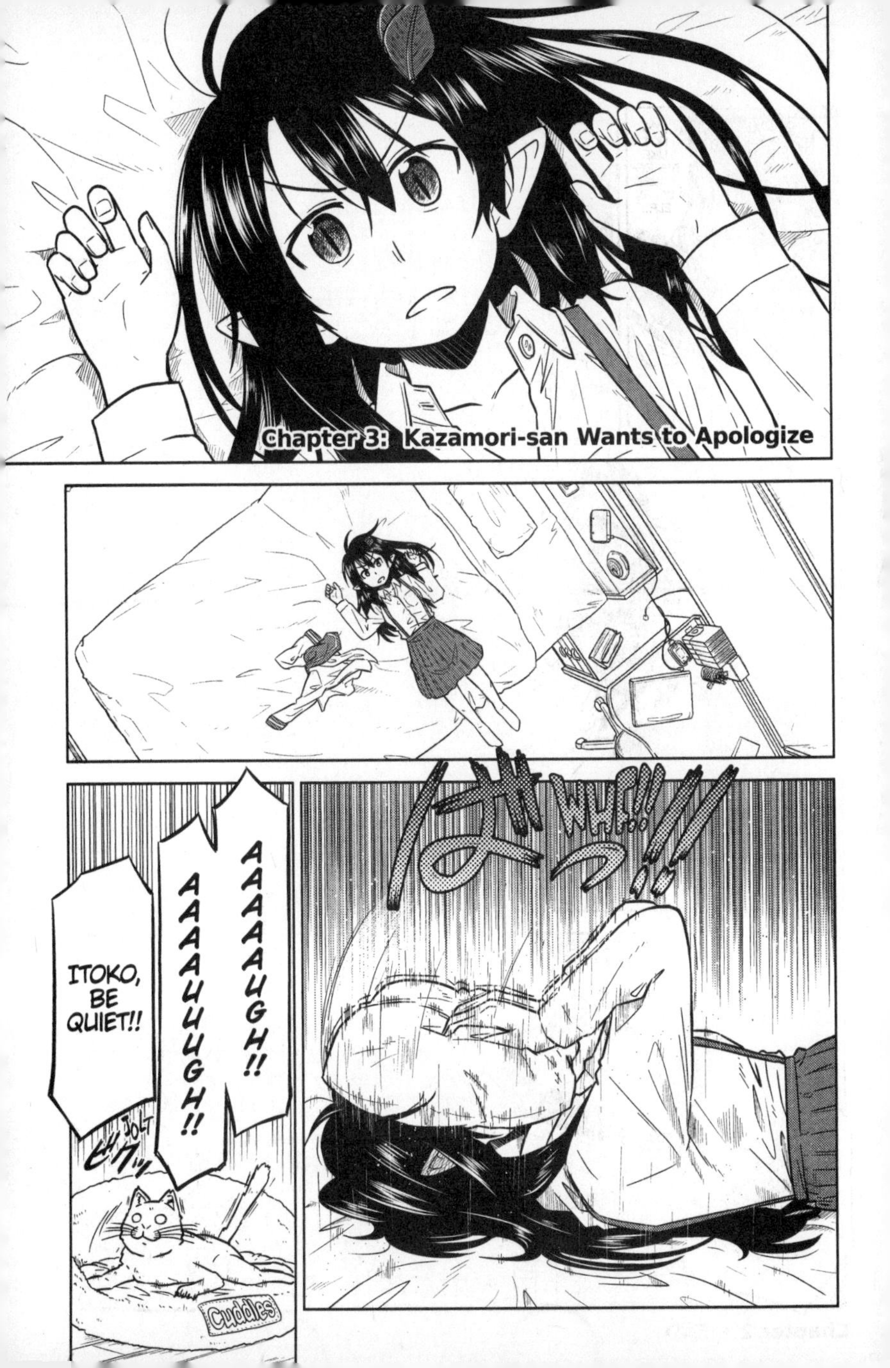
Chapter 3: Kazamori-san Wants to Apologize
WHF!!
AAAAAAUGH!!
AAAAAUUUGH!!
ITOKO, BE QUIET!!
JOLT
Cuddles

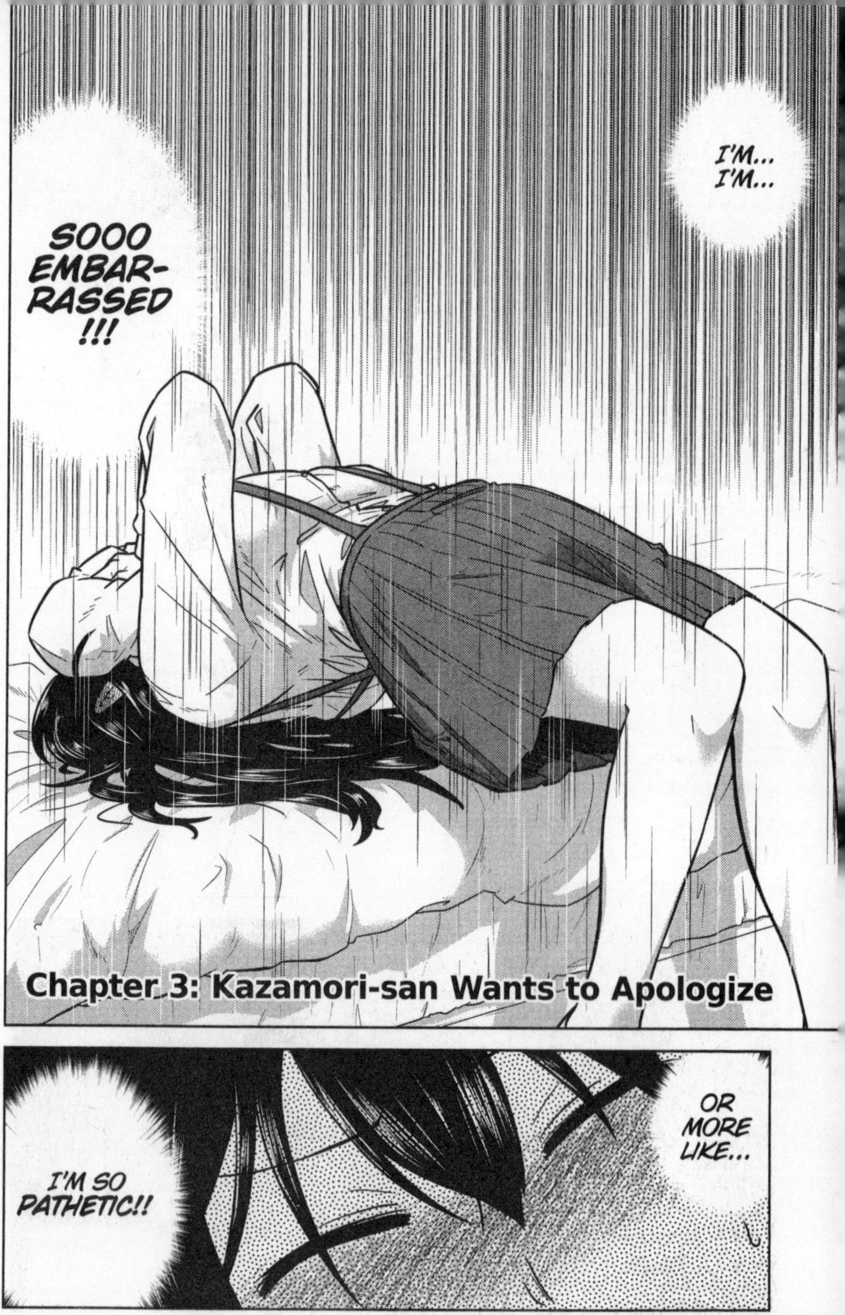
I'M... I'M...
SOOO EMBARRASSED!!!
Chapter 3: Kazamori-san Wants to Apologize
OR MORE LIKE...
I'M SO PATHETIC!!

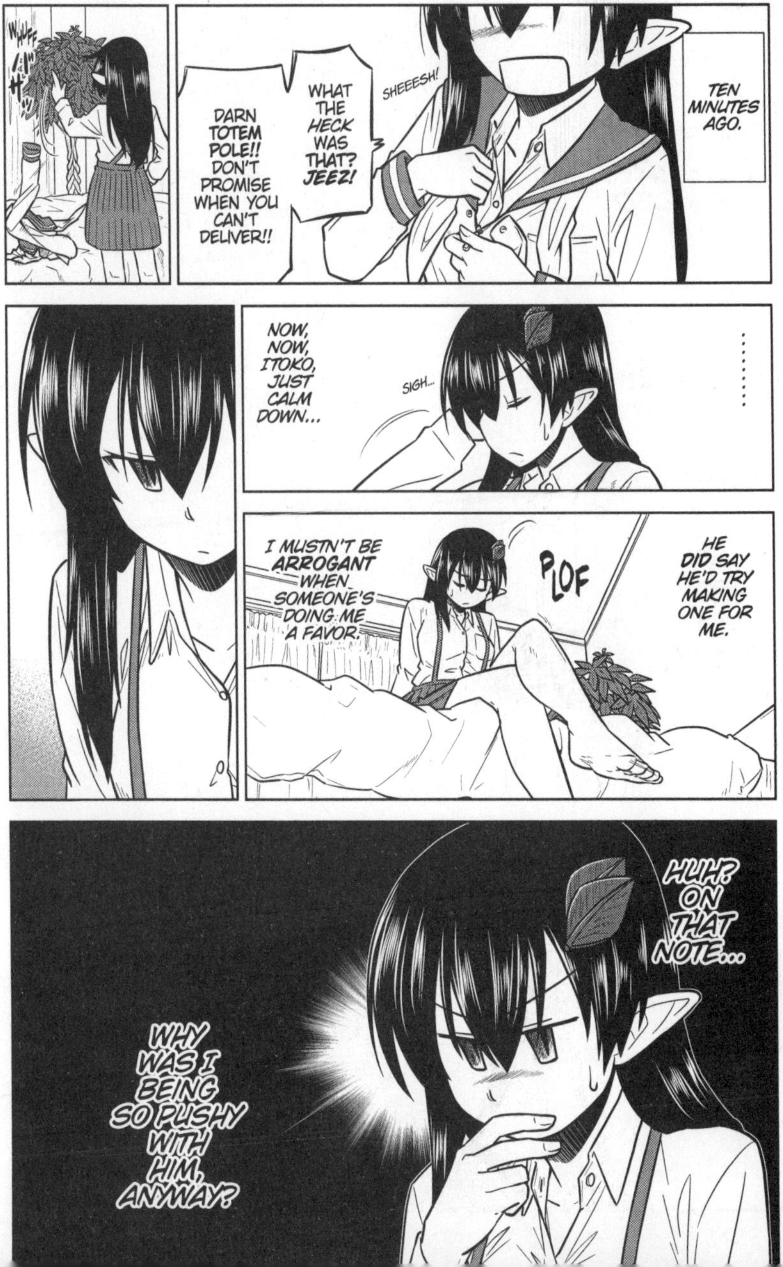
TEN MINUTES AGO.
SHEEESH!
WHAT THE HECK WAS THAT? JEEZ!
DARN TOTEM POLE!! DON'T PROMISE WHEN YOU CAN'T DELIVER!!
WHUFF
......
SIGH...
NOW, NOW, ITOKO, JUST CALM DOWN...
HE DID SAY HE'D TRY MAKING ONE FOR ME.
PLOF
I MUSTN'T BE ARROGANT WHEN SOMEONE'S DOING ME A FAVOR.
HUH? ON THAT NOTE...
WHY WAS I BEING SO PUSHY WITH HIM, ANYWAY?

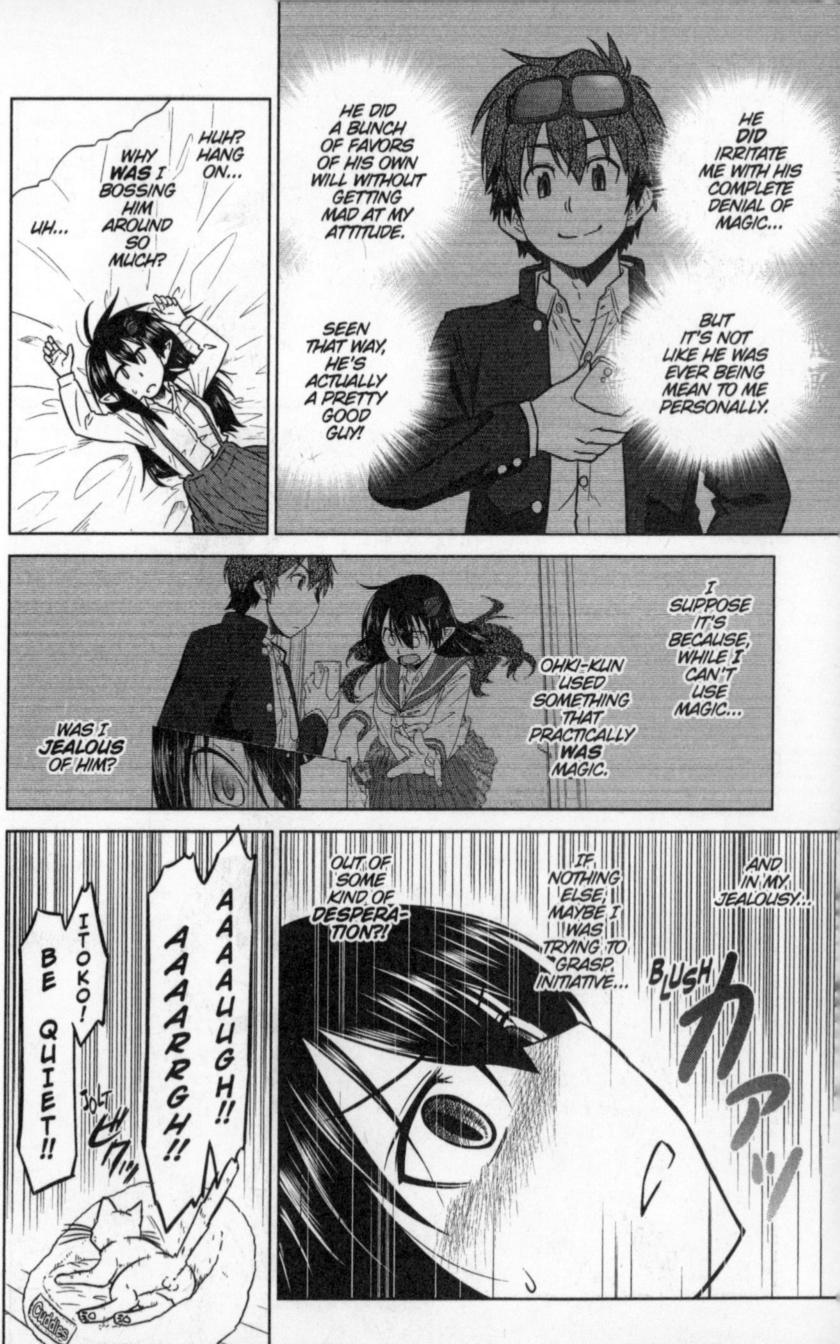
HE DID IRRITATE ME WITH HIS COMPLETE DENIAL OF MAGIC...
HE DID A BUNCH OF FAVORS OF HIS OWN WILL WITHOUT GETTING MAD AT MY ATTITUDE.
BUT IT'S NOT LIKE HE WAS EVER BEING MEAN TO ME PERSONALLY.
SEEN THAT WAY, HE'S ACTUALLY A PRETTY GOOD GUY!
HUH? HANG ON...
WHY WAS I BOSSING HIM AROUND SO MUCH?
UH...
I SUPPOSE IT'S BECAUSE, WHILE I CAN'T USE MAGIC...
OHKI-KUN USED SOMETHING THAT PRACTICALLY WAS MAGIC.
WAS I JEALOUS OF HIM?
AND IN MY JEALOUSY...
BLUSH
カァッ
IF NOTHING ELSE, MAYBE I WAS TRYING TO GRASP INITIATIVE...
OUT OF SOME KIND OF DESPERA-TION?!
AAAAUGH!!
AAAARRGH!!
ITOKO! BE QUIET!!
JOLT
Cuddles

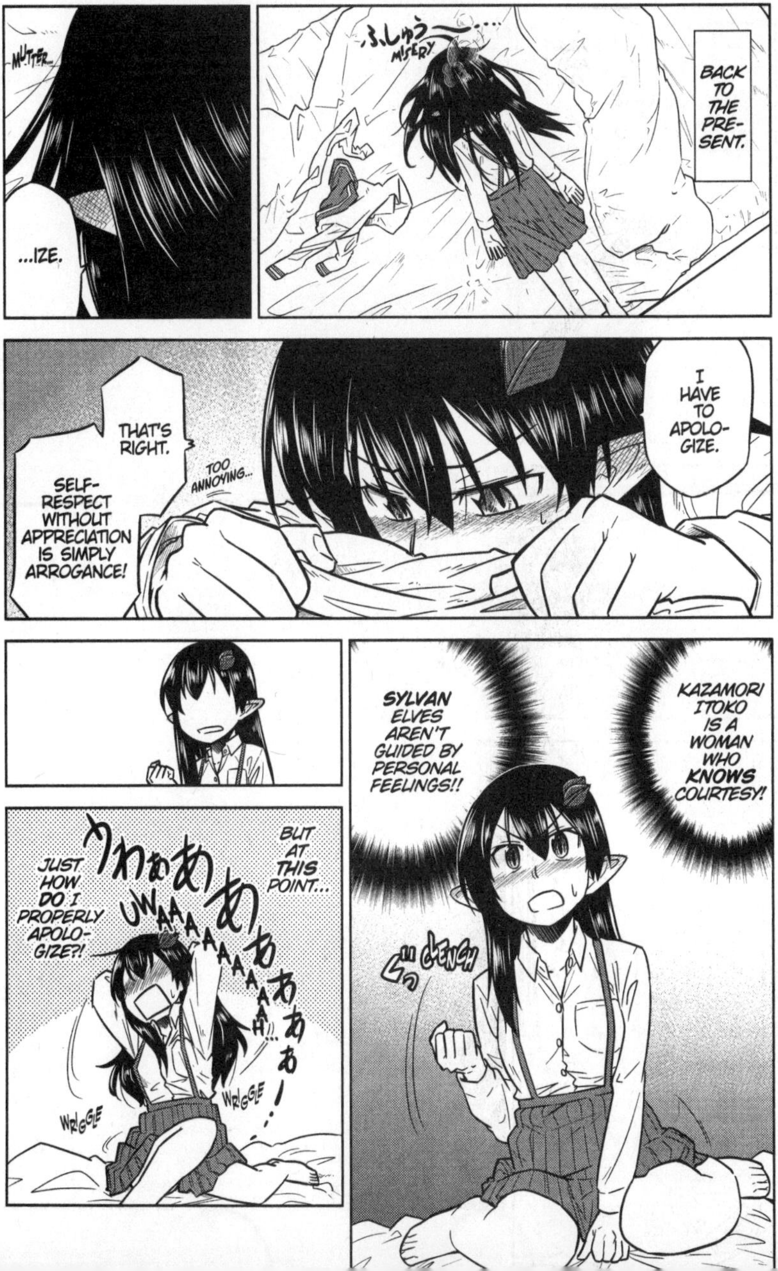

BACK TO THE PRESENT.
ふしゅう~…
MISERY
MUTTER...
...IZE.
I HAVE TO APOLOGIZE.
TOO ANNOYING...
THAT'S RIGHT.
SELF-RESPECT WITHOUT APPRECIATION IS SIMPLY ARROGANCE!
KAZAMORI ITOKO IS A WOMAN WHO KNOWS COURTESY!
SYLVAN ELVES AREN'T GUIDED BY PERSONAL FEELINGS!!
ぐっ
CLENCH
BUT AT THIS POINT...
うわぁああああああ
UWAAAAAAAAAH!!...
JUST HOW DO I PROPERLY APOLOGIZE?!
WRIGGLE
WRIGGLE

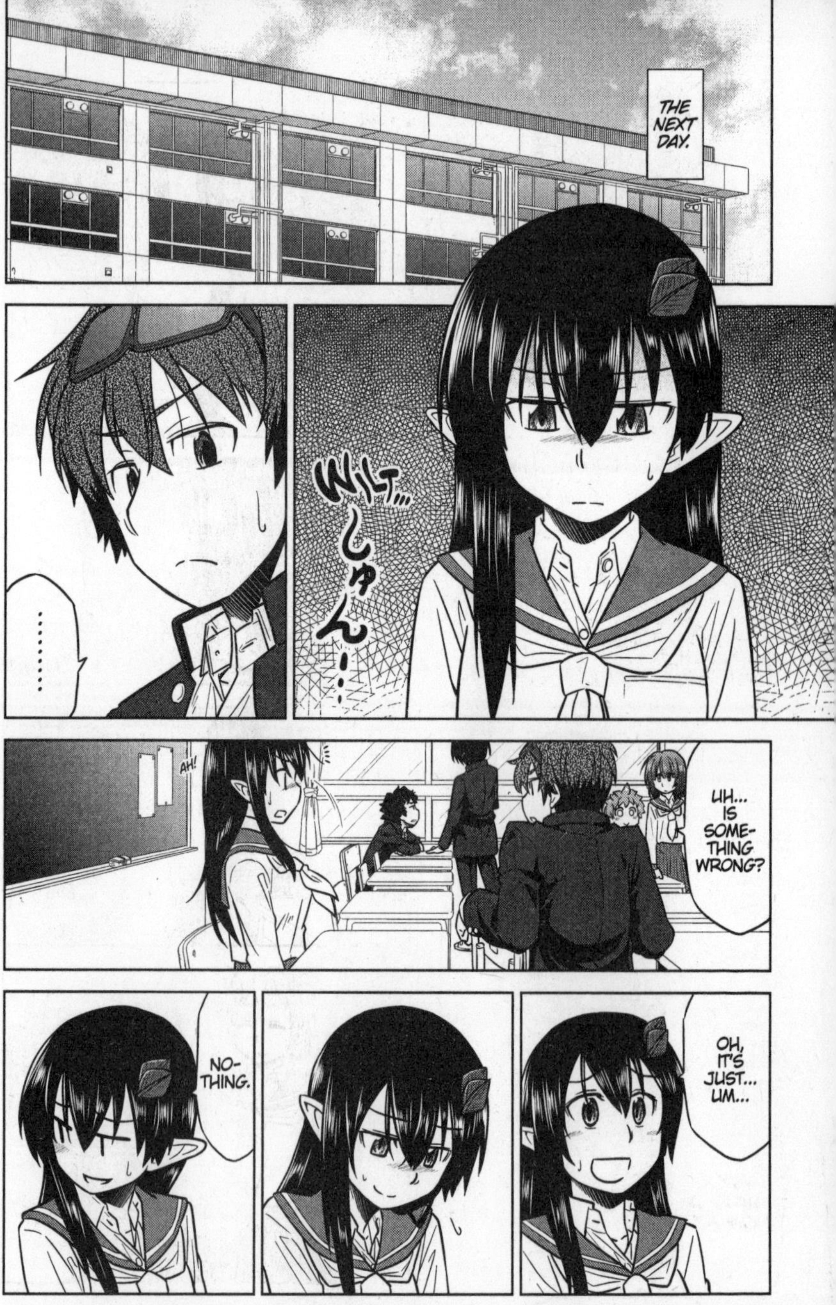
THE NEXT DAY.
WILT...
しゅん…!!
......
UH... IS SOME-THING WRONG?
AH!
OH, IT'S JUST... UM...
NO-THING.

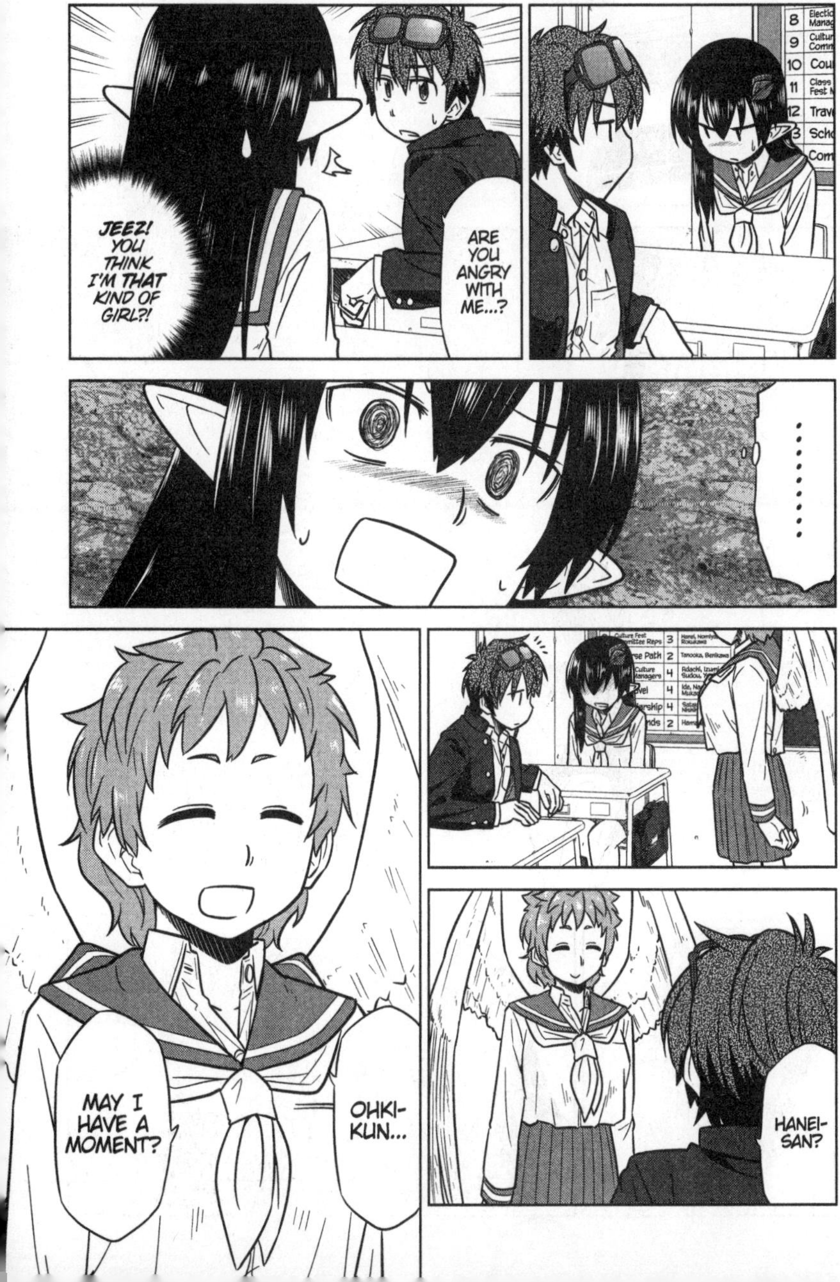
ARE YOU ANGRY WITH ME...?
JEEZ! YOU THINK I'M THAT KIND OF GIRL?!
......
HANEI-SAN?
OHKI-KUN...
MAY I HAVE A MOMENT?

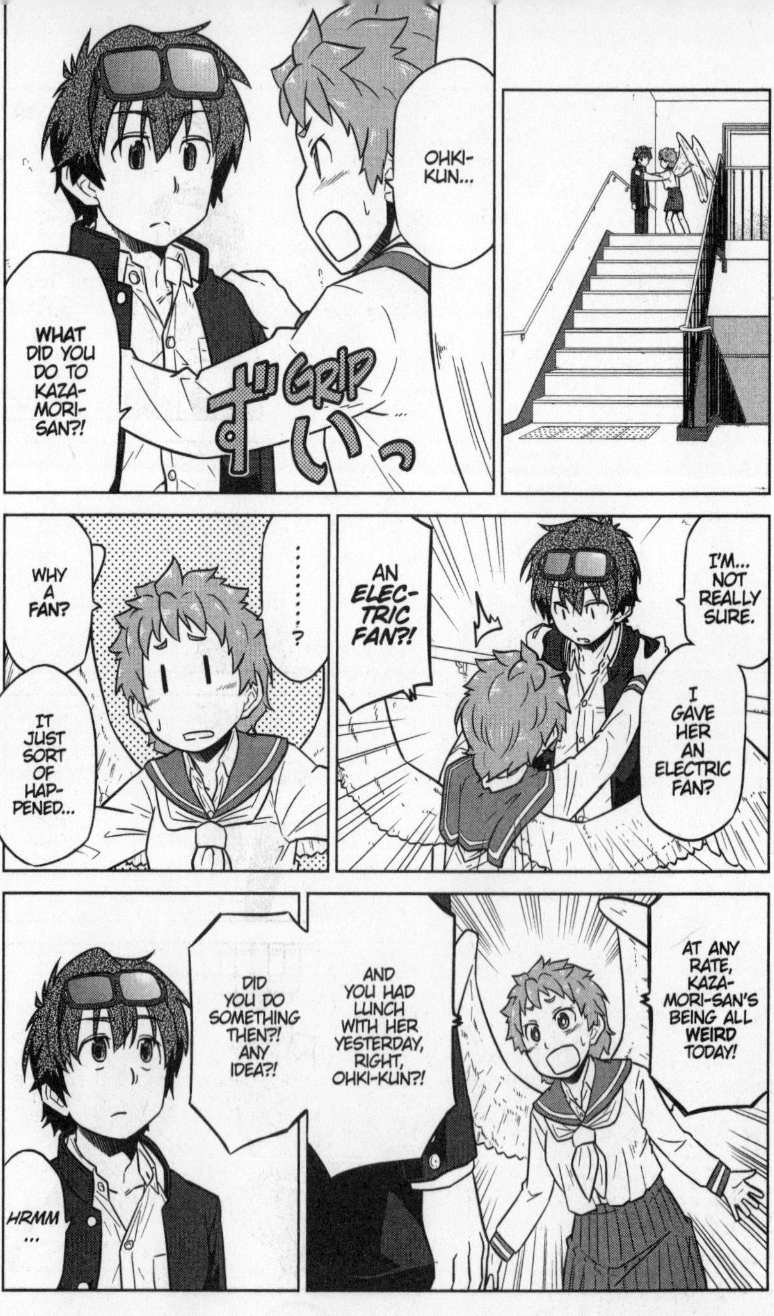
OHKI-KUN...
WHAT DID YOU DO TO KAZAMORI-SAN?!
GRIP
ずいっ
I'M... NOT REALLY SURE.
I GAVE HER AN ELECTRIC FAN?
AN ELECTRIC FAN?!
......?
WHY A FAN?
IT JUST SORT OF HAPPENED...
AT ANY RATE, KAZAMORI-SAN'S BEING ALL WEIRD TODAY!
AND YOU HAD LUNCH WITH HER YESTERDAY, RIGHT, OHKI-KUN?!
DID YOU DO SOMETHING THEN?! ANY IDEA?!
HRMM...

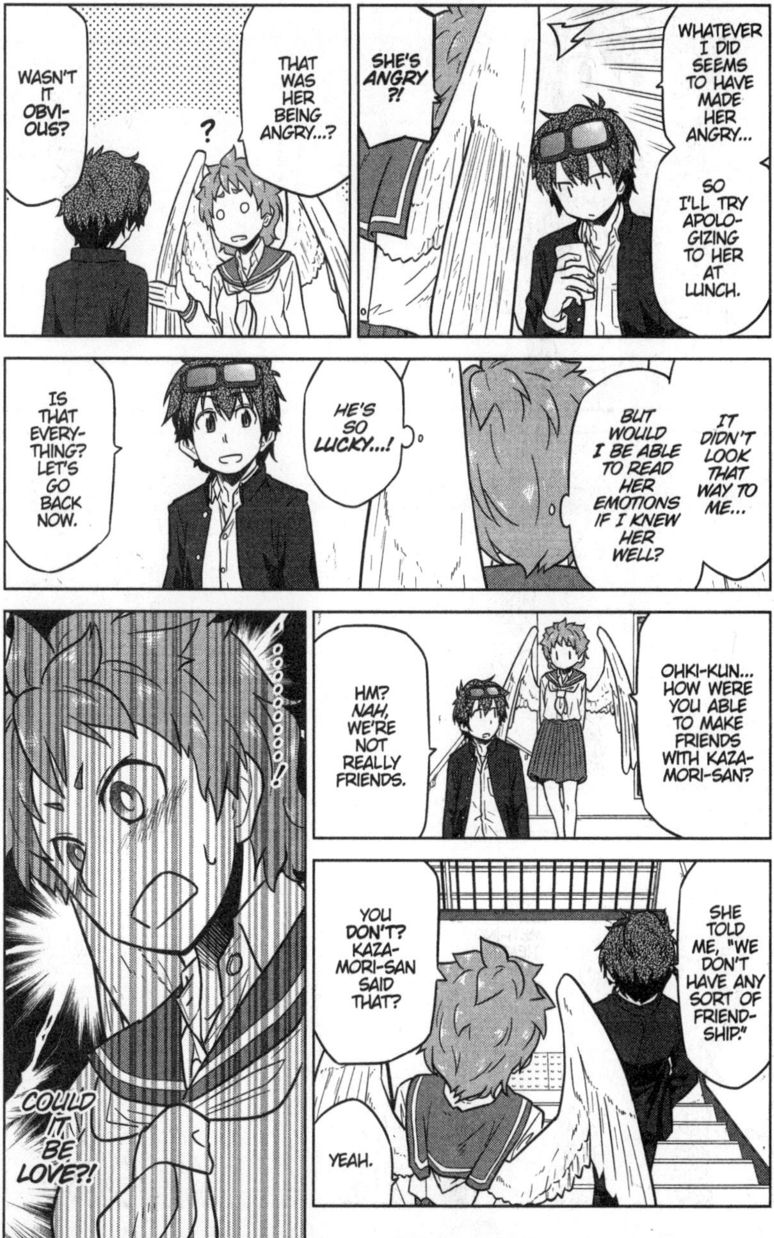
WHATEVER I DID SEEMS TO HAVE MADE HER ANGRY...
SO I'LL TRY APOLOGIZING TO HER AT LUNCH.
SHE'S ANGRY?!
THAT WAS HER BEING ANGRY...?
?
WASN'T IT OBVIOUS?
IT DIDN'T LOOK THAT WAY TO ME...
BUT WOULD I BE ABLE TO READ HER EMOTIONS IF I KNEW HER WELL?
HE'S SO LUCKY...!
IS THAT EVERYTHING? LET'S GO BACK NOW.
OHKI-KUN... HOW WERE YOU ABLE TO MAKE FRIENDS WITH KAZAMORI-SAN?
HM? NAH, WE'RE NOT REALLY FRIENDS.
SHE TOLD ME, "WE DON'T HAVE ANY SORT OF FRIENDSHIP."
YOU DON'T? KAZAMORI-SAN SAID THAT?
YEAH.
OOOOOOOOOOO!
COULD IT BE LOVE?!

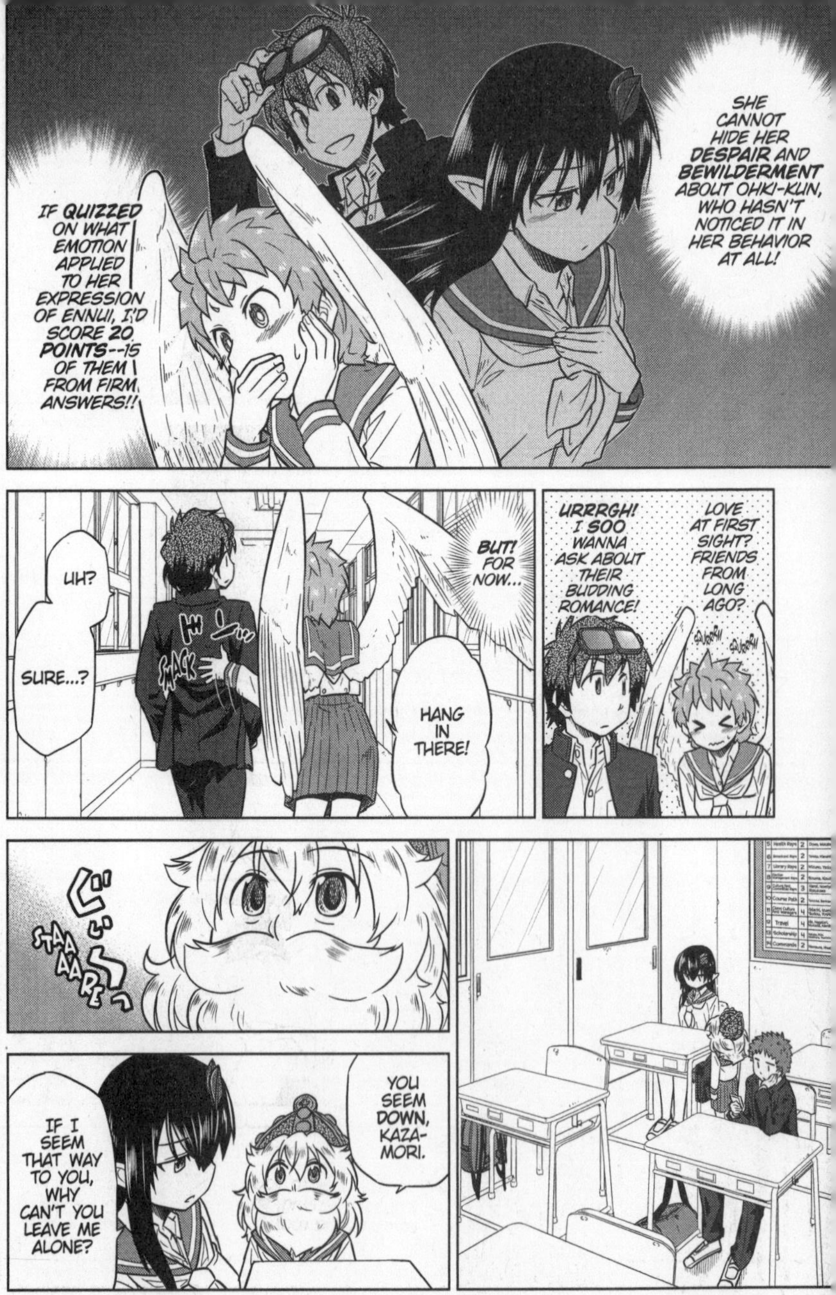
SHE CANNOT HIDE HER DESPAIR AND BEWILDERMENT ABOUT OHKI-KUN, WHO HASN'T NOTICED IT IN HER BEHAVIOR AT ALL!
IF QUIZZED ON WHAT EMOTION APPLIED TO HER EXPRESSION OF ENNUI, I'D SCORE 20 POINTS--15 OF THEM FROM FIRM ANSWERS!!
LOVE AT FIRST SIGHT? FRIENDS FROM LONG AGO?
URRRGH! I SOO WANNA ASK ABOUT THEIR BUDDING ROMANCE!
SQUIRM SQUIRM
BUT! FOR NOW...
HANG IN THERE!
SMACK
UH?
SURE...?
STAAARE
YOU SEEM DOWN, KAZAMORI.
IF I SEEM THAT WAY TO YOU, WHY CAN'T YOU LEAVE ME ALONE?

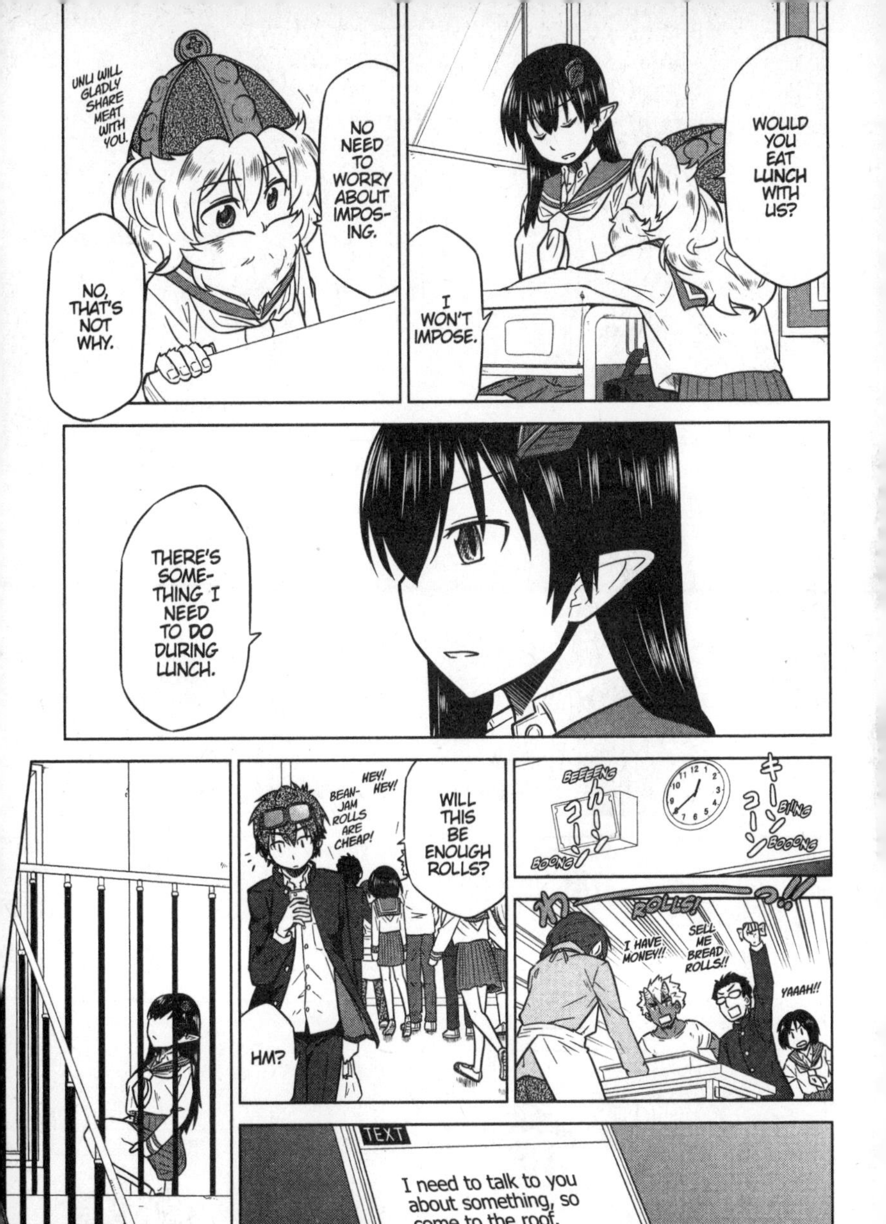
WOULD YOU EAT LUNCH WITH US?
I WON'T IMPOSE.
NO NEED TO WORRY ABOUT IMPOSING.
UNLI WILL GLADLY SHARE MEAT WITH YOU.
NO, THAT'S NOT WHY.
THERE'S SOMETHING I NEED TO DO DURING LUNCH.
BIING
BOOONG
BEEEENG
BOONG
ROLLS!
SELL ME BREAD ROLLS!!
I HAVE MONEY!!
YAAAH!!
WILL THIS BE ENOUGH ROLLS?
HEY! HEY! BEAN-JAM ROLLS ARE CHEAP!
HM?
TEXT
I need to talk to you about something, so come to the roof.

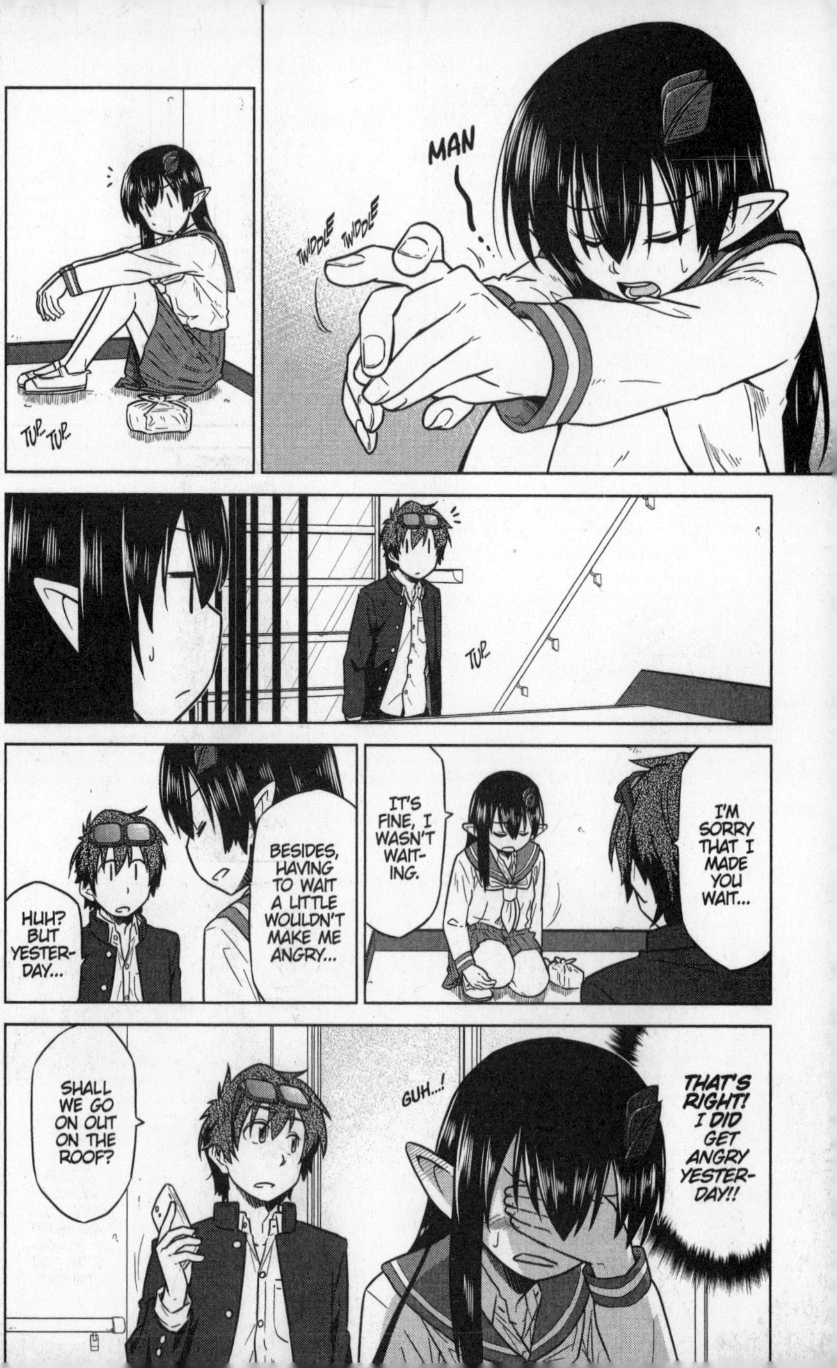
MAN
TWIDDLE TWIDDLE
TUP... TUP...
TUP...
I'M SORRY THAT I MADE YOU WAIT...
IT'S FINE, I WASN'T WAITING.
BESIDES, HAVING TO WAIT A LITTLE WOULDN'T MAKE ME ANGRY...
HUH? BUT YESTERDAY...
THAT'S RIGHT! I DID GET ANGRY YESTERDAY!!
GUH...!
SHALL WE GO ON OUT ON THE ROOF?

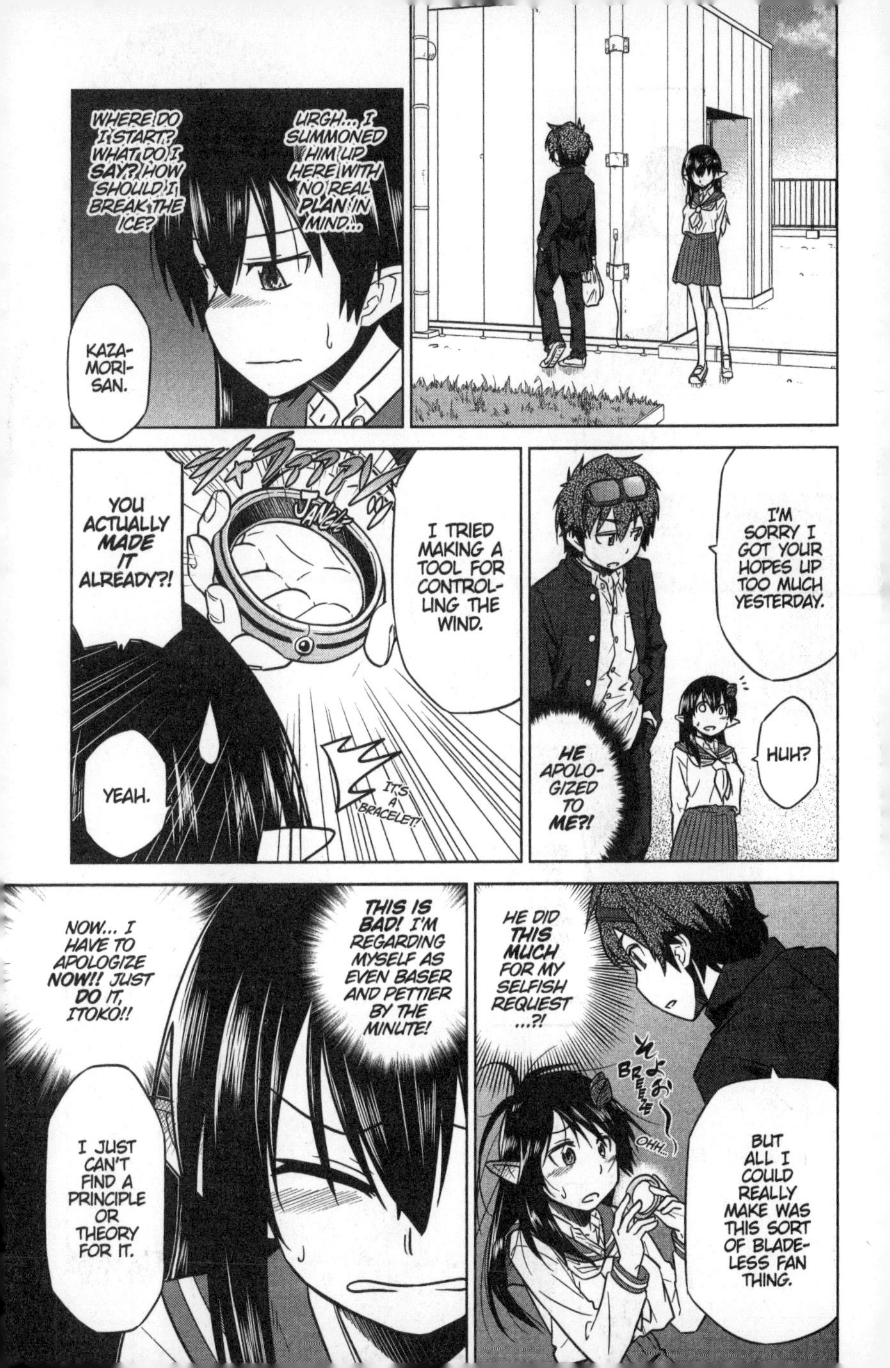
URGH... I SUMMONED HIM UP HERE WITH NO REAL PLAN IN MIND...
WHERE DO I START? WHAT DO I SAY? HOW SHOULD I BREAK THE ICE?
KAZAMORI-SAN.
I'M SORRY I GOT YOUR HOPES UP TOO MUCH YESTERDAY.
HUH?
HE APOLOGIZED TO ME?!
I TRIED MAKING A TOOL FOR CONTROLLING THE WIND.
JANGLE
YOU ACTUALLY MADE IT ALREADY?!
IT'S A BRACELET!
YEAH.
HE DID THIS MUCH FOR MY SELFISH REQUEST...?!
BREEZE
OHH...
BUT ALL I COULD REALLY MAKE WAS THIS SORT OF BLADELESS FAN THING.
THIS IS BAD! I'M REGARDING MYSELF AS EVEN BASER AND PETTIER BY THE MINUTE!
NOW... I HAVE TO APOLOGIZE NOW!! JUST DO IT, ITOKO!!
I JUST CAN'T FIND A PRINCIPLE OR THEORY FOR IT.

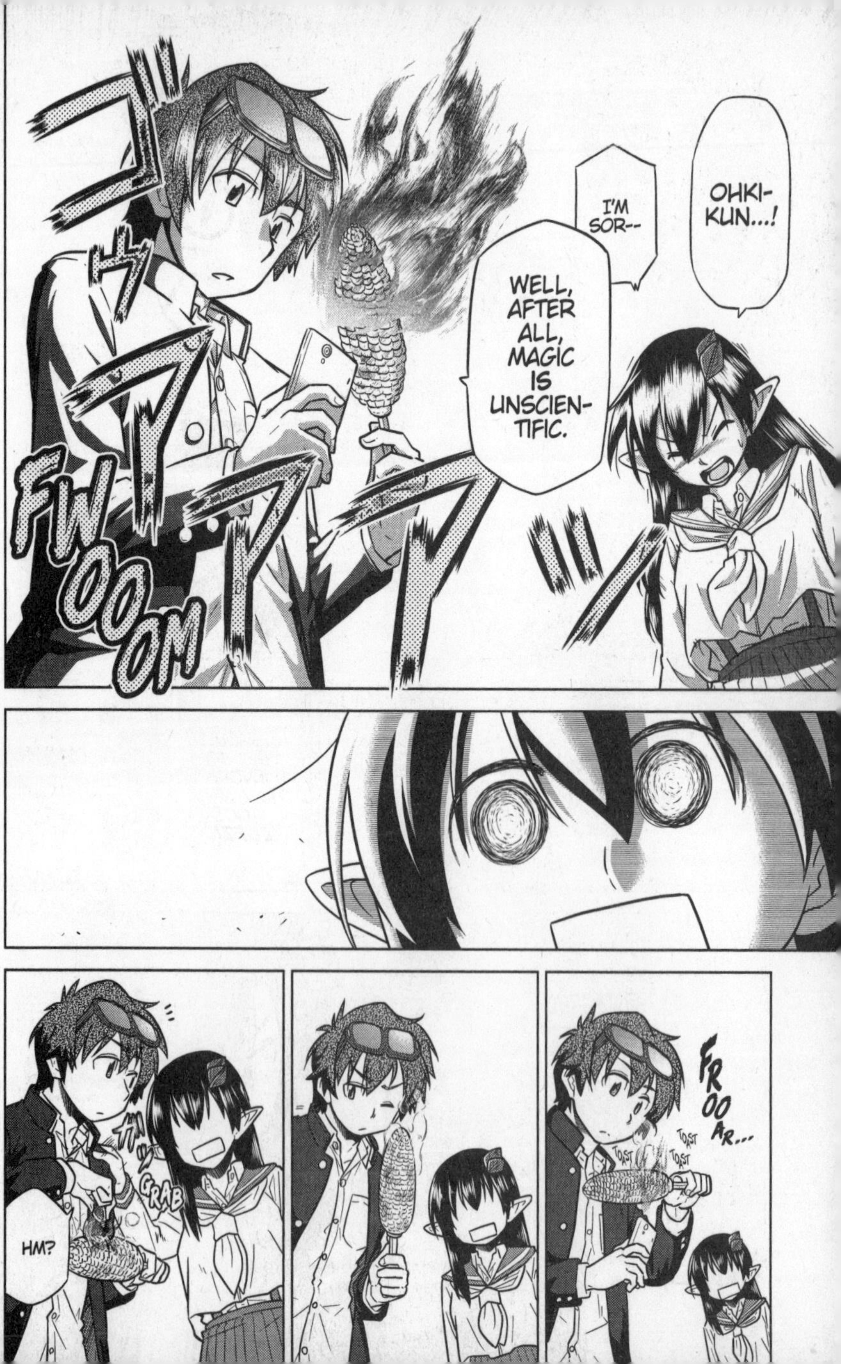

OHKI-KUN...!
I'M SOR--
WELL, AFTER ALL, MAGIC IS UNSCIENTIFIC.
FWOOOOM
FROOAR...
TOAST
TOAST
TOAST
GRAB
HM?

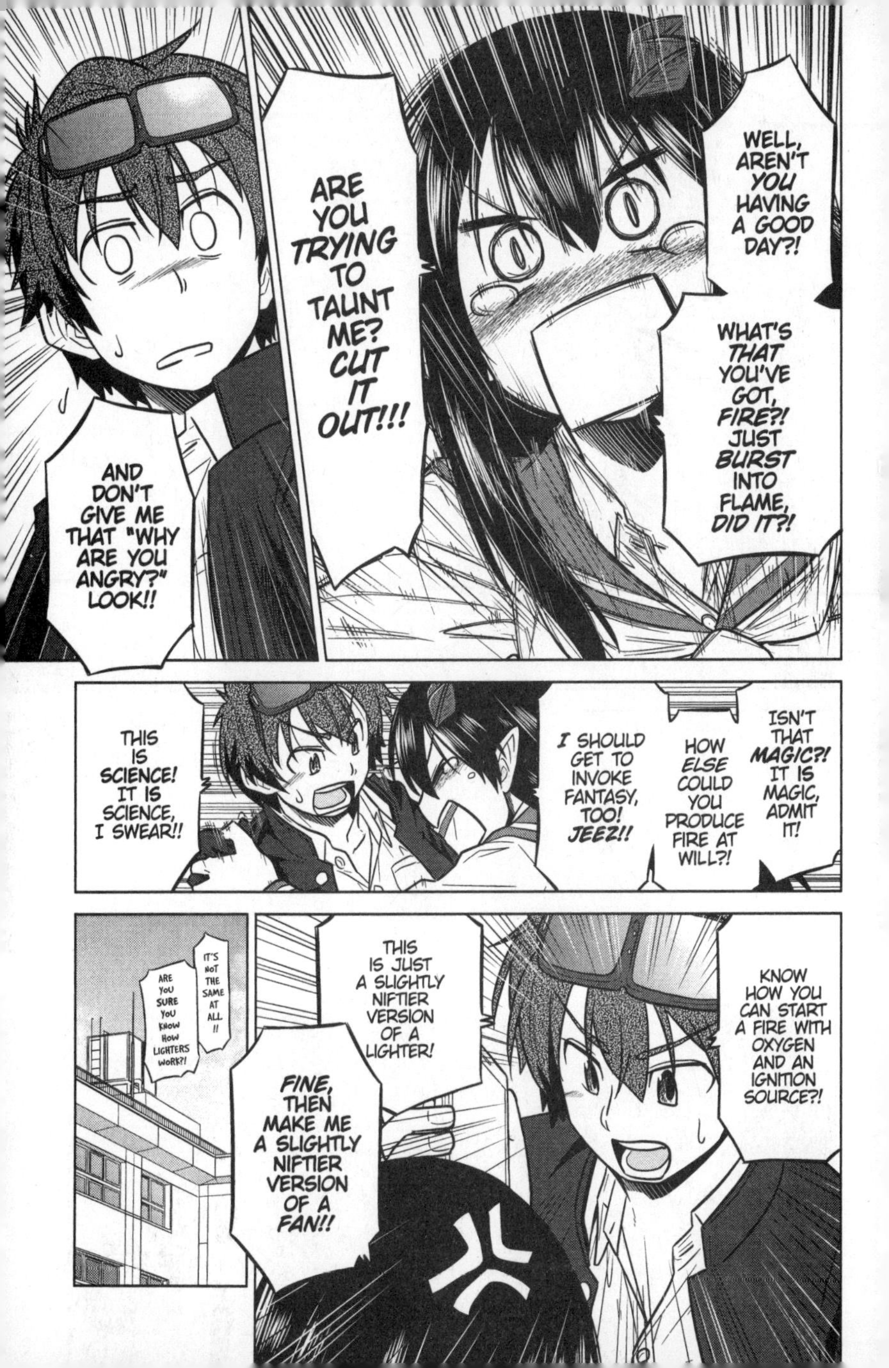
WELL, AREN'T YOU HAVING A GOOD DAY?!
WHAT'S THAT YOU'VE GOT, FIRE?! JUST BURST INTO FLAME, DID IT?!
ARE YOU TRYING TO TAUNT ME? CUT IT OUT!!!
AND DON'T GIVE ME THAT "WHY ARE YOU ANGRY?" LOOK!!
ISN'T THAT MAGIC?! IT IS MAGIC, ADMIT IT!
HOW ELSE COULD YOU PRODUCE FIRE AT WILL?!
I SHOULD GET TO INVOKE FANTASY, TOO! JEEZ!!
THIS IS SCIENCE! IT IS SCIENCE, I SWEAR!!
KNOW HOW YOU CAN START A FIRE WITH OXYGEN AND AN IGNITION SOURCE?!
THIS IS JUST A SLIGHTLY NIFTIER VERSION OF A LIGHTER!
FINE, THEN MAKE ME A SLIGHTLY NIFTIER VERSION OF A FAN!!
IT'S NOT THE SAME AT ALL!!
ARE YOU SURE YOU KNOW HOW LIGHTERS WORK?!

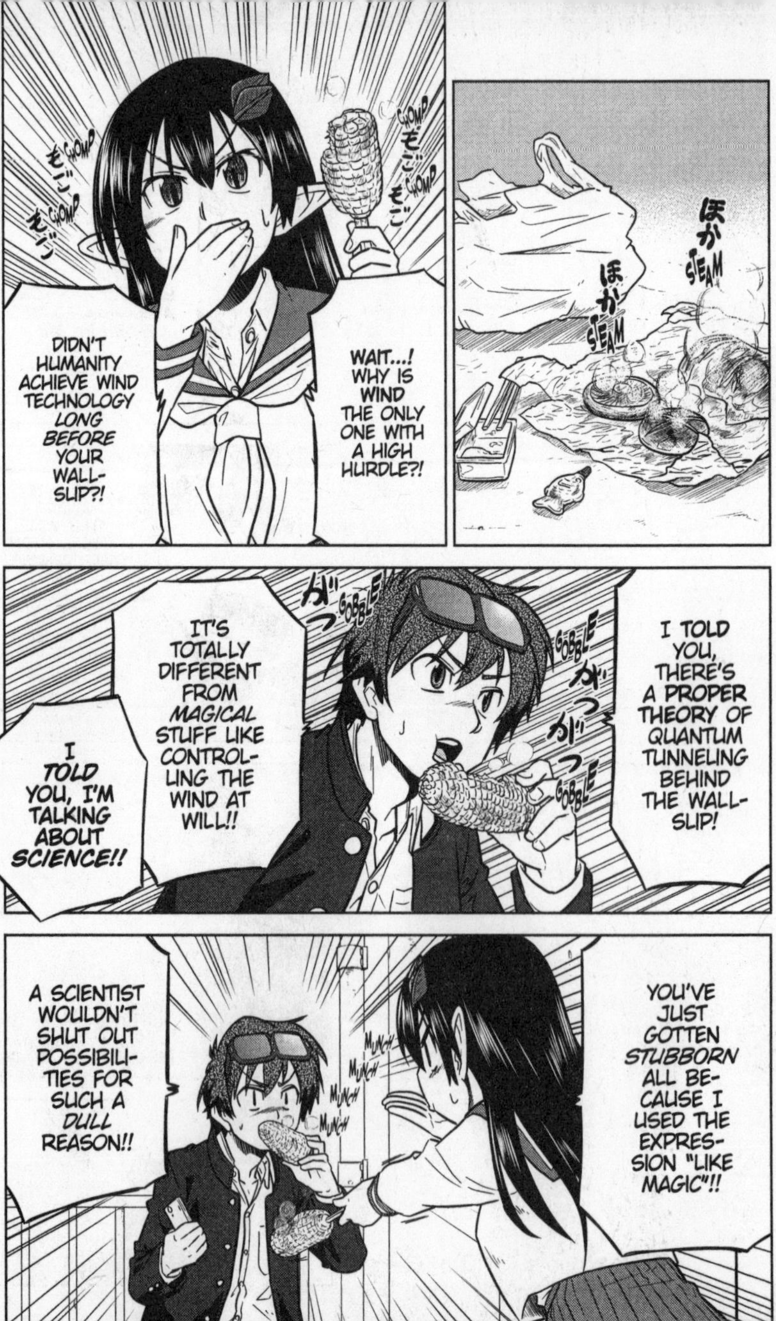
ほか STEAM
ほか STEAM
もご CHOMP
もご CHOMP
もご CHOMP
もご CHOMP
WAIT...! WHY IS WIND THE ONLY ONE WITH A HIGH HURDLE?!
DIDN'T HUMANITY ACHIEVE WIND TECHNOLOGY *LONG BEFORE* YOUR WALL-SLIP?!
がつ GOBBLE
がつ GOBBLE
がつ GOBBLE
I TOLD YOU, THERE'S A PROPER THEORY OF QUANTUM TUNNELING BEHIND THE WALL-SLIP!
IT'S TOTALLY DIFFERENT FROM *MAGICAL* STUFF LIKE CONTROL-LING THE WIND AT WILL!!
I *TOLD* YOU, I'M TALKING ABOUT *SCIENCE!!*
YOU'VE JUST GOTTEN *STUBBORN* ALL BE-CAUSE I USED THE EXPRES-SION "LIKE MAGIC"!!
MUNCH
MUNCH
MUNCH
MUNCH
A SCIENTIST WOULDN'T SHUT OUT POSSIBILI-TIES FOR SUCH A *DULL* REASON!!

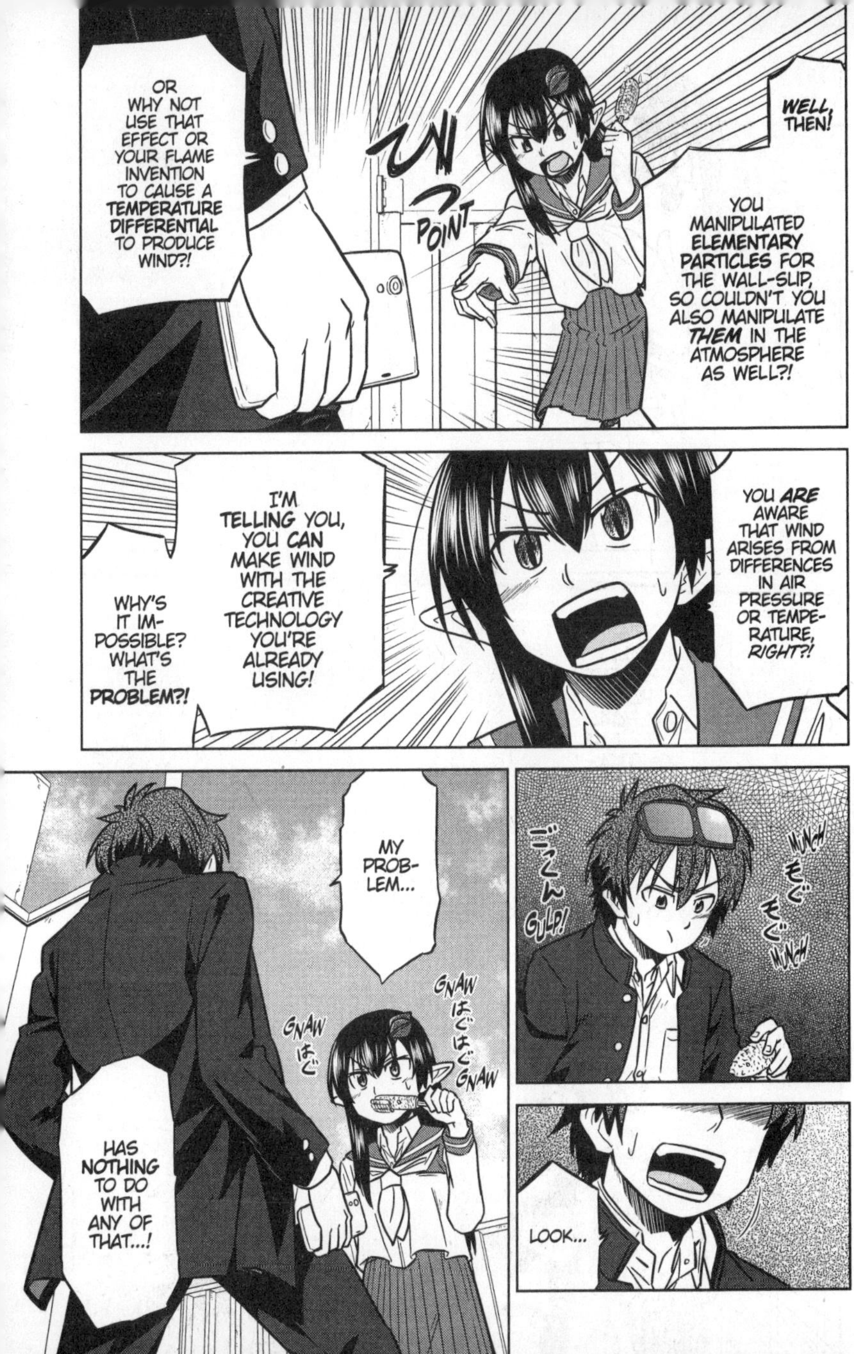
WELL, THEN!
YOU MANIPULATED ELEMENTARY PARTICLES FOR THE WALL-SLIP, SO COULDN'T YOU ALSO MANIPULATE THEM IN THE ATMOSPHERE AS WELL?!
POINT
OR WHY NOT USE THAT EFFECT OR YOUR FLAME INVENTION TO CAUSE A TEMPERATURE DIFFERENTIAL TO PRODUCE WIND?!
YOU ARE AWARE THAT WIND ARISES FROM DIFFERENCES IN AIR PRESSURE OR TEMPE-RATURE, RIGHT?!
I'M TELLING YOU, YOU CAN MAKE WIND WITH THE CREATIVE TECHNOLOGY YOU'RE ALREADY USING!
WHY'S IT IM-POSSIBLE? WHAT'S THE PROBLEM?!
もぐもぐ MUNCH MUNCH
ごくん GULP!
LOOK...
MY PROB-LEM...
GNAW はぐはぐ GNAW
GNAW はぐ
HAS NOTHING TO DO WITH ANY OF THAT...!

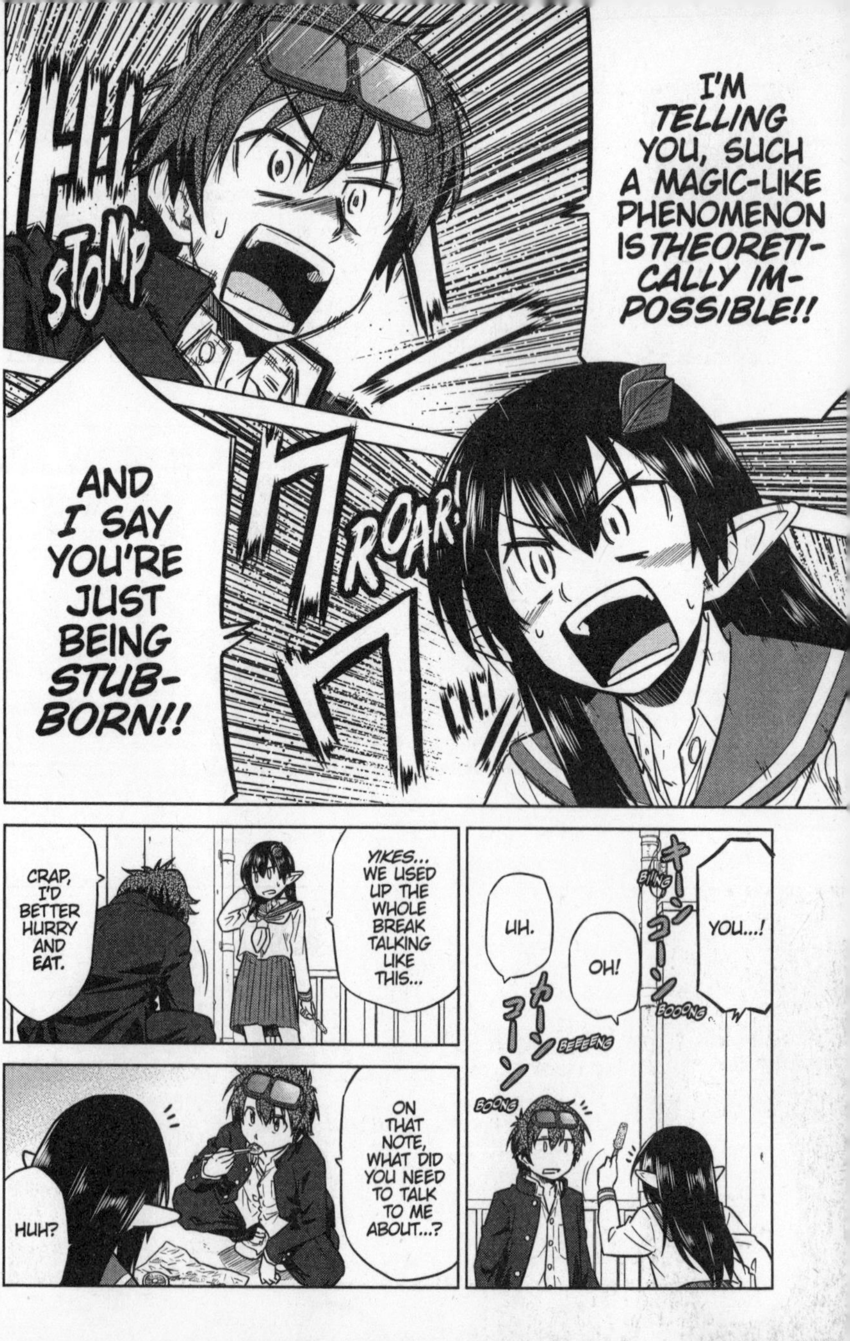
I'M TELLING YOU, SUCH A MAGIC-LIKE PHENOMENON IS THEORETICALLY IMPOSSIBLE!!
STOMP
ROAR!
AND I SAY YOU'RE JUST BEING STUBBORN!!
YOU...!
BING
BOOONG
OH!
UH.
BEEEENG
BOONG
YIKES... WE USED UP THE WHOLE BREAK TALKING LIKE THIS...
CRAP, I'D BETTER HURRY AND EAT.
ON THAT NOTE, WHAT DID YOU NEED TO TALK TO ME ABOUT...?
HUH?

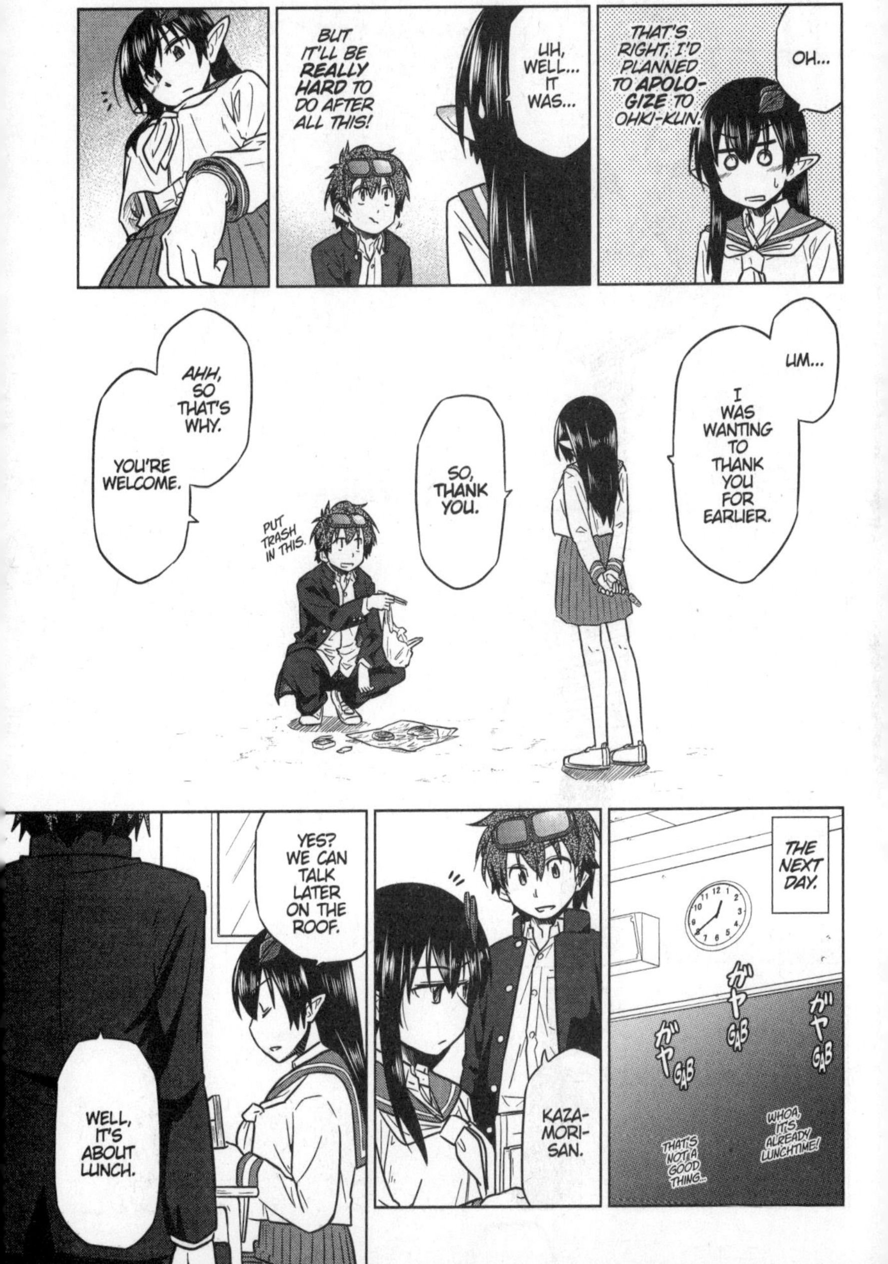
OH...
THAT'S RIGHT, I'D PLANNED TO APOLOGIZE TO OHKI-KUN.
UH, WELL... IT WAS...
BUT IT'LL BE REALLY HARD TO DO AFTER ALL THIS!
UM...
I WAS WANTING TO THANK YOU FOR EARLIER.
SO, THANK YOU.
PUT TRASH IN THIS.
AHH, SO THAT'S WHY.
YOU'RE WELCOME.
THE NEXT DAY.
ガヤ GAB
ガヤ GAB
ガヤ GAB
WHOA, IT'S ALREADY LUNCHTIME!
THAT'S NOT A GOOD THING...
KAZAMORI-SAN.
YES? WE CAN TALK LATER ON THE ROOF.
WELL, IT'S ABOUT LUNCH.

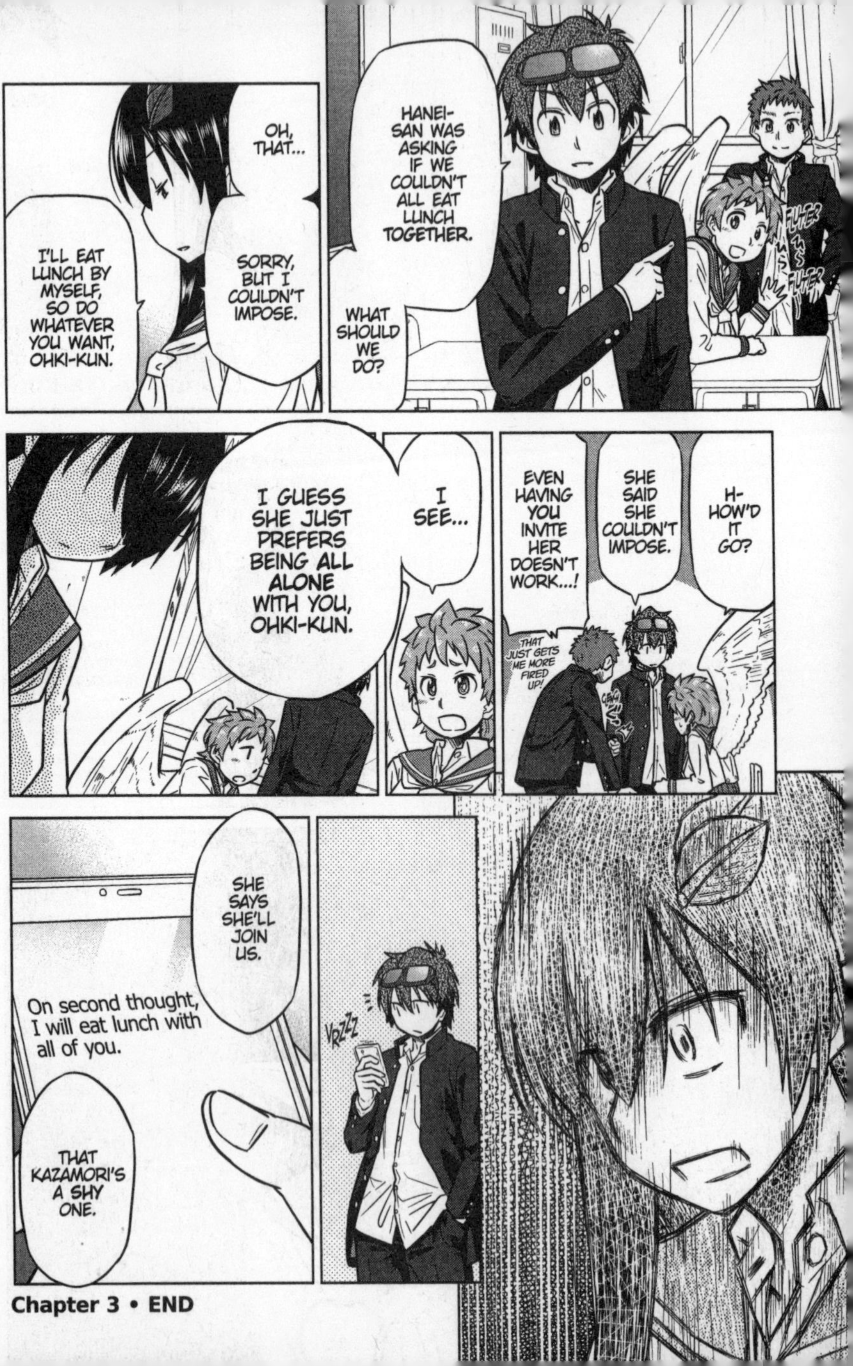
HANEI-SAN WAS ASKING IF WE COULDN'T ALL EAT LUNCH TOGETHER.
WHAT SHOULD WE DO?
OH, THAT...
SORRY, BUT I COULDN'T IMPOSE.
I'LL EAT LUNCH BY MYSELF, SO DO WHATEVER YOU WANT, OHKI-KUN.
H-HOW'D IT GO?
SHE SAID SHE COULDN'T IMPOSE.
EVEN HAVING YOU INVITE HER DOESN'T WORK...!
THAT JUST GETS ME MORE FIRED UP!
I SEE...
I GUESS SHE JUST PREFERS BEING ALL ALONE WITH YOU, OHKI-KUN.
VRZZZ
SHE SAYS SHE'LL JOIN US.
On second thought, I will eat lunch with all of you.
THAT KAZAMORI'S A SHY ONE.

Chapter 3 • END

Chapter 4: Dowa-san and Tanaka-kun

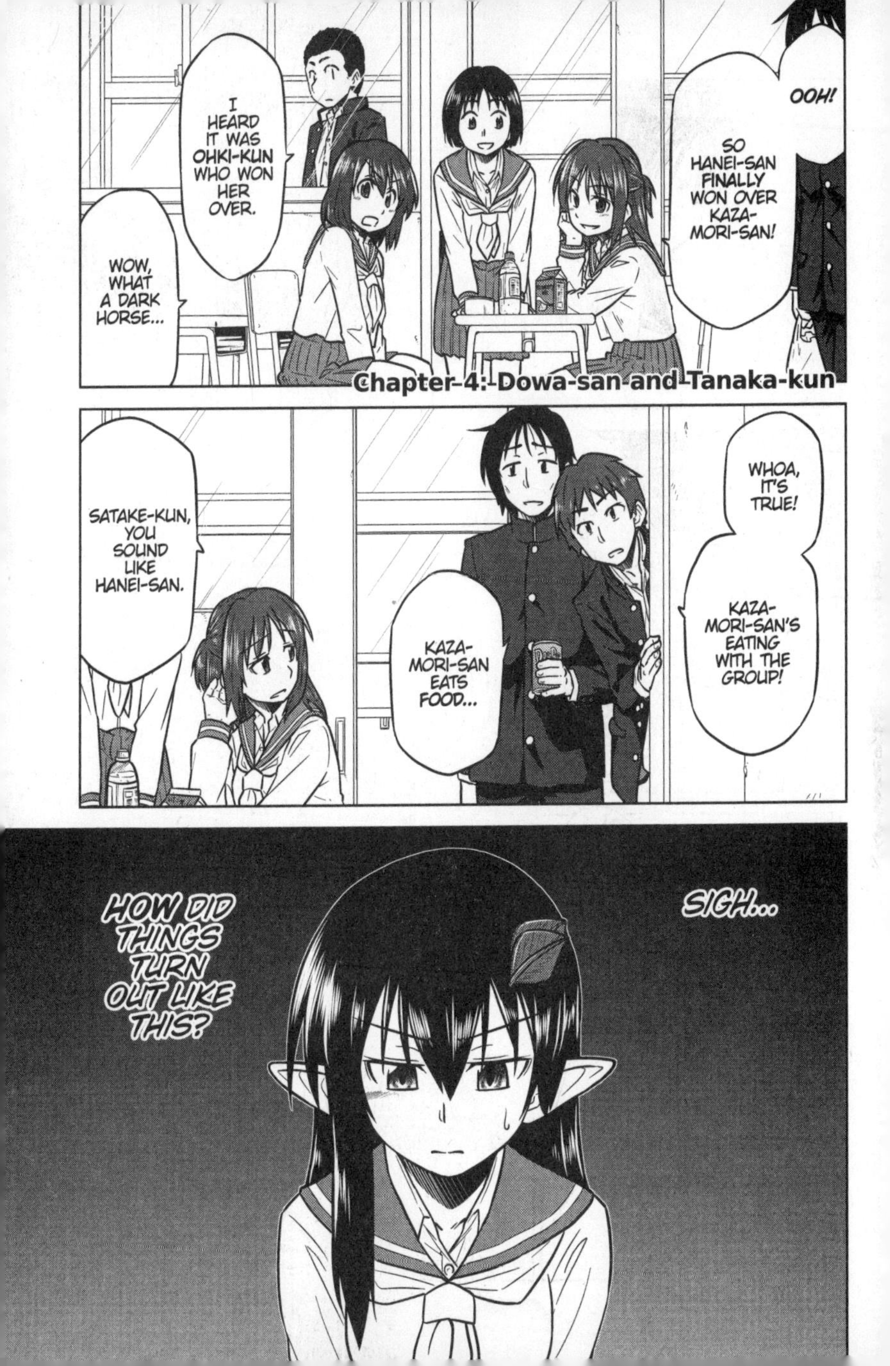
OOH!
SO HANEI-SAN FINALLY WON OVER KAZA-MORI-SAN!
I HEARD IT WAS OHKI-KUN WHO WON HER OVER.
WOW, WHAT A DARK HORSE...
WHOA, IT'S TRUE!
KAZA-MORI-SAN'S EATING WITH THE GROUP!
KAZA-MORI-SAN EATS FOOD...
SATAKE-KUN, YOU SOUND LIKE HANEI-SAN.
SIGH...
HOW DID THINGS TURN OUT LIKE THIS?

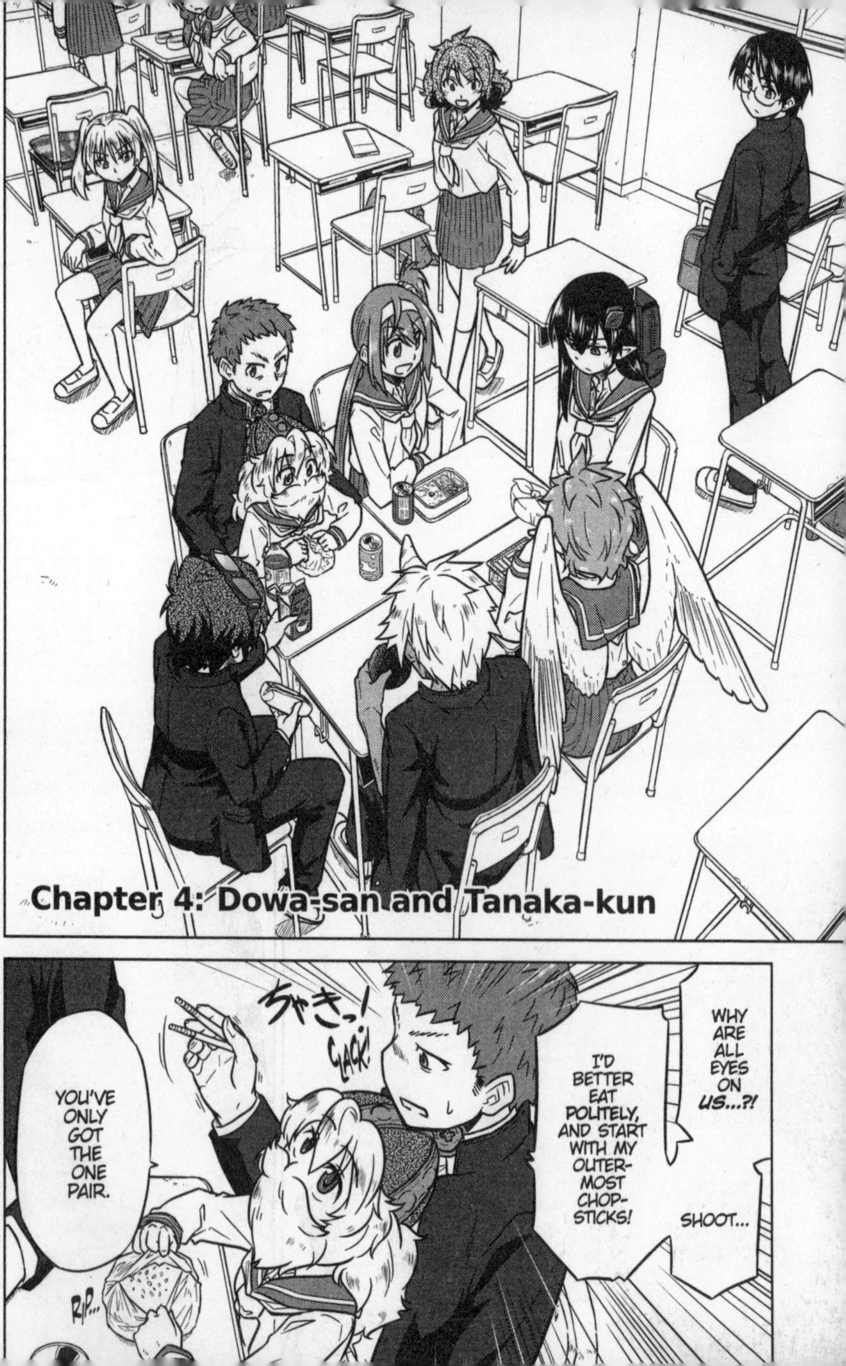
Chapter 4: Dowa-san and Tanaka-kun
WHY ARE ALL EYES ON US...?!
SHOOT...
I'D BETTER EAT POLITELY, AND START WITH MY OUTER-MOST CHOP-STICKS!
ちゃきっ!
CLACK!
YOU'VE ONLY GOT THE ONE PAIR.
RIP...

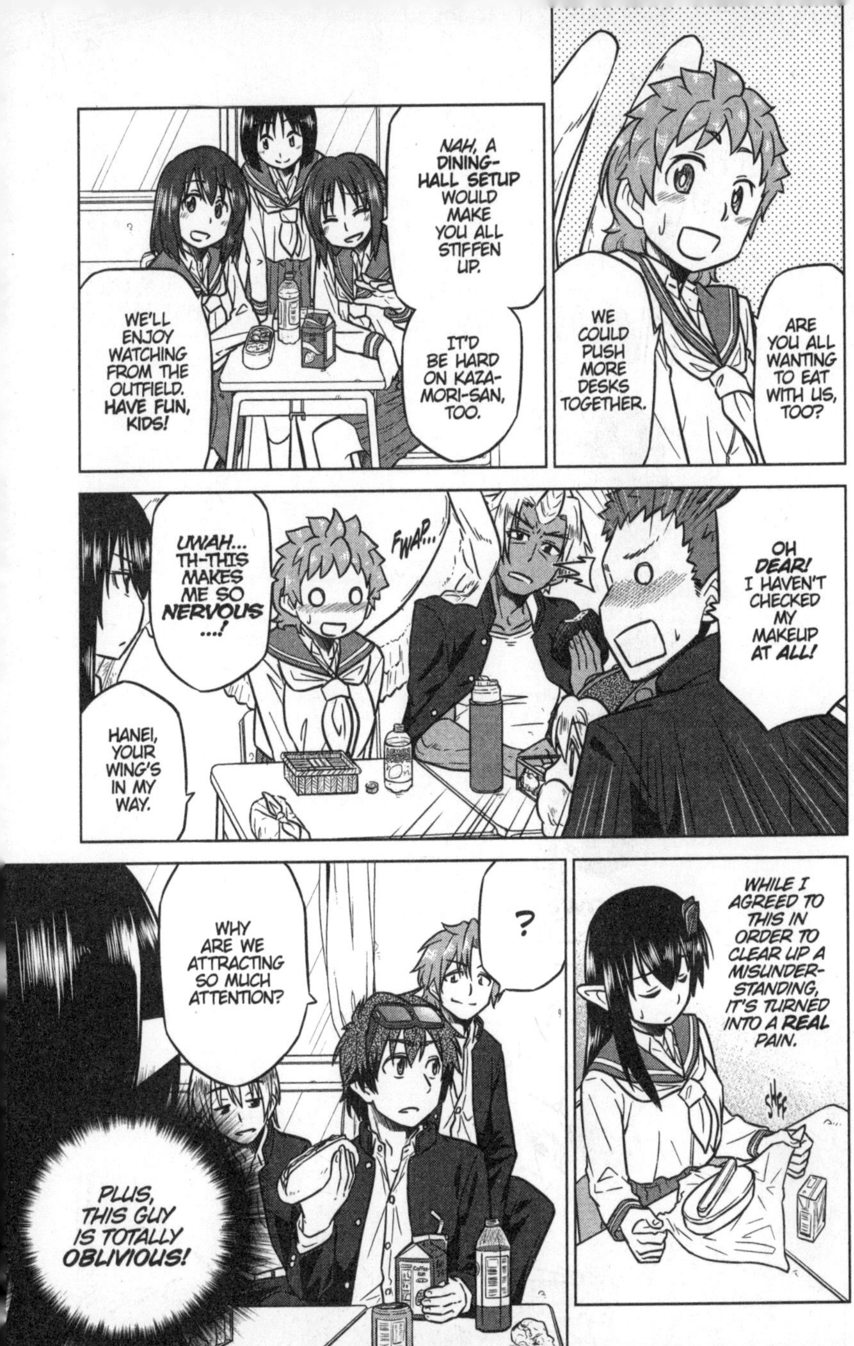
ARE YOU ALL WANTING TO EAT WITH US, TOO?
WE COULD PUSH MORE DESKS TOGETHER.
NAH, A DINING-HALL SETUP WOULD MAKE YOU ALL STIFFEN UP.
IT'D BE HARD ON KAZAMORI-SAN, TOO.
WE'LL ENJOY WATCHING FROM THE OUTFIELD. HAVE FUN, KIDS!
OH DEAR! I HAVEN'T CHECKED MY MAKEUP AT ALL!
FWAP...
UWAH... TH-THIS MAKES ME SO NERVOUS...!
HANEI, YOUR WING'S IN MY WAY.
WHILE I AGREED TO THIS IN ORDER TO CLEAR UP A MISUNDERSTANDING, IT'S TURNED INTO A REAL PAIN.
?
WHY ARE WE ATTRACTING SO MUCH ATTENTION?
PLUS, THIS GUY IS TOTALLY OBLIVIOUS!

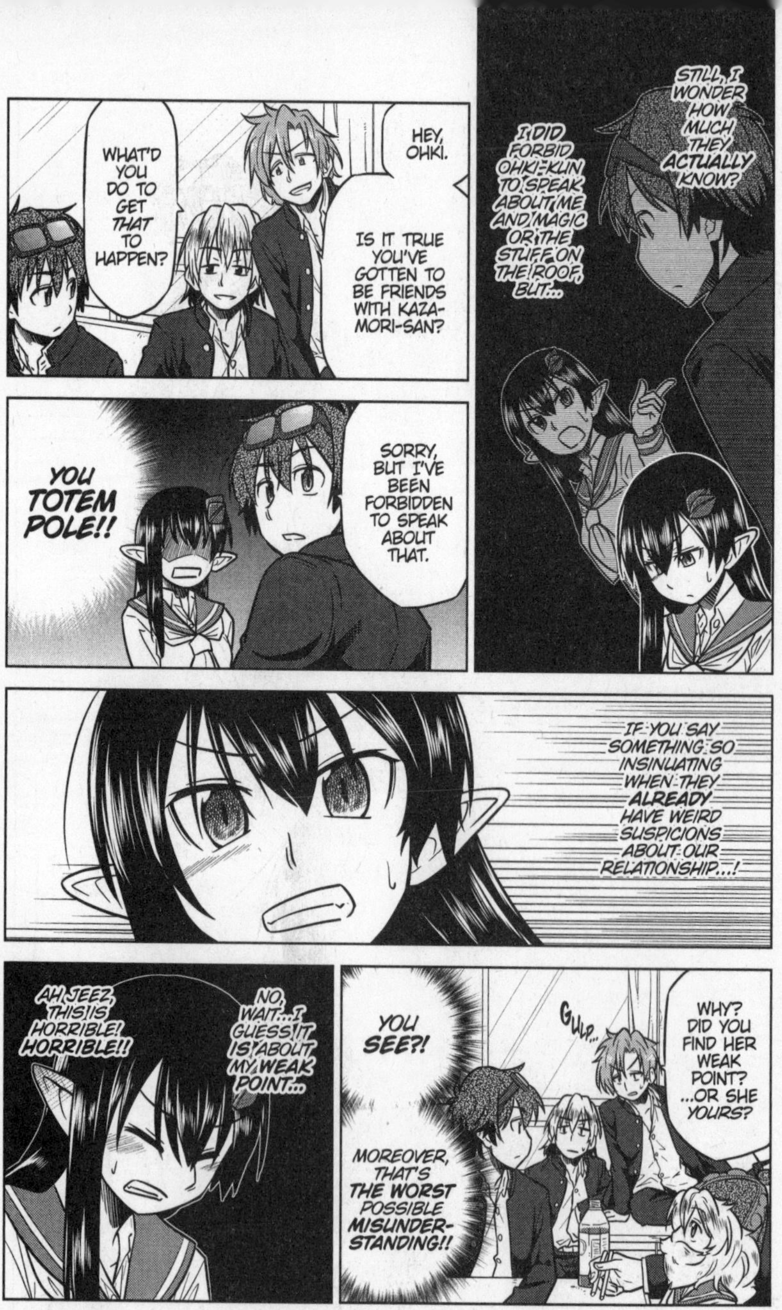
STILL, I WONDER HOW MUCH THEY ACTUALLY KNOW?
I DID FORBID OHKI-KUN TO SPEAK ABOUT ME AND MAGIC OR THE STUFF ON THE ROOF, BUT...
HEY, OHKI.
IS IT TRUE YOU'VE GOTTEN TO BE FRIENDS WITH KAZA-MORI-SAN?
WHAT'D YOU DO TO GET THAT TO HAPPEN?
SORRY, BUT I'VE BEEN FORBIDDEN TO SPEAK ABOUT THAT.
YOU TOTEM POLE!!
IF YOU SAY SOMETHING SO INSINUATING WHEN THEY ALREADY HAVE WEIRD SUSPICIONS ABOUT OUR RELATIONSHIP...!
WHY? DID YOU FIND HER WEAK POINT? ...OR SHE YOURS?
GULP...
YOU SEE?!
MOREOVER, THAT'S THE WORST POSSIBLE MISUNDER-STANDING!!
NO, WAIT...I GUESS IT IS ABOUT MY WEAK POINT...
AH JEEZ, THIS IS HORRIBLE! HORRIBLE!!

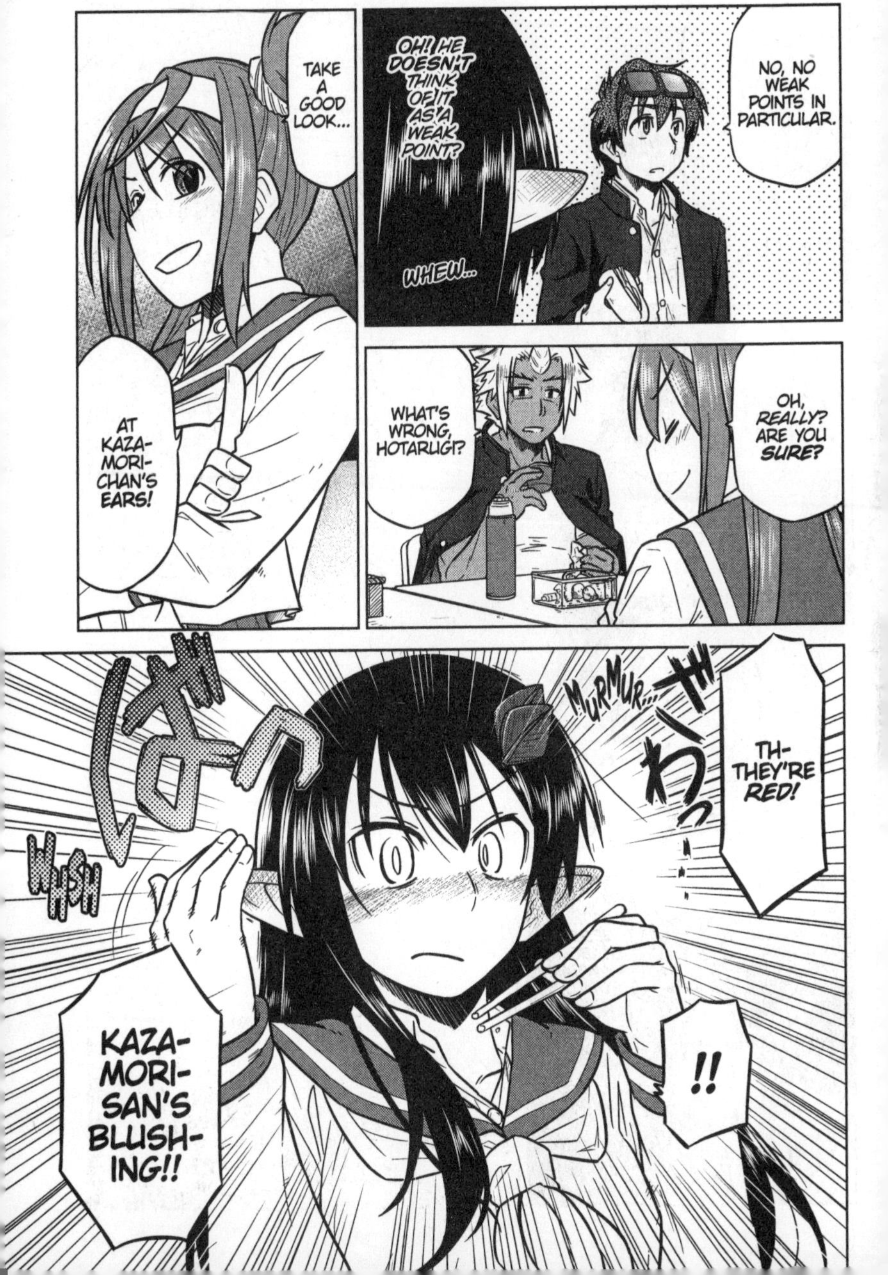
NO, NO WEAK POINTS IN PARTICULAR.
OH! HE DOESN'T THINK OF IT AS A WEAK POINT?
WHEW...
OH, *REALLY*? ARE YOU *SURE*?
WHAT'S WRONG, HOTARUGI?
TAKE A GOOD LOOK...
AT KAZAMORI-CHAN'S EARS!
TH-THEY'RE *RED!*
MURMUR...
わっ
!!
ぱっ
WHSH
KAZAMORI-SAN'S BLUSHING!!

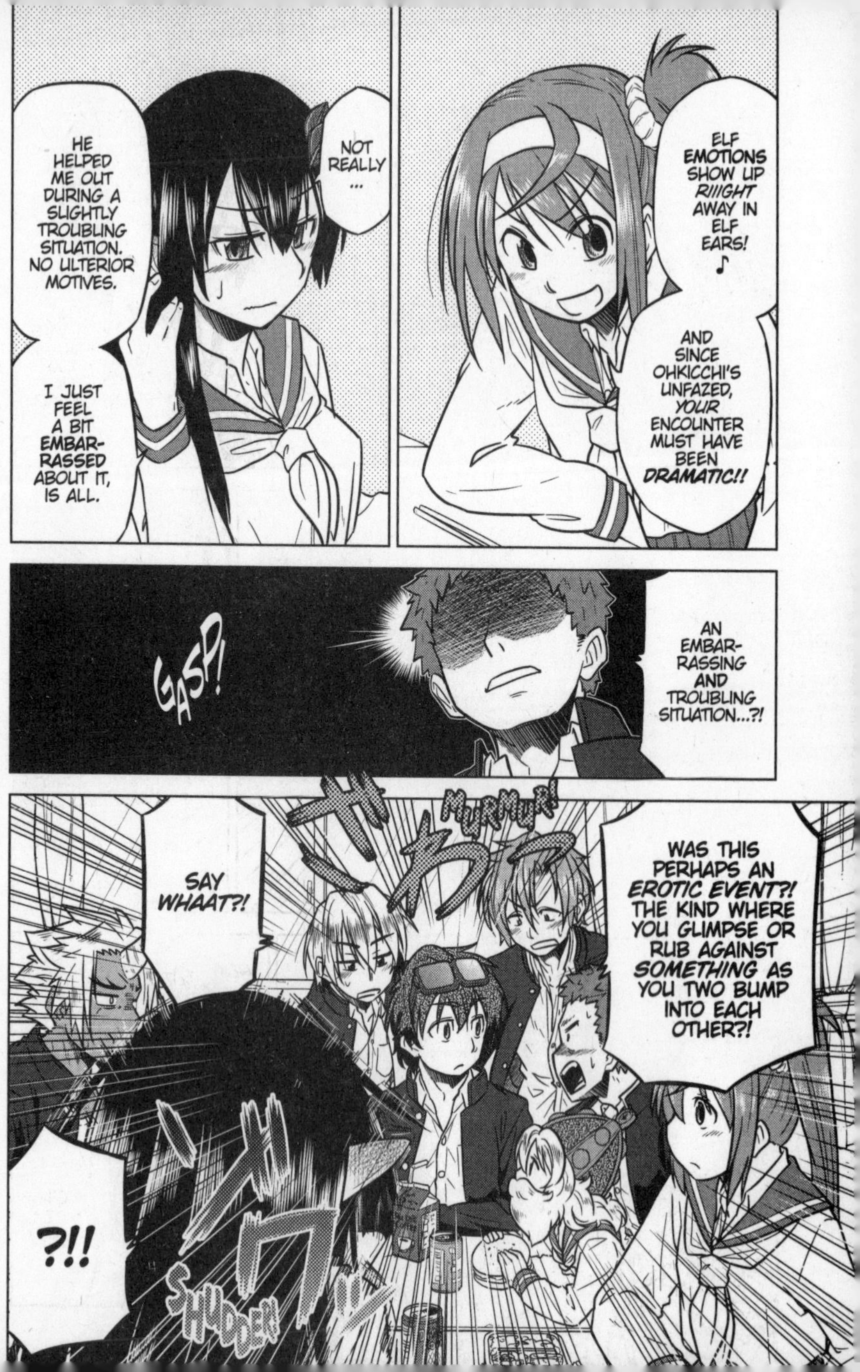
ELF EMOTIONS SHOW UP RIIIGHT AWAY IN ELF EARS! ♪
AND SINCE OHKICCHI'S UNFAZED, YOUR ENCOUNTER MUST HAVE BEEN DRAMATIC!!
NOT REALLY ...
HE HELPED ME OUT DURING A SLIGHTLY TROUBLING SITUATION. NO ULTERIOR MOTIVES.
I JUST FEEL A BIT EMBARRASSED ABOUT IT, IS ALL.
AN EMBARRASSING AND TROUBLING SITUATION...?!
GASP!
MURMUR
WAS THIS PERHAPS AN EROTIC EVENT?! THE KIND WHERE YOU GLIMPSE OR RUB AGAINST SOMETHING AS YOU TWO BUMP INTO EACH OTHER?!
SAY WHAAT?!
?!!
SHUDDER

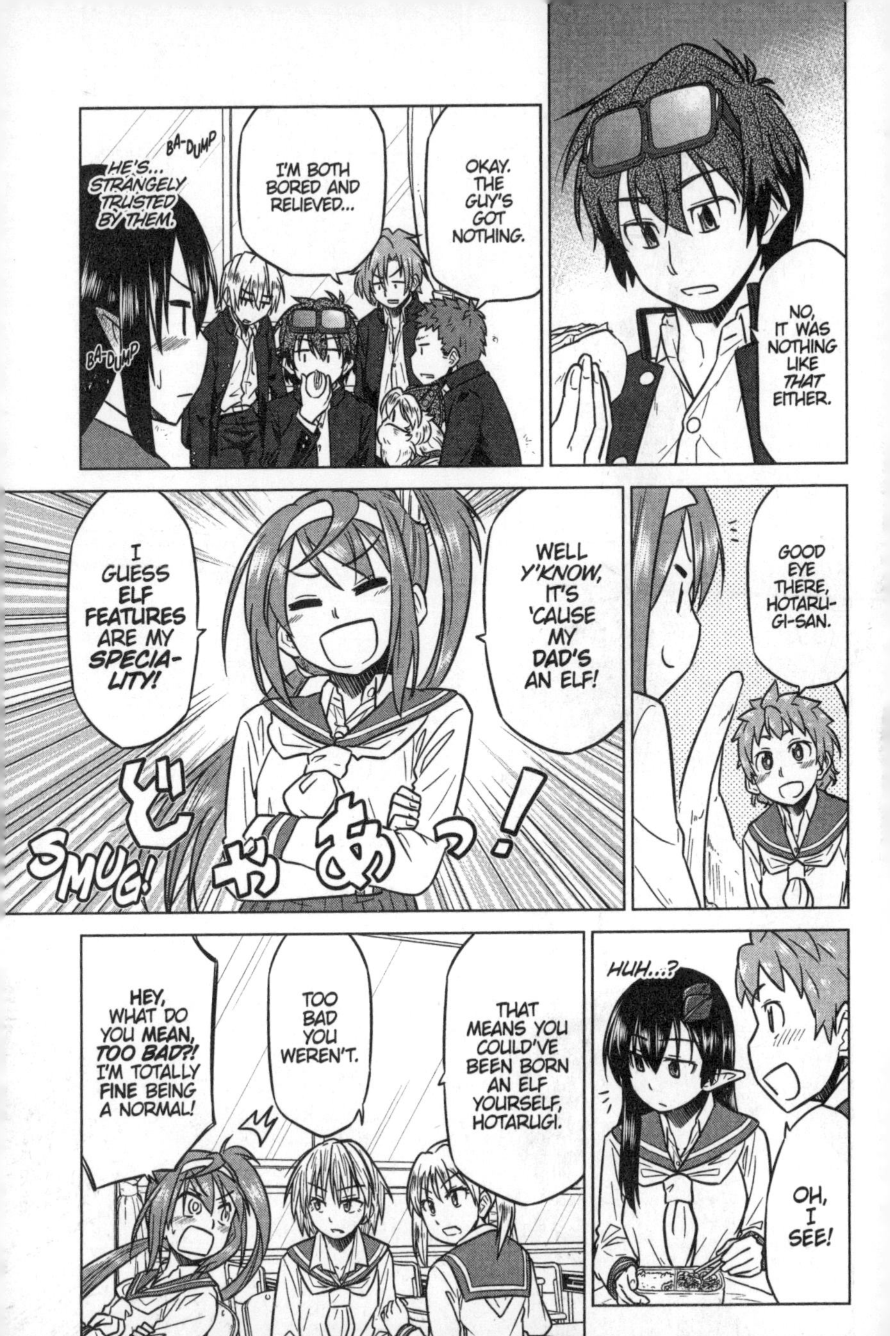
NO, IT WAS NOTHING LIKE THAT EITHER.
OKAY. THE GUY'S GOT NOTHING.
I'M BOTH BORED AND RELIEVED...
BA-DUMP
HE'S... STRANGELY TRUSTED BY THEM.
BA-DUMP
GOOD EYE THERE, HOTARUGI-SAN.
WELL Y'KNOW, IT'S 'CAUSE MY DAD'S AN ELF!
I GUESS ELF FEATURES ARE MY SPECIALITY!
どやあっ!
SMUG!
HUH...?
OH, I SEE!
THAT MEANS YOU COULD'VE BEEN BORN AN ELF YOURSELF, HOTARUGI.
TOO BAD YOU WEREN'T.
HEY, WHAT DO YOU MEAN, TOO BAD?! I'M TOTALLY FINE BEING A NORMAL!

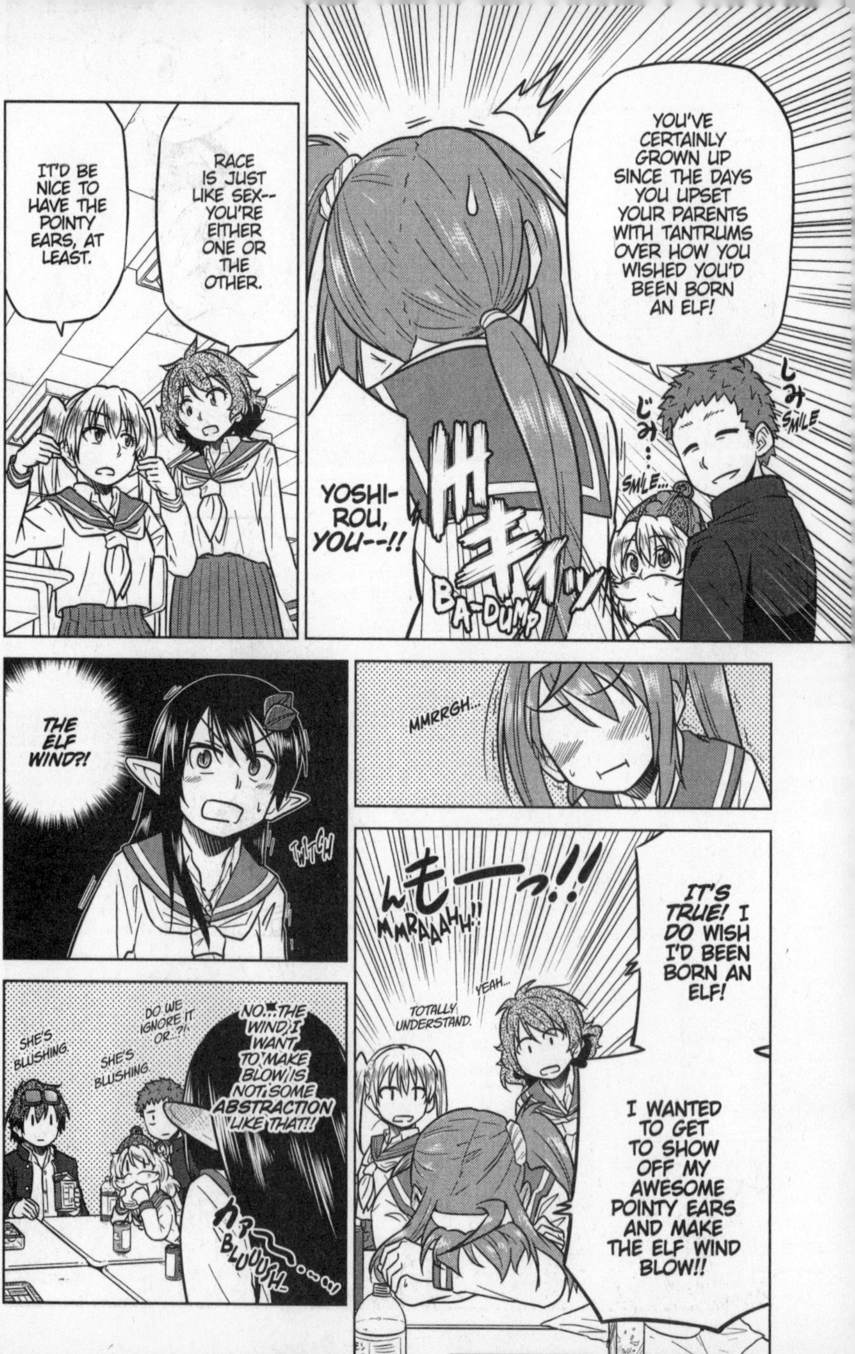
YOU'VE CERTAINLY GROWN UP SINCE THE DAYS YOU UPSET YOUR PARENTS WITH TANTRUMS OVER HOW YOU WISHED YOU'D BEEN BORN AN ELF!
しみ
SMILE
じみ…
SMILE...
YOSHI-ROU, YOU--!!
ピキィッ
BA-DUMP
RACE IS JUST LIKE SEX-- YOU'RE EITHER ONE OR THE OTHER.
IT'D BE NICE TO HAVE THE POINTY EARS, AT LEAST.
MMRRGH...
んもーっ!!
MMRAAAHH!!
IT'S TRUE! I DO WISH I'D BEEN BORN AN ELF!
YEAH...
TOTALLY UNDERSTAND.
I WANTED TO GET TO SHOW OFF MY AWESOME POINTY EARS AND MAKE THE ELF WIND BLOW!!
THE ELF WIND?!
TWITCH
NO... THE WIND I WANT TO MAKE BLOW IS NOT SOME ABSTRACTION LIKE THAT!!
DO WE IGNORE IT OR...?!
SHE'S BLUSHING.
SHE'S BLUSHING.
カァ～～
BLUUUSH...

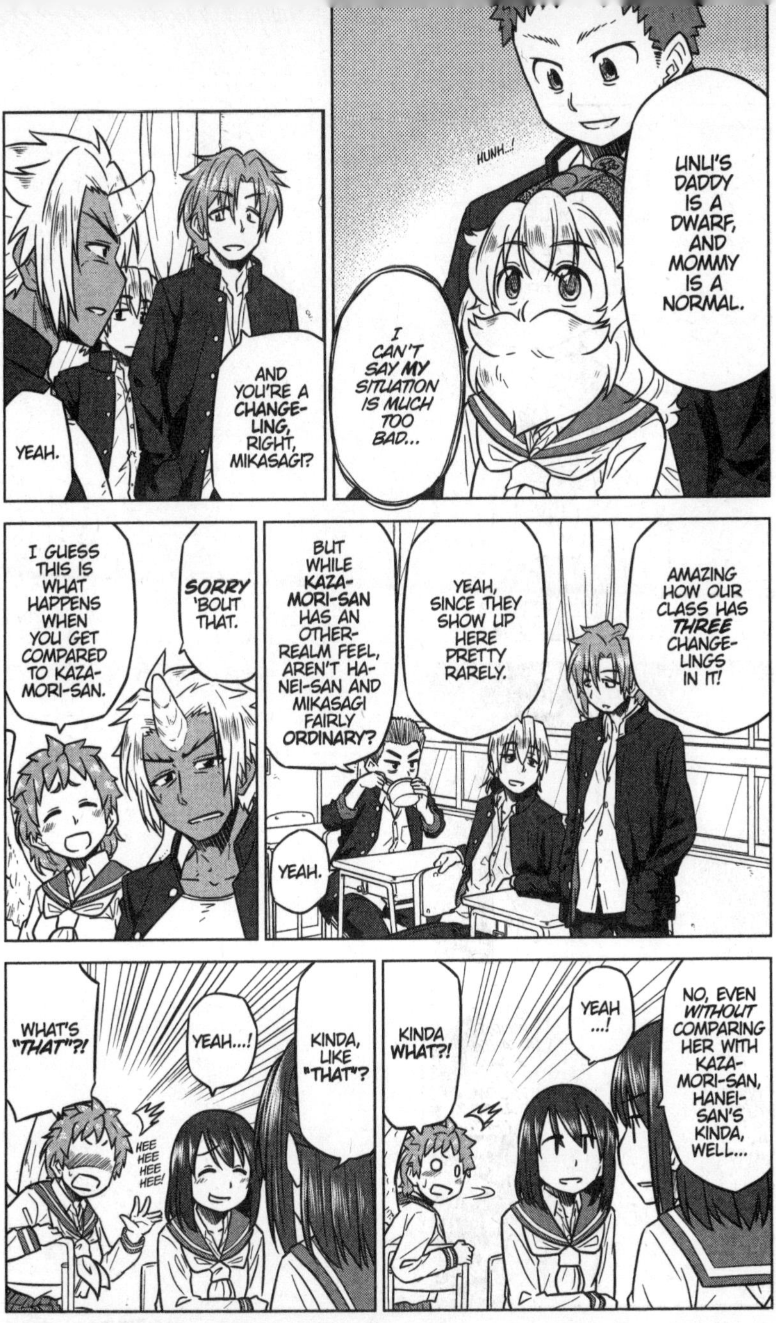
HUNH...!
UNLI'S DADDY IS A DWARF, AND MOMMY IS A NORMAL.
I CAN'T SAY MY SITUATION IS MUCH TOO BAD...
AND YOU'RE A CHANGELING, RIGHT, MIKASAGI?
YEAH.
AMAZING HOW OUR CLASS HAS THREE CHANGELINGS IN IT!
YEAH, SINCE THEY SHOW UP HERE PRETTY RARELY.
BUT WHILE KAZAMORI-SAN HAS AN OTHER-REALM FEEL, AREN'T HANEI-SAN AND MIKASAGI FAIRLY ORDINARY?
YEAH.
SORRY 'BOUT THAT.
I GUESS THIS IS WHAT HAPPENS WHEN YOU GET COMPARED TO KAZAMORI-SAN.
NO, EVEN WITHOUT COMPARING HER WITH KAZAMORI-SAN, HANEI-SAN'S KINDA, WELL...
YEAH...!
KINDA WHAT?!
KINDA, LIKE "THAT"?
YEAH...!
WHAT'S "THAT"?!
HEE HEE HEE HEE!

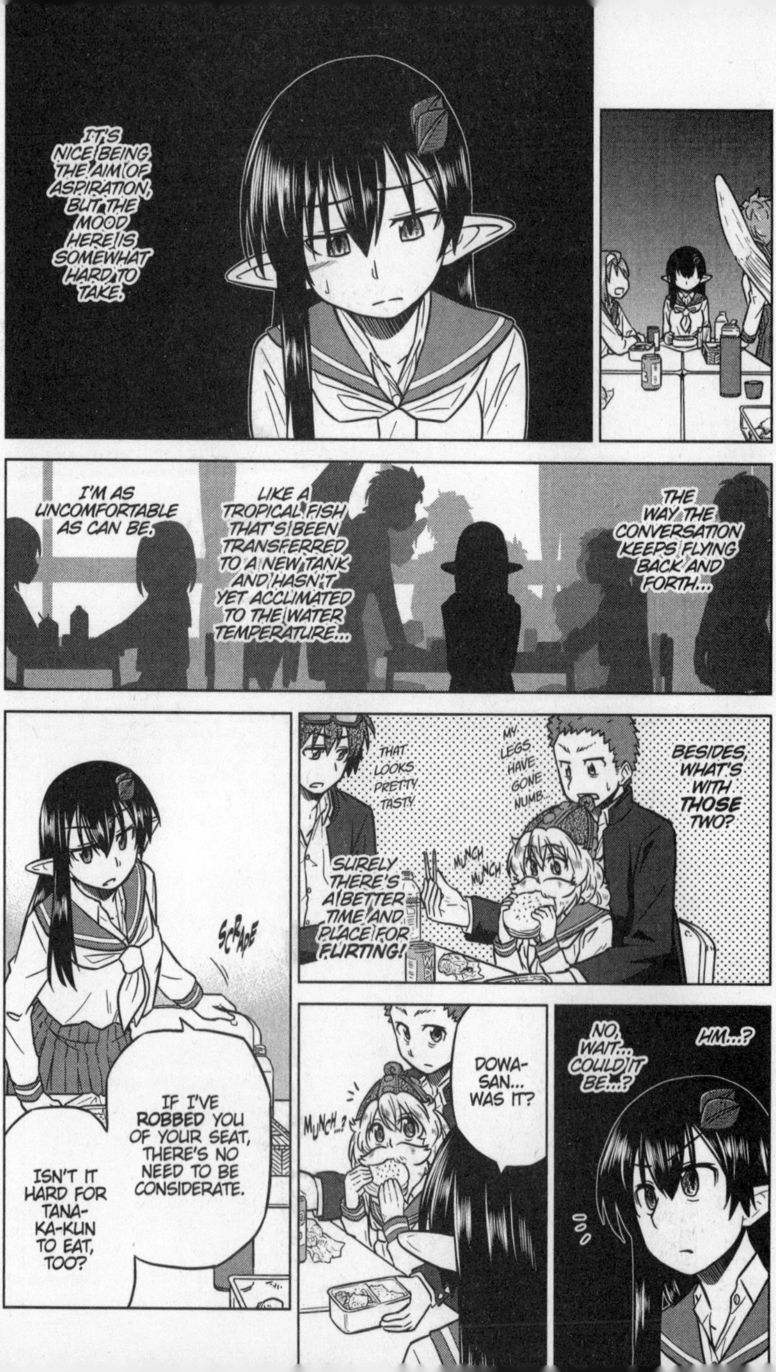
IT'S NICE BEING THE AIM OF ASPIRATION, BUT THE MOOD HERE IS SOMEWHAT HARD TO TAKE.
THE WAY THE CONVERSATION KEEPS FLYING BACK AND FORTH...
LIKE A TROPICAL FISH THAT'S BEEN TRANSFERRED TO A NEW TANK AND HASN'T YET ACCLIMATED TO THE WATER TEMPERATURE...
I'M AS UNCOMFORTABLE AS CAN BE.
BESIDES, WHAT'S WITH THOSE TWO?
MY LEGS HAVE GONE NUMB.
THAT LOOKS PRETTY TASTY.
MUNCH MUNCH
SURELY THERE'S A BETTER TIME AND PLACE FOR FLIRTING!
HM...?
NO, WAIT... COULD IT BE...?
DOWA-SAN... WAS IT?
MUNCH...?
SCRAPE
IF I'VE ROBBED YOU OF YOUR SEAT, THERE'S NO NEED TO BE CONSIDERATE.
ISN'T IT HARD FOR TANAKA-KUN TO EAT, TOO?

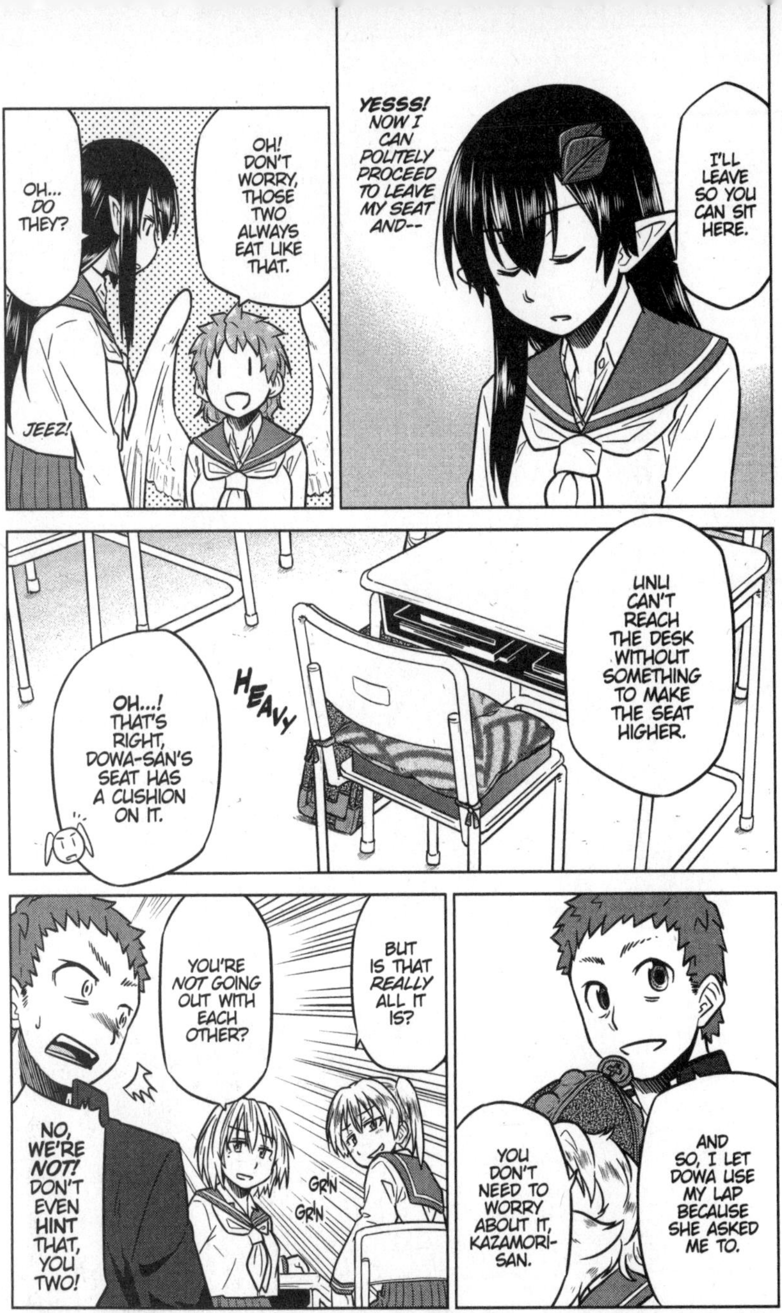
I'LL LEAVE SO YOU CAN SIT HERE.
YESSS! NOW I CAN POLITELY PROCEED TO LEAVE MY SEAT AND--
OH! DON'T WORRY, THOSE TWO ALWAYS EAT LIKE THAT.
OH... DO THEY?
JEEZ!
UNLI CAN'T REACH THE DESK WITHOUT SOMETHING TO MAKE THE SEAT HIGHER.
HEAVY
OH...! THAT'S RIGHT, DOWA-SAN'S SEAT HAS A CUSHION ON IT.
AND SO, I LET DOWA USE MY LAP BECAUSE SHE ASKED ME TO.
YOU DON'T NEED TO WORRY ABOUT IT, KAZAMORI-SAN.
BUT IS THAT REALLY ALL IT IS?
YOU'RE NOT GOING OUT WITH EACH OTHER?
GR'N
GR'N
NO, WE'RE NOT! DON'T EVEN HINT THAT, YOU TWO!

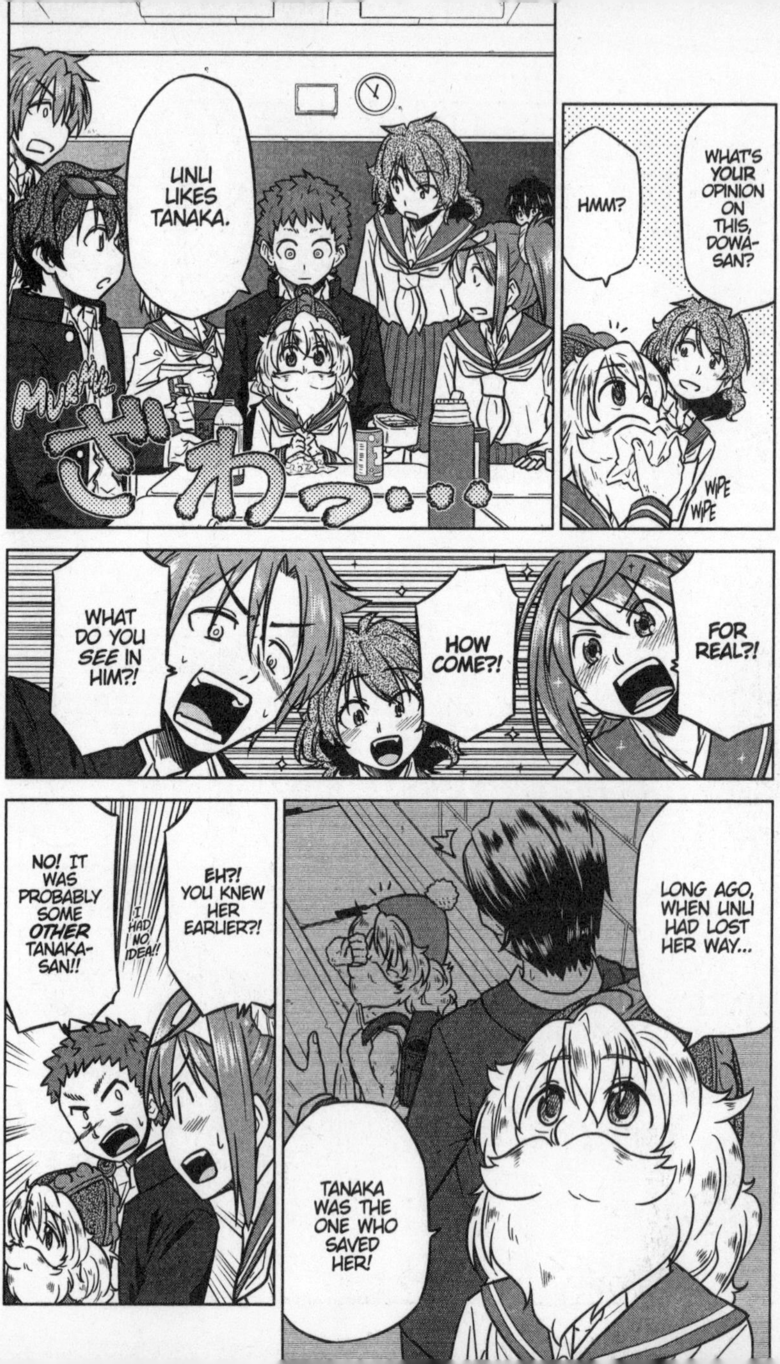
WHAT'S YOUR OPINION ON THIS, DOWA-SAN?
HMM?
WIPE WIPE
UNLI LIKES TANAKA.
MURMUR...
ざわっ…
FOR REAL?!
HOW COME?!
WHAT DO YOU SEE IN HIM?!
LONG AGO, WHEN UNLI HAD LOST HER WAY...
TANAKA WAS THE ONE WHO SAVED HER!
EH?! YOU KNEW HER EARLIER?!
I HAD NO IDEA!!
NO! IT WAS PROBABLY SOME *OTHER* TANAKA-SAN!!

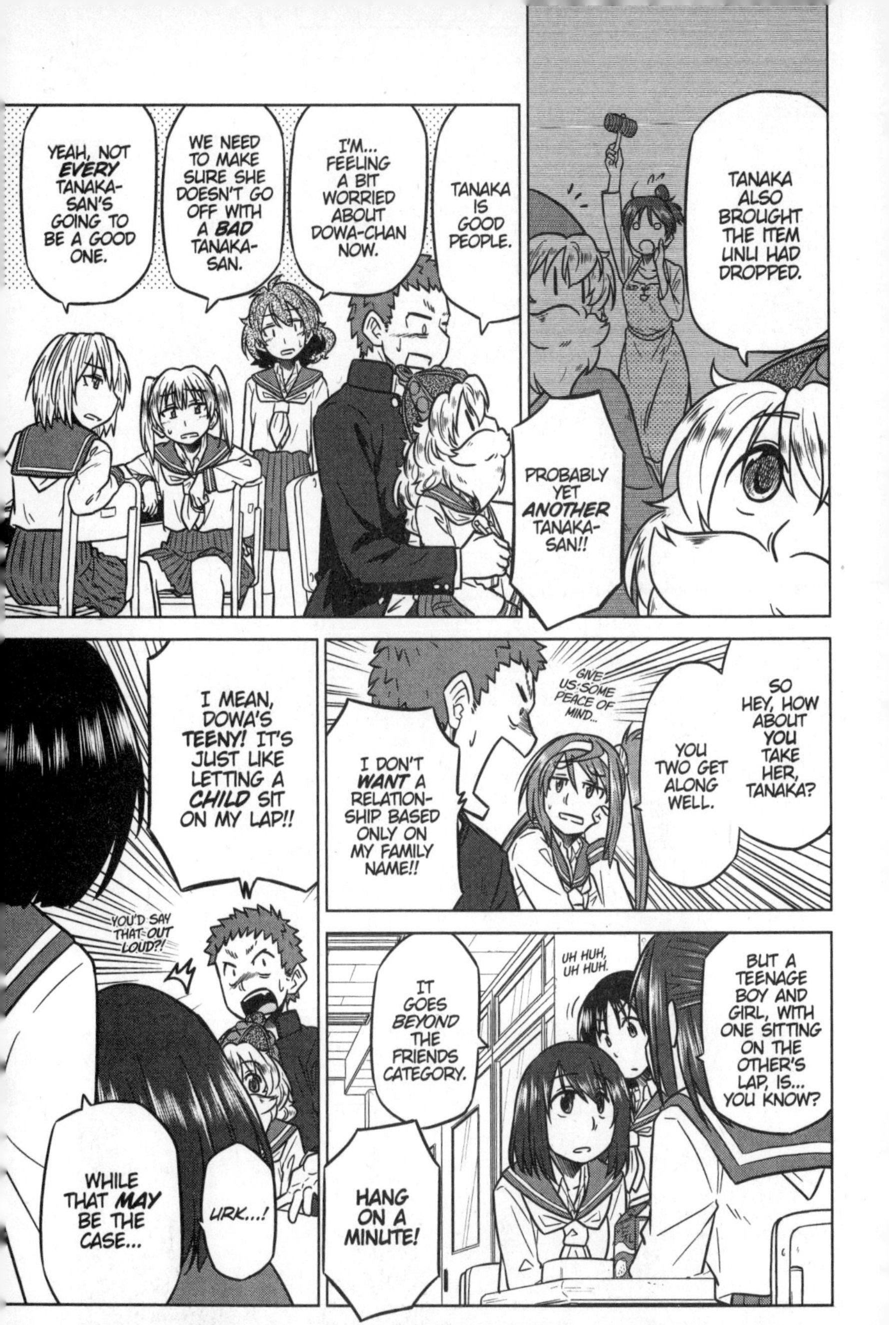
TANAKA ALSO BROUGHT THE ITEM UNLI HAD DROPPED.
PROBABLY YET ANOTHER TANAKA-SAN!!
TANAKA IS GOOD PEOPLE.
I'M... FEELING A BIT WORRIED ABOUT DOWA-CHAN NOW.
WE NEED TO MAKE SURE SHE DOESN'T GO OFF WITH A BAD TANAKA-SAN.
YEAH, NOT EVERY TANAKA-SAN'S GOING TO BE A GOOD ONE.
SO HEY, HOW ABOUT YOU TAKE HER, TANAKA?
YOU TWO GET ALONG WELL.
GIVE US SOME PEACE OF MIND...
I DON'T WANT A RELATIONSHIP BASED ONLY ON MY FAMILY NAME!!
BUT A TEENAGE BOY AND GIRL, WITH ONE SITTING ON THE OTHER'S LAP, IS... YOU KNOW?
UH HUH, UH HUH.
IT GOES BEYOND THE FRIENDS CATEGORY.
HANG ON A MINUTE!
I MEAN, DOWA'S TEENY! IT'S JUST LIKE LETTING A CHILD SIT ON MY LAP!!
YOU'D SAY THAT OUT LOUD?!
URK...!
WHILE THAT MAY BE THE CASE...

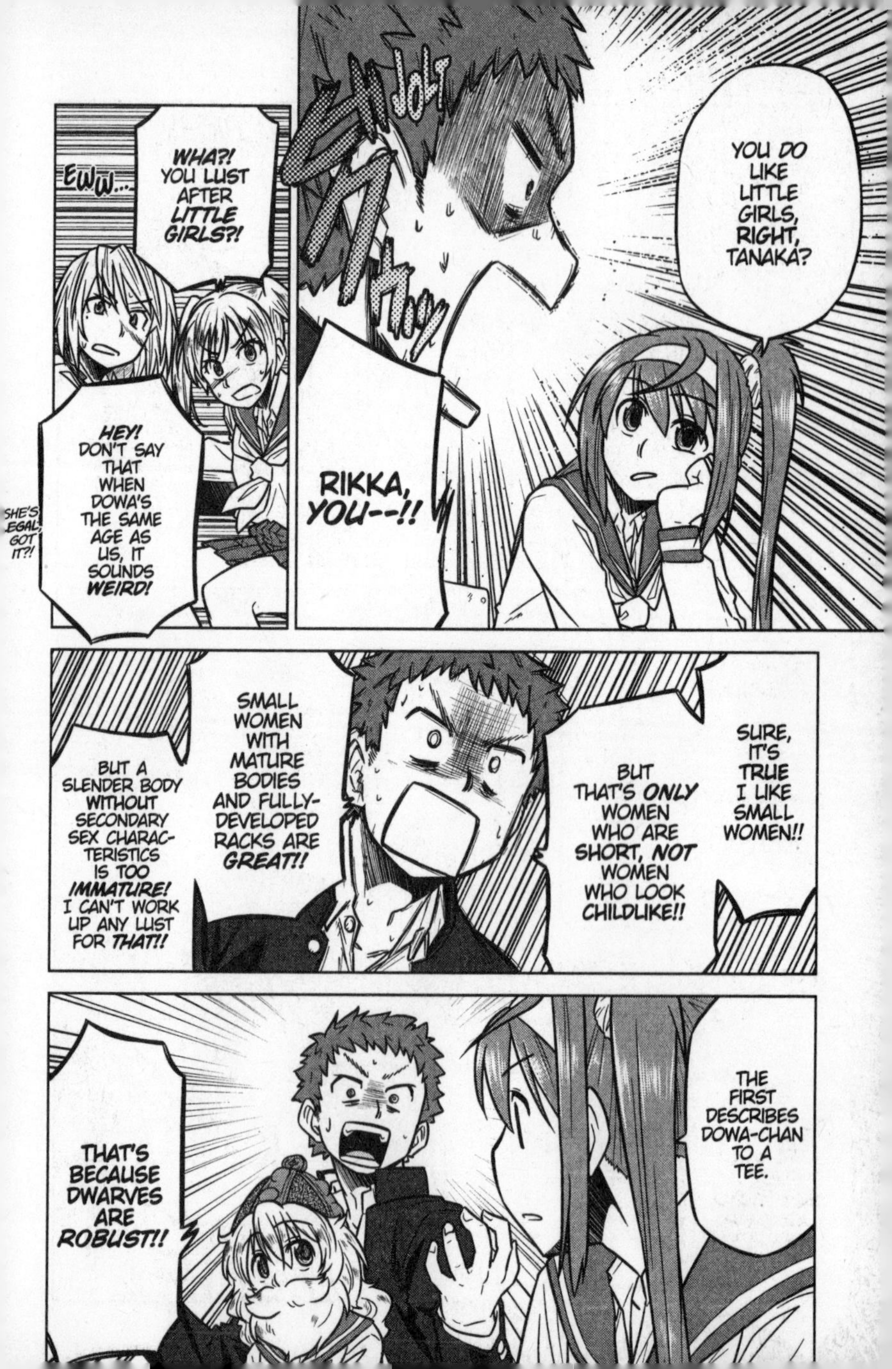
YOU DO LIKE LITTLE GIRLS, RIGHT, TANAKA?
JOLT
RIKKA, YOU--!!
WHA?! YOU LUST AFTER LITTLE GIRLS?!
EWW...
HEY! DON'T SAY THAT WHEN DOWA'S THE SAME AGE AS US, IT SOUNDS WEIRD!
SHE'S EGAL, GOT IT?!
SURE, IT'S TRUE I LIKE SMALL WOMEN!!
BUT THAT'S ONLY WOMEN WHO ARE SHORT, NOT WOMEN WHO LOOK CHILDLIKE!!
SMALL WOMEN WITH MATURE BODIES AND FULLY-DEVELOPED RACKS ARE GREAT!!
BUT A SLENDER BODY WITHOUT SECONDARY SEX CHARAC-TERISTICS IS TOO IMMATURE! I CAN'T WORK UP ANY LUST FOR THAT!!
THE FIRST DESCRIBES DOWA-CHAN TO A TEE.
THAT'S BECAUSE DWARVES ARE ROBUST!!

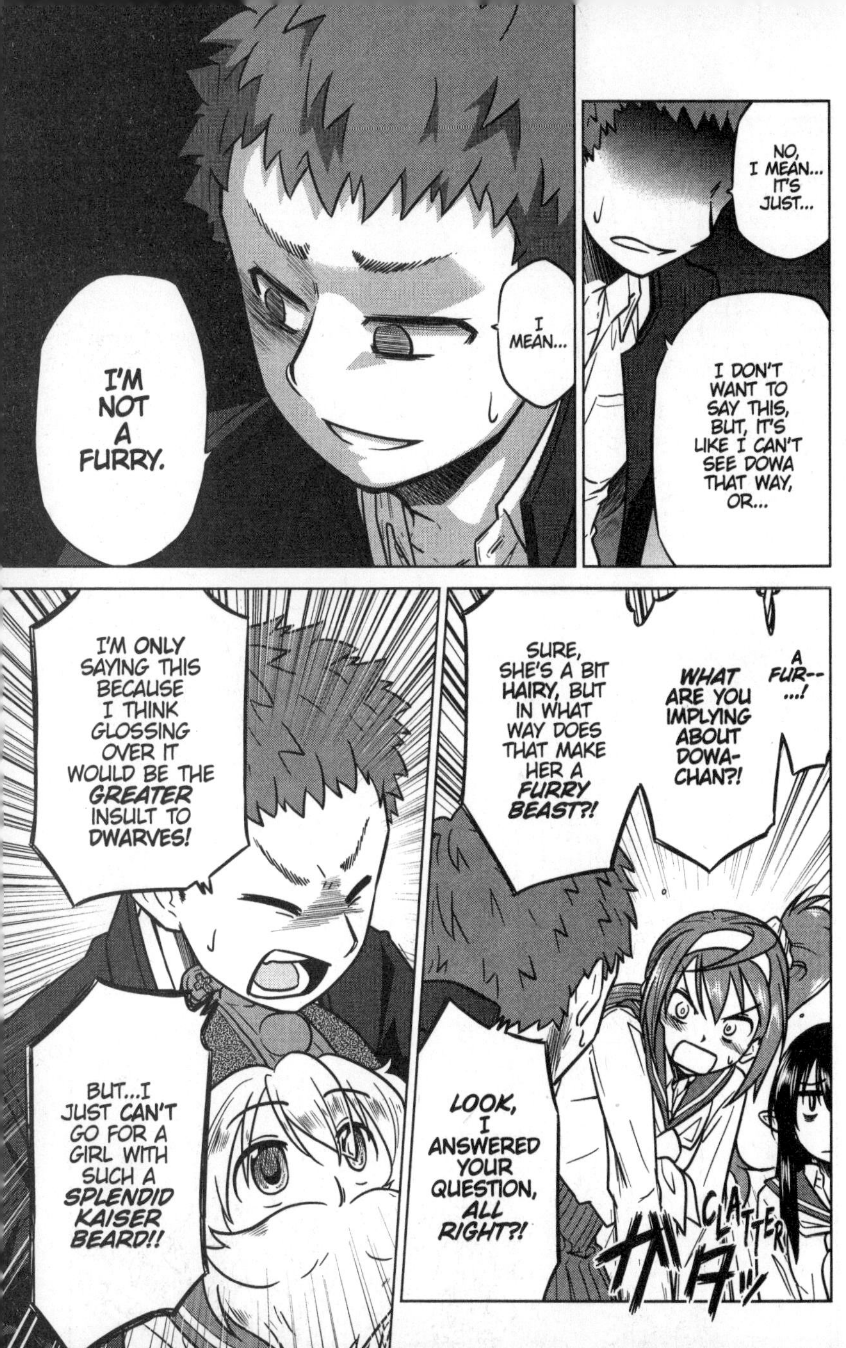
NO, I MEAN... IT'S JUST...
I DON'T WANT TO SAY THIS, BUT, IT'S LIKE I CAN'T SEE DOWA THAT WAY, OR...
I MEAN...
I'M NOT A FURRY.
A FUR-- ...!
WHAT ARE YOU IMPLYING ABOUT DOWA-CHAN?!
SURE, SHE'S A BIT HAIRY, BUT IN WHAT WAY DOES THAT MAKE HER A FURRY BEAST?!
LOOK, I ANSWERED YOUR QUESTION, ALL RIGHT?!
CLATTER
I'M ONLY SAYING THIS BECAUSE I THINK GLOSSING OVER IT WOULD BE THE GREATER INSULT TO DWARVES!
BUT...I JUST CAN'T GO FOR A GIRL WITH SUCH A SPLENDID KAISER BEARD!!

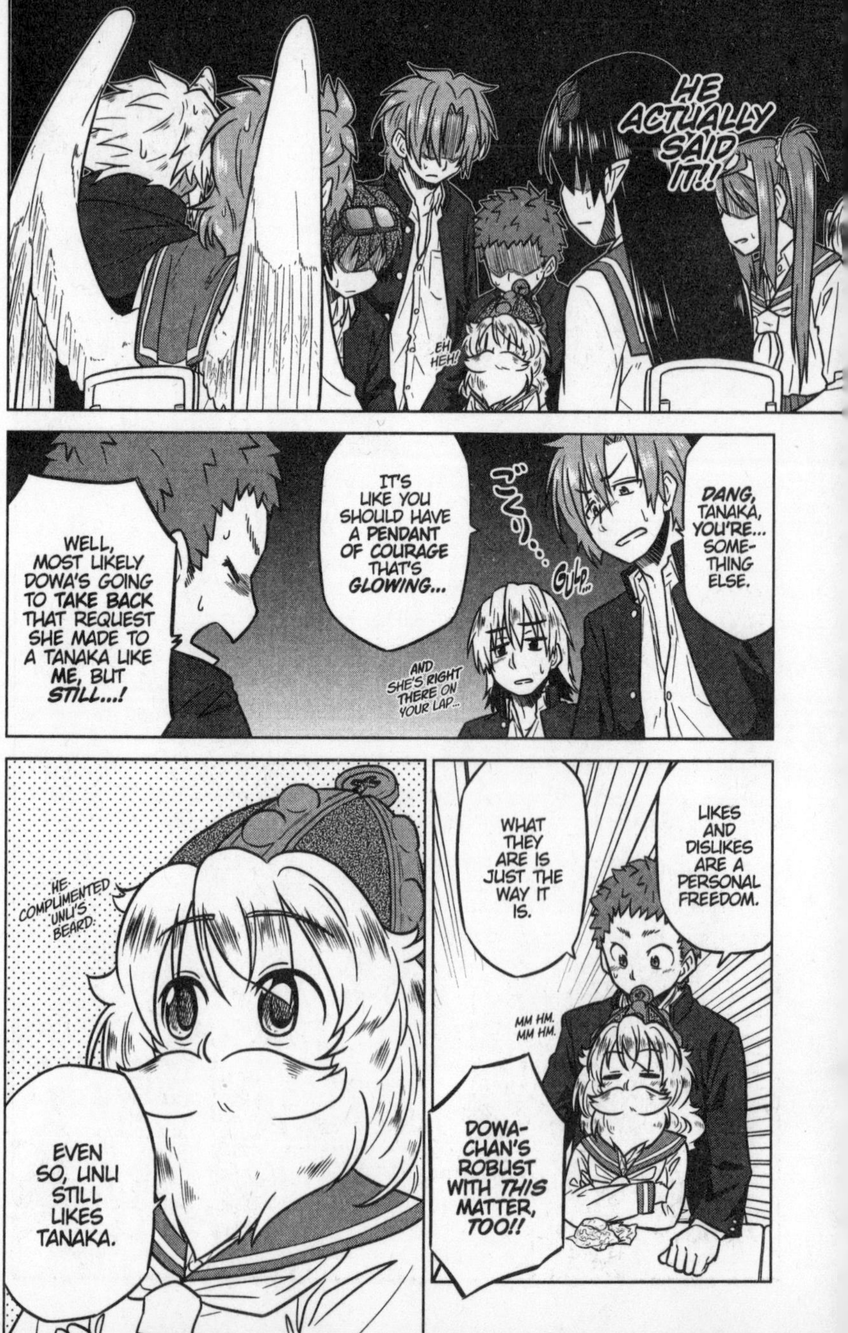
HE ACTUALLY SAID IT!!
EH HEH!
DANG, TANAKA, YOU'RE... SOMETHING ELSE.
GULP...
IT'S LIKE YOU SHOULD HAVE A PENDANT OF COURAGE THAT'S GLOWING...
AND SHE'S RIGHT THERE ON YOUR LAP...
WELL, MOST LIKELY DOWA'S GOING TO TAKE BACK THAT REQUEST SHE MADE TO A TANAKA LIKE ME, BUT STILL...!
LIKES AND DISLIKES ARE A PERSONAL FREEDOM.
WHAT THEY ARE IS JUST THE WAY IT IS.
MM HM. MM HM.
DOWA-CHAN'S ROBUST WITH THIS MATTER, TOO!!
HE COMPLIMENTED UNLI'S BEARD.
EVEN SO, UNLI STILL LIKES TANAKA.

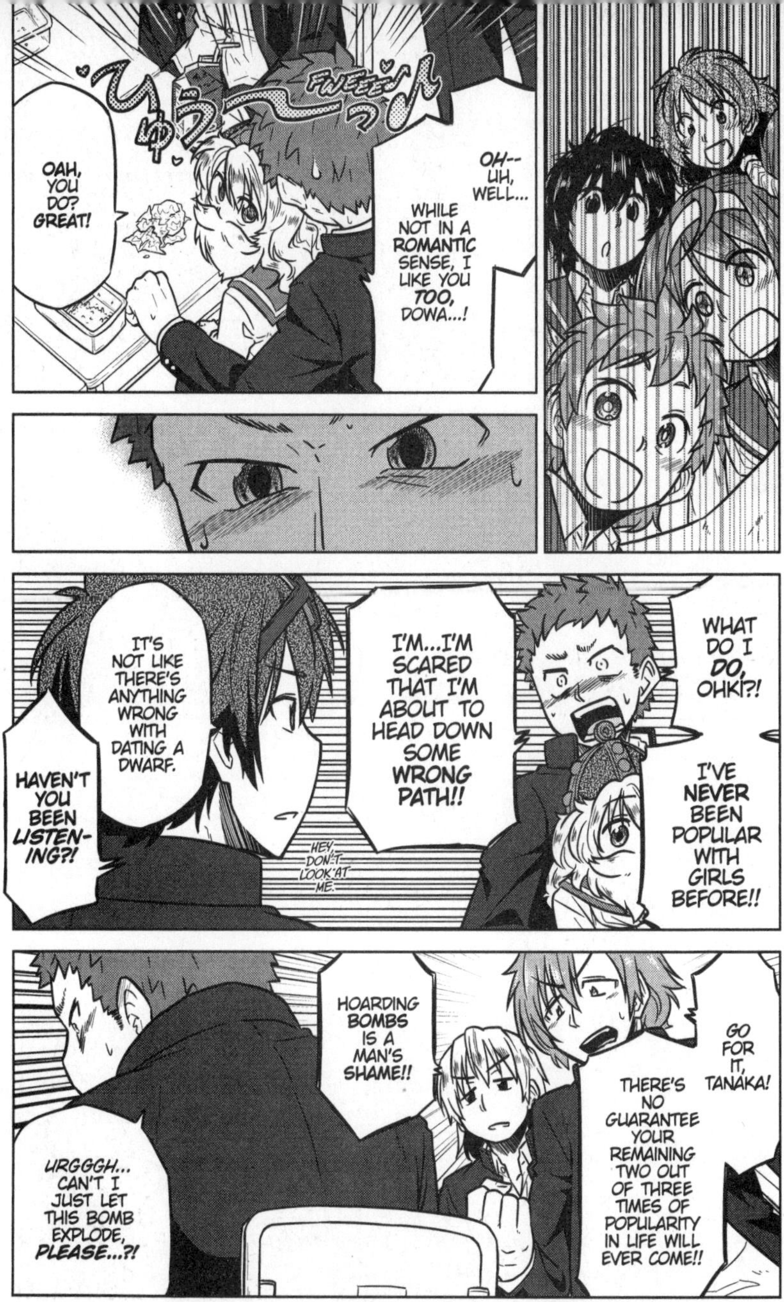
OH-- UH, WELL...
WHILE NOT IN A ROMANTIC SENSE, I LIKE YOU TOO, DOWA...!
ひゅう〜〜っん
FWEEE
OAH, YOU DO? GREAT!
WHAT DO I DO, OHKI?!
I'VE NEVER BEEN POPULAR WITH GIRLS BEFORE!!
I'M...I'M SCARED THAT I'M ABOUT TO HEAD DOWN SOME WRONG PATH!!
HEY, DON'T LOOK AT ME.
IT'S NOT LIKE THERE'S ANYTHING WRONG WITH DATING A DWARF.
HAVEN'T YOU BEEN LISTEN-ING?!
GO FOR IT, TANAKA!
THERE'S NO GUARANTEE YOUR REMAINING TWO OUT OF THREE TIMES OF POPULARITY IN LIFE WILL EVER COME!!
HOARDING BOMBS IS A MAN'S SHAME!!
URGGGH... CAN'T I JUST LET THIS BOMB EXPLODE, PLEASE...?!

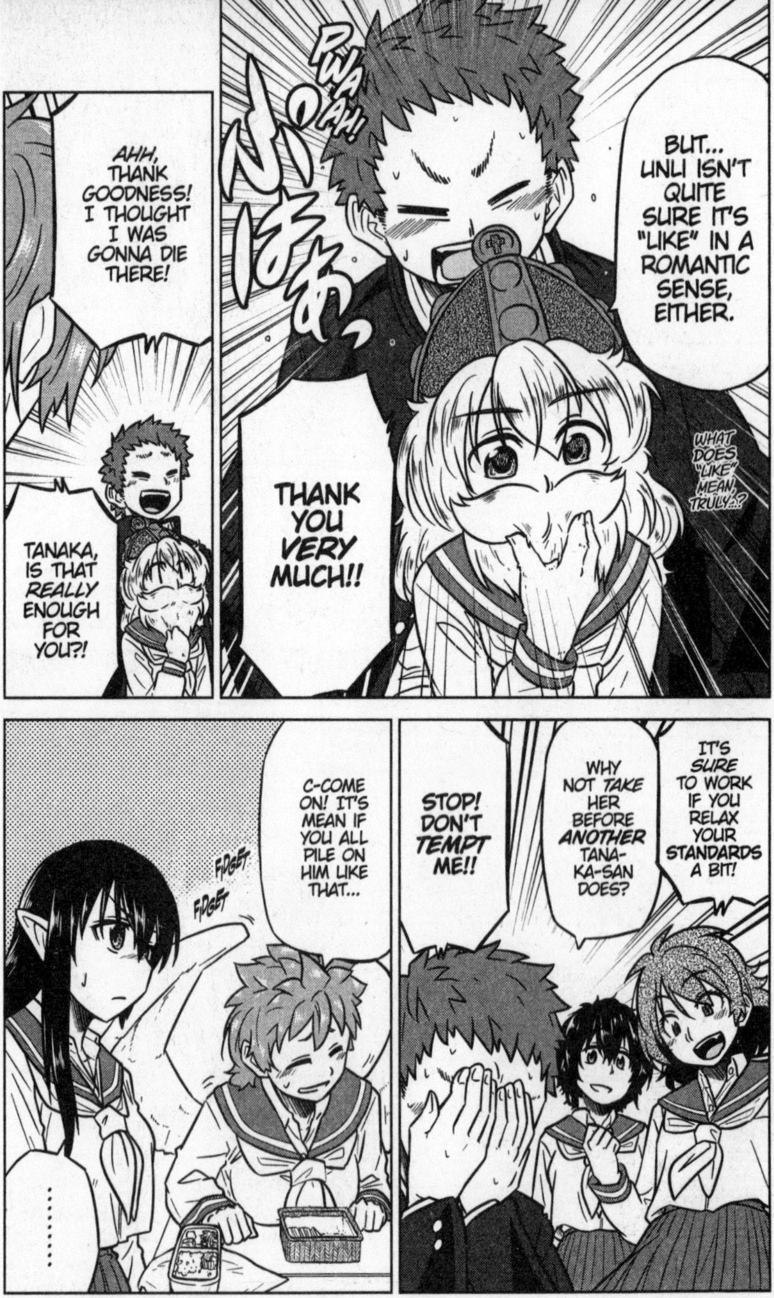
BUT... UNLI ISN'T QUITE SURE IT'S "LIKE" IN A ROMANTIC SENSE, EITHER.
PWAAH!
WHAT DOES "LIKE" MEAN, TRULY...?
THANK YOU *VERY* MUCH!!
AHH, THANK GOODNESS! I THOUGHT I WAS GONNA DIE THERE!
TANAKA, IS THAT *REALLY* ENOUGH FOR YOU?!
IT'S *SURE* TO WORK IF YOU RELAX YOUR STANDARDS A BIT!
WHY NOT *TAKE* HER BEFORE *ANOTHER* TANA-KA-SAN DOES?
STOP! DON'T *TEMPT* ME!!
C-COME ON! IT'S MEAN IF YOU ALL PILE ON HIM LIKE THAT...
FIDGET
FIDGET
......

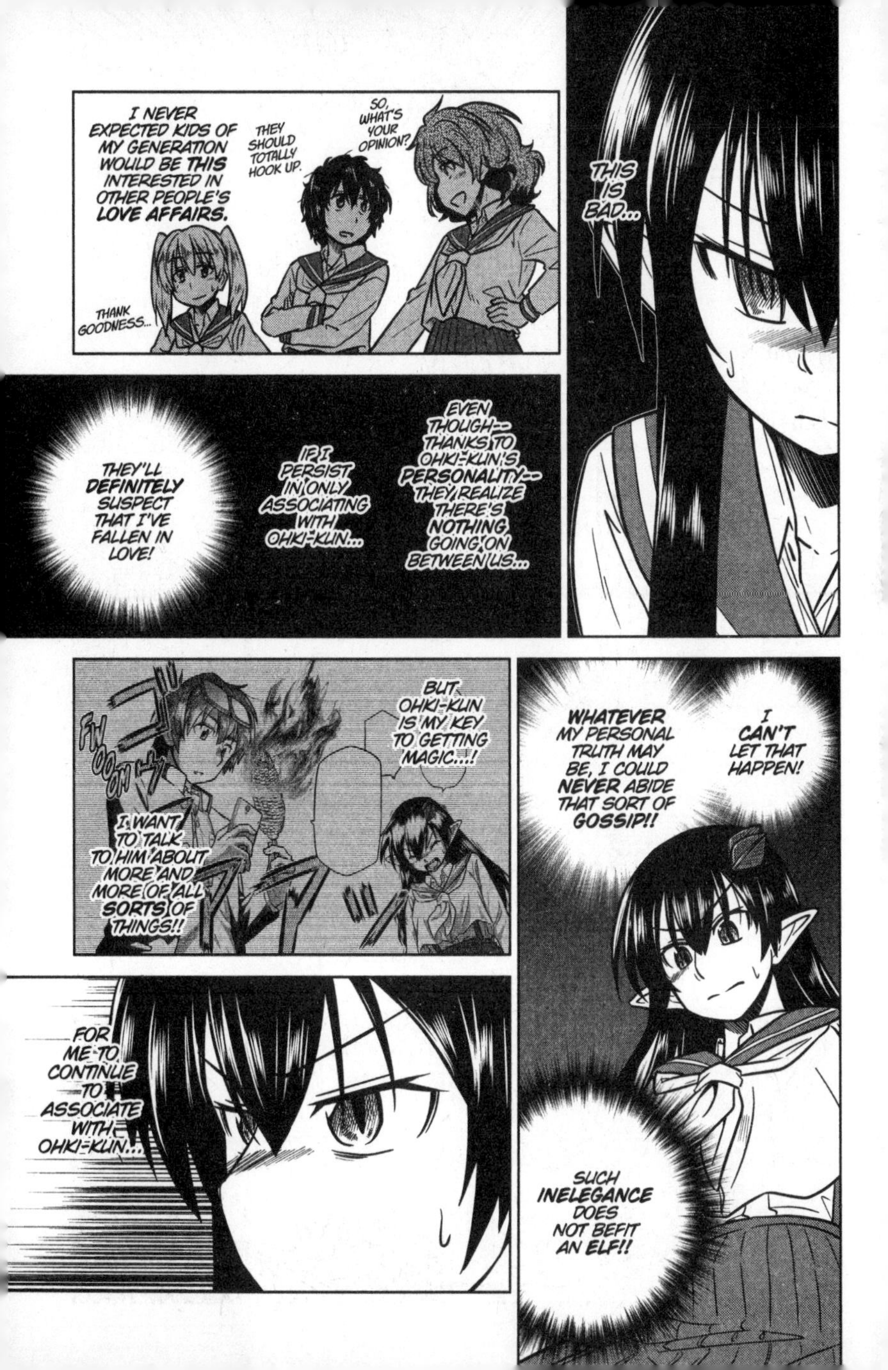
THIS IS BAD...
SO, WHAT'S YOUR OPINION?
THEY SHOULD TOTALLY HOOK UP.
I NEVER EXPECTED KIDS OF MY GENERATION WOULD BE THIS INTERESTED IN OTHER PEOPLE'S LOVE AFFAIRS.
THANK GOODNESS...
EVEN THOUGH-- THANKS TO OHKI-KUN'S PERSONALITY-- THEY REALIZE THERE'S NOTHING GOING ON BETWEEN US...
IF I PERSIST IN ONLY ASSOCIATING WITH OHKI-KUN...
THEY'LL DEFINITELY SUSPECT THAT I'VE FALLEN IN LOVE!
I CAN'T LET THAT HAPPEN!
WHATEVER MY PERSONAL TRUTH MAY BE, I COULD NEVER ABIDE THAT SORT OF GOSSIP!!
BUT OHKI-KUN IS MY KEY TO GETTING MAGIC...!
I WANT TO TALK TO HIM ABOUT MORE AND MORE OF ALL SORTS OF THINGS!!
FWOOOM
FOR ME TO CONTINUE TO ASSOCIATE WITH OHKI-KUN...
SUCH INELEGANCE DOES NOT BEFIT AN ELF!!

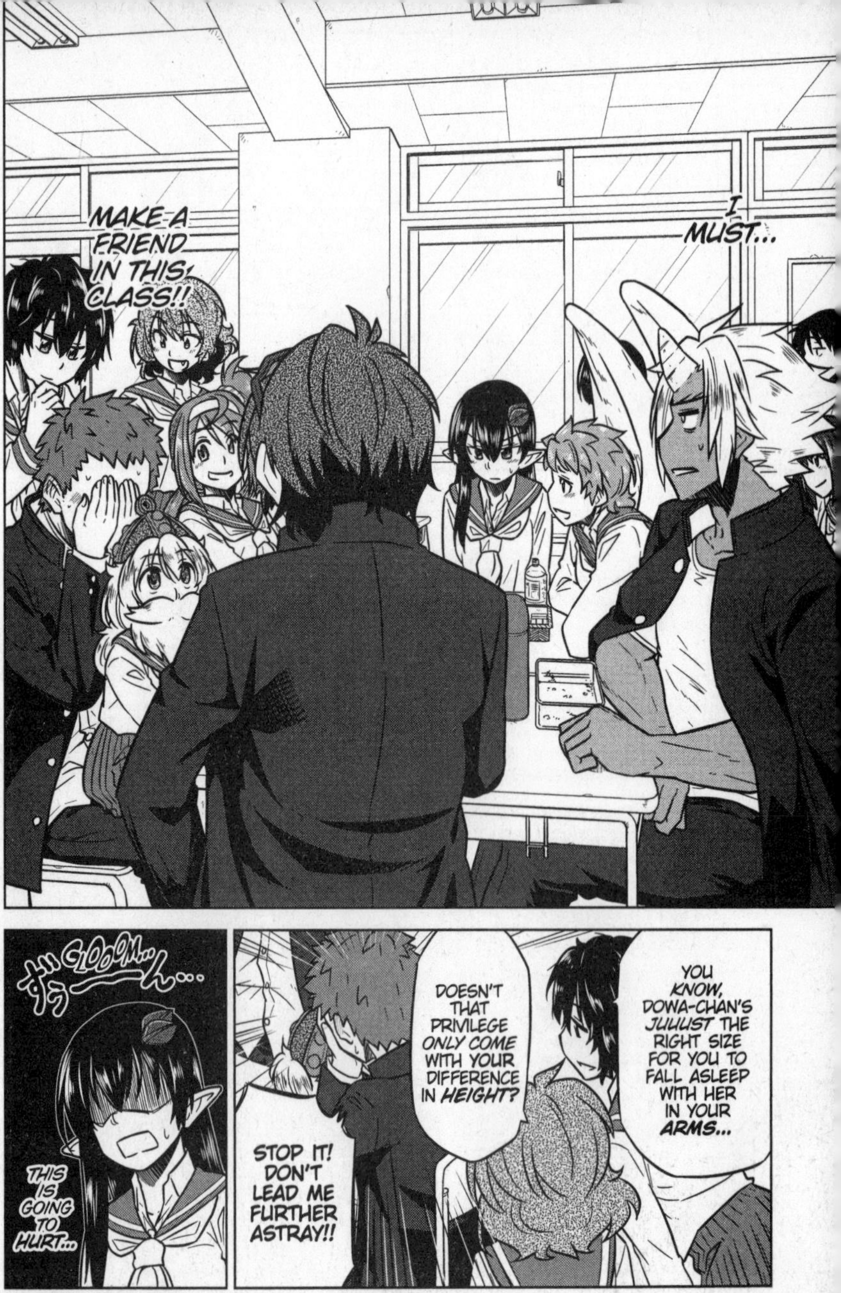
I MUST...
MAKE A FRIEND IN THIS CLASS!!
YOU KNOW, DOWA-CHAN'S JUUUST THE RIGHT SIZE FOR YOU TO FALL ASLEEP WITH HER IN YOUR ARMS...
DOESN'T THAT PRIVILEGE ONLY COME WITH YOUR DIFFERENCE IN HEIGHT?
STOP IT! DON'T LEAD ME FURTHER ASTRAY!!
GLOOOM...
THIS IS GOING TO HURT...

Chapter 4 • END

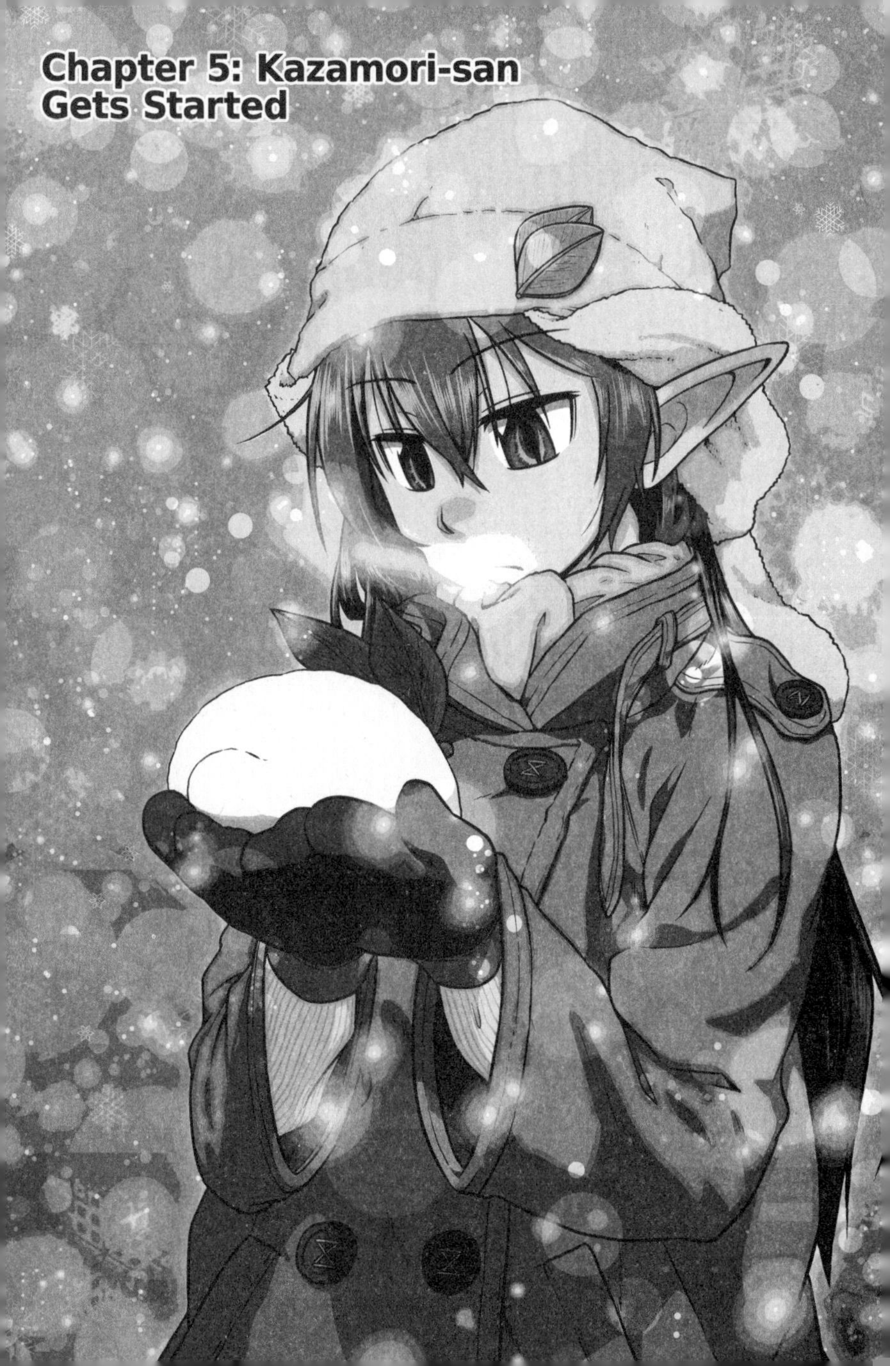
Chapter 5: Kazamori-san
Gets Started

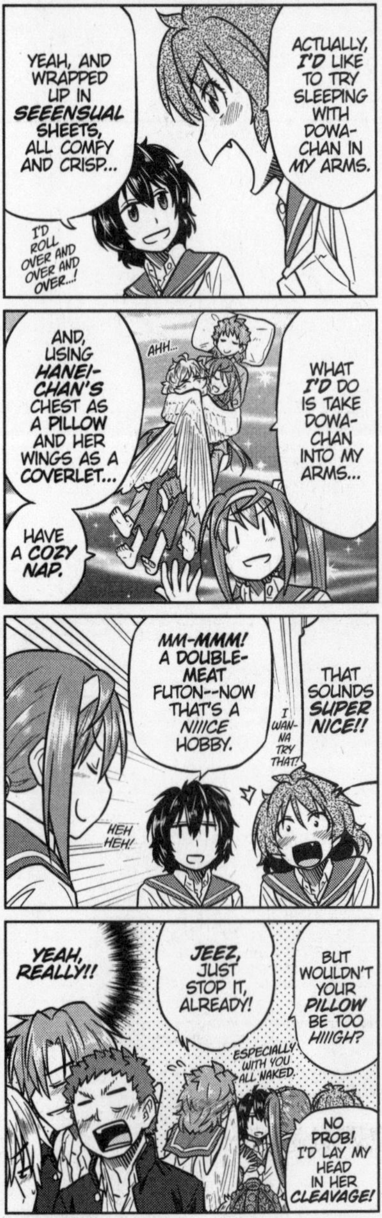
ACTUALLY, I'D LIKE TO TRY SLEEPING WITH DOWA-CHAN IN MY ARMS.
YEAH, AND WRAPPED UP IN SEEENSUAL SHEETS, ALL COMFY AND CRISP...
I'D ROLL OVER AND OVER AND OVER...!
WHAT I'D DO IS TAKE DOWA-CHAN INTO MY ARMS...
AHH...
AND, USING HANEI-CHAN'S CHEST AS A PILLOW AND HER WINGS AS A COVERLET...
HAVE A COZY NAP.
THAT SOUNDS SUPER NICE!!
I WAN-NA TRY THAT!
MM-MMM! A DOUBLE-MEAT FUTON--NOW THAT'S A NIIICE HOBBY.
HEH HEH!
BUT WOULDN'T YOUR PILLOW BE TOO HIIIGH?
JEEZ, JUST STOP IT, ALREADY!
YEAH, REALLY!!
ESPECIALLY WITH YOU ALL NAKED.
NO PROB! I'D LAY MY HEAD IN HER CLEAVAGE!

Awkward

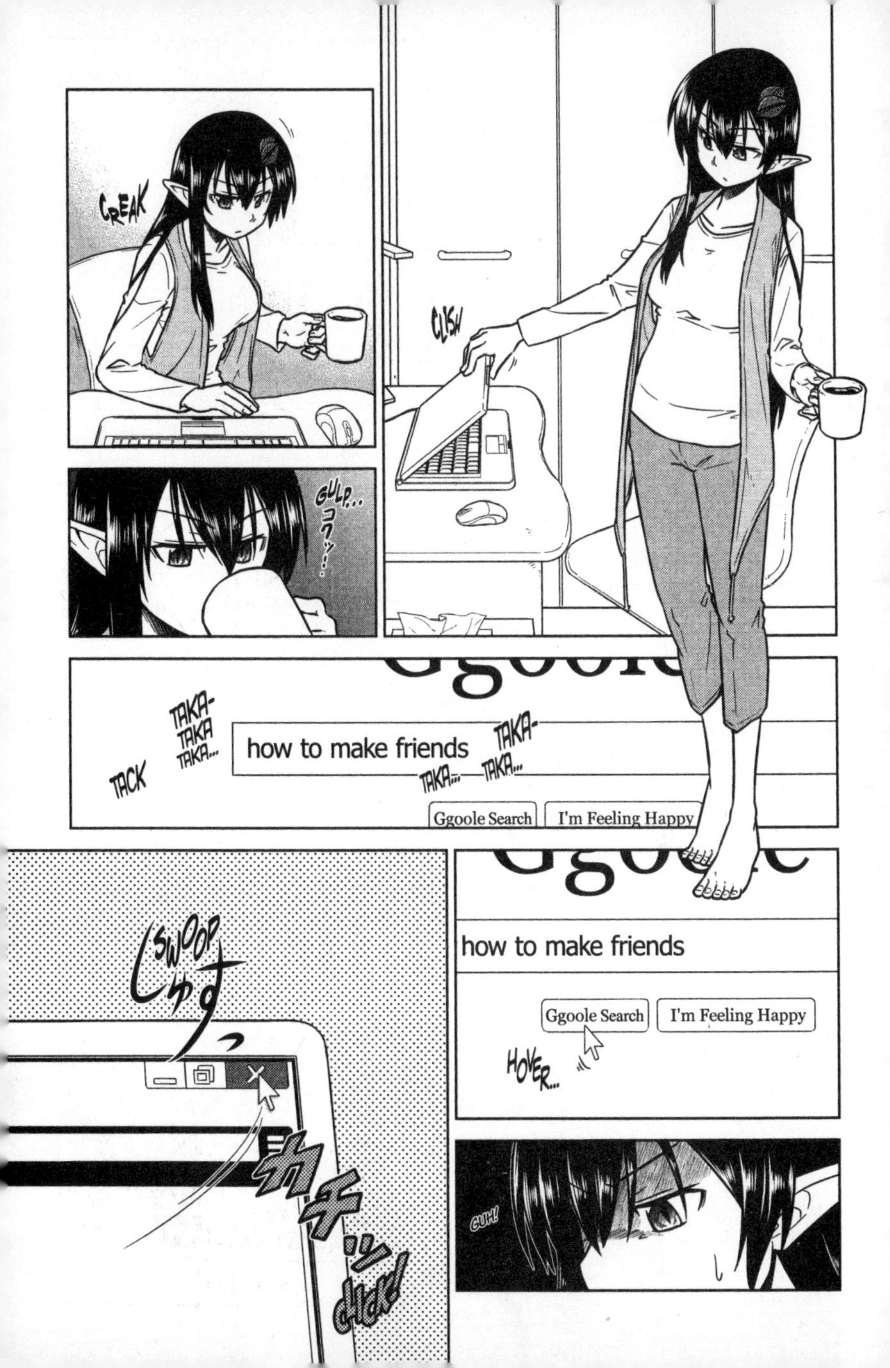
CLISH
CREAK
GULP...
コクッ…
TAKA-
TAKA...
TAKA...
how to make friends
TAKA-
TAKA
TAKA...
TACK
Ggoole Search
I'm Feeling Happy
how to make friends
Ggoole Search
I'm Feeling Happy
HOVER...
GUH!
SWOOP
しゅっ
カチッ
CLICK!

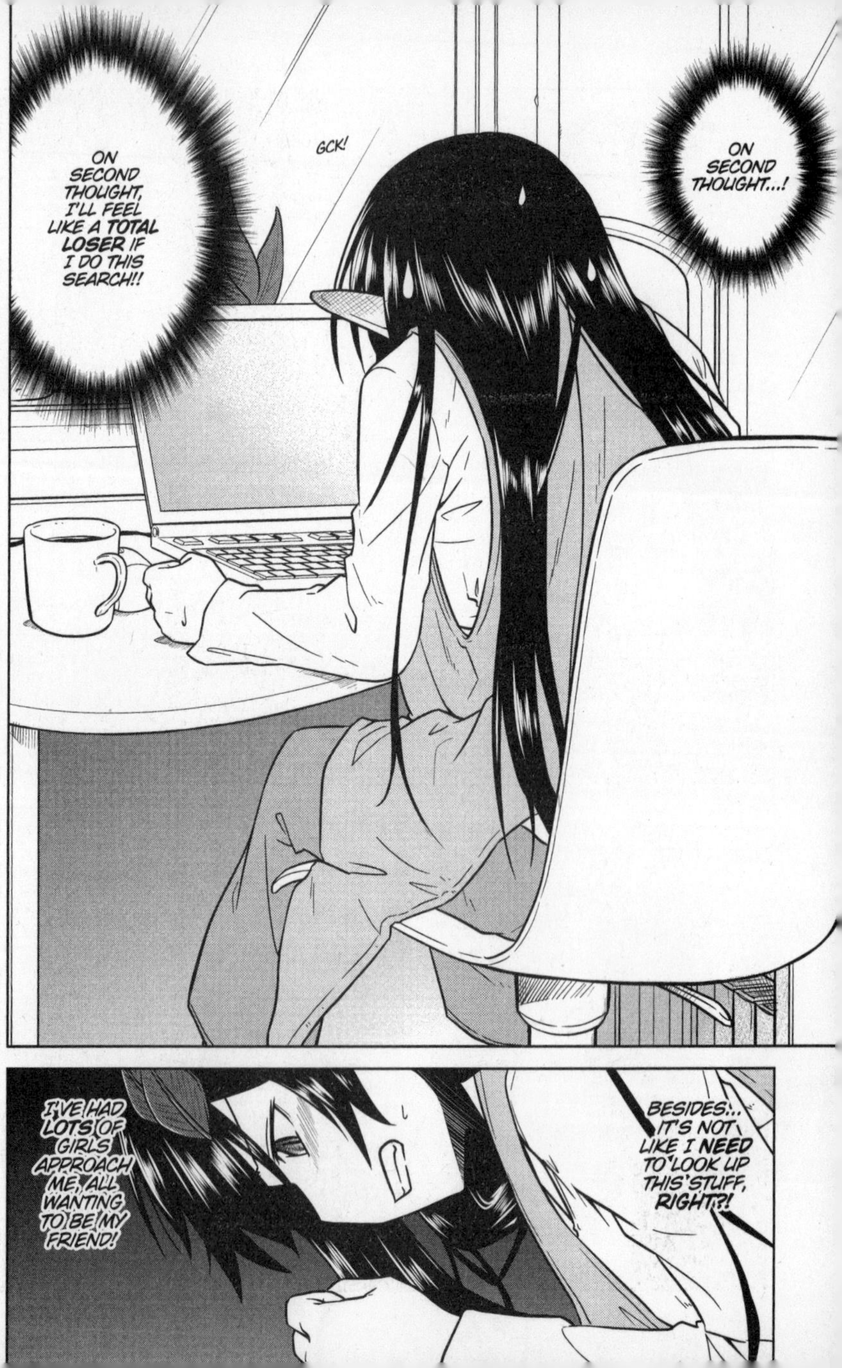
ON SECOND THOUGHT...!
GCK!
ON SECOND THOUGHT, I'LL FEEL LIKE A TOTAL LOSER IF I DO THIS SEARCH!!
BESIDES... IT'S NOT LIKE I NEED TO LOOK UP THIS STUFF, RIGHT?!
I'VE HAD LOTS OF GIRLS APPROACH ME, ALL WANTING TO BE MY FRIEND!

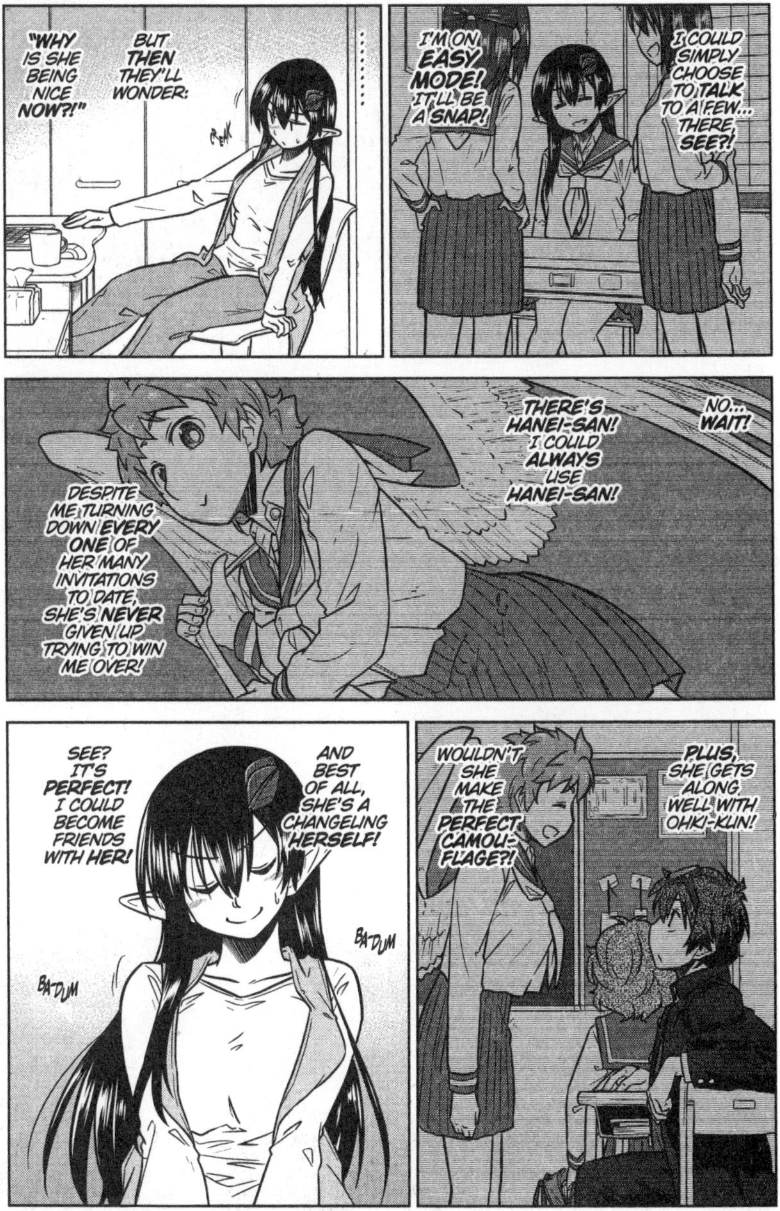
I COULD SIMPLY CHOOSE TO TALK TO A FEW... THERE, SEE?!
I'M ON EASY MODE! IT'LL BE A SNAP!
......
BUT THEN THEY'LL WONDER:
"WHY IS SHE BEING NICE NOW?!"
CREAK
NO... WAIT!
THERE'S HANEI-SAN! I COULD ALWAYS USE HANEI-SAN!
DESPITE ME TURNING DOWN EVERY ONE OF HER MANY INVITATIONS TO DATE, SHE'S NEVER GIVEN UP TRYING TO WIN ME OVER!
PLUS, SHE GETS ALONG WELL WITH OHKI-KUN!
WOULDN'T SHE MAKE THE PERFECT CAMOU-FLAGE?!
AND BEST OF ALL, SHE'S A CHANGELING HERSELF!
SEE? IT'S PERFECT! I COULD BECOME FRIENDS WITH HER!
BA-DUM
BA-DUM

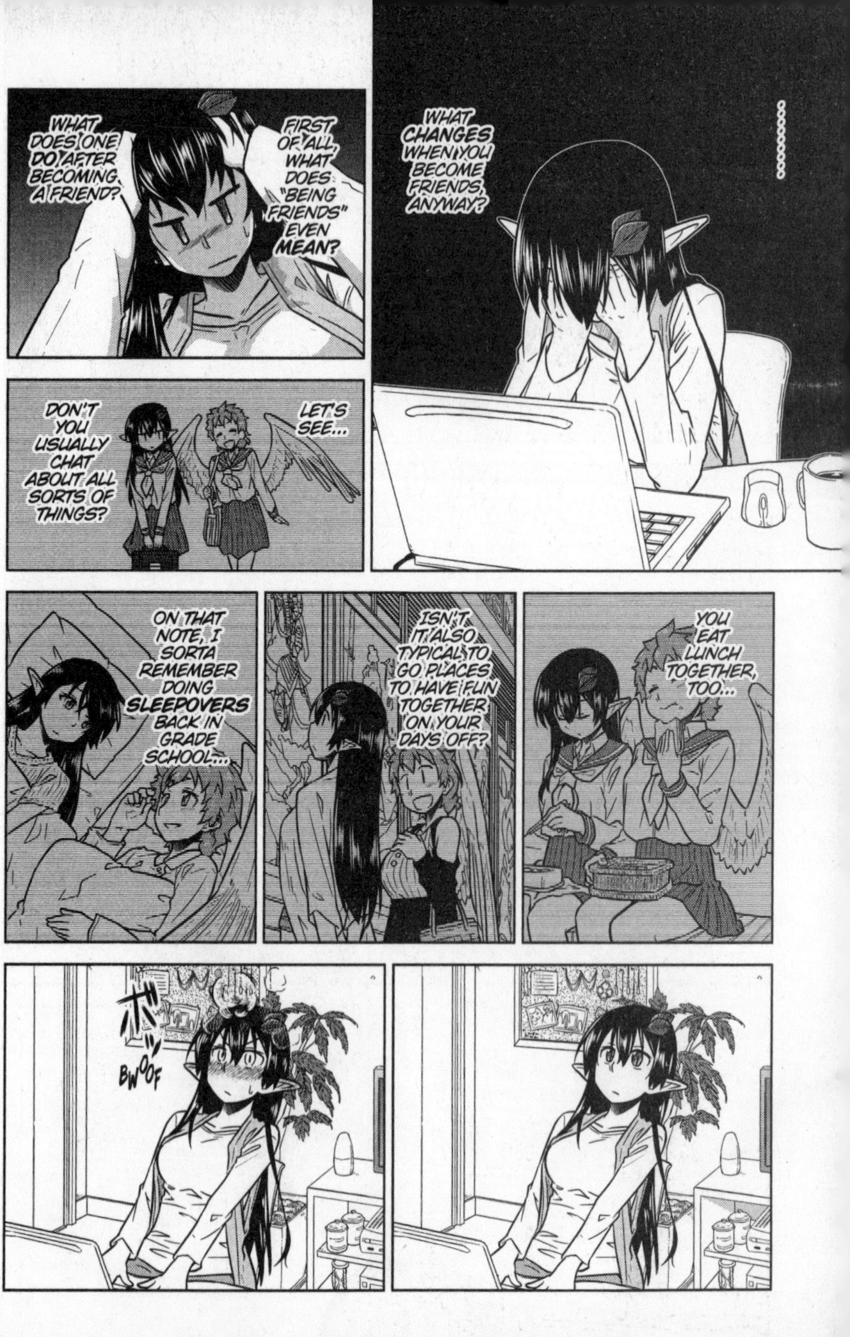

....
WHAT CHANGES WHEN YOU BECOME FRIENDS, ANYWAY?
FIRST OF ALL, WHAT DOES "BEING FRIENDS" EVEN MEAN?
WHAT DOES ONE DO AFTER BECOMING A FRIEND?
LET'S SEE...
DON'T YOU USUALLY CHAT ABOUT ALL SORTS OF THINGS?
YOU EAT LUNCH TOGETHER, TOO...
ISN'T IT ALSO TYPICAL TO GO PLACES TO HAVE FUN TOGETHER ON YOUR DAYS OFF?
ON THAT NOTE, I SORTA REMEMBER DOING SLEEPOVERS BACK IN GRADE SCHOOL...
BWOOF

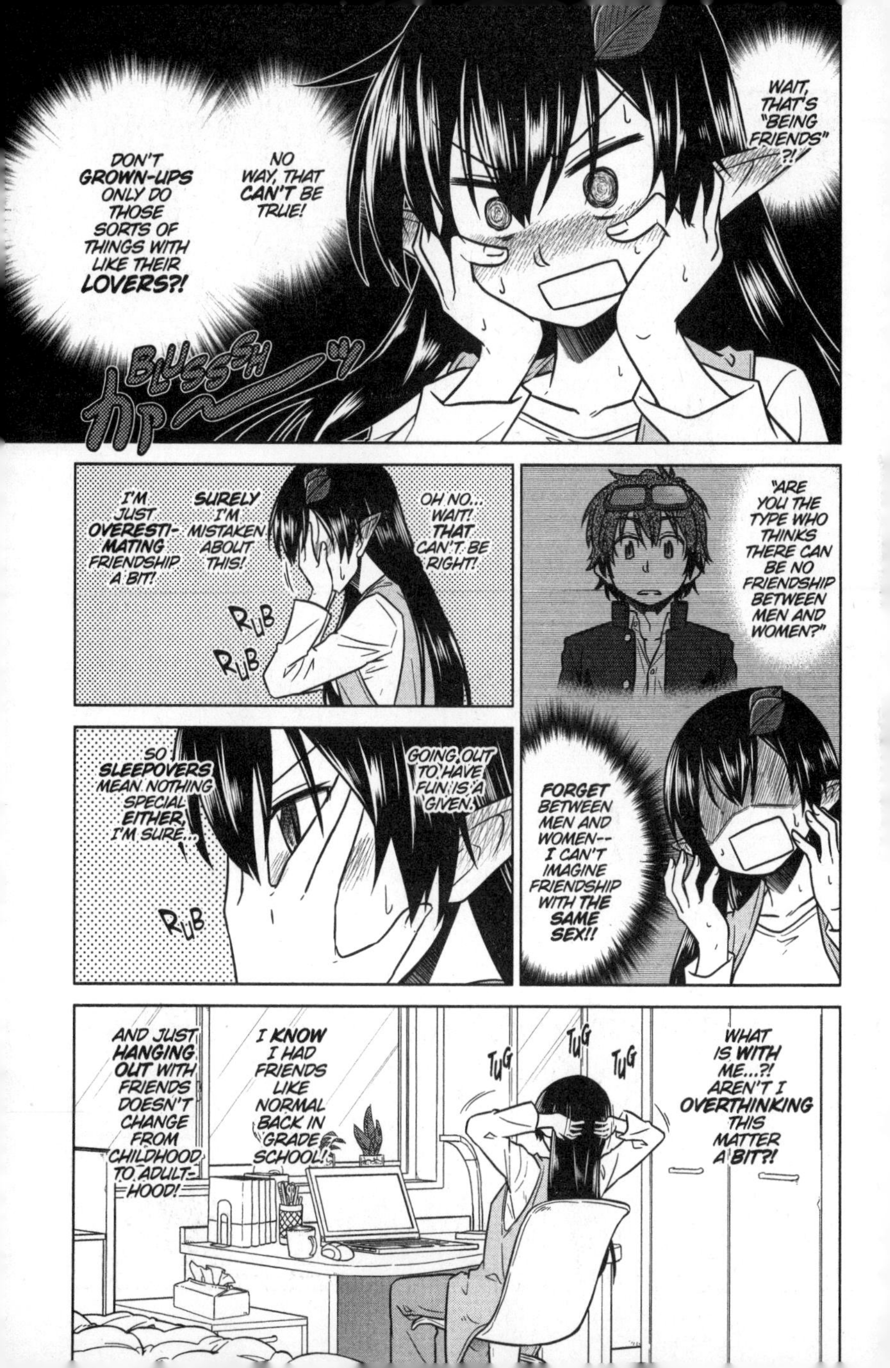
WAIT, THAT'S "BEING FRIENDS"?!
NO WAY, THAT CAN'T BE TRUE!
DON'T GROWN-UPS ONLY DO THOSE SORTS OF THINGS WITH LIKE THEIR LOVERS?!
BLUSSSH
カア~ッ
"ARE YOU THE TYPE WHO THINKS THERE CAN BE NO FRIENDSHIP BETWEEN MEN AND WOMEN?"
OH NO... WAIT! THAT CAN'T BE RIGHT!
SURELY I'M MISTAKEN ABOUT THIS!
I'M JUST OVERESTIMATING FRIENDSHIP A BIT!
RUB
RUB
FORGET BETWEEN MEN AND WOMEN-- I CAN'T IMAGINE FRIENDSHIP WITH THE SAME SEX!!
GOING OUT TO HAVE FUN IS A GIVEN.
SO SLEEPOVERS MEAN NOTHING SPECIAL EITHER, I'M SURE...!
RUB
WHAT IS WITH ME...?! AREN'T I OVERTHINKING THIS MATTER A BIT?!
TUG
TUG
TUG
I KNOW I HAD FRIENDS LIKE NORMAL BACK IN GRADE SCHOOL!
AND JUST HANGING OUT WITH FRIENDS DOESN'T CHANGE FROM CHILDHOOD TO ADULTHOOD!

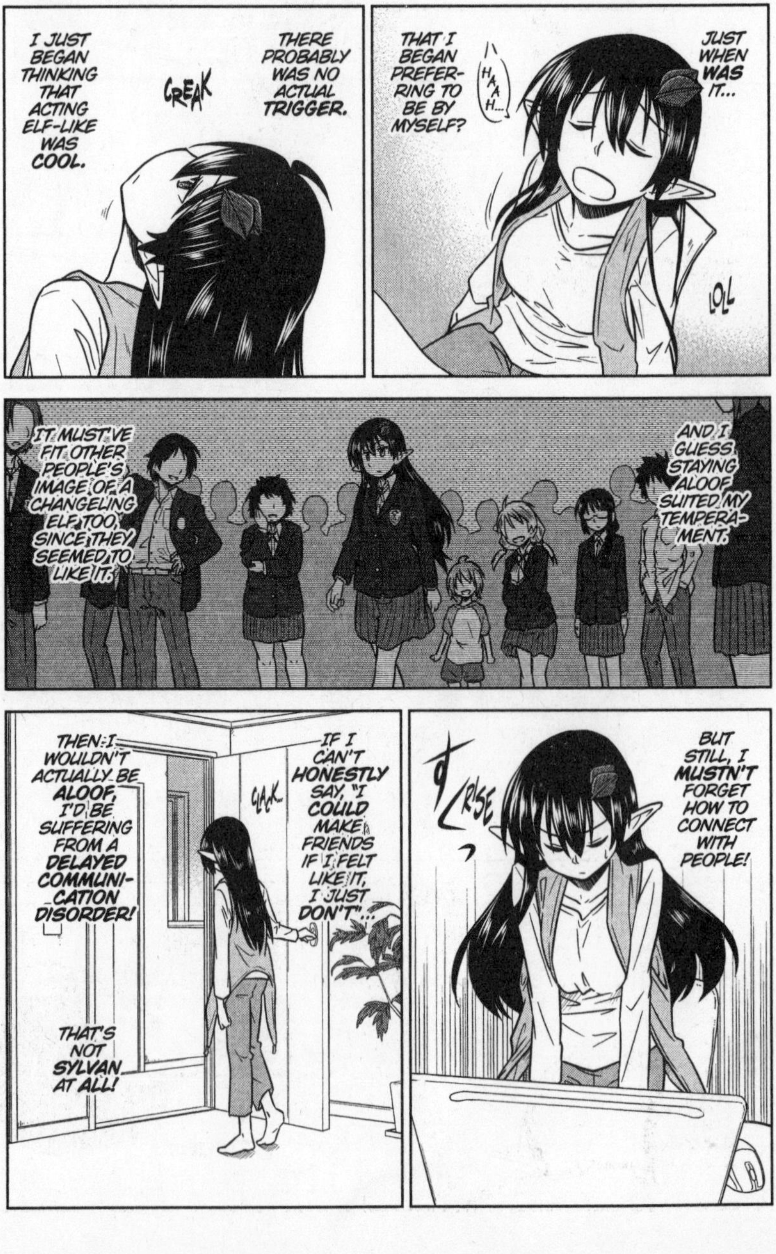
JUST WHEN WAS IT...
THAT I BEGAN PREFERRING TO BE BY MYSELF?
HAAH...
LOLL
THERE PROBABLY WAS NO ACTUAL TRIGGER.
CREAK
I JUST BEGAN THINKING THAT ACTING ELF-LIKE WAS COOL.
AND I GUESS STAYING ALOOF SUITED MY TEMPERAMENT.
IT MUST'VE FIT OTHER PEOPLE'S IMAGE OF A CHANGELING ELF TOO, SINCE THEY SEEMED TO LIKE IT.
RISE
BUT STILL, I MUSTN'T FORGET HOW TO CONNECT WITH PEOPLE!
IF I CAN'T HONESTLY SAY, "I COULD MAKE FRIENDS IF I FELT LIKE IT, I JUST DON'T"...
CLACK...
THEN I WOULDN'T ACTUALLY BE ALOOF, I'D BE SUFFERING FROM A DELAYED COMMUNICATION DISORDER!
THAT'S NOT SYLVAN AT ALL!

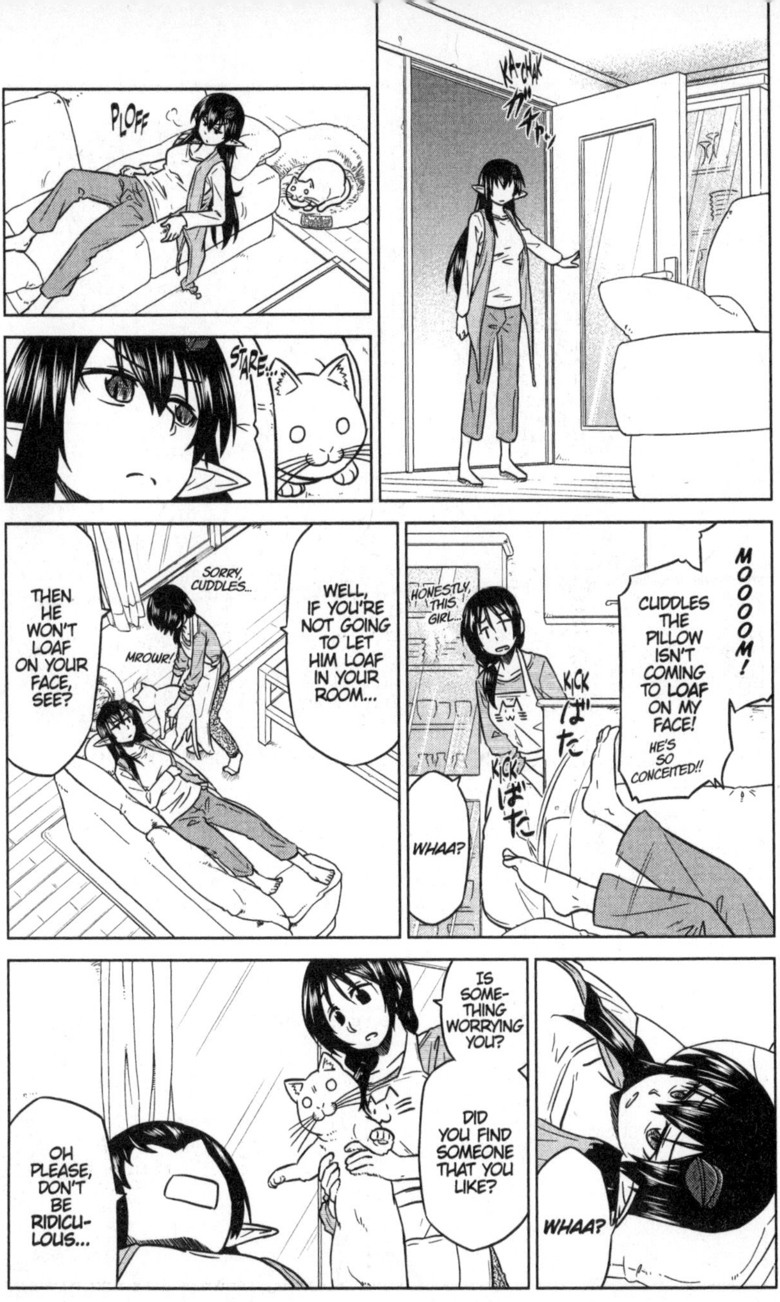
KA-CHAK
ガチャッ
PLOFF
STARE...
MOOOOOM!
CUDDLES THE PILLOW ISN'T COMING TO LOAF ON MY FACE!
HE'S SO CONCEITED!!
KICK
ばた
KICK
ばた
HONESTLY, THIS GIRL...
WHAA?
WELL, IF YOU'RE NOT GOING TO LET HIM LOAF IN YOUR ROOM...
SORRY, CUDDLES...
MROWR!
THEN HE WON'T LOAF ON YOUR FACE, SEE?
WHAA?
IS SOMETHING WORRYING YOU?
DID YOU FIND SOMEONE THAT YOU LIKE?
OH PLEASE, DON'T BE RIDICULOUS...

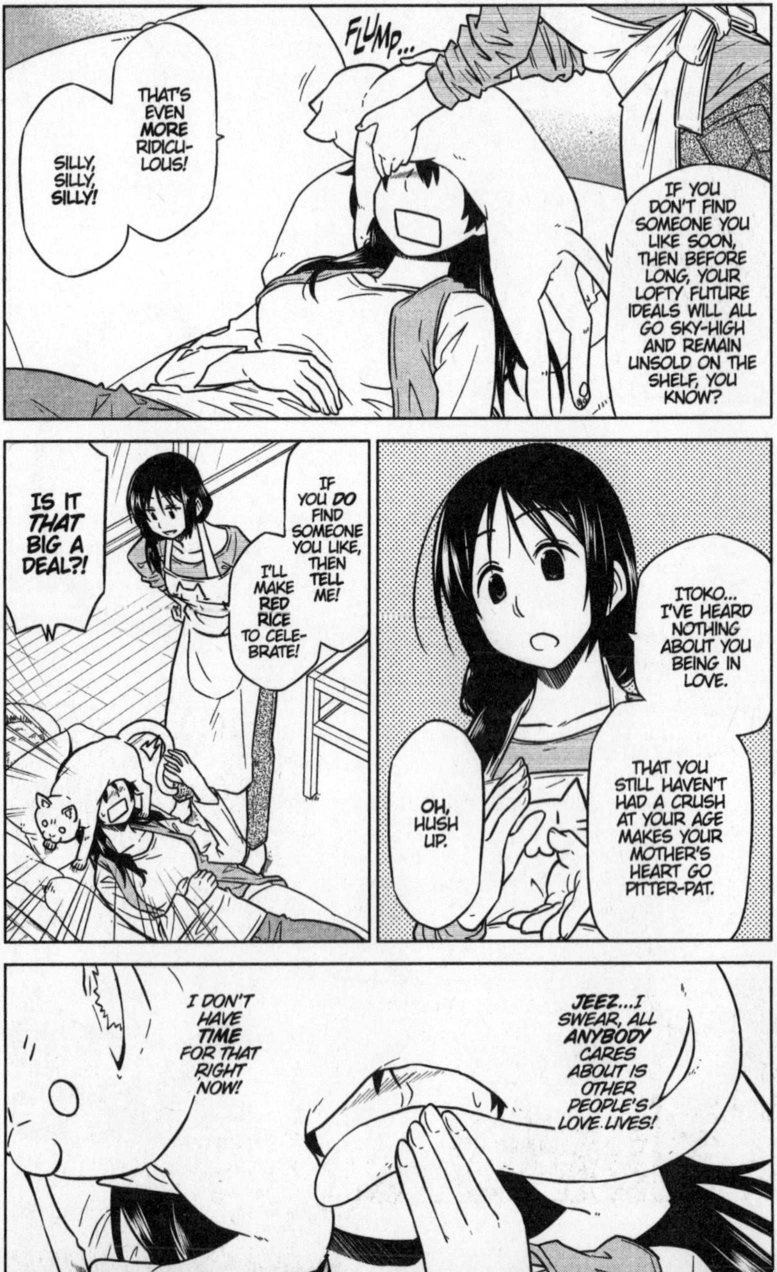
FLUMP...
IF YOU DON'T FIND SOMEONE YOU LIKE SOON, THEN BEFORE LONG, YOUR LOFTY FUTURE IDEALS WILL ALL GO SKY-HIGH AND REMAIN UNSOLD ON THE SHELF, YOU KNOW?
THAT'S EVEN MORE RIDICULOUS!
SILLY, SILLY, SILLY!
ITOKO... I'VE HEARD NOTHING ABOUT YOU BEING IN LOVE.
THAT YOU STILL HAVEN'T HAD A CRUSH AT YOUR AGE MAKES YOUR MOTHER'S HEART GO PITTER-PAT.
OH, HUSH UP.
IF YOU DO FIND SOMEONE YOU LIKE, THEN TELL ME!
I'LL MAKE RED RICE TO CELEBRATE!
IS IT THAT BIG A DEAL?!
JEEZ...I SWEAR, ALL ANYBODY CARES ABOUT IS OTHER PEOPLE'S LOVE LIVES!
I DON'T HAVE TIME FOR THAT RIGHT NOW!

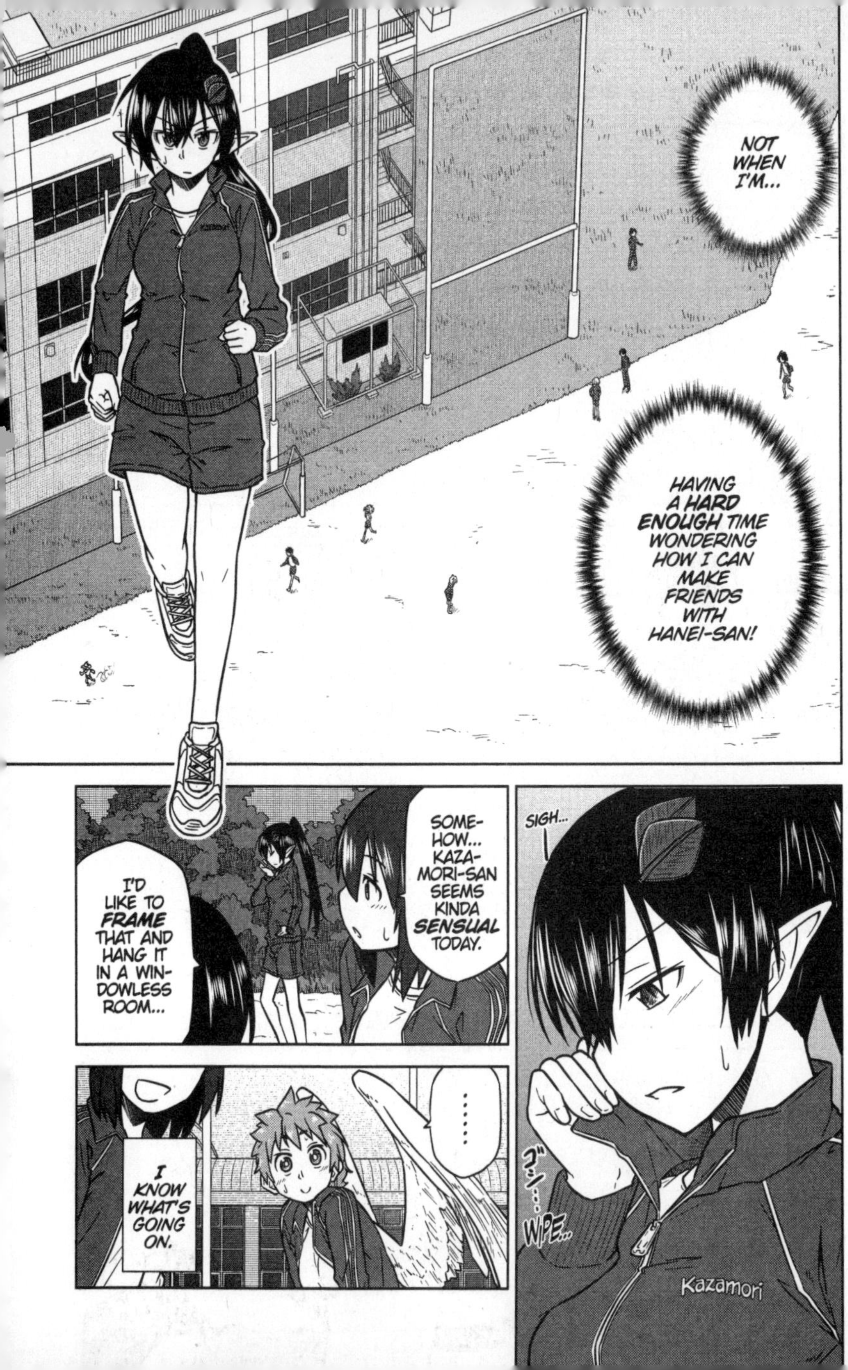
NOT WHEN I'M...
HAVING A HARD ENOUGH TIME WONDERING HOW I CAN MAKE FRIENDS WITH HANEI-SAN!
SIGH...
ゴシ…
WIPE...
Kazamori
SOME-HOW... KAZA-MORI-SAN SEEMS KINDA SENSUAL TODAY.
I'D LIKE TO FRAME THAT AND HANG IT IN A WIN-DOWLESS ROOM...
......
I KNOW WHAT'S GOING ON.

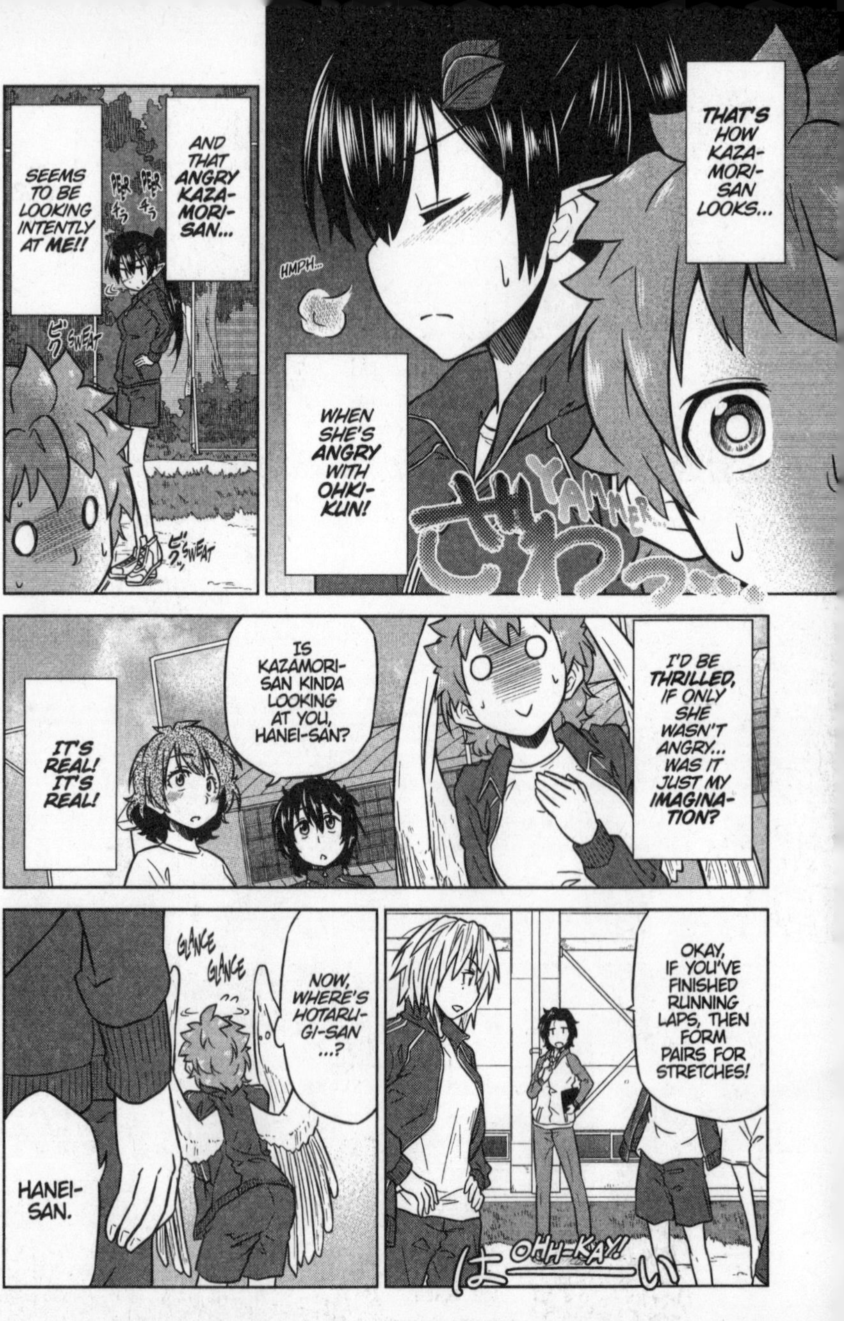

THAT'S HOW KAZAMORI-SAN LOOKS...
HMPH...
WHEN SHE'S ANGRY WITH OHKI-KUN!
YAMMER
AND THAT ANGRY KAZAMORI-SAN...
SEEMS TO BE LOOKING INTENTLY AT ME!!
PEER PEER
SWEAT
SWEAT
I'D BE THRILLED, IF ONLY SHE WASN'T ANGRY... WAS IT JUST MY IMAGINATION?
IS KAZAMORI-SAN KINDA LOOKING AT YOU, HANEI-SAN?
IT'S REAL! IT'S REAL!
OKAY, IF YOU'VE FINISHED RUNNING LAPS, THEN FORM PAIRS FOR STRETCHES!
OHH-KAY!
NOW, WHERE'S HOTARUGI-SAN ...?
GLANCE GLANCE
HANEI-SAN.

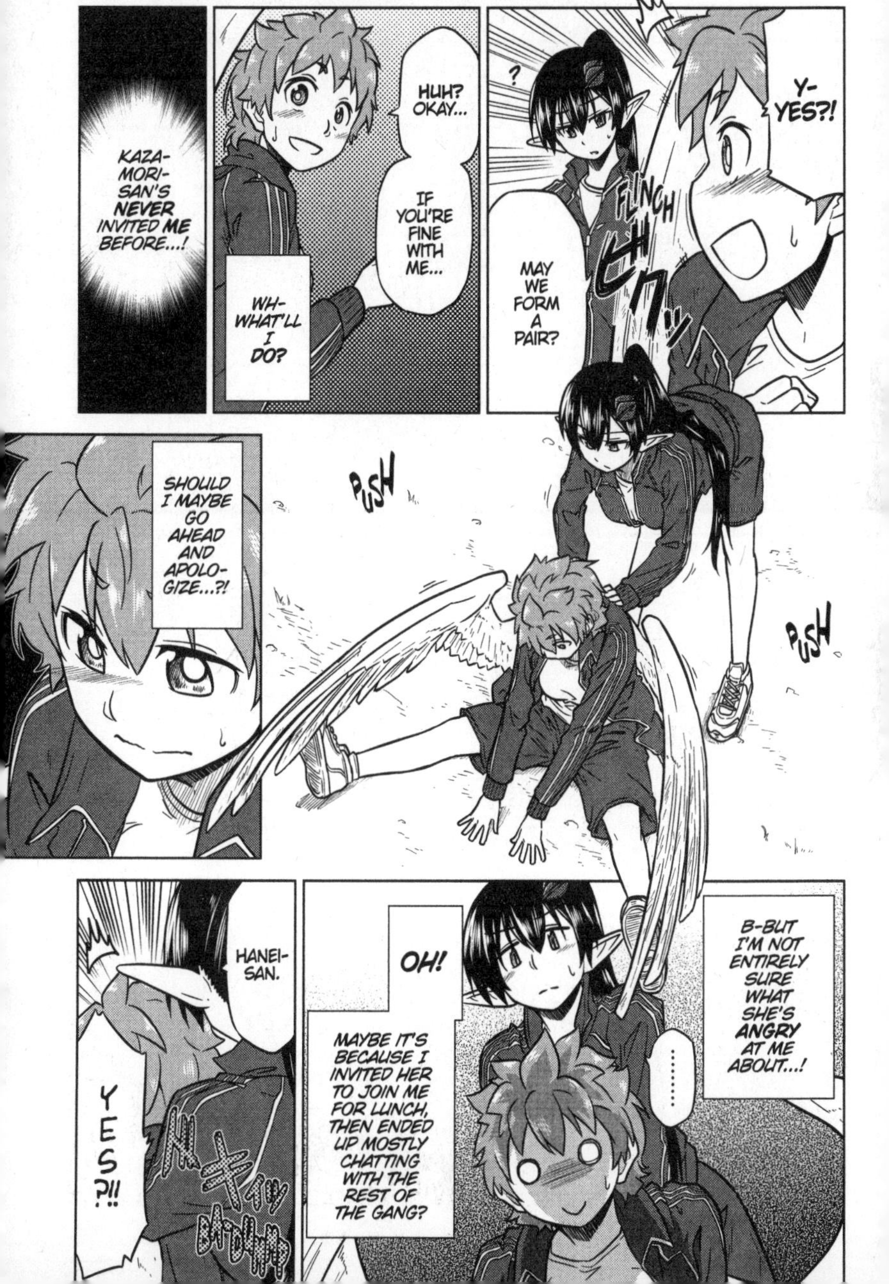
Y-YES?!
?
FLINCH
MAY WE FORM A PAIR?
HUH? OKAY...
IF YOU'RE FINE WITH ME...
WH-WHAT'LL I DO?
KAZAMORI-SAN'S NEVER INVITED ME BEFORE...!
PUSH
PUSH
SHOULD I MAYBE GO AHEAD AND APOLOGIZE...?!
B-BUT I'M NOT ENTIRELY SURE WHAT SHE'S ANGRY AT ME ABOUT...!
OH!
......
MAYBE IT'S BECAUSE I INVITED HER TO JOIN ME FOR LUNCH, THEN ENDED UP MOSTLY CHATTING WITH THE REST OF THE GANG?
HANEI-SAN.
YES?!!

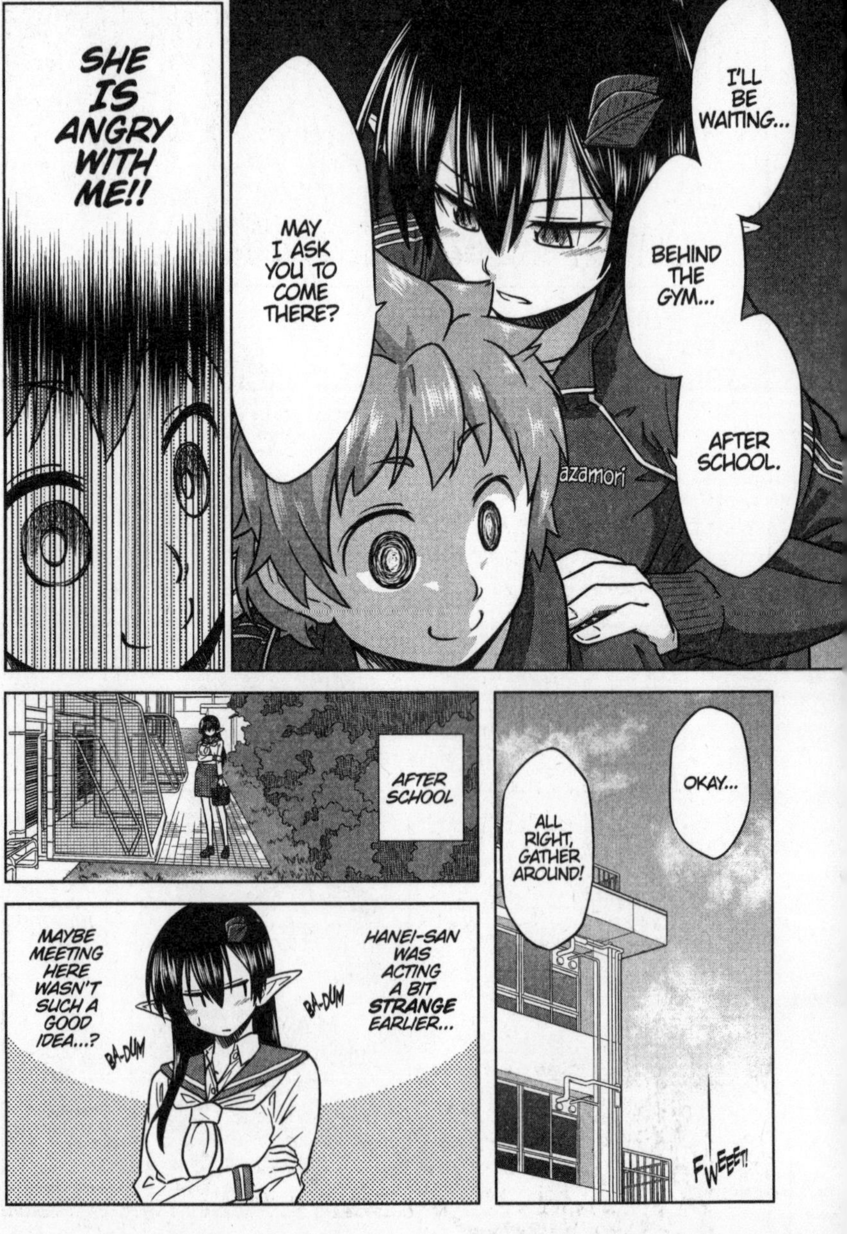
I'LL BE WAITING...
BEHIND THE GYM...
AFTER SCHOOL.
azamori
MAY I ASK YOU TO COME THERE?
SHE IS ANGRY WITH ME!!
OKAY...
ALL RIGHT, GATHER AROUND!
FWEEET!
AFTER SCHOOL
HANEI-SAN WAS ACTING A BIT STRANGE EARLIER...
BA-DUM
MAYBE MEETING HERE WASN'T SUCH A GOOD IDEA...?
BA-DUM

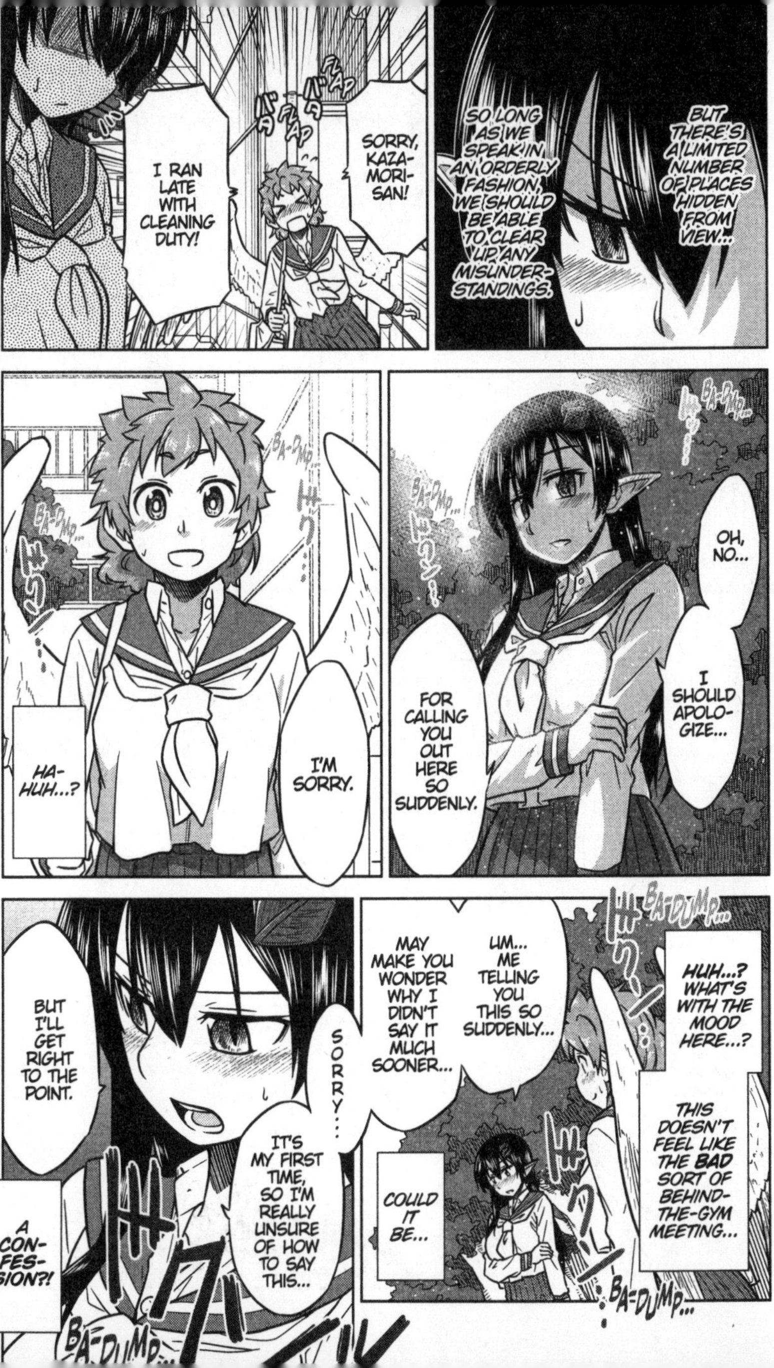
BUT THERE'S A LIMITED NUMBER OF PLACES HIDDEN FROM VIEW...
SO LONG AS WE SPEAK IN AN ORDERLY FASHION, WE SHOULD BE ABLE TO CLEAR UP ANY MISUNDER-STANDINGS.
FLAP FLAP
SORRY, KAZA-MORI-SAN!
I RAN LATE WITH CLEANING DUTY!
BA-DUMP...
OH, NO...
I SHOULD APOLO-GIZE...
FOR CALLING YOU OUT HERE SO SUDDENLY.
BA-DUMP...
I'M SORRY.
HA-HUH...?
BA-DUMP...
HUH...? WHAT'S WITH THE MOOD HERE...?
THIS DOESN'T FEEL LIKE THE BAD SORT OF BEHIND-THE-GYM MEETING...
UM... ME TELLING YOU THIS SO SUDDENLY...
MAY MAKE YOU WONDER WHY I DIDN'T SAY IT MUCH SOONER...
COULD IT BE...
BA-DUMP...
SORRY...
BUT I'LL GET RIGHT TO THE POINT.
IT'S MY FIRST TIME, SO I'M REALLY UNSURE OF HOW TO SAY THIS...
A CON-FES-SION?!
BA-DUMP...

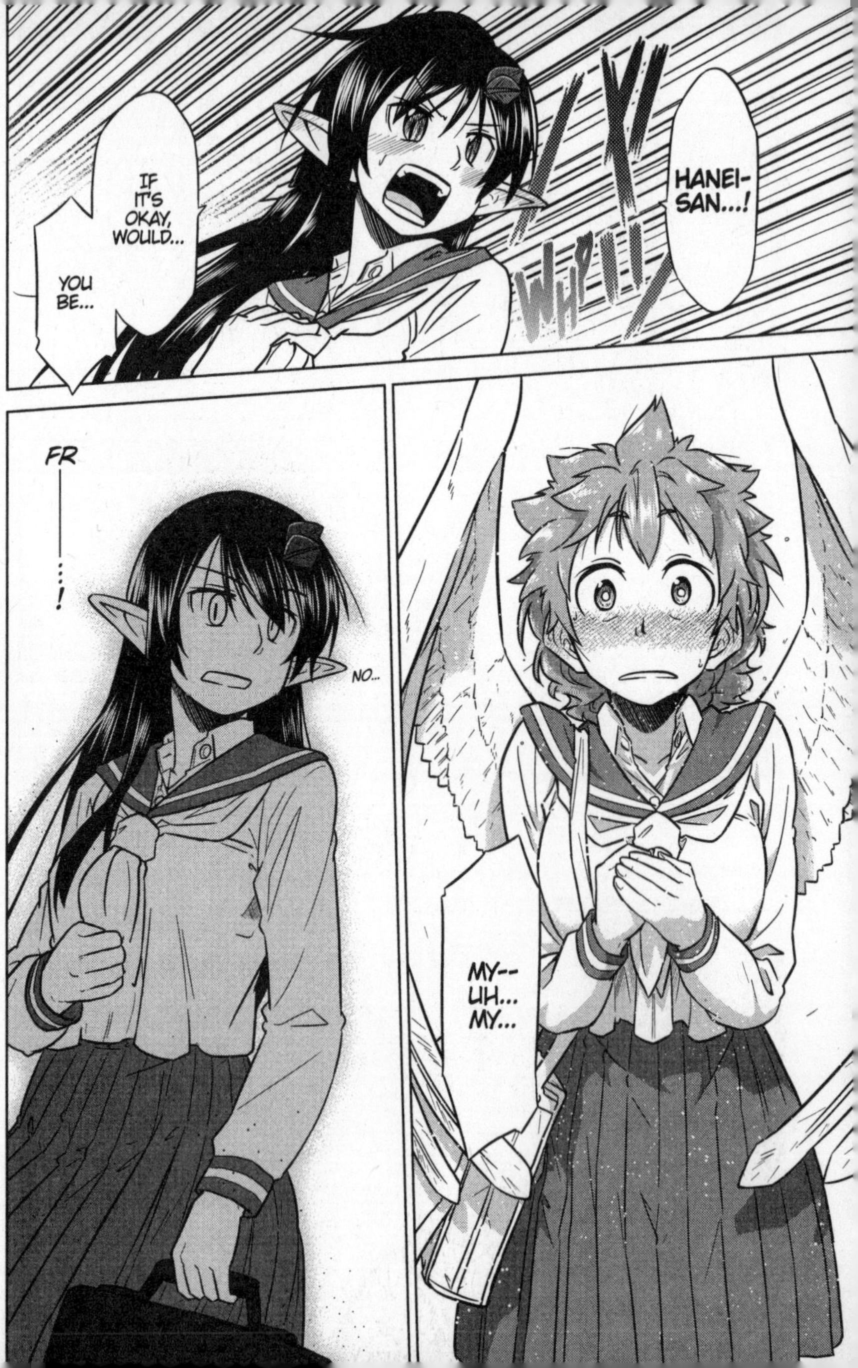
HANEI-SAN...!
WHIP!!!
IF IT'S OKAY, WOULD...
YOU BE...
MY-- UH... MY...
NO...
FR——...!

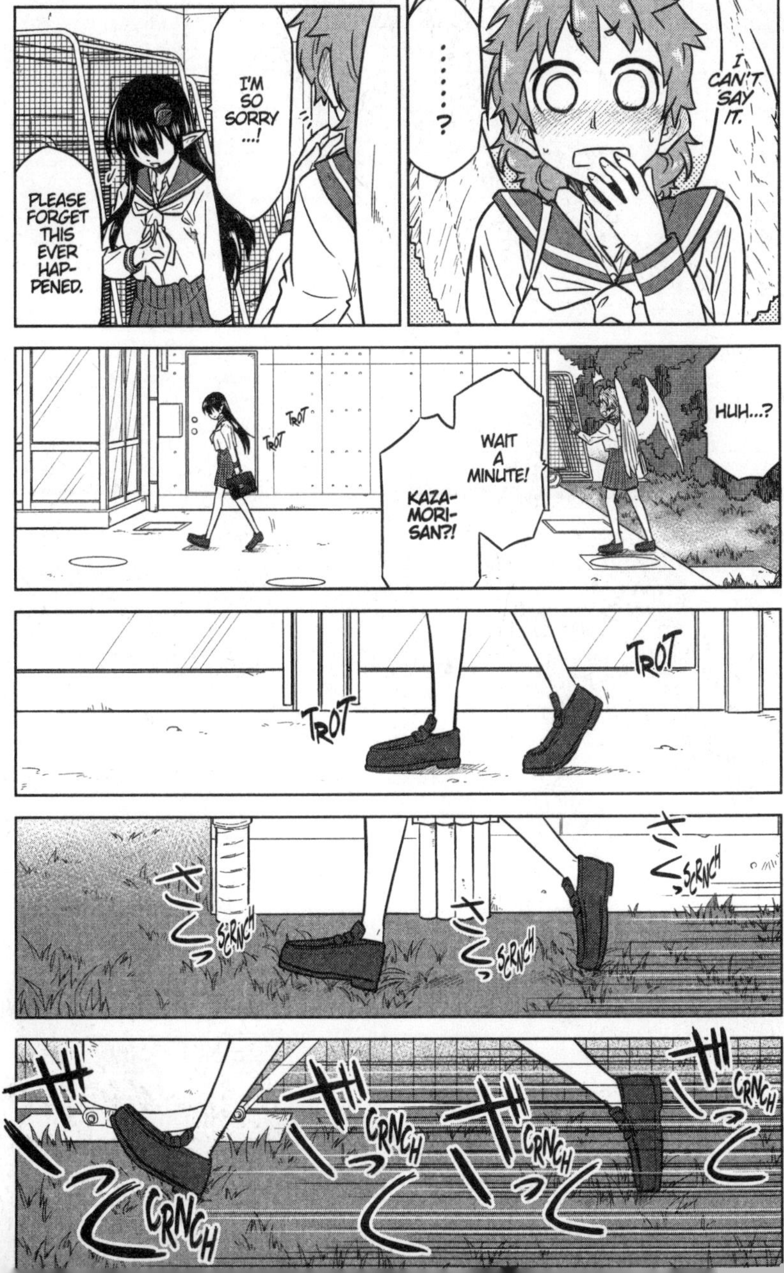
I CAN'T SAY IT.
......?
I'M SO SORRY ...!
PLEASE FORGET THIS EVER HAPPENED.
HUH...?
WAIT A MINUTE! KAZAMORI-SAN?!
TROT
TROT
TROT
TROT
さくっ SCRNCH
さくっ SCRNCH
さくっ SCRNCH
ざっ CRNCH
ざっ CRNCH
ざっ CRNCH
ざっ CRNCH

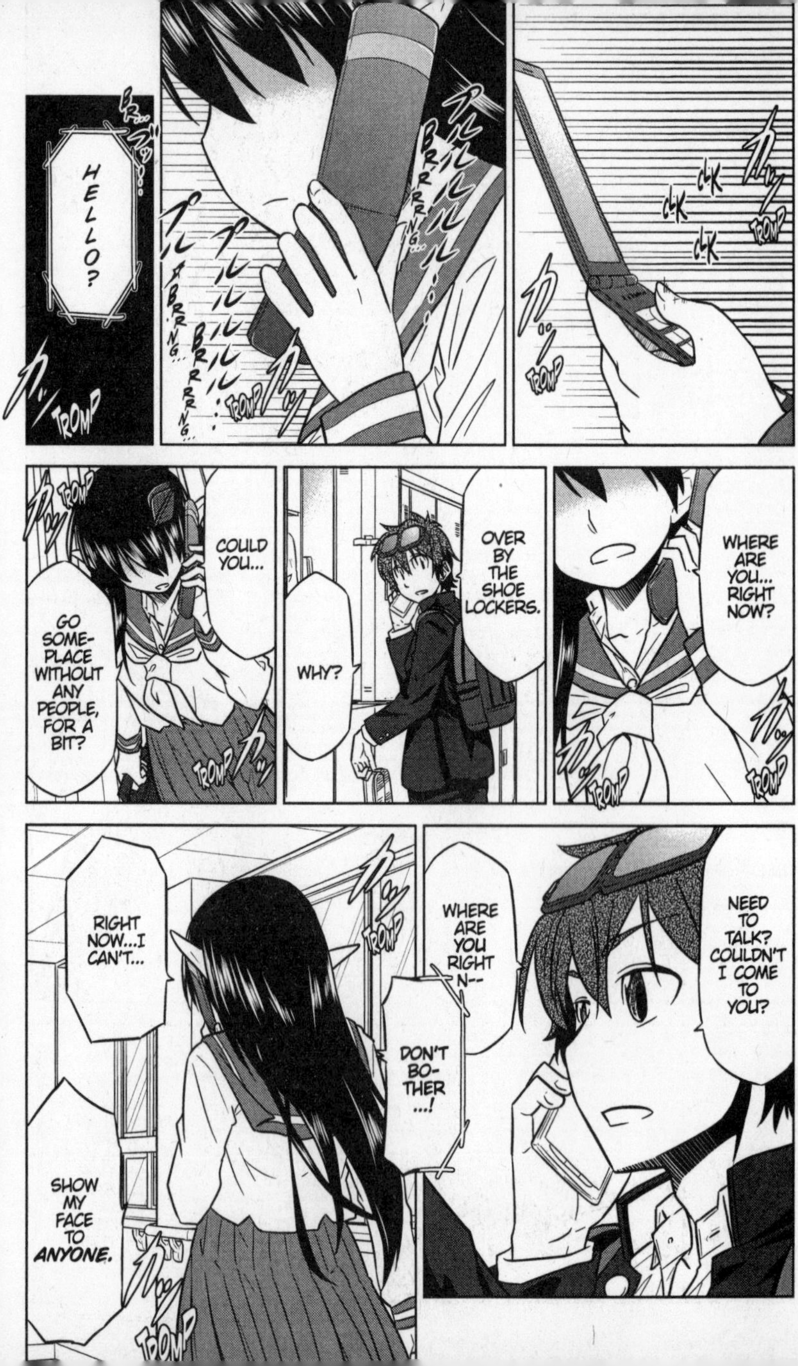

CLK
CLK
CLK
TROMP
TROMP
BRRRRNG...
TROMP
BRRRNG...
BRRRRRNG...
HELLO?
TROMP
WHERE ARE YOU... RIGHT NOW?
TROMP
TROMP
OVER BY THE SHOE LOCKERS.
WHY?
TROMP
COULD YOU...
GO SOME-PLACE WITHOUT ANY PEOPLE, FOR A BIT?
TROMP
NEED TO TALK? COULDN'T I COME TO YOU?
WHERE ARE YOU RIGHT N--
DON'T BO-THER ...!
TROMP
RIGHT NOW...I CAN'T...
SHOW MY FACE TO ANYONE.
TROMP

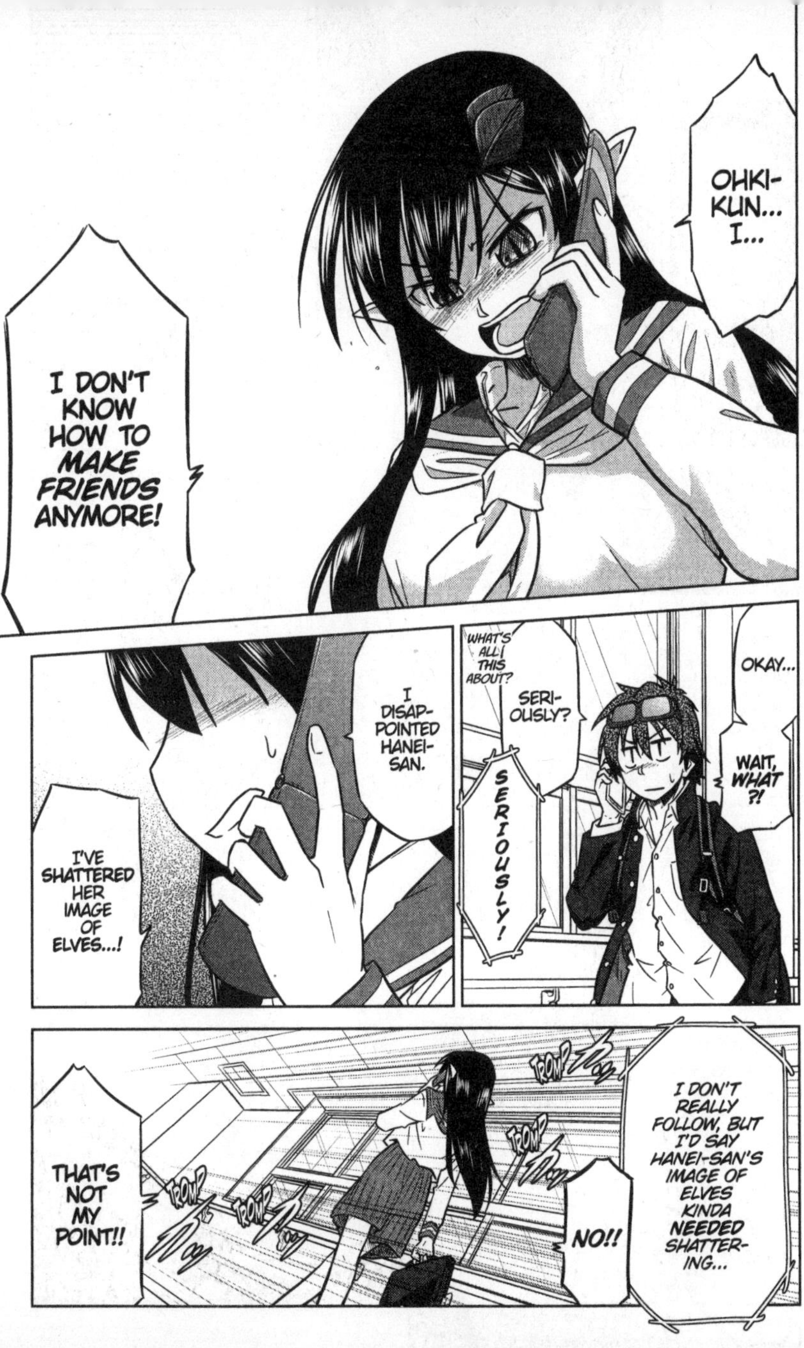
OHKI-KUN... I...
I DON'T KNOW HOW TO MAKE FRIENDS ANYMORE!
OKAY...
WHAT'S ALL THIS ABOUT?
SERI-OUSLY?
WAIT, WHAT?!
SERIOUSLY!
I DISAP-POINTED HANEI-SAN.
I'VE SHATTERED HER IMAGE OF ELVES...!
I DON'T REALLY FOLLOW, BUT I'D SAY HANEI-SAN'S IMAGE OF ELVES KINDA NEEDED SHATTER-ING...
TROMP
TROMP
NO!!
TROMP
TROMP
THAT'S NOT MY POINT!!

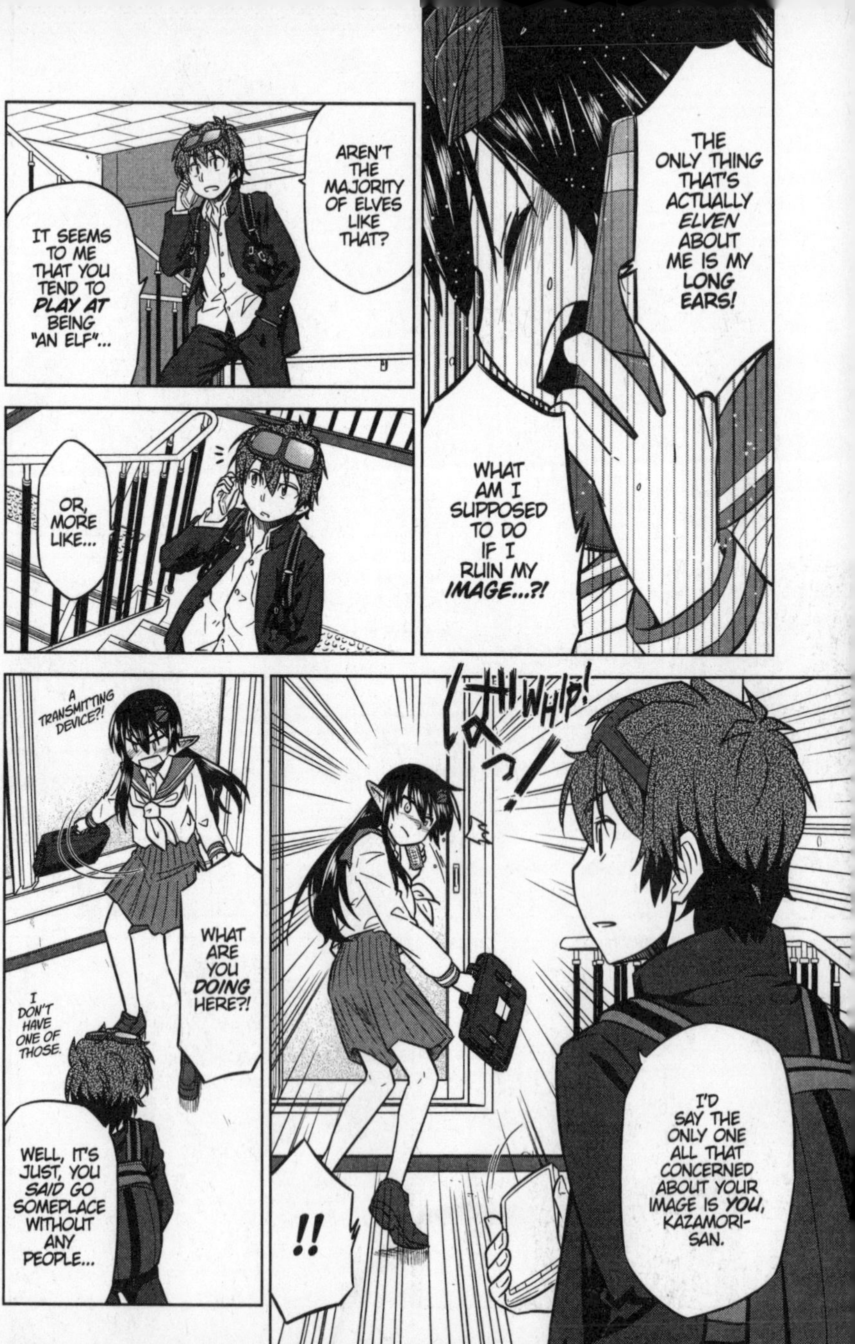
THE ONLY THING THAT'S ACTUALLY *ELVEN* ABOUT ME IS MY LONG EARS!
WHAT AM I SUPPOSED TO DO IF I RUIN MY *IMAGE*...?!
AREN'T THE MAJORITY OF ELVES LIKE THAT?
IT SEEMS TO ME THAT YOU TEND TO *PLAY AT* BEING "AN ELF"...
OR, MORE LIKE...
WHIP!
I'D SAY THE ONLY ONE ALL THAT CONCERNED ABOUT YOUR IMAGE IS *YOU*, KAZAMORI-SAN.
!!
A TRANSMITTING DEVICE?!
WHAT ARE YOU *DOING* HERE?!
I DON'T HAVE ONE OF THOSE.
WELL, IT'S JUST, YOU *SAID* GO SOMEPLACE WITHOUT ANY PEOPLE...

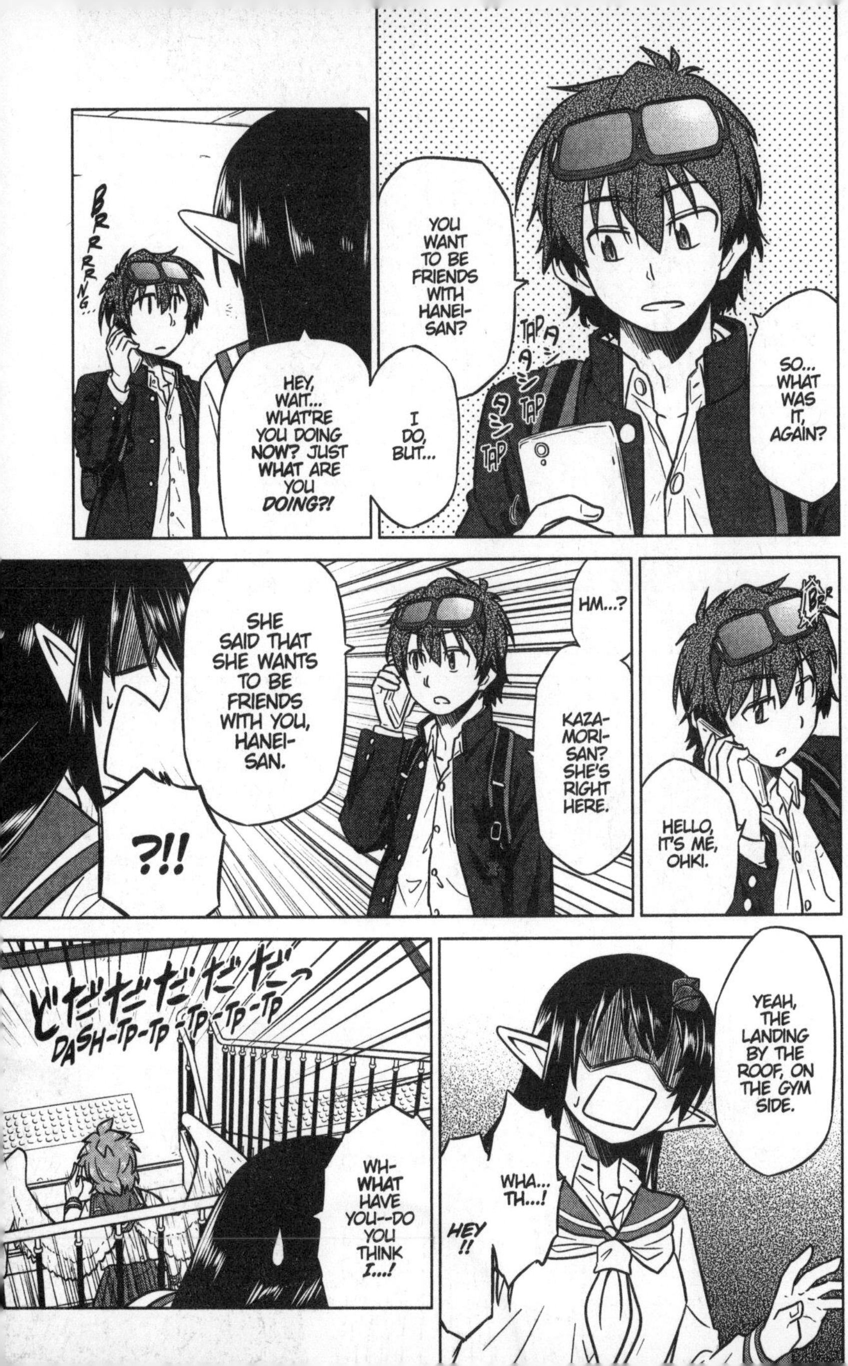
SO... WHAT WAS IT, AGAIN?
TAP TAP TAP TAP
YOU WANT TO BE FRIENDS WITH HANEI-SAN?
I DO, BUT...
HEY, WAIT... WHAT'RE YOU DOING NOW? JUST WHAT ARE YOU *DOING?!*
BRRRRRING...
BRR
HELLO, IT'S ME, OHKI.
HM...?
KAZAMORI-SAN? SHE'S RIGHT HERE.
SHE SAID THAT SHE WANTS TO BE FRIENDS WITH YOU, HANEI-SAN.
?!!
YEAH, THE LANDING BY THE ROOF, ON THE GYM SIDE.
WHA... TH...!
HEY!!
どだだだだだっ
DASH-TP-TP-TP-TP-TP
WH- WHAT HAVE YOU--DO YOU THINK *I...!*

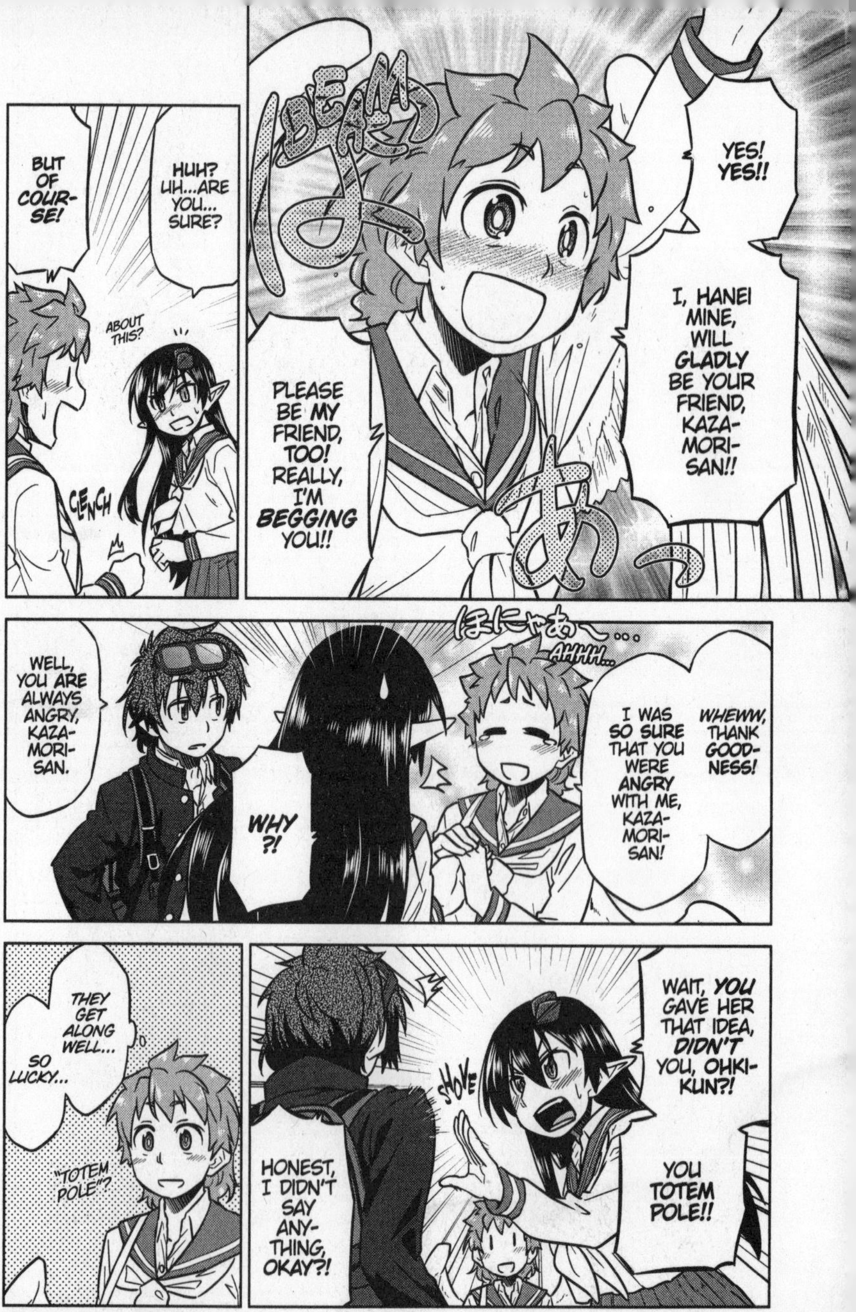

YES! YES!!
BEAM
I, HANEI MINE, WILL GLADLY BE YOUR FRIEND, KAZAMORI-SAN!!
PLEASE BE MY FRIEND, TOO! REALLY, I'M BEGGING YOU!!
あっ
HUH? UH...ARE YOU... SURE?
BUT OF COURSE!
ABOUT THIS?
CLENCH
ほにゃあ~...
AHHHH...
WHEWW, THANK GOODNESS!
I WAS SO SURE THAT YOU WERE ANGRY WITH ME, KAZAMORI-SAN!
WHY?!
WELL, YOU ARE ALWAYS ANGRY, KAZAMORI-SAN.
WAIT, YOU GAVE HER THAT IDEA, DIDN'T YOU, OHKI-KUN?!
SHOVE
YOU TOTEM POLE!!
HONEST, I DIDN'T SAY ANYTHING, OKAY?!
THEY GET ALONG WELL... SO LUCKY...
"TOTEM POLE"?

Chapter 5 • END

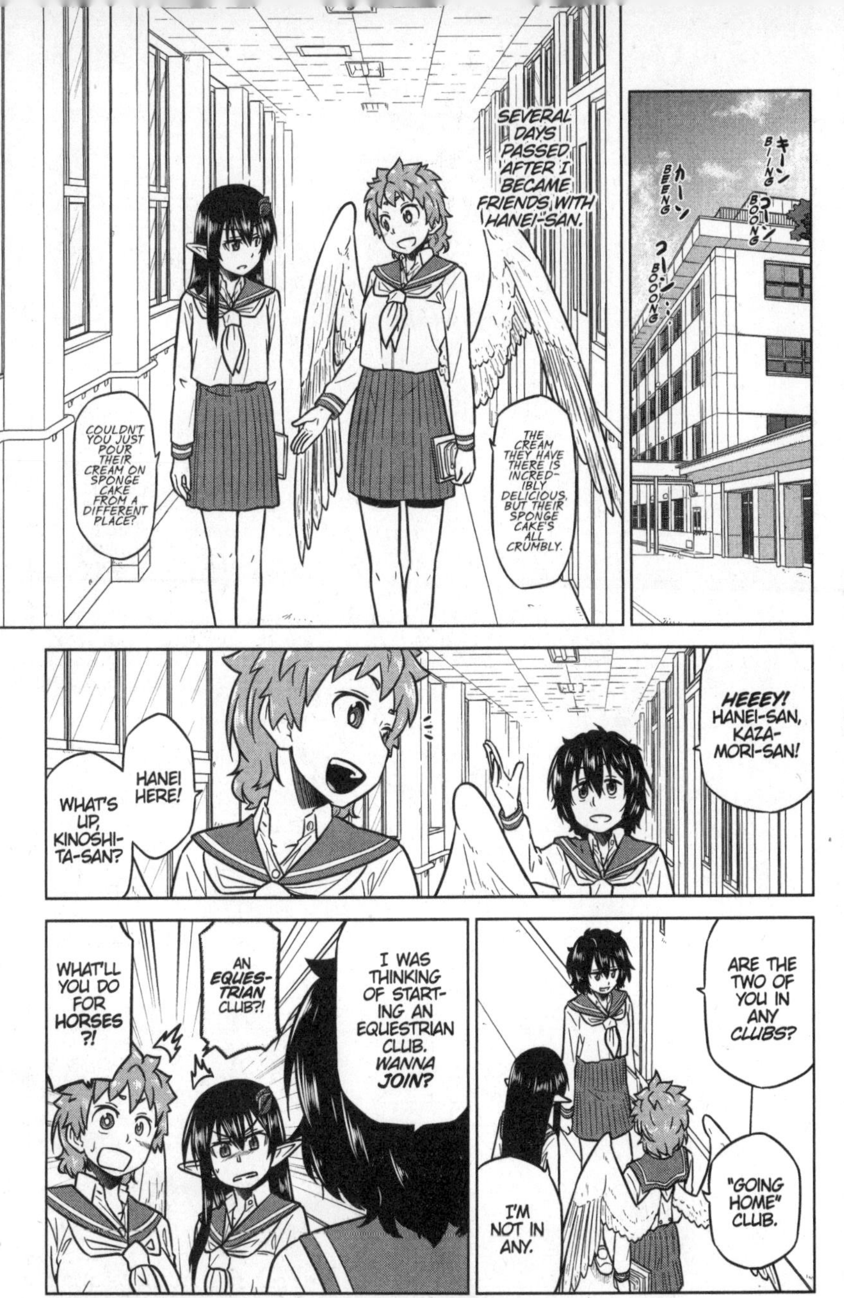
キーン BIING
カーン BEENG
コーン BOOONG
コーン… BOOOONG
SEVERAL DAYS PASSED AFTER I BECAME FRIENDS WITH HANEI-SAN.
THE CREAM THEY HAVE THERE IS INCRED-IBLY DELICIOUS, BUT THEIR SPONGE CAKE'S ALL CRUMBLY.
COULDN'T YOU JUST POUR THEIR CREAM ON SPONGE CAKE FROM A DIFFERENT PLACE?
HEEEY! HANEI-SAN, KAZA-MORI-SAN!
HANEI HERE!
WHAT'S UP, KINOSHI-TA-SAN?
ARE THE TWO OF YOU IN ANY CLUBS?
"GOING HOME" CLUB.
I'M NOT IN ANY.
I WAS THINKING OF START-ING AN EQUESTRIAN CLUB. WANNA JOIN?
AN EQUES-TRIAN CLUB?!
WHAT'LL YOU DO FOR HORSES ?!

Chapter 6: Kazamori-san Wants to Talk

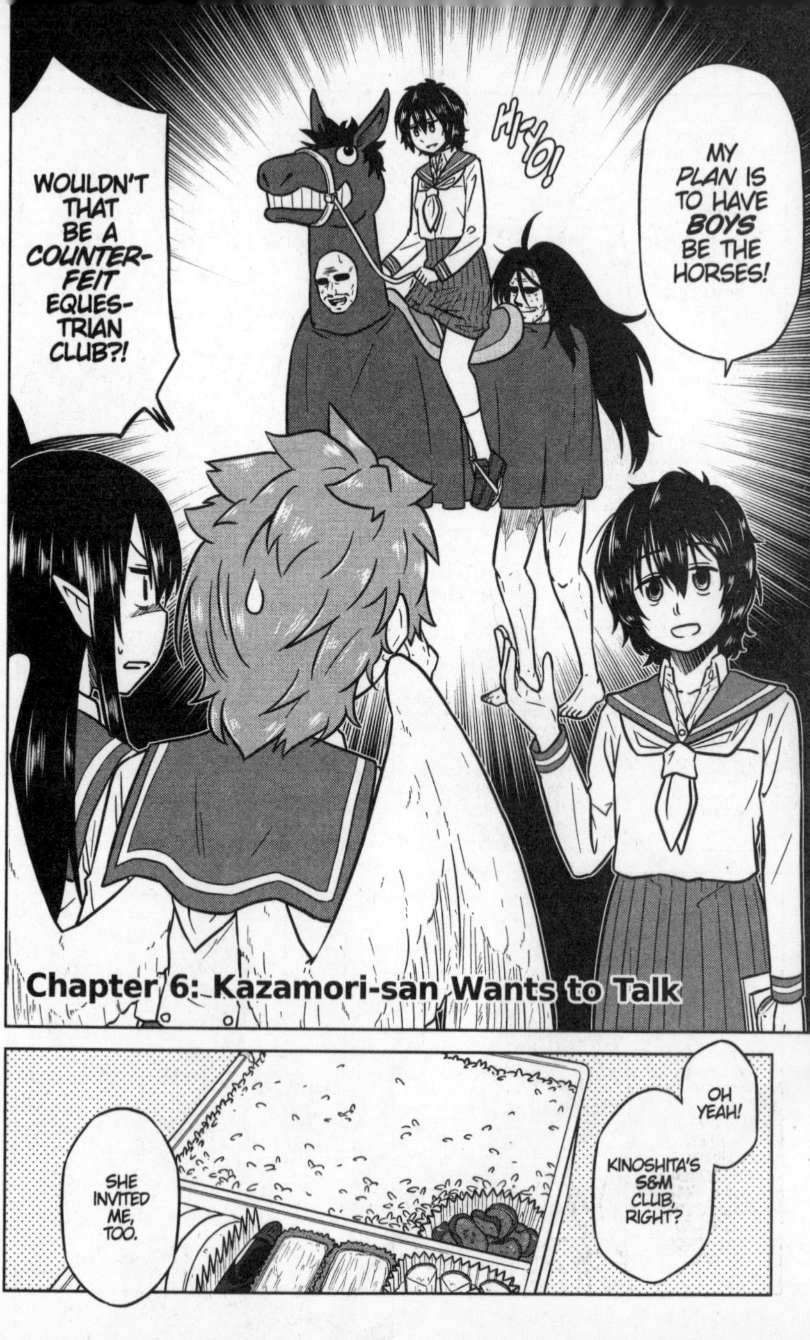
MY PLAN IS TO HAVE BOYS BE THE HORSES!
HI-HO!
WOULDN'T THAT BE A COUNTERFEIT EQUESTRIAN CLUB?!
Chapter 6: Kazamori-san Wants to Talk
OH YEAH!
KINOSHITA'S S&M CLUB, RIGHT?
SHE INVITED ME, TOO.

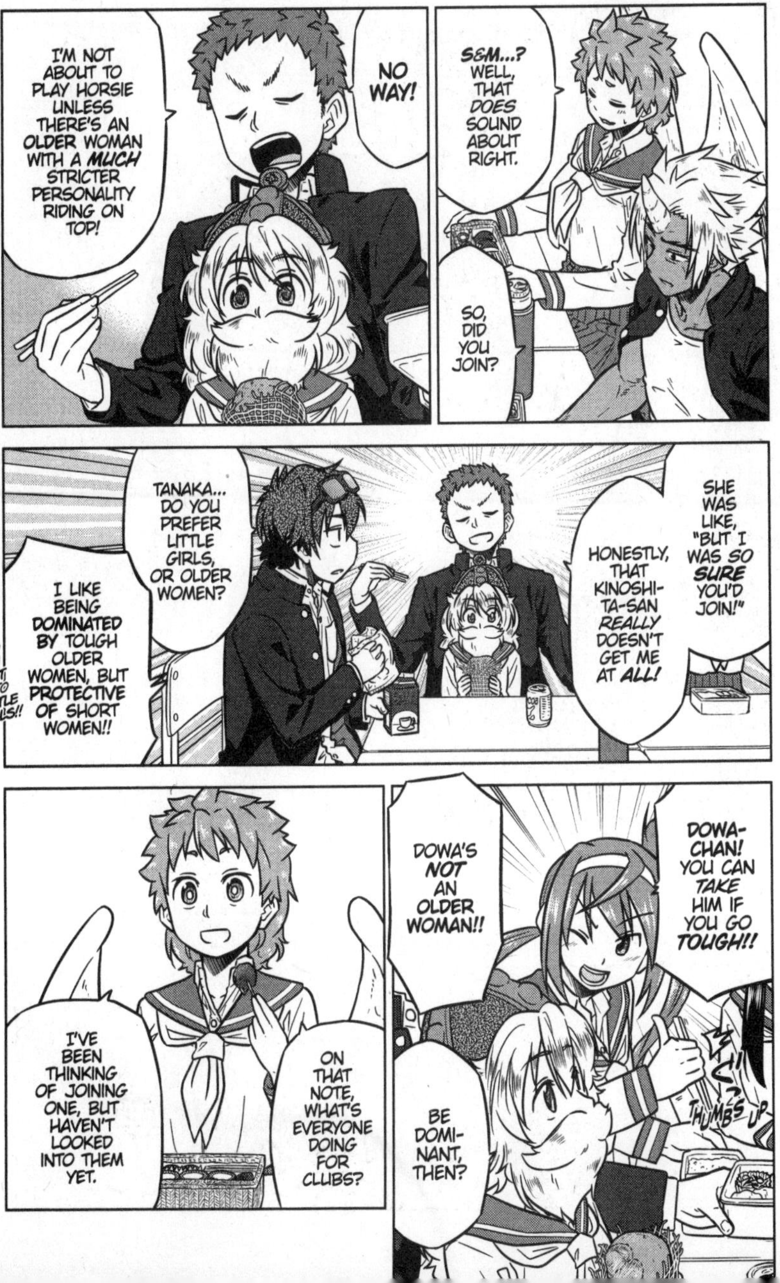
S&M...? WELL, THAT DOES SOUND ABOUT RIGHT.
SO, DID YOU JOIN?
NO WAY!
I'M NOT ABOUT TO PLAY HORSIE UNLESS THERE'S AN OLDER WOMAN WITH A MUCH STRICTER PERSONALITY RIDING ON TOP!
SHE WAS LIKE, "BUT I WAS SO SURE YOU'D JOIN!"
HONESTLY, THAT KINOSHITA-SAN REALLY DOESN'T GET ME AT ALL!
TANAKA... DO YOU PREFER LITTLE GIRLS, OR OLDER WOMEN?
I LIKE BEING DOMINATED BY TOUGH OLDER WOMEN, BUT PROTECTIVE OF SHORT WOMEN!!
AND I'M NOT INTO LITTLE GIRLS!!
DOWA-CHAN! YOU CAN TAKE HIM IF YOU GO TOUGH!!
DOWA'S NOT AN OLDER WOMAN!!
THUMBS UP
BE DOMINANT, THEN?
ON THAT NOTE, WHAT'S EVERYONE DOING FOR CLUBS?
I'VE BEEN THINKING OF JOINING ONE, BUT HAVEN'T LOOKED INTO THEM YET.

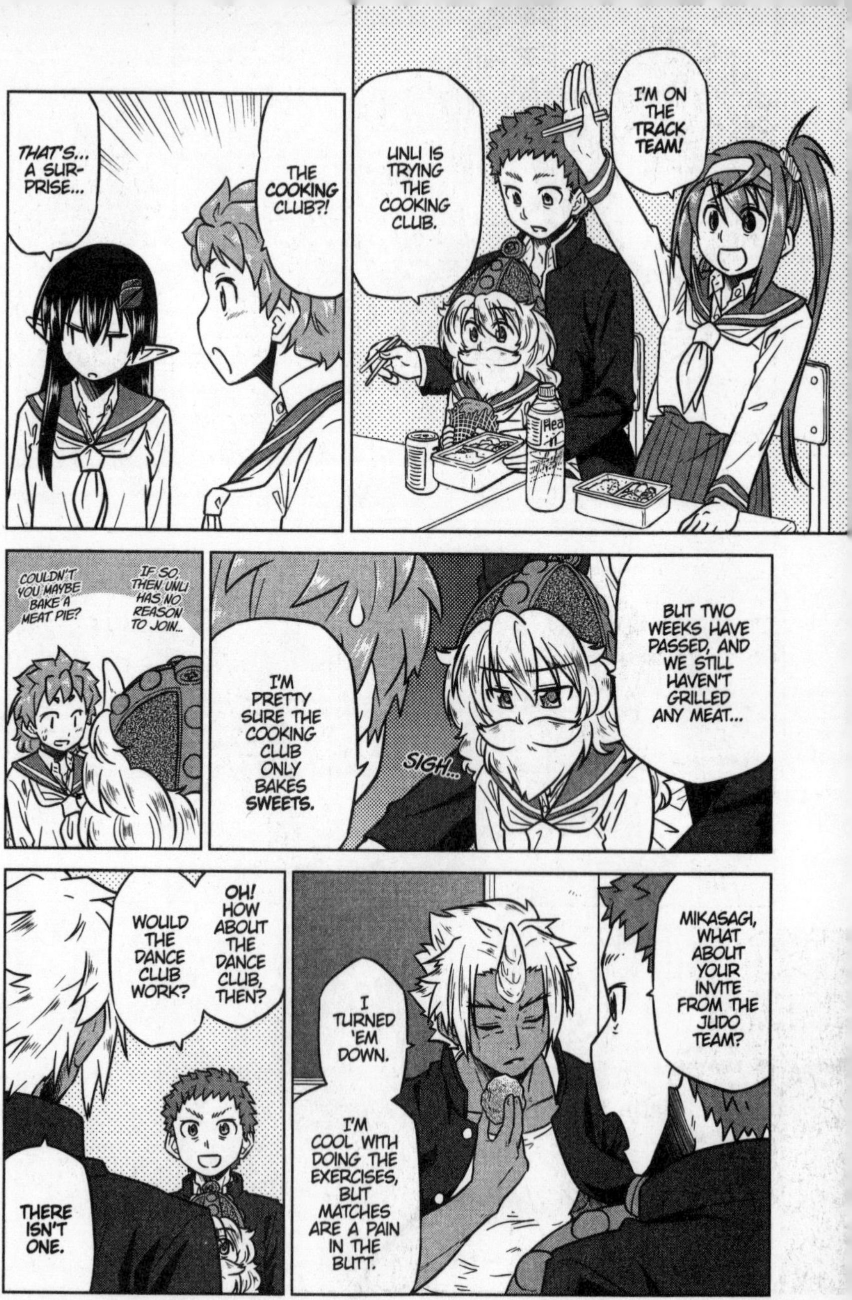
I'M ON THE TRACK TEAM!
UNLI IS TRYING THE COOKING CLUB.
THE COOKING CLUB?!
THAT'S... A SURPRISE...
BUT TWO WEEKS HAVE PASSED, AND WE STILL HAVEN'T GRILLED ANY MEAT...
SIGH...
I'M PRETTY SURE THE COOKING CLUB ONLY BAKES SWEETS.
IF SO, THEN UNLI HAS NO REASON TO JOIN...
COULDN'T YOU MAYBE BAKE A MEAT PIE?
MIKASAGI, WHAT ABOUT YOUR INVITE FROM THE JUDO TEAM?
I TURNED 'EM DOWN.
I'M COOL WITH DOING THE EXERCISES, BUT MATCHES ARE A PAIN IN THE BUTT.
OH! HOW ABOUT THE DANCE CLUB, THEN?
WOULD THE DANCE CLUB WORK?
THERE ISN'T ONE.

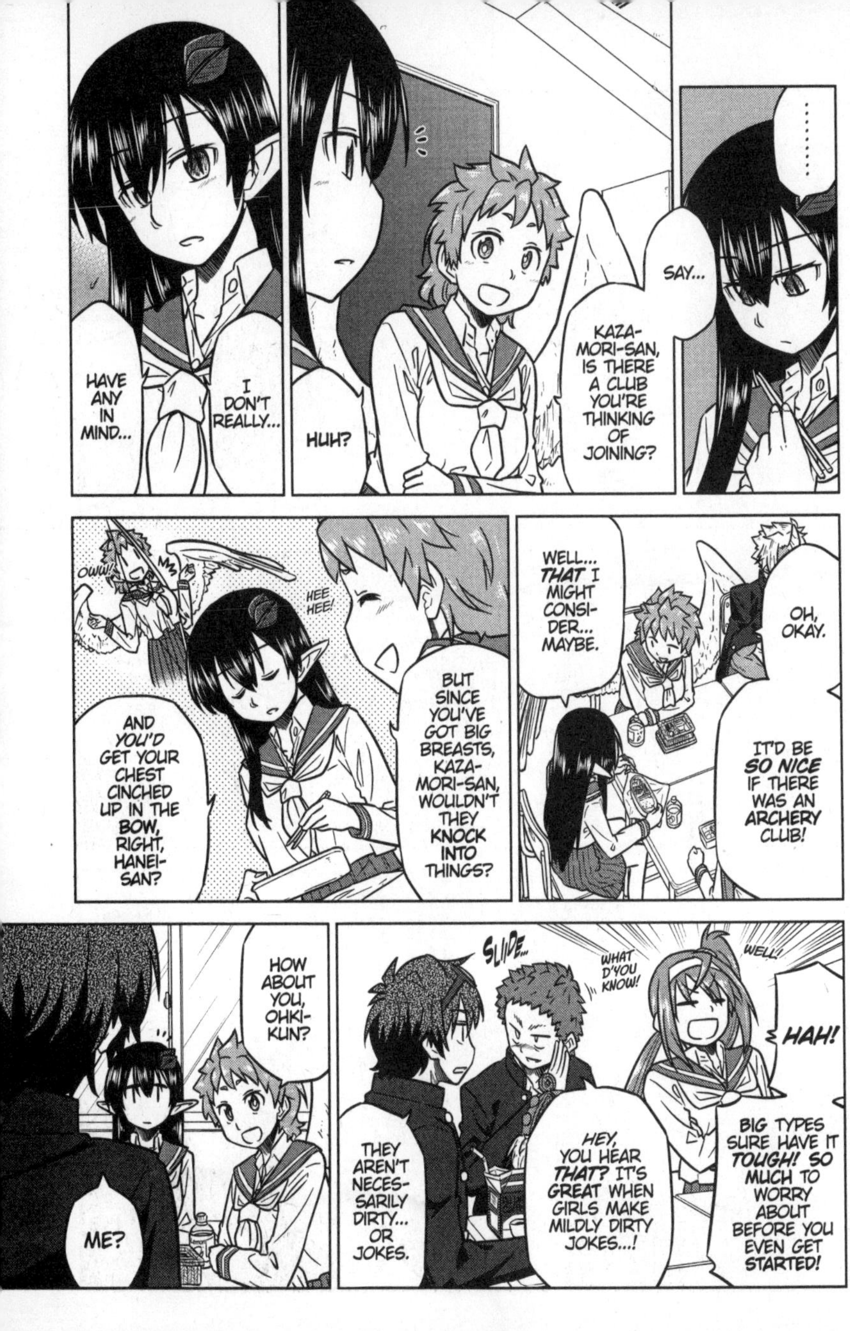
……
SAY...
KAZA-MORI-SAN, IS THERE A CLUB YOU'RE THINKING OF JOINING?
HUH?
I DON'T REALLY...
HAVE ANY IN MIND...
OH, OKAY.
IT'D BE SO NICE IF THERE WAS AN ARCHERY CLUB!
WELL... THAT I MIGHT CONSIDER... MAYBE.
BUT SINCE YOU'VE GOT BIG BREASTS, KAZA-MORI-SAN, WOULDN'T THEY KNOCK INTO THINGS?
HEE HEE!
AND YOU'D GET YOUR CHEST CINCHED UP IN THE BOW, RIGHT, HANEI-SAN?
OWW!
WELL...
HAH!
BIG TYPES SURE HAVE IT TOUGH! SO MUCH TO WORRY ABOUT BEFORE YOU EVEN GET STARTED!
WHAT D'YOU KNOW!
SLIDE...
HEY, YOU HEAR THAT? IT'S GREAT WHEN GIRLS MAKE MILDLY DIRTY JOKES...!
THEY AREN'T NECES-SARILY DIRTY... OR JOKES.
HOW ABOUT YOU, OHKI-KUN?
ME?

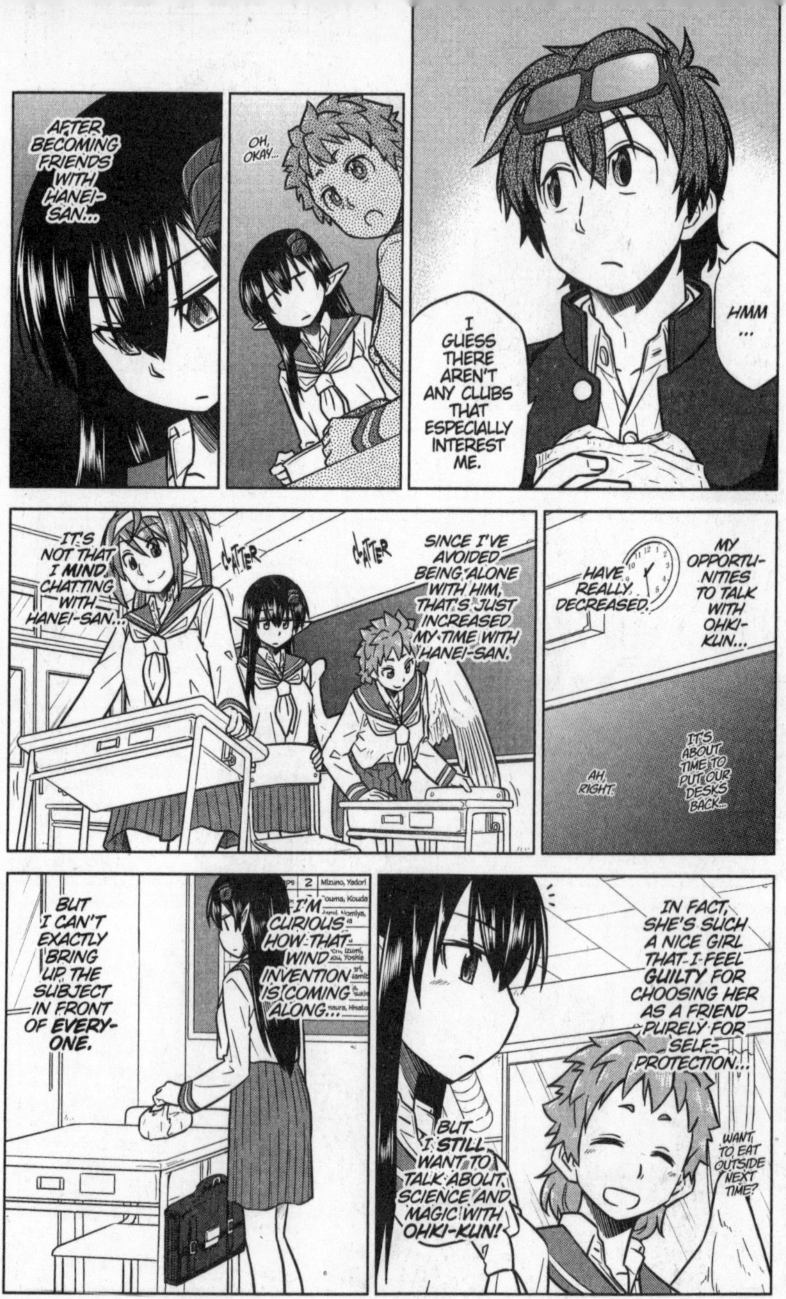
HMM ...
I GUESS THERE AREN'T ANY CLUBS THAT ESPECIALLY INTEREST ME.
OH, OKAY...
AFTER BECOMING FRIENDS WITH HANEI-SAN...
MY OPPORTUNITIES TO TALK WITH OHKI-KUN...
HAVE REALLY DECREASED.
IT'S ABOUT TIME TO PUT OUR DESKS BACK...
AH, RIGHT.
SINCE I'VE AVOIDED BEING ALONE WITH HIM, THAT'S JUST INCREASED MY TIME WITH HANEI-SAN.
CHATTER
CHATTER
IT'S NOT THAT I MIND CHATTING WITH HANEI-SAN...
IN FACT, SHE'S SUCH A NICE GIRL THAT I FEEL GUILTY FOR CHOOSING HER AS A FRIEND PURELY FOR SELF-PROTECTION...
WANT TO EAT OUTSIDE NEXT TIME?
BUT I STILL WANT TO TALK ABOUT SCIENCE AND MAGIC WITH OHKI-KUN!
I'M CURIOUS HOW THAT WIND INVENTION IS COMING ALONG...
BUT I CAN'T EXACTLY BRING UP THE SUBJECT IN FRONT OF EVERYONE.

8	Election Management Reps	2	Souma, Kouda
9	Culture Fest Committee Reps	3	Hanei, Nomiya, Rokuzawa
10			Tanooka, Berikawa

Adachi, Izumi, Sudou, Yoshii, Ide, Nagata, Mukada, Namba, Sataka, Rida, Nishihara, Tsu...maura, H...

MAYBE IF I LEAVE SCHOOL THE SAME TIME HE DOES, THEN ASK RIGHT AWAY?

BUT OUR HOMES ARE IN DIFFERENT DIRECTIONS, SO THERE WON'T BE MUCH TIME...

BUT I'D FEEL LIKE I'VE LOST IF I ADMIT TO EXPECTING THE AMAZING!

I COULD ALWAYS ASK ABOUT HIS PROGRESS BY TEXT OR PHONE...

CLUNK

GRIN...

GRR...

WHAT'S YOUR DEAL?!

IT KINDA TICKS ME OFF!

JUST SAY SOMETHING TO ME!

HEH HEH!

HUH...? WHAT'S WITH THAT WEIRDLY MEANINGFUL SMILE?!

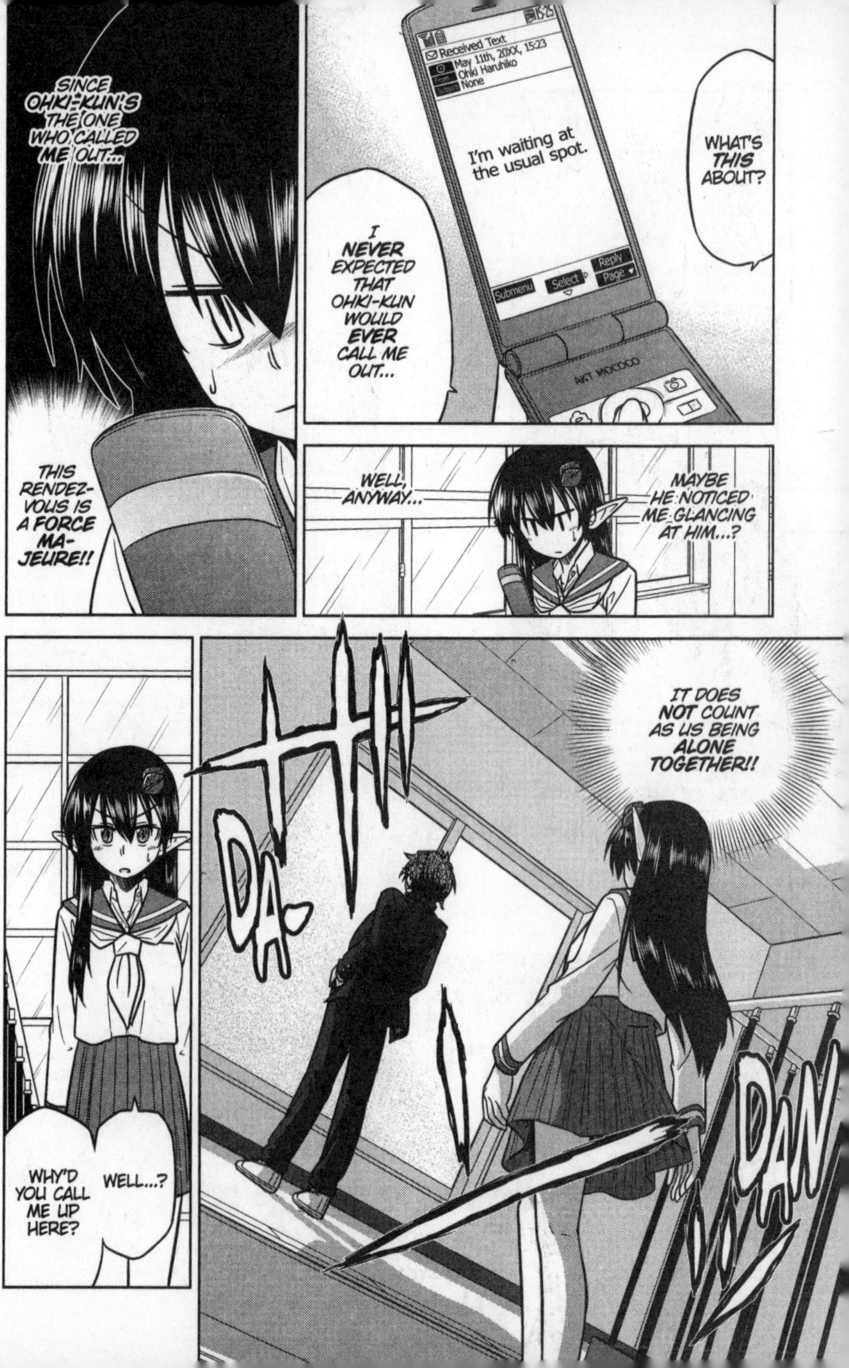
15:25
Received Text
May 11th, 20XX, 15:23
Ohki Haruhiko
None
I'm waiting at the usual spot.
Reply
Submenu
Select
Page
WHAT'S THIS ABOUT?
I NEVER EXPECTED THAT OHKI-KUN WOULD EVER CALL ME OUT...
MAYBE HE NOTICED ME GLANCING AT HIM...?
WELL, ANYWAY...
SINCE OHKI-KUN'S THE ONE WHO CALLED ME OUT...
THIS RENDEZVOUS IS A FORCE MAJEURE!!
IT DOES NOT COUNT AS US BEING ALONE TOGETHER!!
DAN
DA
WELL...?
WHY'D YOU CALL ME UP HERE?

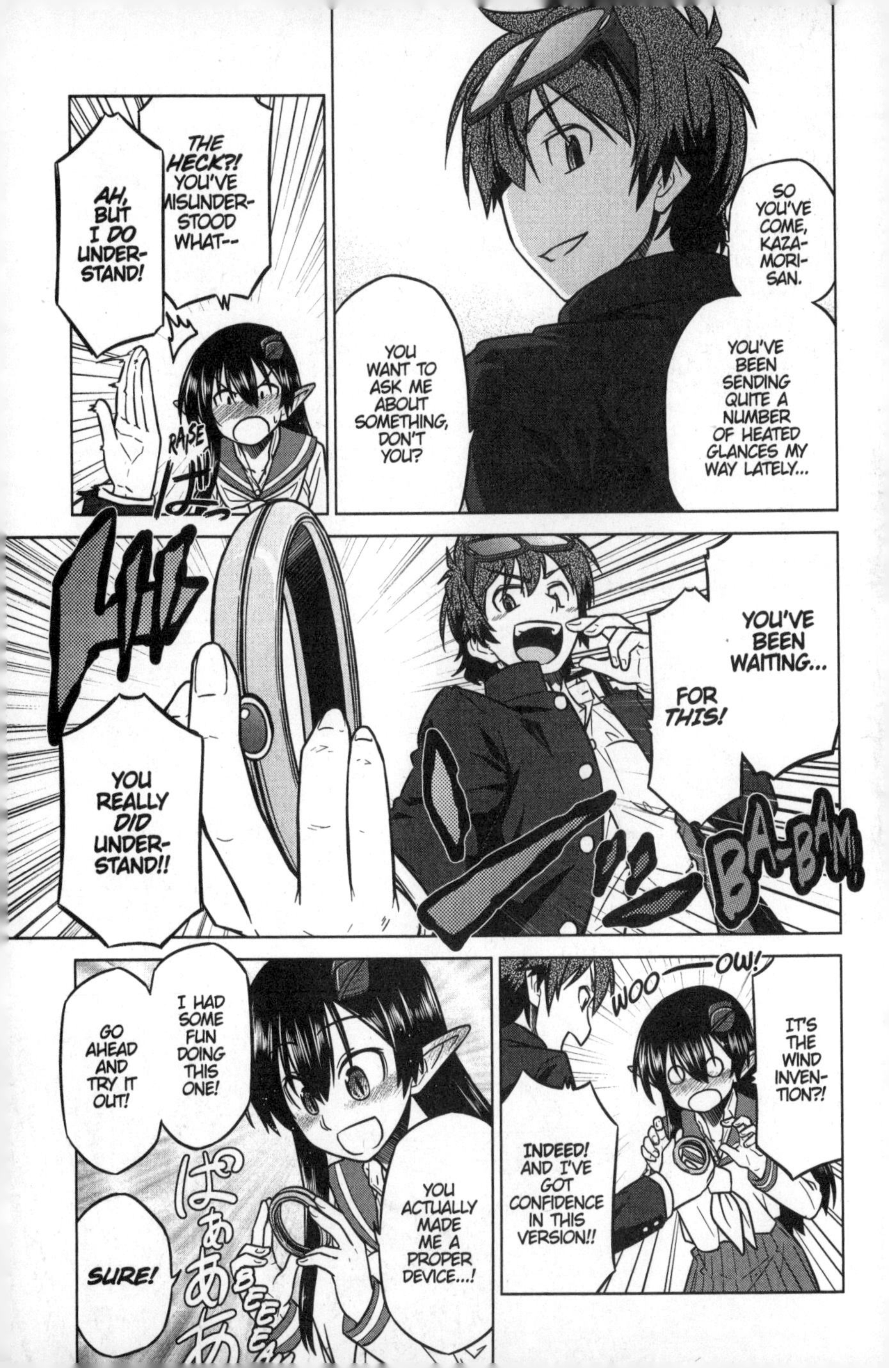
SO YOU'VE COME, KAZAMORI-SAN.
YOU'VE BEEN SENDING QUITE A NUMBER OF HEATED GLANCES MY WAY LATELY...
YOU WANT TO ASK ME ABOUT SOMETHING, DON'T YOU?
THE HECK?! YOU'VE MISUNDERSTOOD WHAT--
AH, BUT I DO UNDERSTAND!
RAISE
YOU'VE BEEN WAITING...
FOR THIS!
BA-BAM!!
YOU REALLY DID UNDERSTAND!!
WOO—OW!
IT'S THE WIND INVENTION?!
INDEED! AND I'VE GOT CONFIDENCE IN THIS VERSION!!
I HAD SOME FUN DOING THIS ONE!
GO AHEAD AND TRY IT OUT!
YOU ACTUALLY MADE ME A PROPER DEVICE...!
SURE!

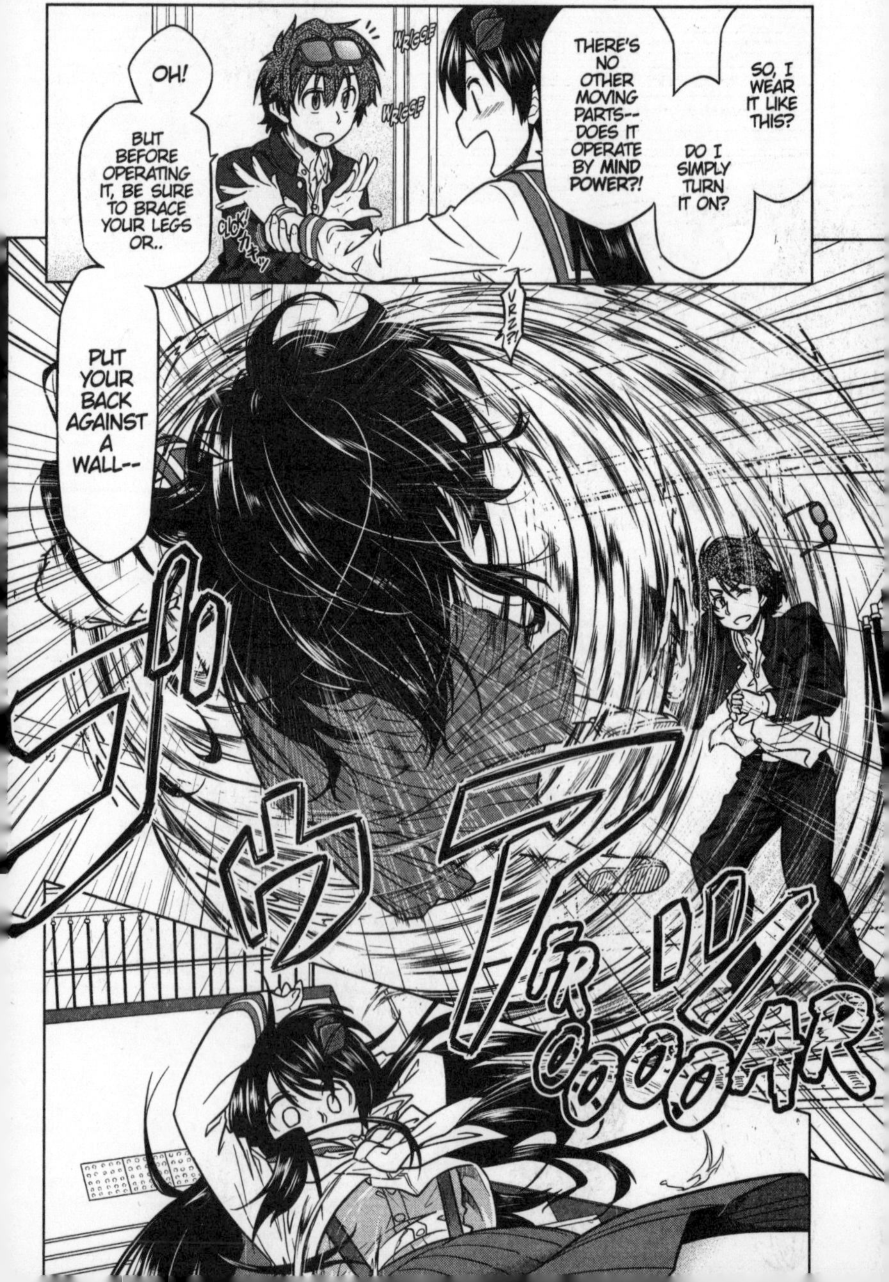
SO, I WEAR IT LIKE THIS?
DO I SIMPLY TURN IT ON?
THERE'S NO OTHER MOVING PARTS-- DOES IT OPERATE BY MIND POWER?!
WRIGGLE
WRIGGLE
OH!
BUT BEFORE OPERATING IT, BE SURE TO BRACE YOUR LEGS OR..
CLICK!
VRZZ?!
PUT YOUR BACK AGAINST A WALL--
FROOOOAR

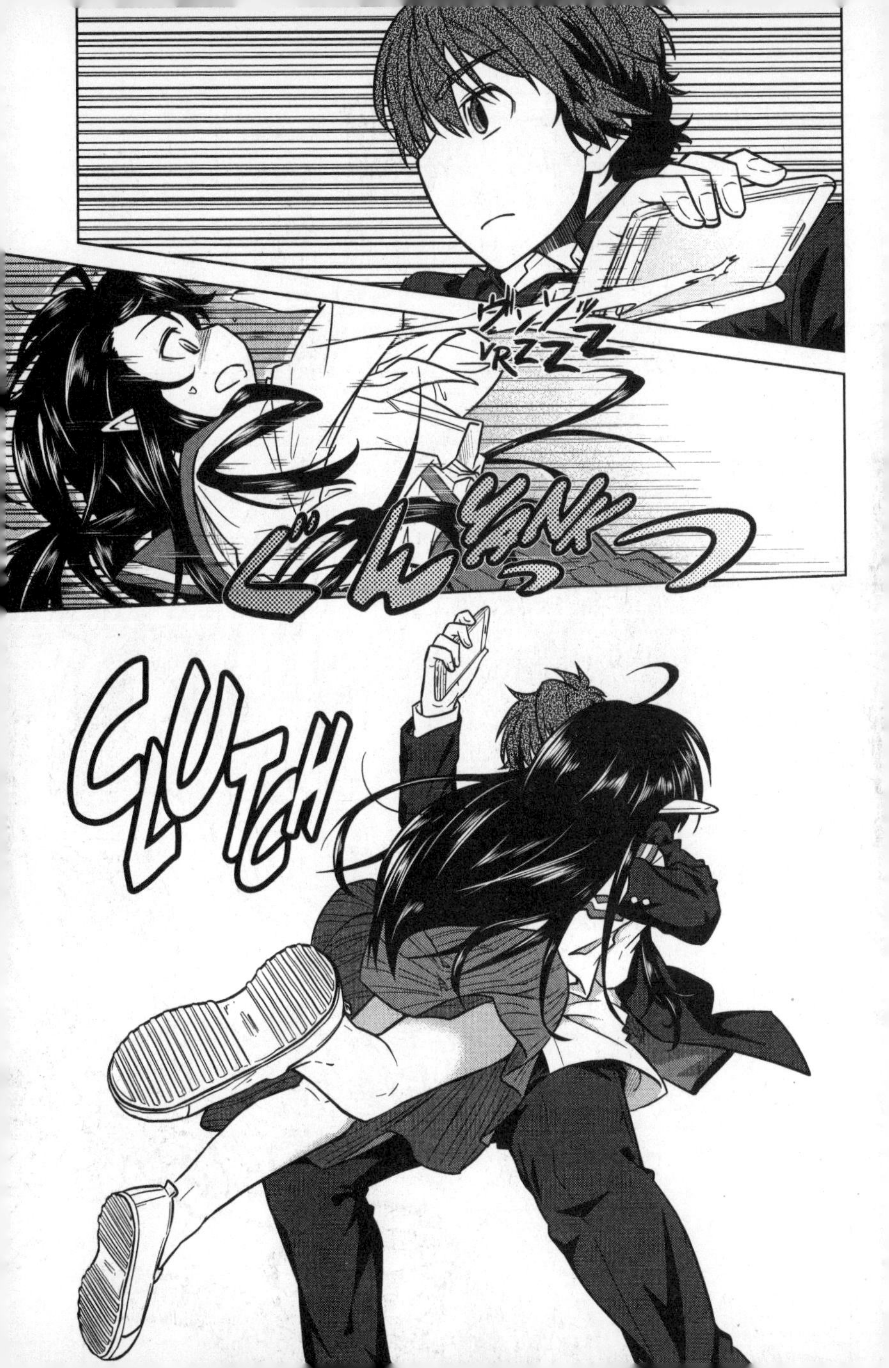
VRZZZ
ぐんっ
YANK
CLUTCH

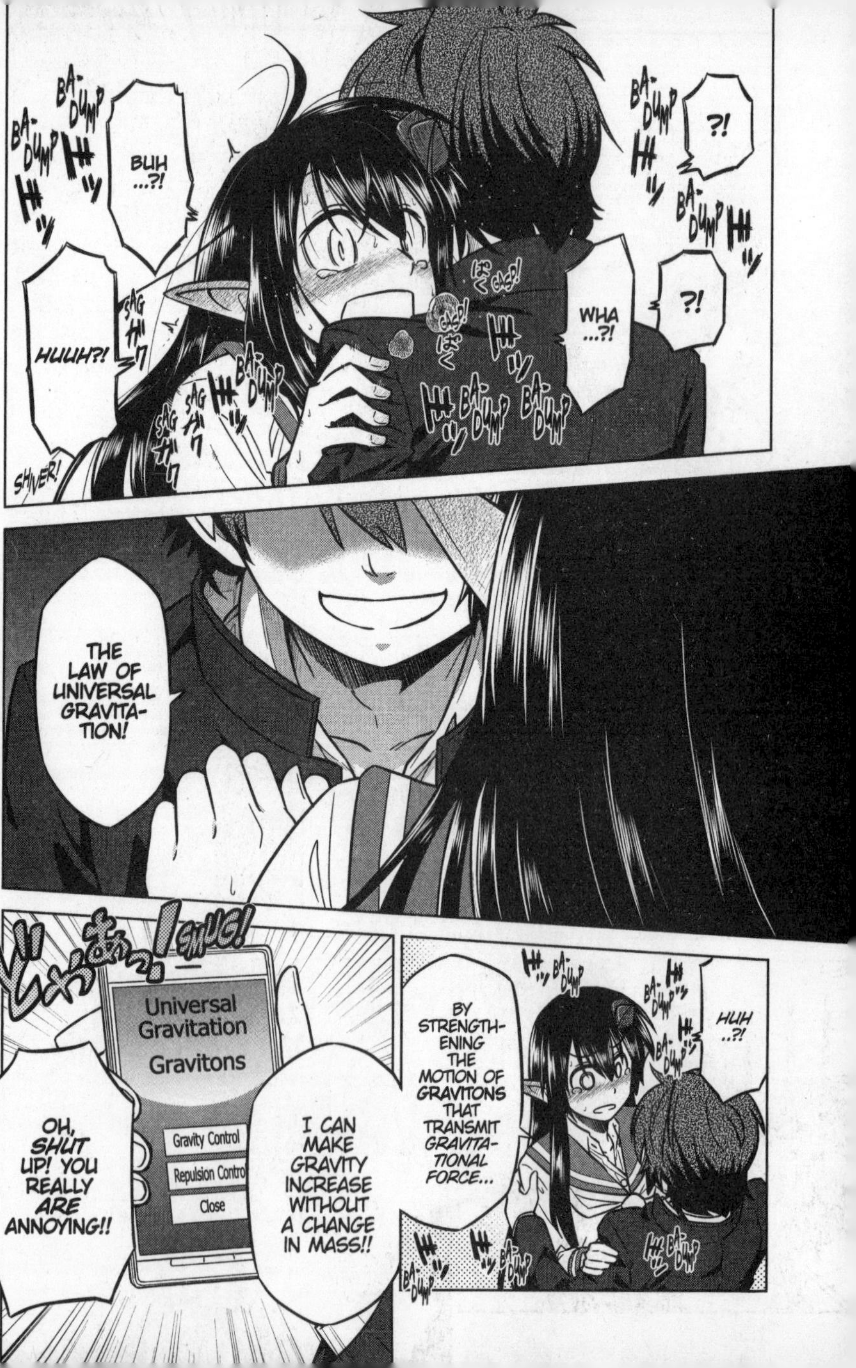

BA-DUMP
?!
BA-DUMP
?!
WHA...?!
GASP!
BA-DUMP
BA-DUMP
BA-DUMP
BA-DUMP
BUH...?!
BA-DUMP
HUUH?!
SAG
SAG
SAG
SHIVER!
THE LAW OF UNIVERSAL GRAVITA-TION!
BA-DUMP
HUH..?!
BA-DUMP
BA-DUMP
BY STRENGTH-ENING THE MOTION OF GRAVITONS THAT TRANSMIT GRAVITA-TIONAL FORCE...
BA-DUMP
BA-DUMP
BA-DUMP
SMUG!
Universal Gravitation
Gravitons
Gravity Control
Repulsion Control
Close
I CAN MAKE GRAVITY INCREASE WITHOUT A CHANGE IN MASS!!
OH, SHUT UP! YOU REALLY ARE ANNOYING!!

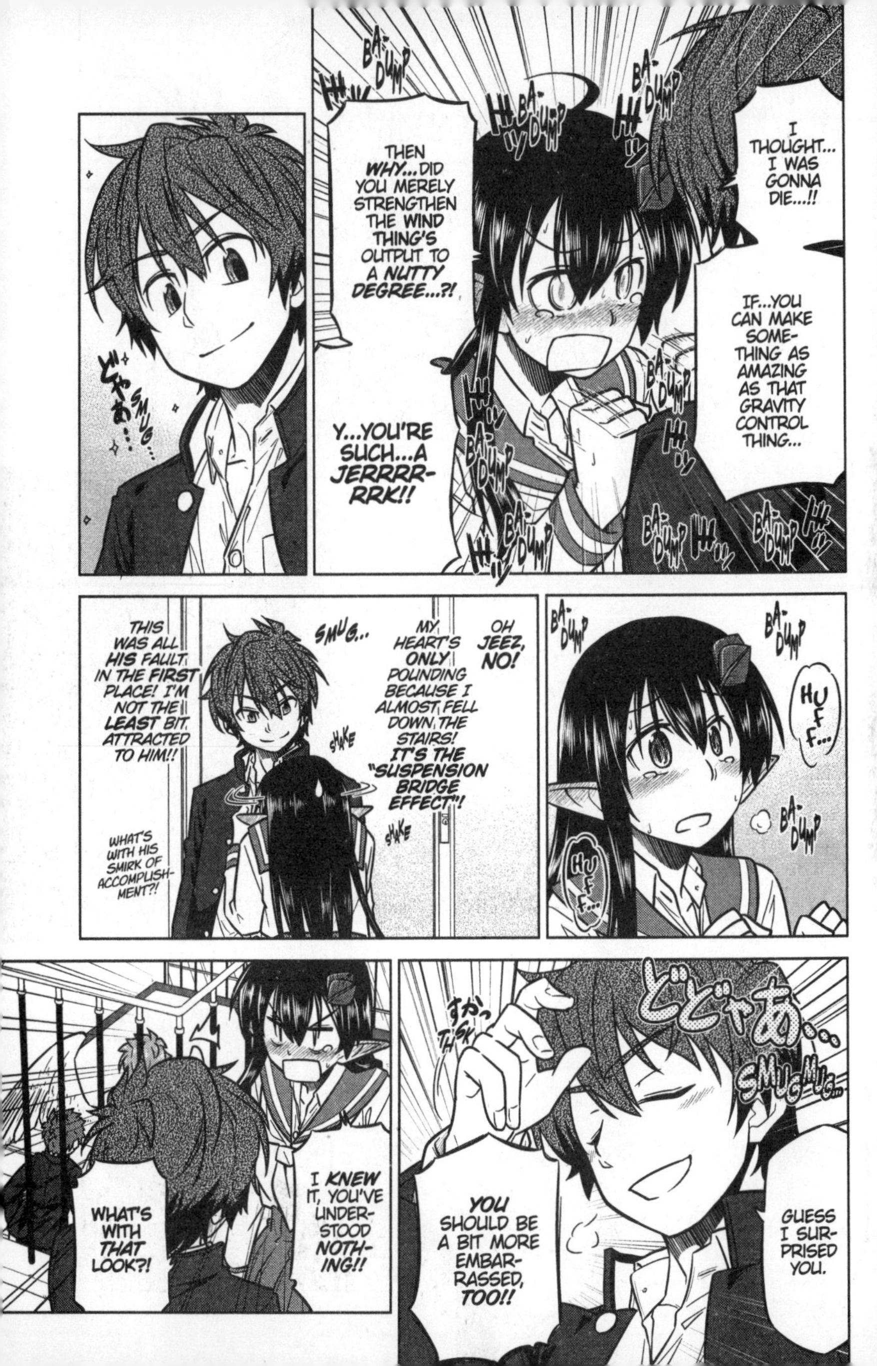
I THOUGHT... I WAS GONNA DIE...!!
IF...YOU CAN MAKE SOME-THING AS AMAZING AS THAT GRAVITY CONTROL THING...
THEN WHY...DID YOU MERELY STRENGTHEN THE WIND THING'S OUTPUT TO A NUTTY DEGREE...?!
Y...YOU'RE SUCH...A JERRRRR-RRK!!
BA-DUMP
SMUG...
HUFF...
HUFF...
BA-DUMP
OH JEEZ, NO!
MY HEART'S ONLY POUNDING BECAUSE I ALMOST FELL DOWN THE STAIRS! IT'S THE "SUSPENSION BRIDGE EFFECT"!
SMUG...
SHAKE
SHAKE
THIS WAS ALL HIS FAULT IN THE FIRST PLACE! I'M NOT THE LEAST BIT ATTRACTED TO HIM!!
WHAT'S WITH HIS SMIRK OF ACCOMPLISH-MENT?!
どどやあ…
SMUG SMUG...
すかっ
TSK
GUESS I SUR-PRISED YOU.
YOU SHOULD BE A BIT MORE EMBAR-RASSED, TOO!!
I KNEW IT, YOU'VE UNDER-STOOD NOTH-ING!!
WHAT'S WITH THAT LOOK?!

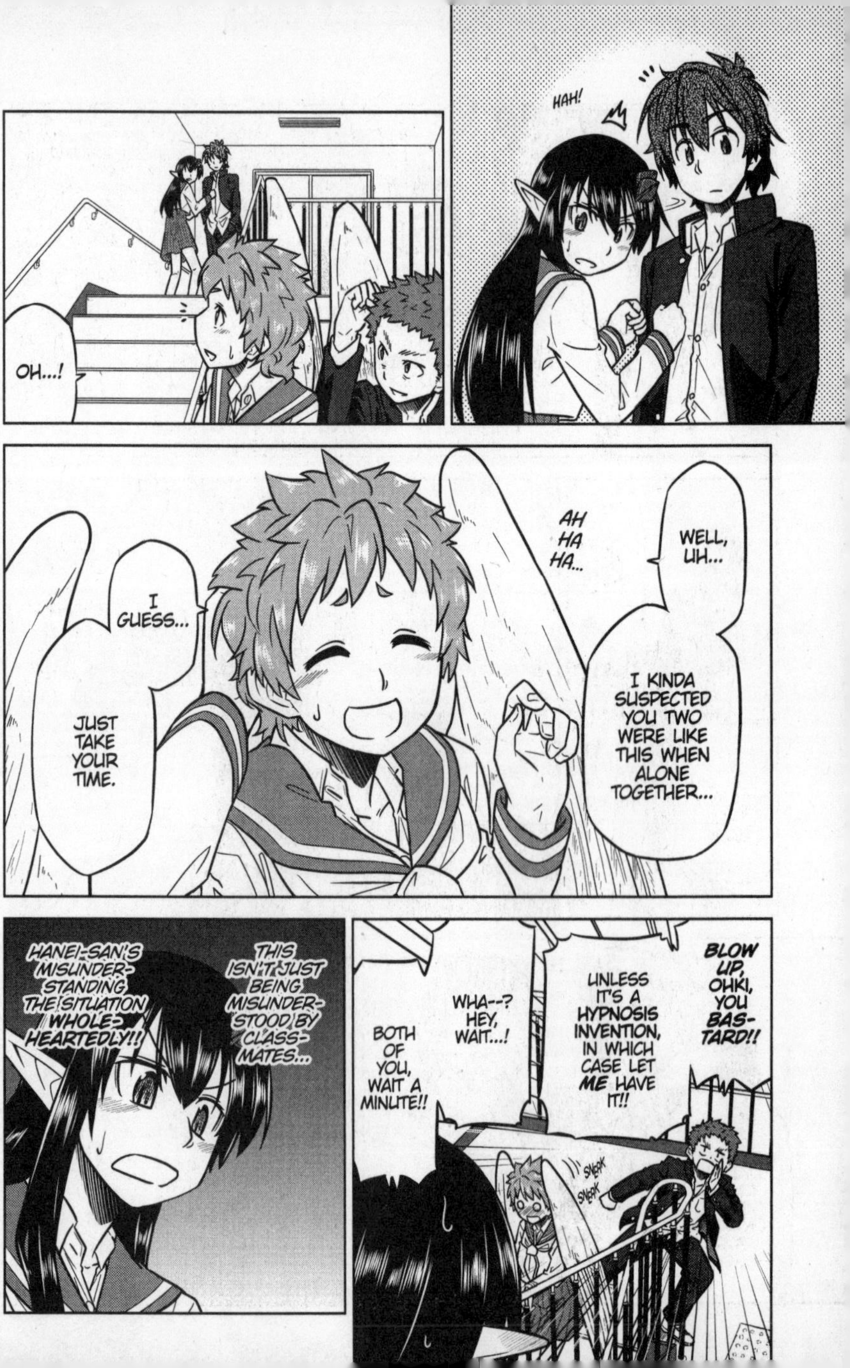
HAH!
OH...!
WELL, UH...
AH HA HA...
I KINDA SUSPECTED YOU TWO WERE LIKE THIS WHEN ALONE TOGETHER...
I GUESS...
JUST TAKE YOUR TIME.
BLOW UP, OHKI, YOU BASTARD!!
UNLESS IT'S A HYPNOSIS INVENTION, IN WHICH CASE LET *ME* HAVE IT!!
WHA--? HEY, WAIT...!
BOTH OF YOU, WAIT A MINUTE!!
SNEAK
SNEAK
THIS ISN'T JUST BEING MISUNDER-STOOD BY CLASS-MATES...
HANEI-SAN'S MISUNDER-STANDING THE SITUATION WHOLE-HEARTEDLY!!

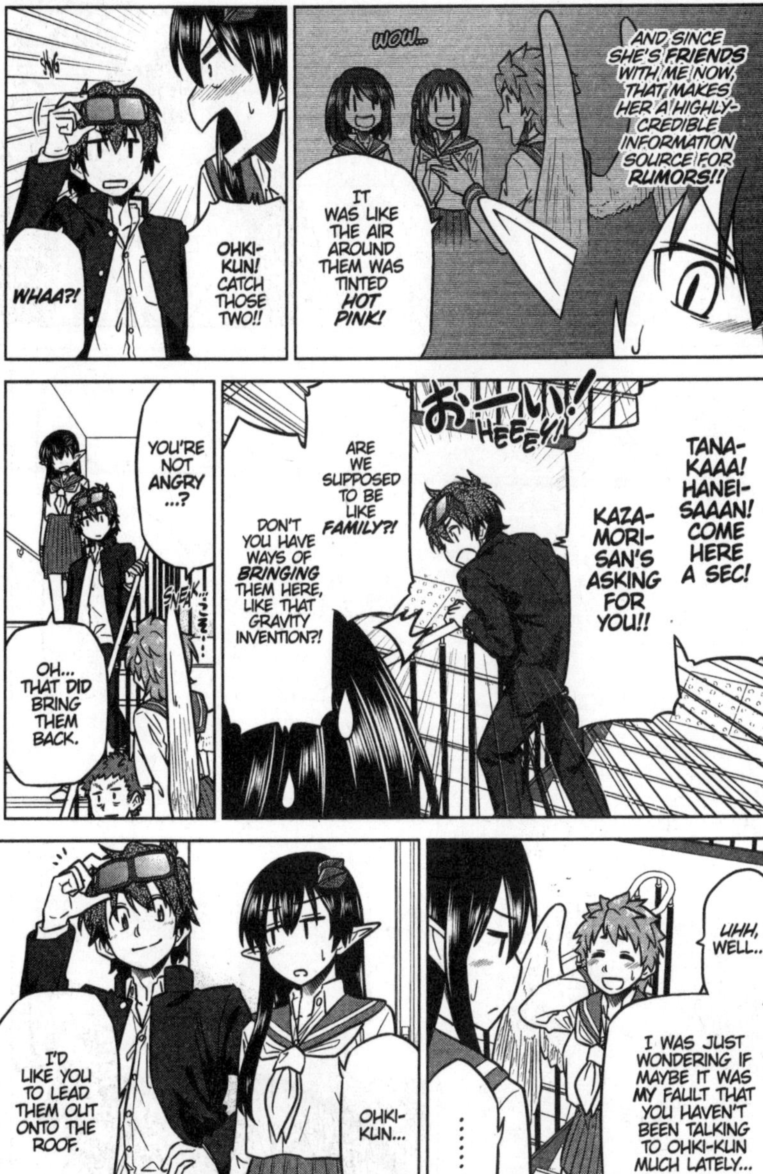

AND SINCE SHE'S FRIENDS WITH ME NOW, THAT MAKES HER A HIGHLY-CREDIBLE INFORMATION SOURCE FOR RUMORS!!
WOW...
IT WAS LIKE THE AIR AROUND THEM WAS TINTED HOT PINK!
OHKI-KUN! CATCH THOSE TWO!!
WHAA?!
TANA-KAAA! HANEI-SAAAN! COME HERE A SEC!
おーい! HEEEY!
KAZA-MORI-SAN'S ASKING FOR YOU!!
ARE WE SUPPOSED TO BE LIKE FAMILY?!
DON'T YOU HAVE WAYS OF BRINGING THEM HERE, LIKE THAT GRAVITY INVENTION?!
YOU'RE NOT ANGRY ...?
OH... THAT DID BRING THEM BACK.
UHH, WELL...
I WAS JUST WONDERING IF MAYBE IT WAS MY FAULT THAT YOU HAVEN'T BEEN TALKING TO OHKI-KUN MUCH LATELY...
......
OHKI-KUN...
I'D LIKE YOU TO LEAD THEM OUT ONTO THE ROOF.

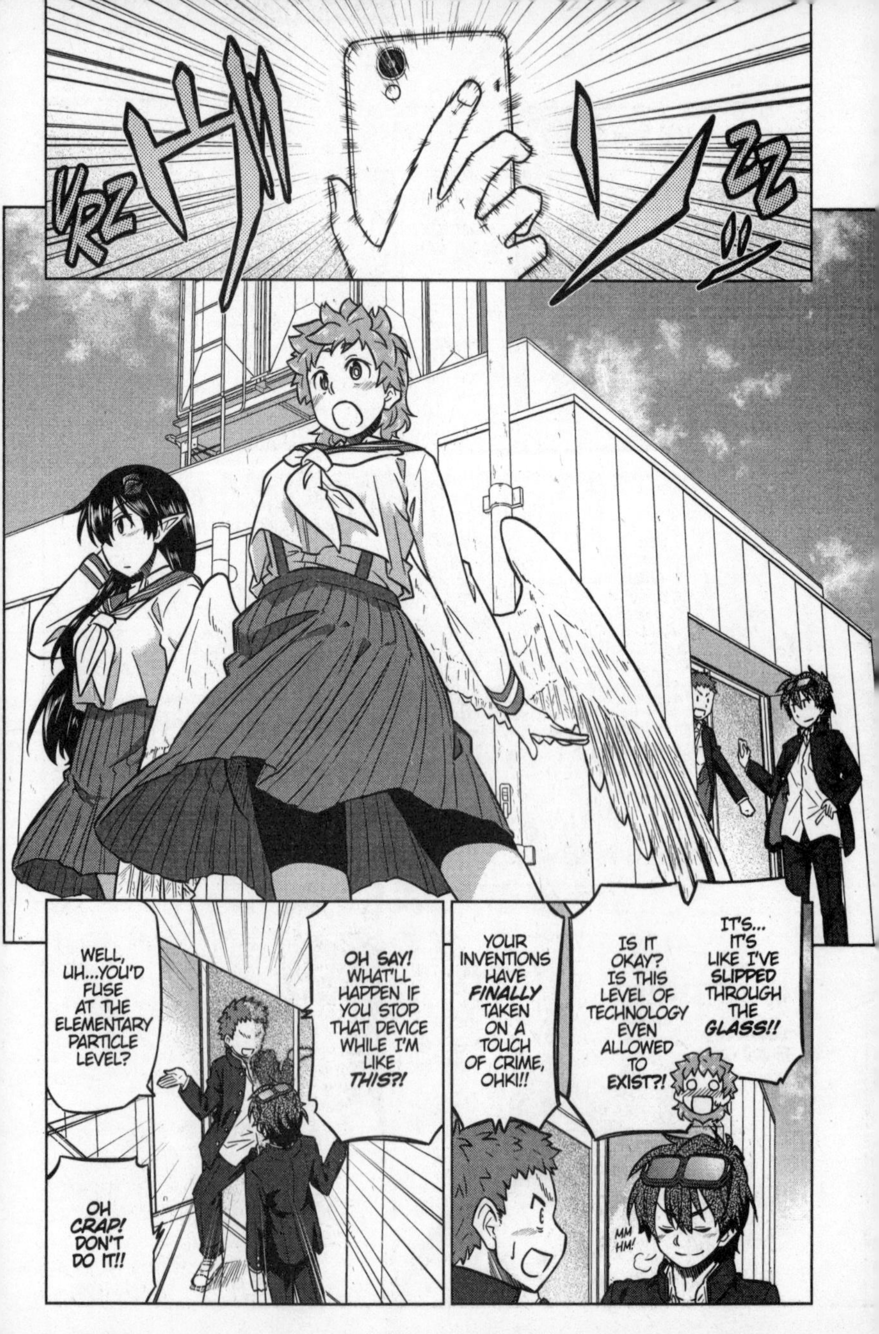
VRZZZ!!
IT'S... IT'S LIKE I'VE SLIPPED THROUGH THE *GLASS!!*
IS IT OKAY? IS THIS LEVEL OF TECHNOLOGY EVEN ALLOWED TO EXIST?!
YOUR INVENTIONS HAVE *FINALLY* TAKEN ON A TOUCH OF CRIME, OHKI!!
MM HM!
OH SAY! WHAT'LL HAPPEN IF YOU STOP THAT DEVICE WHILE I'M LIKE *THIS?!*
WELL, UH...YOU'D FUSE AT THE ELEMENTARY PARTICLE LEVEL?
OH *CRAP!* DON'T DO IT!!

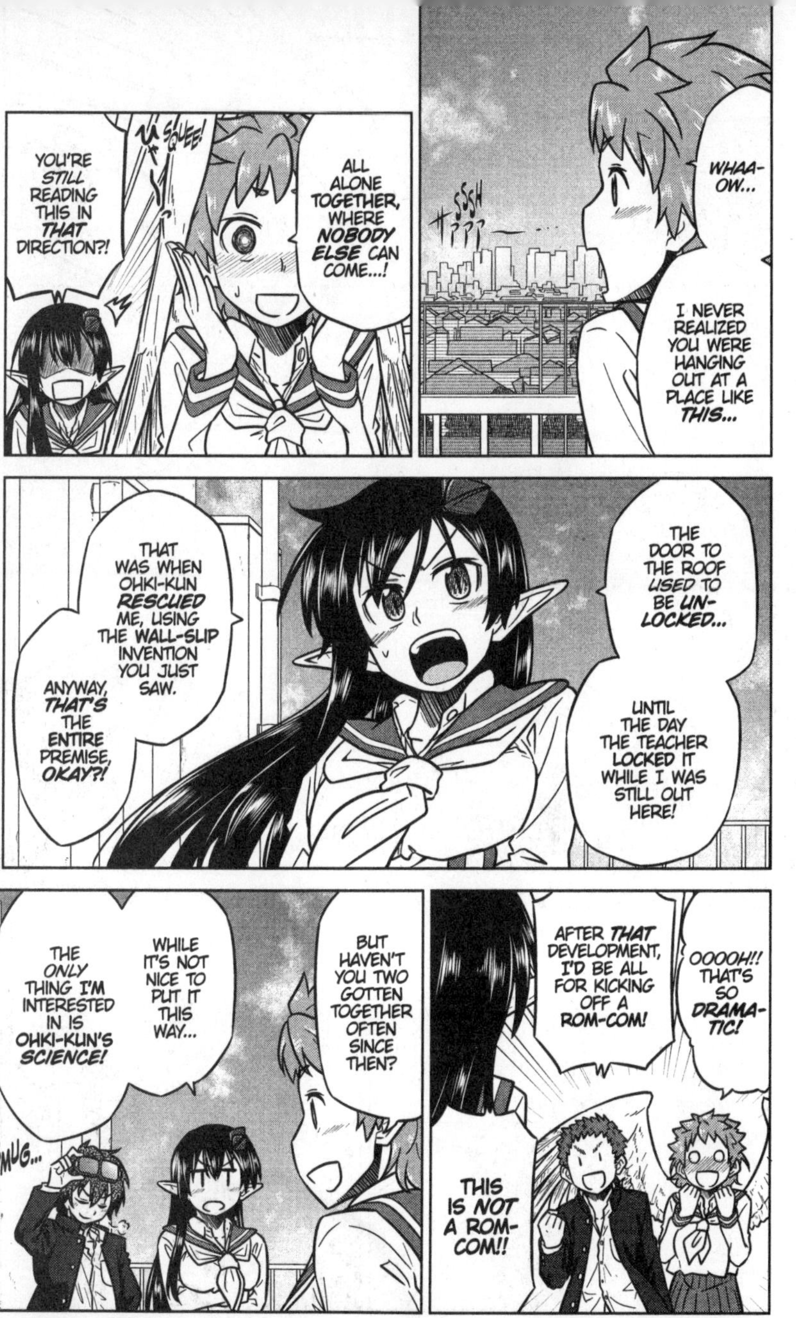
WHAA-OW...
SSSH
I NEVER REALIZED YOU WERE HANGING OUT AT A PLACE LIKE THIS...
ALL ALONE TOGETHER, WHERE NOBODY ELSE CAN COME...!
SQUEE!
YOU'RE STILL READING THIS IN THAT DIRECTION?!
THE DOOR TO THE ROOF USED TO BE UN-LOCKED...
UNTIL THE DAY THE TEACHER LOCKED IT WHILE I WAS STILL OUT HERE!
THAT WAS WHEN OHKI-KUN RESCUED ME, USING THE WALL-SLIP INVENTION YOU JUST SAW.
ANYWAY, THAT'S THE ENTIRE PREMISE, OKAY?!
OOOOH!! THAT'S SO DRAMA-TIC!
AFTER THAT DEVELOPMENT, I'D BE ALL FOR KICKING OFF A ROM-COM!
THIS IS NOT A ROM-COM!!
BUT HAVEN'T YOU TWO GOTTEN TOGETHER OFTEN SINCE THEN?
WHILE IT'S NOT NICE TO PUT IT THIS WAY...
THE ONLY THING I'M INTERESTED IN IS OHKI-KUN'S SCIENCE!
SMUG...

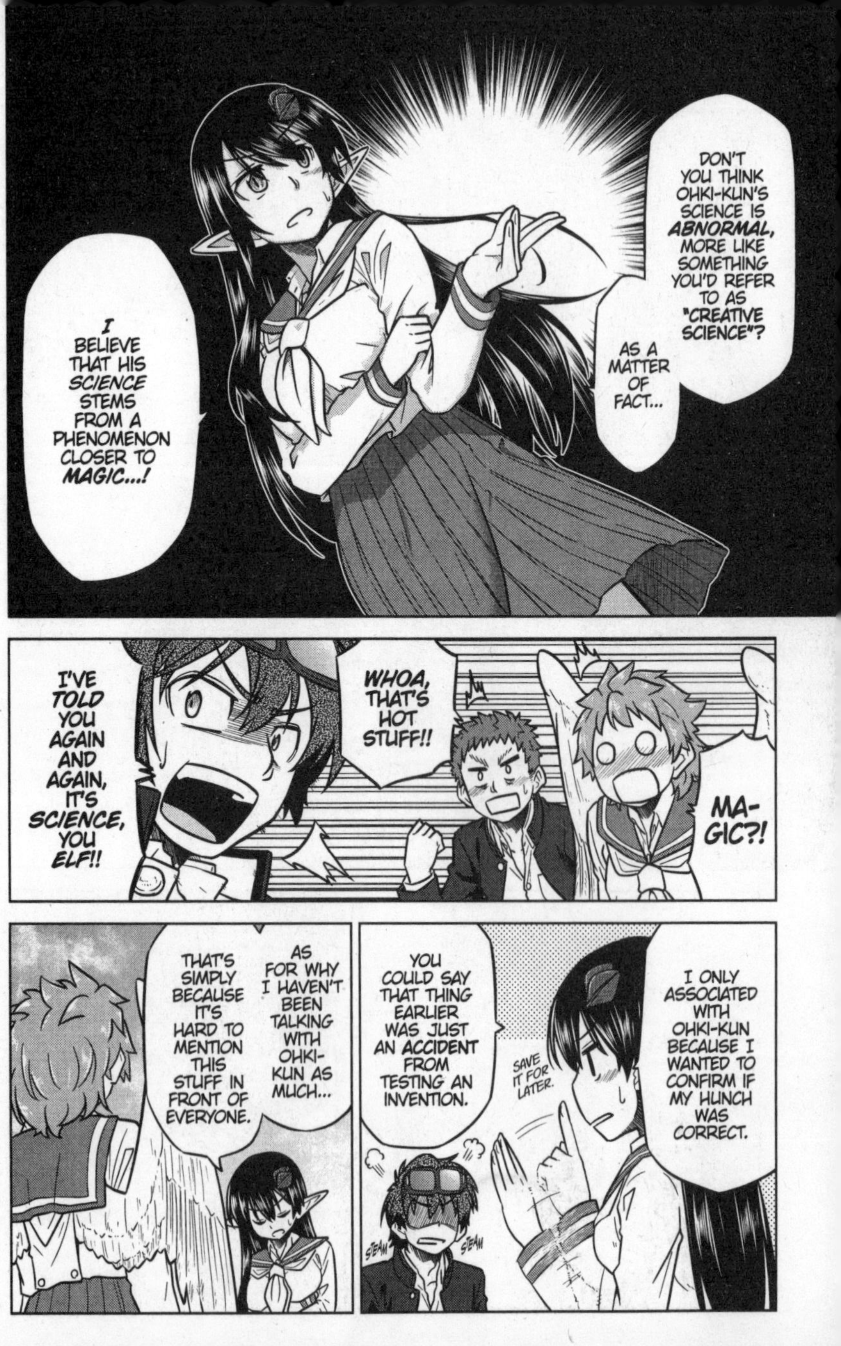
DON'T YOU THINK OHKI-KUN'S SCIENCE IS ABNORMAL, MORE LIKE SOMETHING YOU'D REFER TO AS "CREATIVE SCIENCE"?
AS A MATTER OF FACT...
I BELIEVE THAT HIS SCIENCE STEMS FROM A PHENOMENON CLOSER TO MAGIC...!
MA-GIC?!
WHOA, THAT'S HOT STUFF!!
I'VE TOLD YOU AGAIN AND AGAIN, IT'S SCIENCE, YOU ELF!!
I ONLY ASSOCIATED WITH OHKI-KUN BECAUSE I WANTED TO CONFIRM IF MY HUNCH WAS CORRECT.
SAVE IT FOR LATER.
YOU COULD SAY THAT THING EARLIER WAS JUST AN ACCIDENT FROM TESTING AN INVENTION.
STEAM STEAM
AS FOR WHY I HAVEN'T BEEN TALKING WITH OHKI-KUN AS MUCH...
THAT'S SIMPLY BECAUSE IT'S HARD TO MENTION THIS STUFF IN FRONT OF EVERYONE.

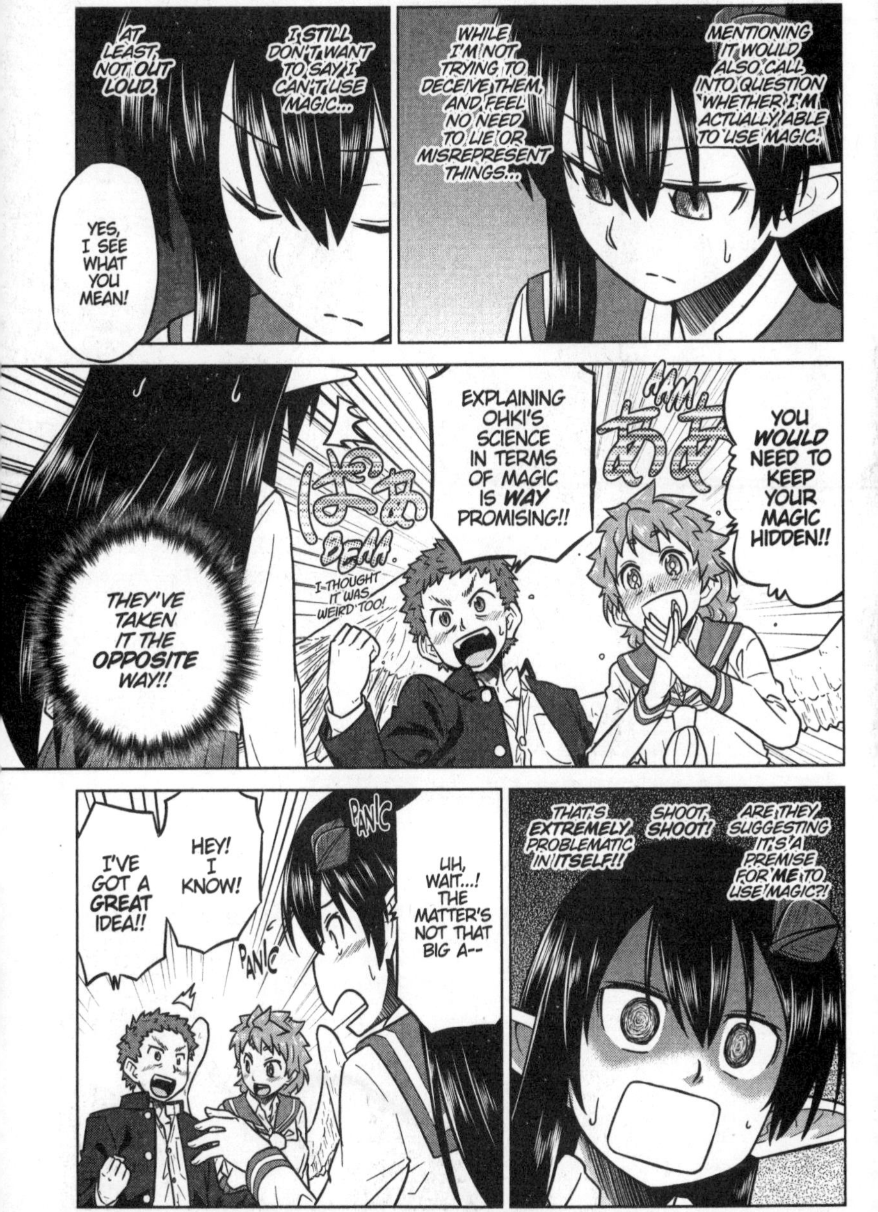
MENTIONING IT WOULD ALSO CALL INTO QUESTION WHETHER I'M ACTUALLY ABLE TO USE MAGIC.
WHILE I'M NOT TRYING TO DECEIVE THEM, AND FEEL NO NEED TO LIE OR MISREPRESENT THINGS...
I STILL DON'T WANT TO SAY I CAN'T USE MAGIC...
AT LEAST, NOT OUT LOUD.
YES, I SEE WHAT YOU MEAN!
YOU WOULD NEED TO KEEP YOUR MAGIC HIDDEN!!
EXPLAINING OHKI'S SCIENCE IN TERMS OF MAGIC IS WAY PROMISING!!
I-THOUGHT IT WAS WEIRD TOO!
THEY'VE TAKEN IT THE OPPOSITE WAY!!
ARE THEY SUGGESTING IT'S A PREMISE FOR ME TO USE MAGIC?!
SHOOT, SHOOT!
THAT'S EXTREMELY PROBLEMATIC IN ITSELF!!
PANIC
UH, WAIT...! THE MATTER'S NOT THAT BIG A--
PANIC
HEY! I KNOW!
I'VE GOT A GREAT IDEA!!

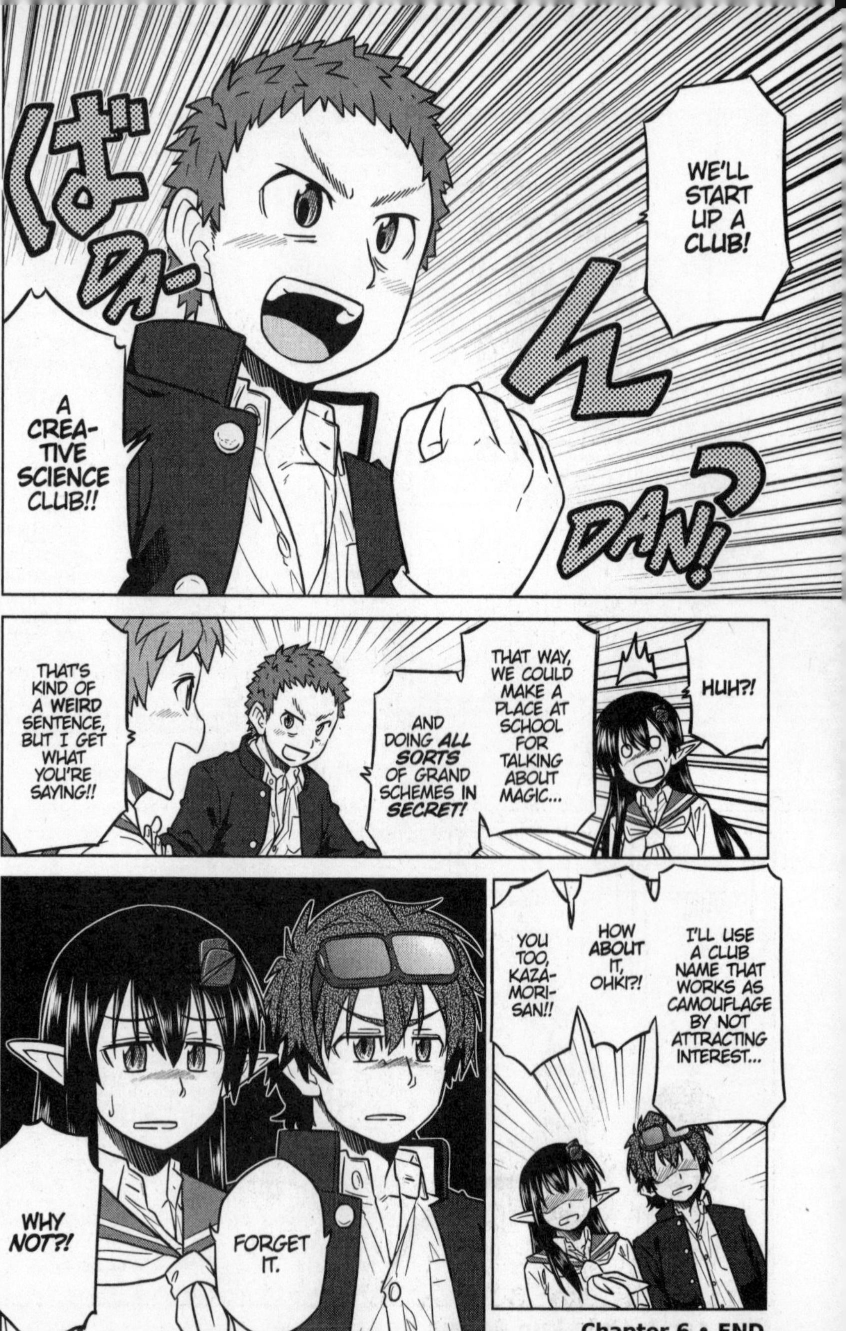
WE'LL START UP A CLUB!
DAN!
A CREATIVE SCIENCE CLUB!!
HUH?!
THAT WAY, WE COULD MAKE A PLACE AT SCHOOL FOR TALKING ABOUT MAGIC...
AND DOING ALL SORTS OF GRAND SCHEMES IN SECRET!
THAT'S KIND OF A WEIRD SENTENCE, BUT I GET WHAT YOU'RE SAYING!!
I'LL USE A CLUB NAME THAT WORKS AS CAMOUFLAGE BY NOT ATTRACTING INTEREST...
HOW ABOUT IT, OHKI?!
YOU TOO, KAZAMORI-SAN!!
FORGET IT.
WHY NOT?!

Chapter 6 • END

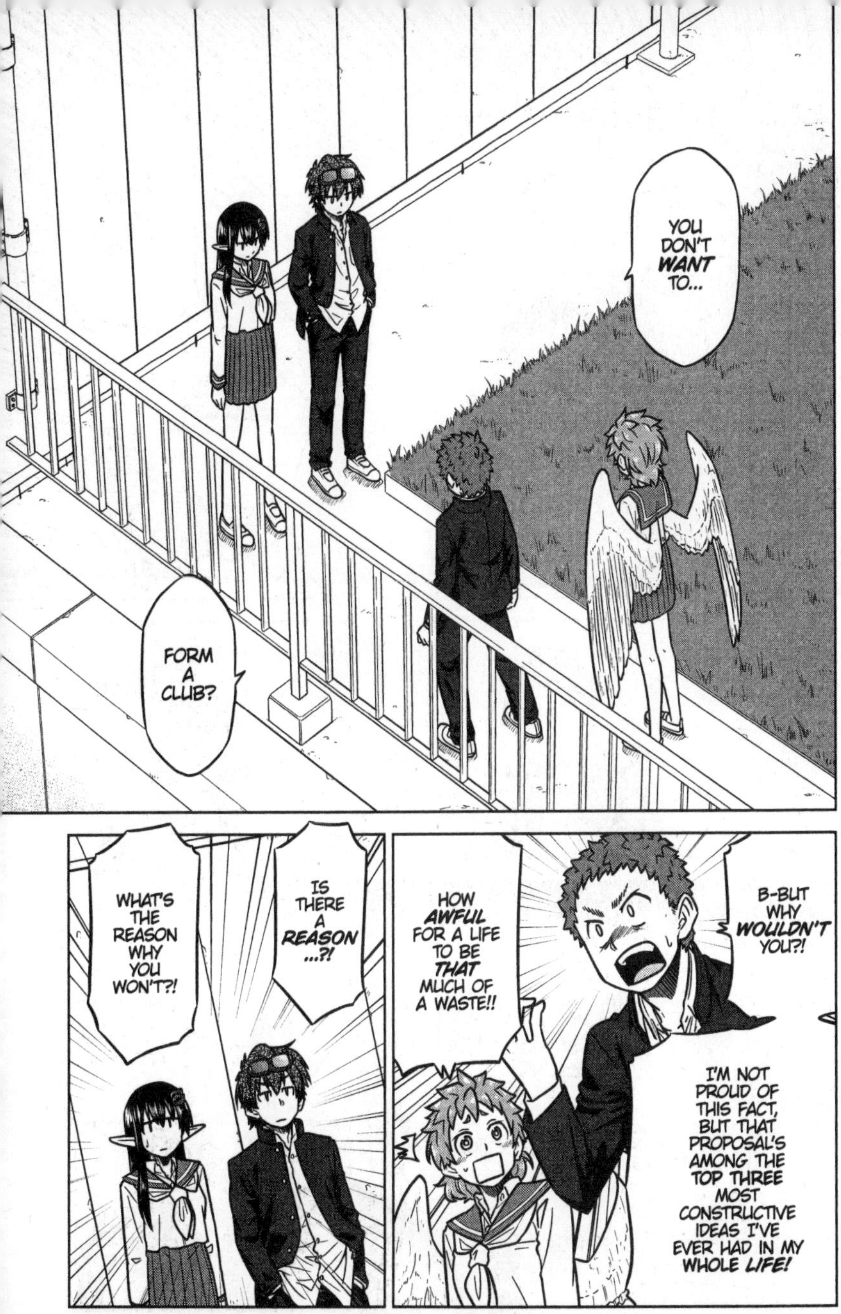
YOU DON'T WANT TO...
FORM A CLUB?
B-BUT WHY WOULDN'T YOU?!
HOW AWFUL FOR A LIFE TO BE THAT MUCH OF A WASTE!!
I'M NOT PROUD OF THIS FACT, BUT THAT PROPOSAL'S AMONG THE TOP THREE MOST CONSTRUCTIVE IDEAS I'VE EVER HAD IN MY WHOLE LIFE!
IS THERE A REASON...?!
WHAT'S THE REASON WHY YOU WON'T?!

Chapter 7: Ohki-kun Revels

Chapter 7: Ohki-kun Revels

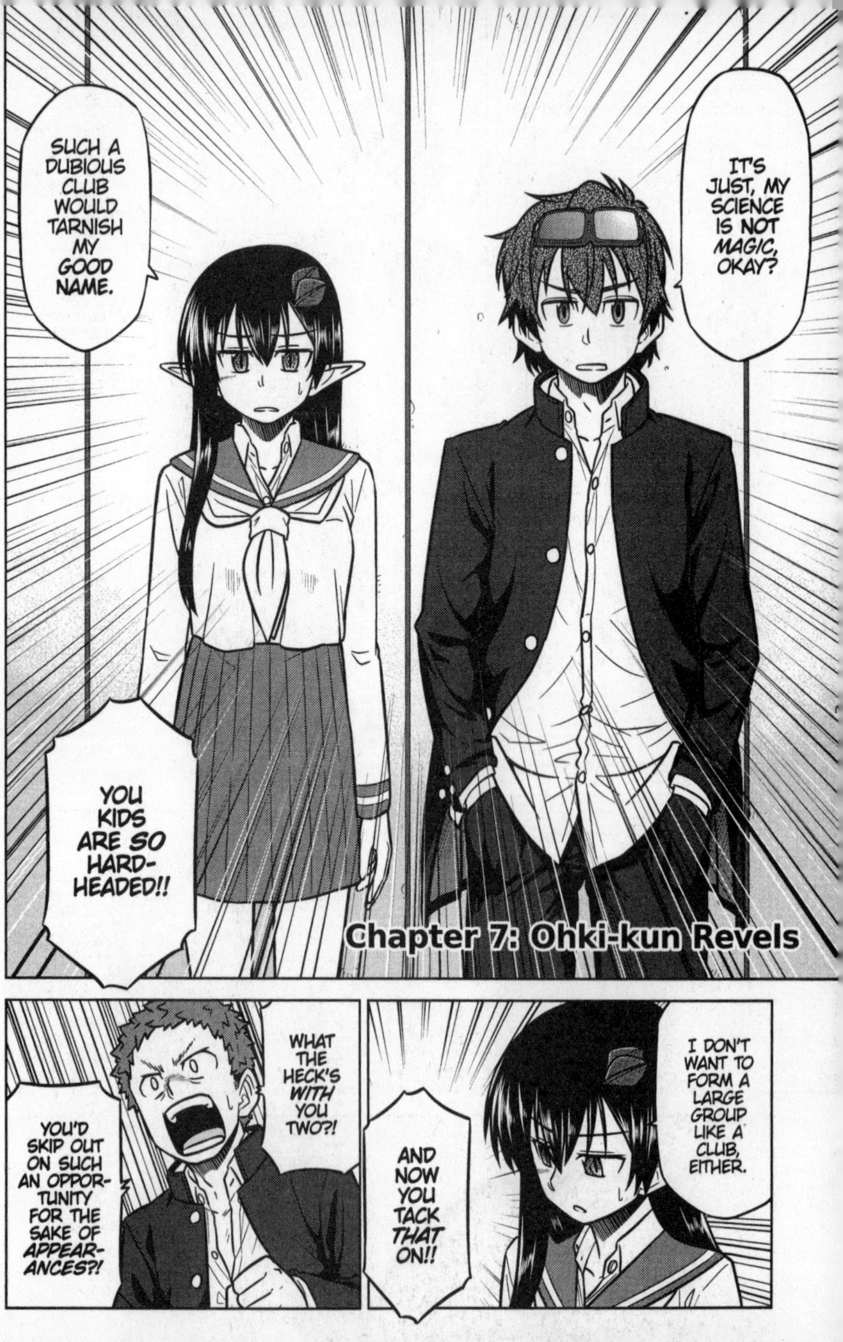
IT'S JUST, MY SCIENCE IS NOT *MAGIC*, OKAY?
SUCH A DUBIOUS CLUB WOULD TARNISH MY GOOD NAME.
YOU KIDS ARE *SO* HARD-HEADED!!
I DON'T WANT TO FORM A LARGE GROUP LIKE A CLUB, EITHER.
AND NOW YOU TACK *THAT* ON!!
WHAT THE HECK'S *WITH* YOU TWO?!
YOU'D SKIP OUT ON SUCH AN OPPORTUNITY FOR THE SAKE OF *APPEARANCES*?!

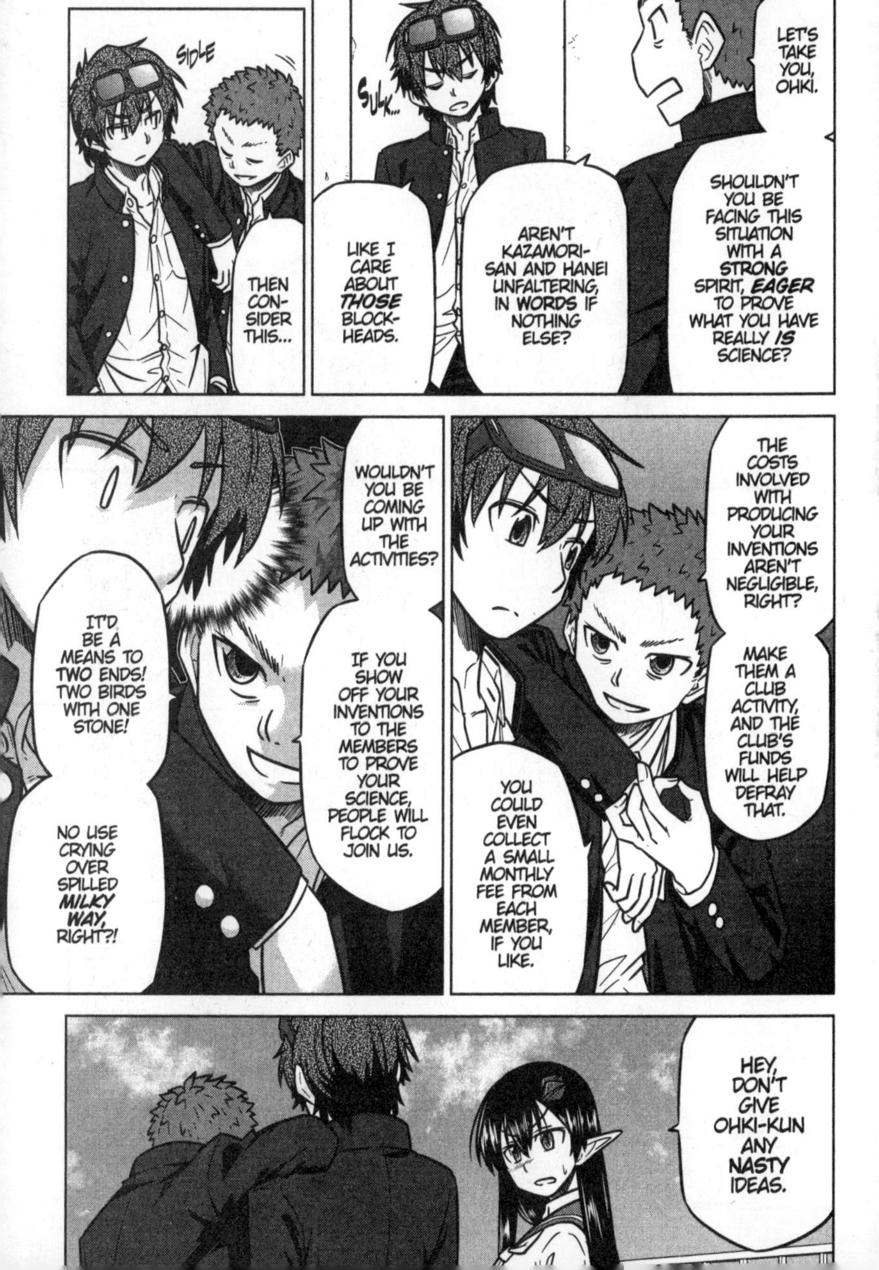

LET'S TAKE YOU, OHKI.
SHOULDN'T YOU BE FACING THIS SITUATION WITH A STRONG SPIRIT, EAGER TO PROVE WHAT YOU HAVE REALLY IS SCIENCE?
SULK...
AREN'T KAZAMORI-SAN AND HANEI UNFALTERING, IN WORDS IF NOTHING ELSE?
LIKE I CARE ABOUT THOSE BLOCK-HEADS.
SIDLE
THEN CON-SIDER THIS...
THE COSTS INVOLVED WITH PRODUCING YOUR INVENTIONS AREN'T NEGLIGIBLE, RIGHT?
MAKE THEM A CLUB ACTIVITY, AND THE CLUB'S FUNDS WILL HELP DEFRAY THAT.
YOU COULD EVEN COLLECT A SMALL MONTHLY FEE FROM EACH MEMBER, IF YOU LIKE.
WOULDN'T YOU BE COMING UP WITH THE ACTIVITIES?
IF YOU SHOW OFF YOUR INVENTIONS TO THE MEMBERS TO PROVE YOUR SCIENCE, PEOPLE WILL FLOCK TO JOIN US.
IT'D BE A MEANS TO TWO ENDS! TWO BIRDS WITH ONE STONE!
NO USE CRYING OVER SPILLED MILKY WAY, RIGHT?!
HEY, DON'T GIVE OHKI-KUN ANY NASTY IDEAS.

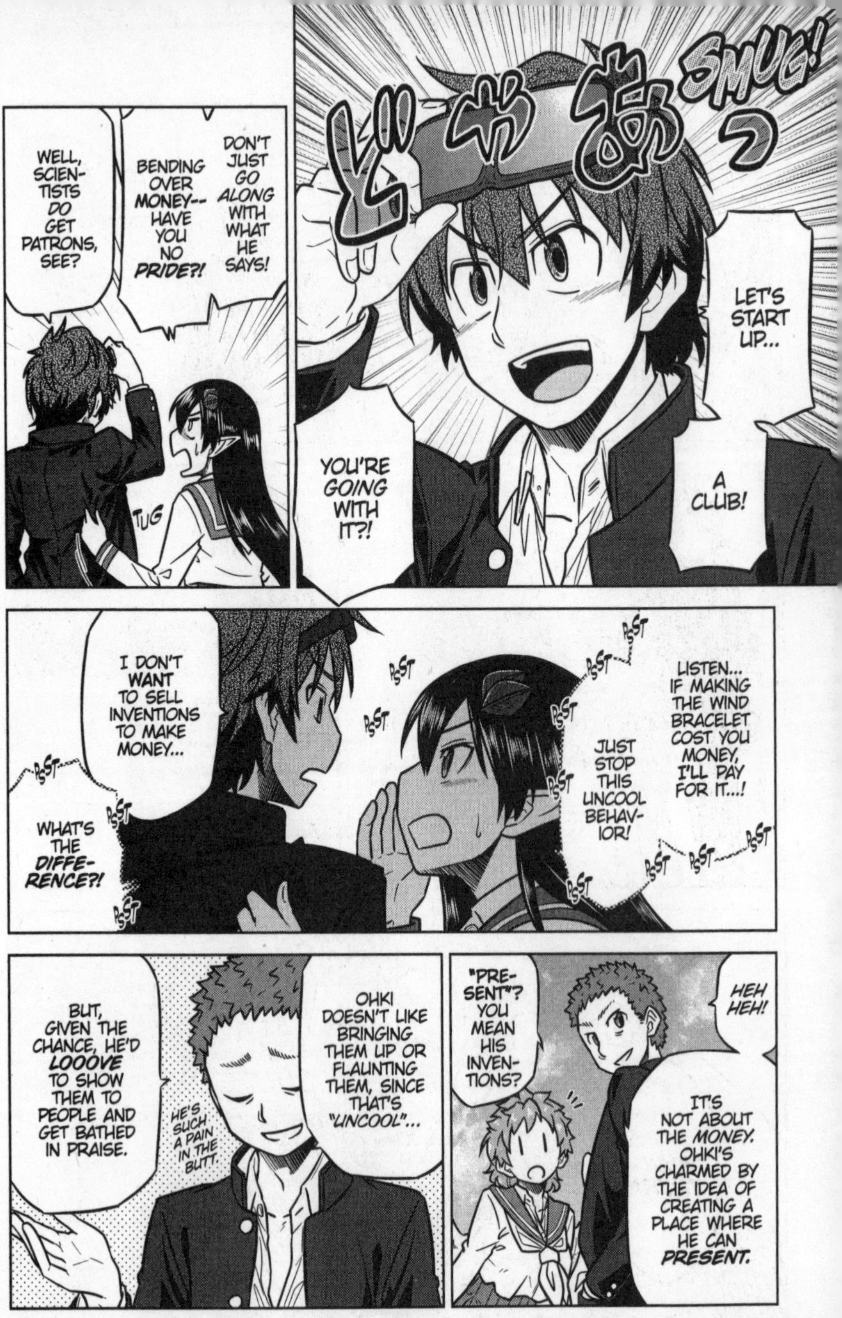
どやあっ
SMUG!
LET'S START UP...
A CLUB!
YOU'RE GOING WITH IT?!
DON'T JUST GO ALONG WITH WHAT HE SAYS!
BENDING OVER MONEY-- HAVE YOU NO PRIDE?!
WELL, SCIENTISTS DO GET PATRONS, SEE?
TUG
LISTEN... IF MAKING THE WIND BRACELET COST YOU MONEY, I'LL PAY FOR IT...!
JUST STOP THIS UNCOOL BEHAVIOR!
PSST
I DON'T WANT TO SELL INVENTIONS TO MAKE MONEY...
WHAT'S THE DIFFERENCE?!
HEH HEH!
IT'S NOT ABOUT THE MONEY. OHKI'S CHARMED BY THE IDEA OF CREATING A PLACE WHERE HE CAN PRESENT.
"PRESENT"? YOU MEAN HIS INVENTIONS?
OHKI DOESN'T LIKE BRINGING THEM UP OR FLAUNTING THEM, SINCE THAT'S "UNCOOL"...
BUT, GIVEN THE CHANCE, HE'D LOOOVE TO SHOW THEM TO PEOPLE AND GET BATHED IN PRAISE.
HE'S SUCH A PAIN IN THE BUTT.

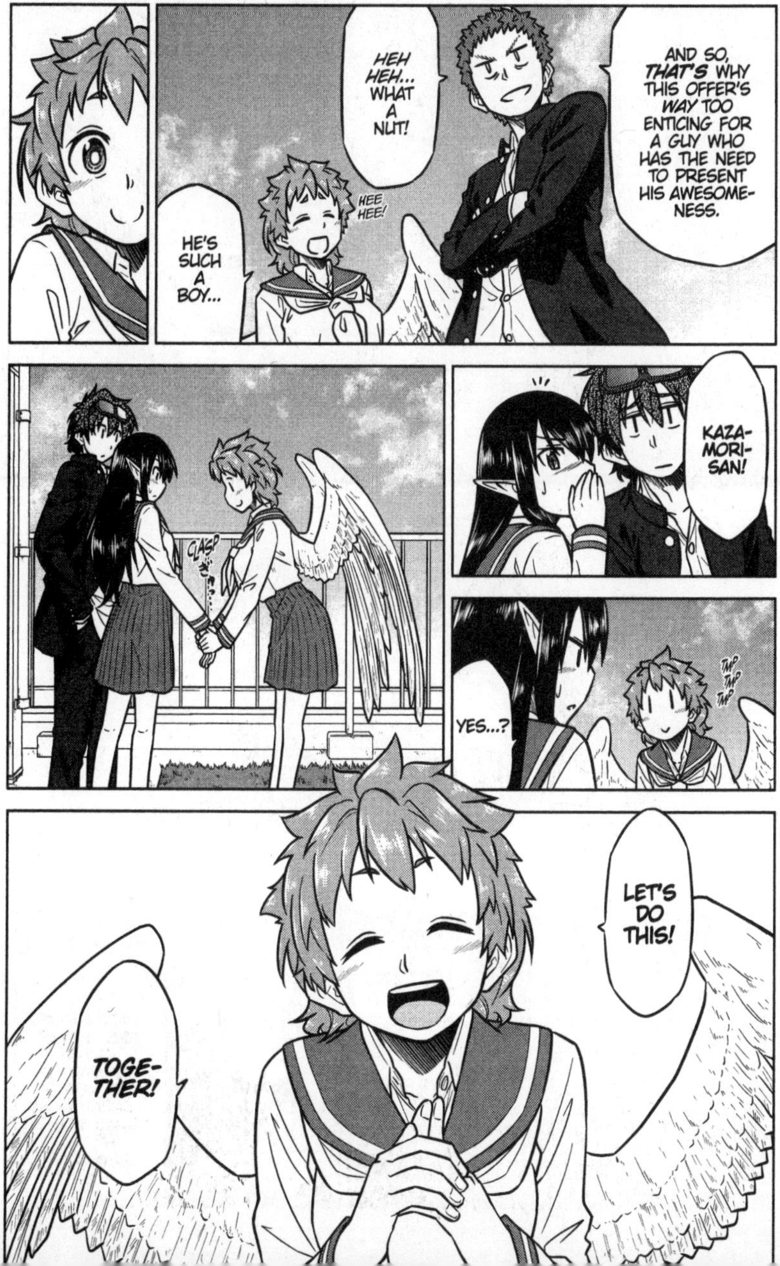
AND SO, THAT'S WHY THIS OFFER'S WAY TOO ENTICING FOR A GUY WHO HAS THE NEED TO PRESENT HIS AWESOMENESS.
HEH HEH... WHAT A NUT!
HEE HEE!
HE'S SUCH A BOY...
KAZAMORI-SAN!
TMP TMP TMP
YES...?
CLASP
LET'S DO THIS!
TOGETHER!

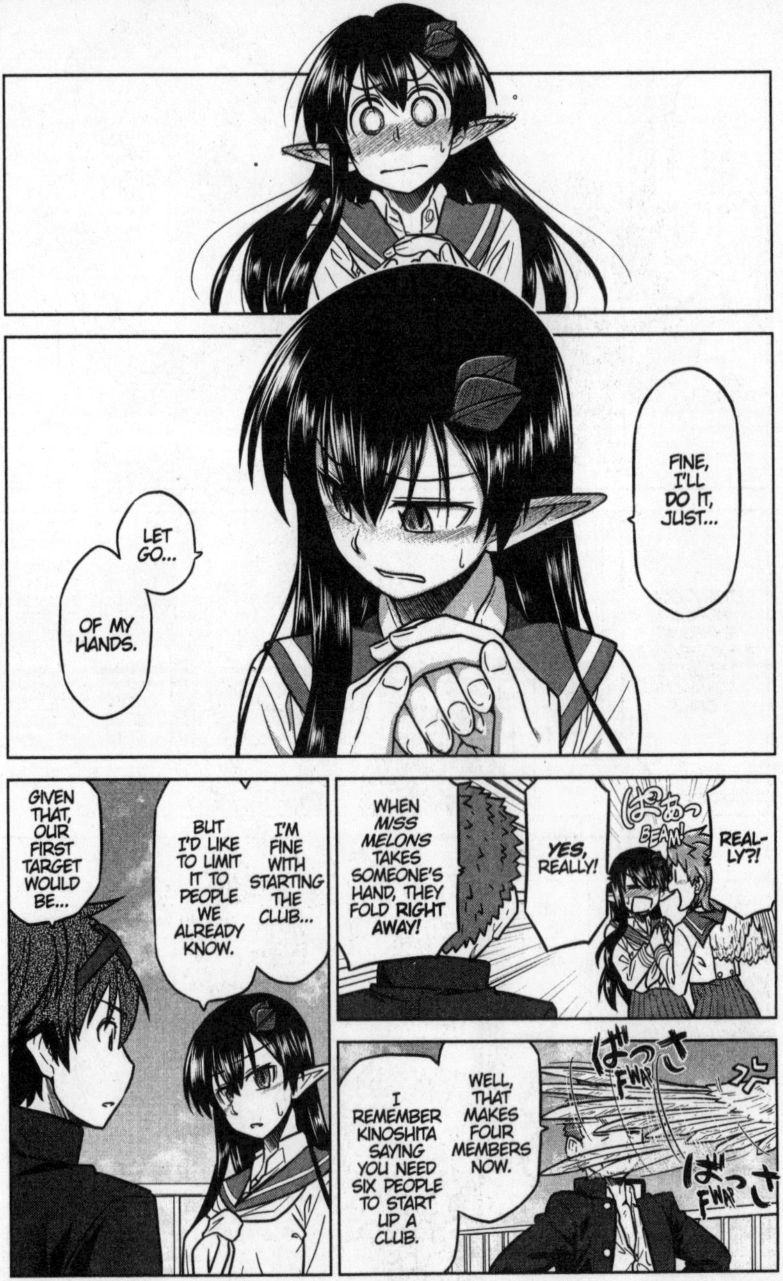
FINE, I'LL DO IT, JUST...
LET GO...
OF MY HANDS.
BEAM!
REAL-LY?!
YES, REALLY!
WHEN *MISS MELONS* TAKES SOMEONE'S HAND, THEY FOLD RIGHT AWAY!
ばっさ
FWAP
ばっさ
FWAP
WELL, THAT MAKES FOUR MEMBERS NOW.
I REMEMBER KINOSHITA SAYING YOU NEED SIX PEOPLE TO START UP A CLUB.
I'M FINE WITH STARTING THE CLUB...
BUT I'D LIKE TO LIMIT IT TO PEOPLE WE ALREADY KNOW.
GIVEN THAT, OUR FIRST TARGET WOULD BE...

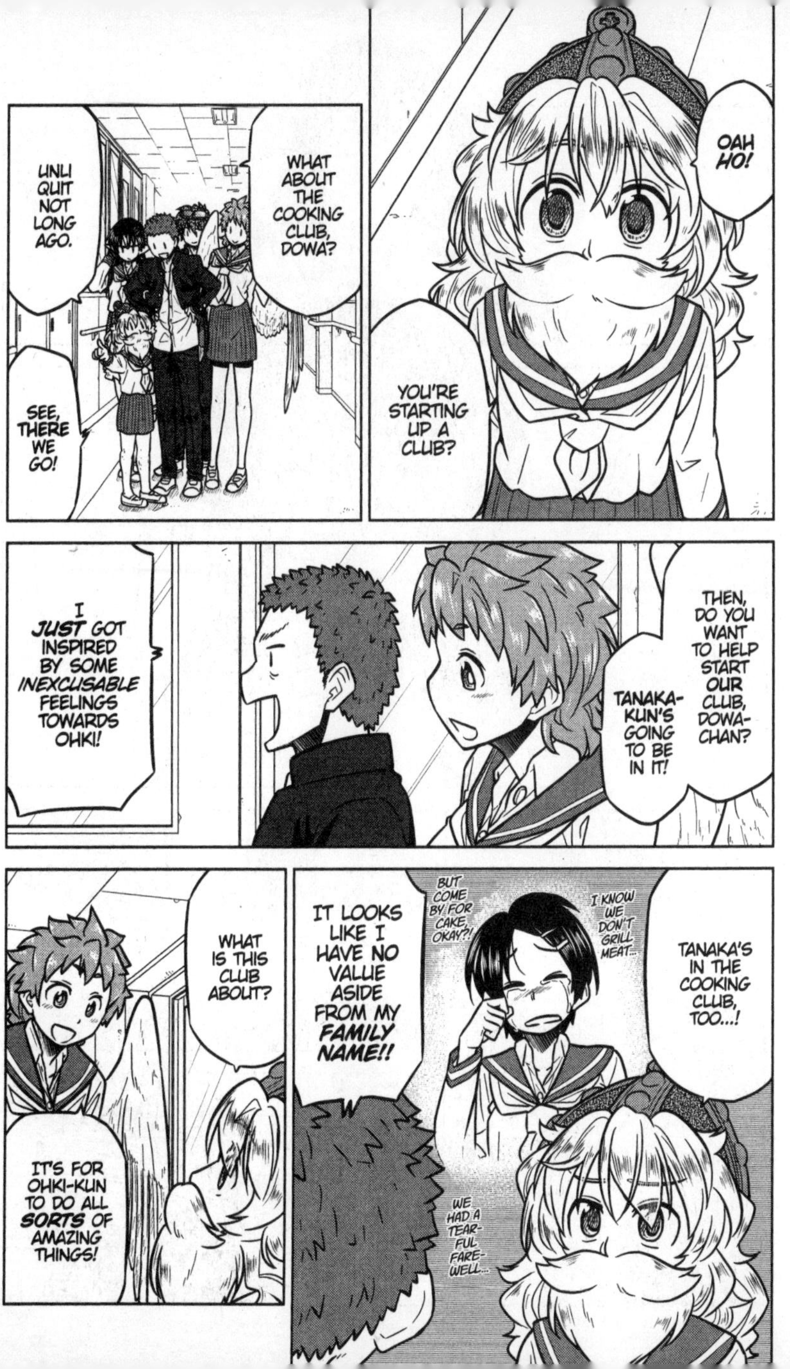
OAH HO!
YOU'RE STARTING UP A CLUB?
WHAT ABOUT THE COOKING CLUB, DOWA?
UNLI QUIT NOT LONG AGO.
SEE, THERE WE GO!
THEN, DO YOU WANT TO HELP START OUR CLUB, DOWA-CHAN?
TANAKA-KUN'S GOING TO BE IN IT!
I JUST GOT INSPIRED BY SOME INEXCUSABLE FEELINGS TOWARDS OHKI!
TANAKA'S IN THE COOKING CLUB, TOO...!
I KNOW WE DON'T GRILL MEAT...
BUT COME BY FOR CAKE, OKAY?!
IT LOOKS LIKE I HAVE NO VALUE ASIDE FROM MY FAMILY NAME!!
WE HAD A TEARFUL FAREWELL...
WHAT IS THIS CLUB ABOUT?
IT'S FOR OHKI-KUN TO DO ALL SORTS OF AMAZING THINGS!

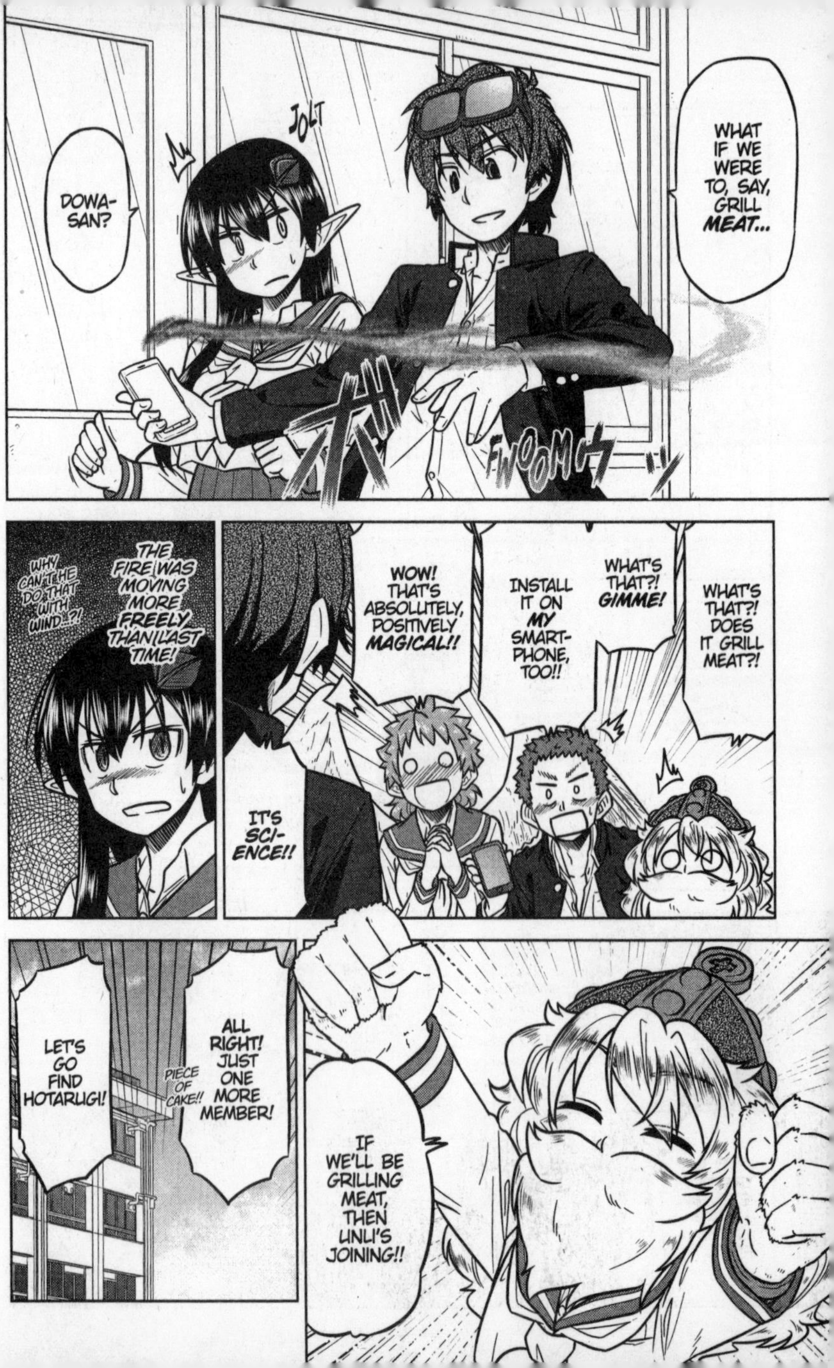

WHAT IF WE WERE TO, SAY, GRILL MEAT...
FWOOM
JOLT
DOWA-SAN?
WHAT'S THAT?! DOES IT GRILL MEAT?!
WHAT'S THAT?! GIMME!
INSTALL IT ON MY SMARTPHONE, TOO!!
WOW! THAT'S ABSOLUTELY, POSITIVELY MAGICAL!!
IT'S SCI-ENCE!!
THE FIRE WAS MOVING MORE FREELY THAN LAST TIME!
WHY CAN'T HE DO THAT WITH WIND...?!
IF WE'LL BE GRILLING MEAT, THEN UNLI'S JOINING!!
ALL RIGHT! JUST ONE MORE MEMBER!
PIECE OF CAKE!!
LET'S GO FIND HOTARUGI!

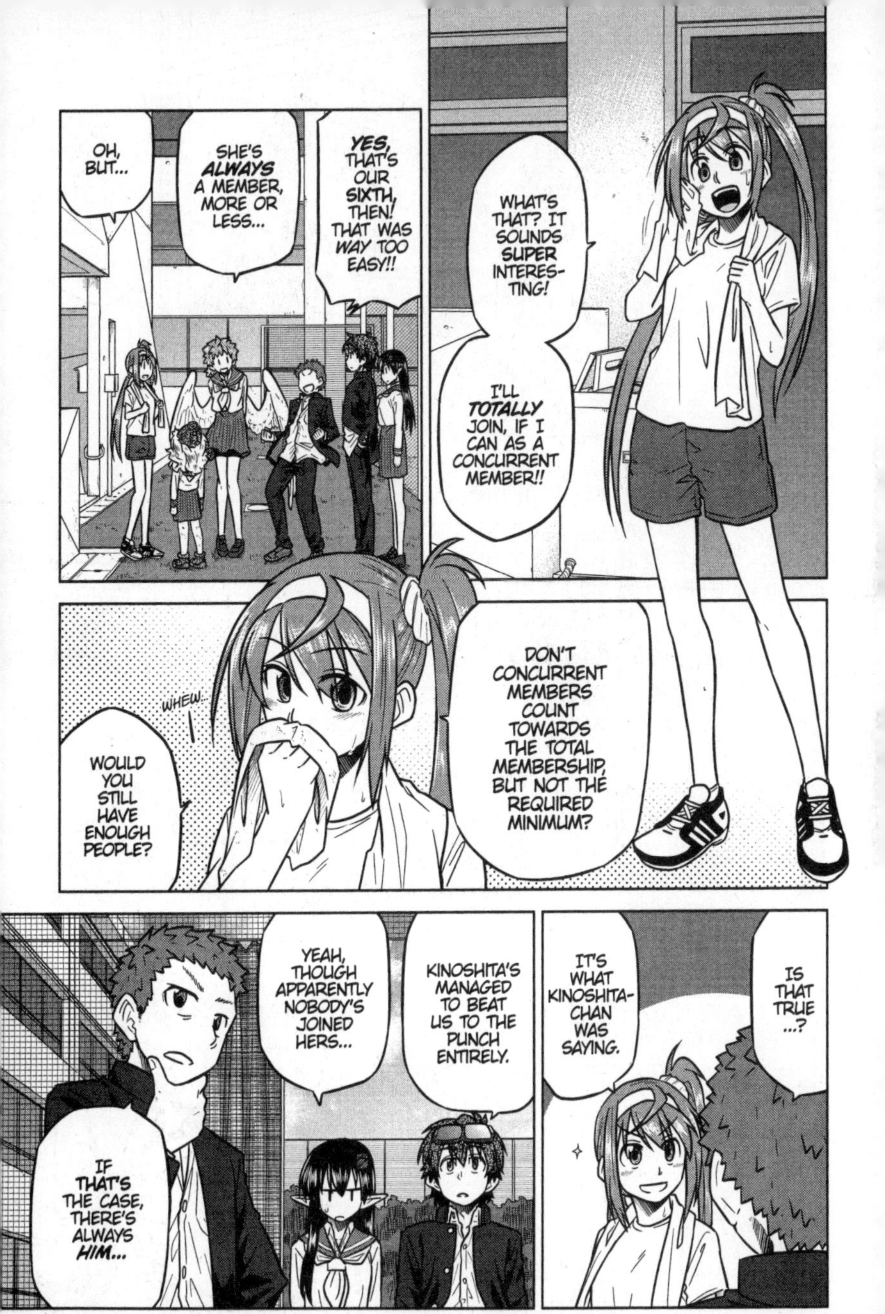
WHAT'S THAT? IT SOUNDS SUPER INTERESTING!
I'LL TOTALLY JOIN, IF I CAN AS A CONCURRENT MEMBER!!
YES, THAT'S OUR SIXTH, THEN! THAT WAS WAY TOO EASY!!
SHE'S ALWAYS A MEMBER, MORE OR LESS...
OH, BUT...
DON'T CONCURRENT MEMBERS COUNT TOWARDS THE TOTAL MEMBERSHIP, BUT NOT THE REQUIRED MINIMUM?
WHEW...
WOULD YOU STILL HAVE ENOUGH PEOPLE?
IS THAT TRUE...?
IT'S WHAT KINOSHITA-CHAN WAS SAYING.
KINOSHITA'S MANAGED TO BEAT US TO THE PUNCH ENTIRELY.
YEAH, THOUGH APPARENTLY NOBODY'S JOINED HERS...
IF THAT'S THE CASE, THERE'S ALWAYS HIM...

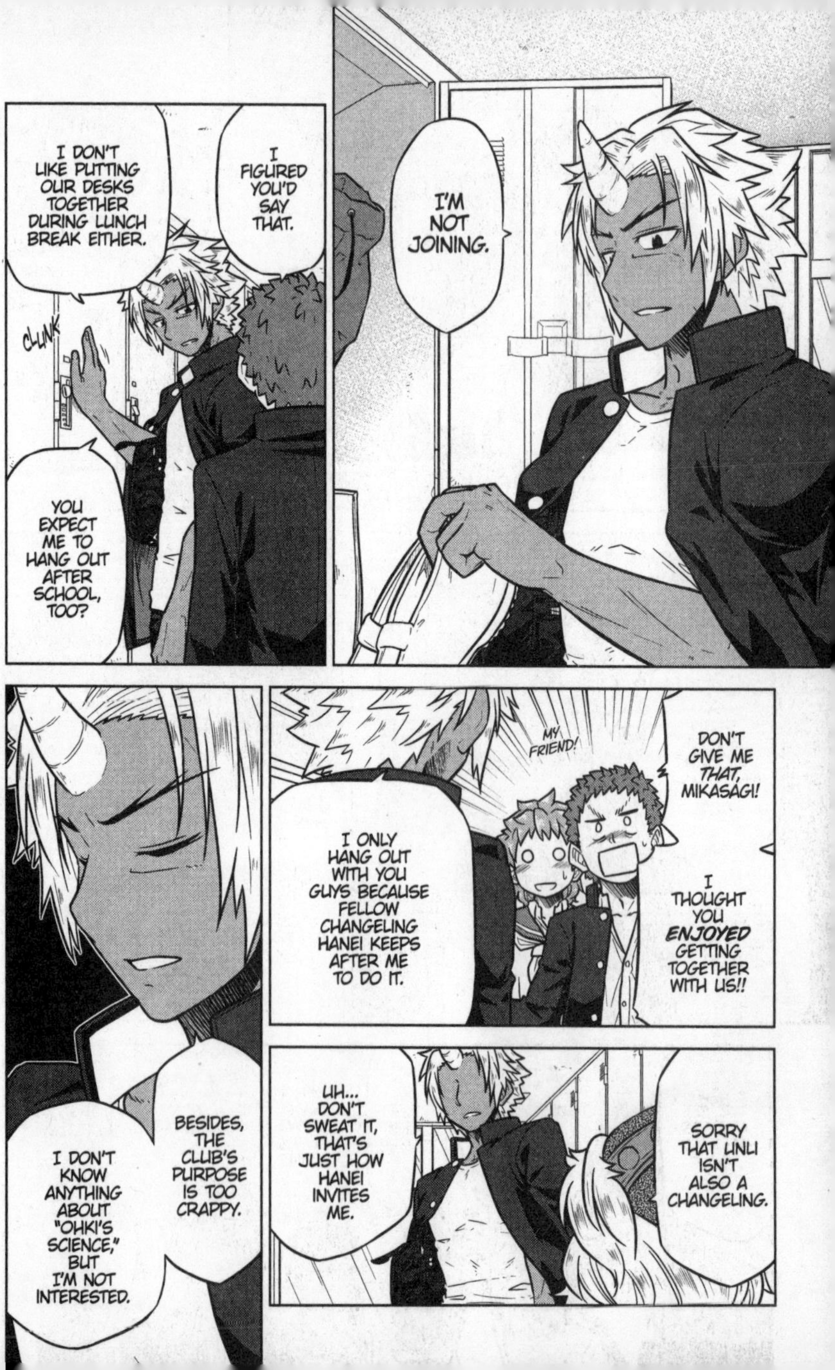
I'M NOT JOINING.
I FIGURED YOU'D SAY THAT.
I DON'T LIKE PUTTING OUR DESKS TOGETHER DURING LUNCH BREAK EITHER.
CLUNK
YOU EXPECT ME TO HANG OUT AFTER SCHOOL, TOO?
DON'T GIVE ME *THAT*, MIKASAGI!
MY FRIEND!
I THOUGHT YOU **ENJOYED** GETTING TOGETHER WITH US!!
I ONLY HANG OUT WITH YOU GUYS BECAUSE FELLOW CHANGELING HANEI KEEPS AFTER ME TO DO IT.
SORRY THAT UNLI ISN'T ALSO A CHANGELING.
UH... DON'T SWEAT IT, THAT'S JUST HOW HANEI INVITES ME.
BESIDES, THE CLUB'S PURPOSE IS TOO CRAPPY.
I DON'T KNOW ANYTHING ABOUT "OHKI'S SCIENCE," BUT I'M NOT INTERESTED.

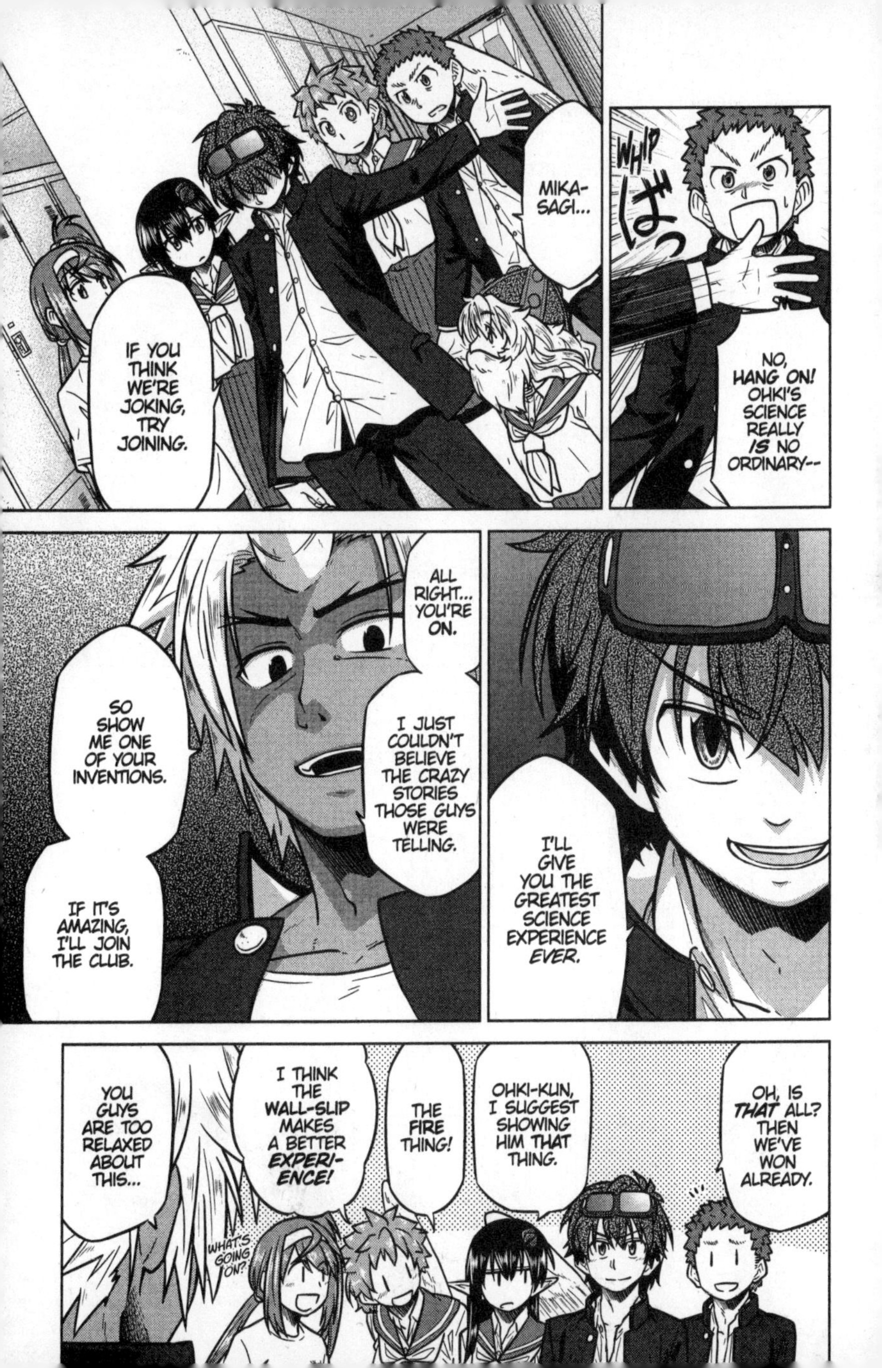
WHIP
ぱっ
NO, HANG ON! OHKI'S SCIENCE REALLY *IS* NO ORDINARY--
MIKA-SAGI...
IF YOU THINK WE'RE JOKING, TRY JOINING.
I'LL GIVE YOU THE GREATEST SCIENCE EXPERIENCE *EVER.*
ALL RIGHT... YOU'RE ON.
I JUST COULDN'T BELIEVE THE CRAZY STORIES THOSE GUYS WERE TELLING.
SO SHOW ME ONE OF YOUR INVENTIONS.
IF IT'S AMAZING, I'LL JOIN THE CLUB.
OH, IS *THAT* ALL? THEN WE'VE WON ALREADY.
OHKI-KUN, I SUGGEST SHOWING HIM THAT THING.
THE FIRE THING!
I THINK THE WALL-SLIP MAKES A BETTER *EXPERI-ENCE!*
WHAT'S GOING ON?
YOU GUYS ARE TOO RELAXED ABOUT THIS...

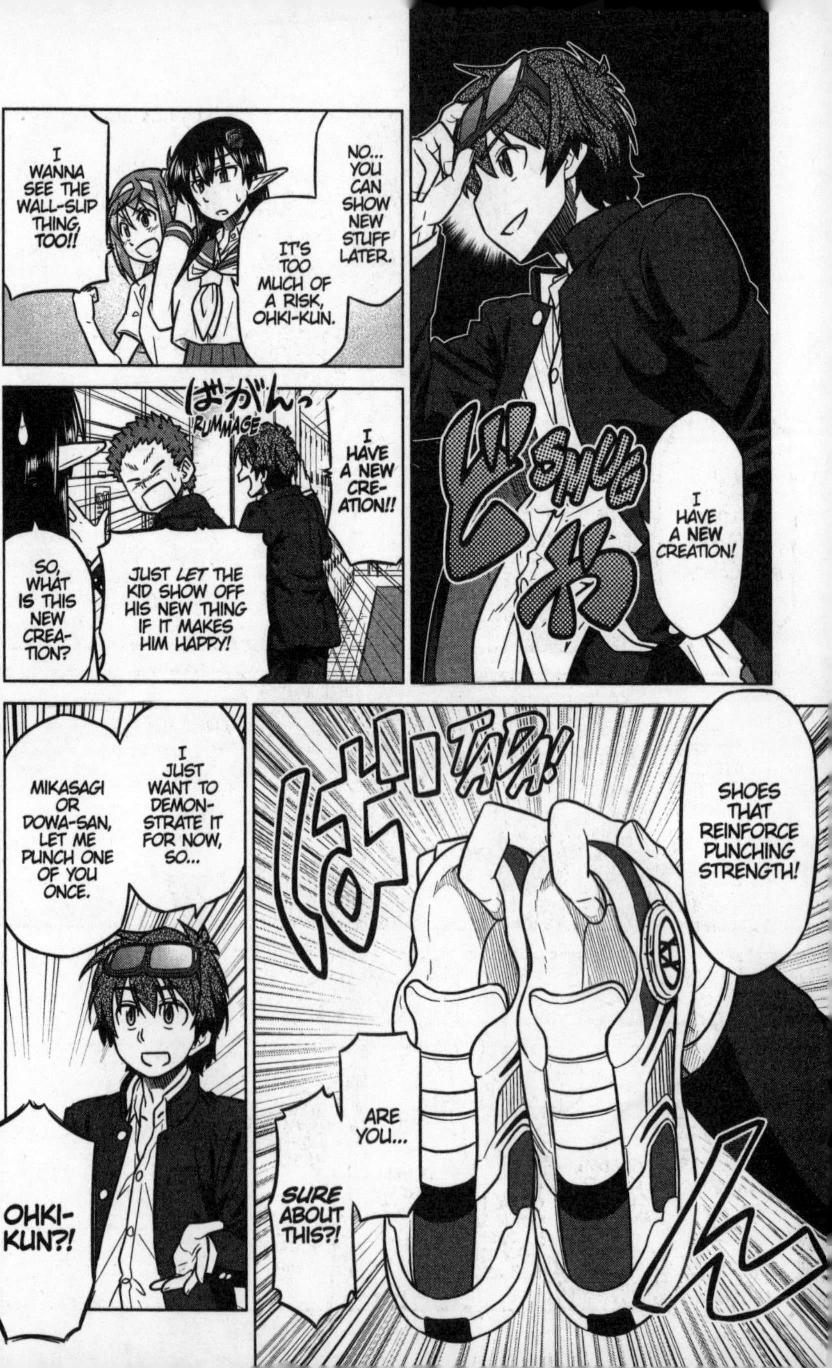
I HAVE A NEW CREATION!
NO... YOU CAN SHOW NEW STUFF LATER.
IT'S TOO MUCH OF A RISK, OHKI-KUN.
I WANNA SEE THE WALL-SLIP THING, TOO!!
ばがんっ
RUMMAGE
I HAVE A NEW CREATION!!
JUST LET THE KID SHOW OFF HIS NEW THING IF IT MAKES HIM HAPPY!
SO, WHAT IS THIS NEW CREATION?
TADA!
SHOES THAT REINFORCE PUNCHING STRENGTH!
ARE YOU...
SURE ABOUT THIS?!
I JUST WANT TO DEMONSTRATE IT FOR NOW, SO...
MIKASAGI OR DOWA-SAN, LET ME PUNCH ONE OF YOU ONCE.
OHKI-KUN?!

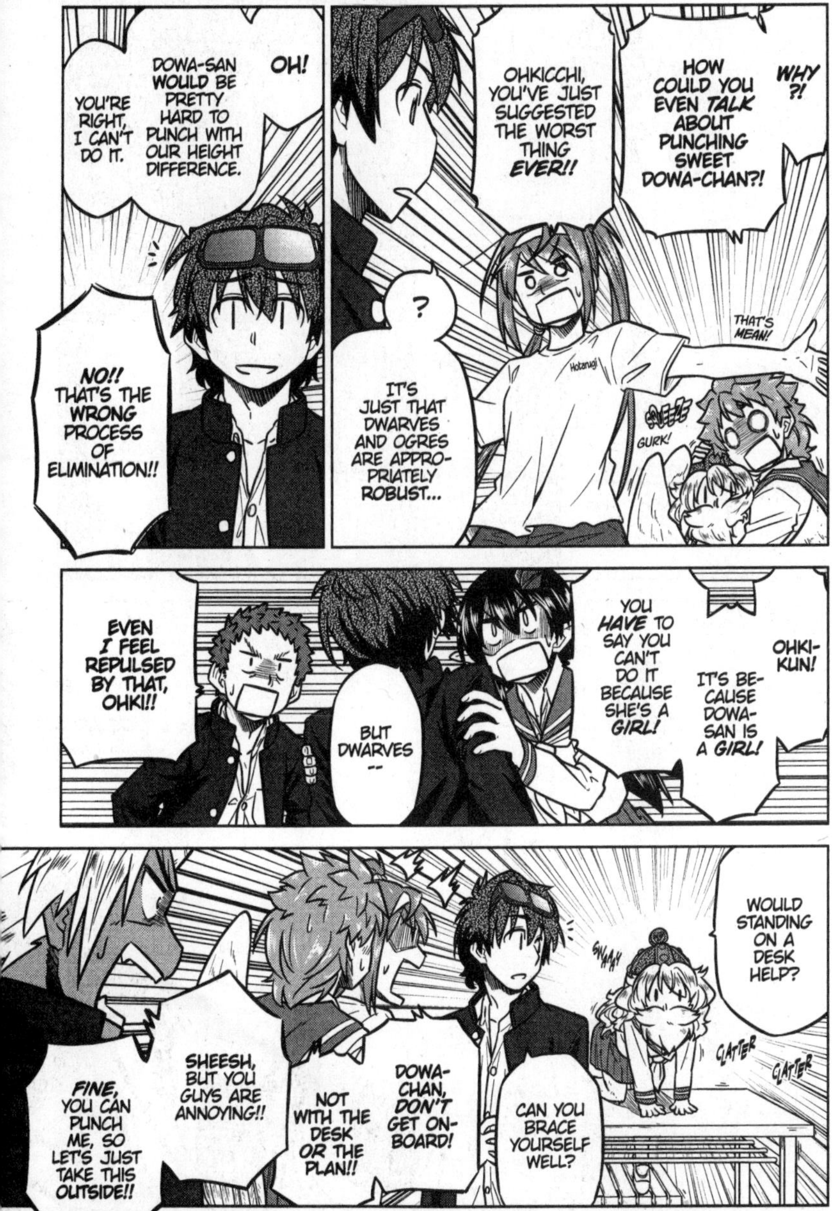
WHY?!
HOW COULD YOU EVEN TALK ABOUT PUNCHING SWEET DOWA-CHAN?!
OHKICCHI, YOU'VE JUST SUGGESTED THE WORST THING EVER!!
THAT'S MEAN!
GURK!
?
IT'S JUST THAT DWARVES AND OGRES ARE APPRO-PRIATELY ROBUST...
OH!
DOWA-SAN WOULD BE PRETTY HARD TO PUNCH WITH OUR HEIGHT DIFFERENCE.
YOU'RE RIGHT, I CAN'T DO IT.
NO!! THAT'S THE WRONG PROCESS OF ELIMINATION!!
OHKI-KUN!
IT'S BE-CAUSE DOWA-SAN IS A GIRL!
YOU HAVE TO SAY YOU CAN'T DO IT BECAUSE SHE'S A GIRL!
BUT DWARVES --
EVEN I FEEL REPULSED BY THAT, OHKI!!
WOULD STANDING ON A DESK HELP?
CLATTER
CLATTER
CAN YOU BRACE YOURSELF WELL?
DOWA-CHAN, DON'T GET ON-BOARD!
NOT WITH THE DESK OR THE PLAN!!
SHEESH, BUT YOU GUYS ARE ANNOYING!!
FINE, YOU CAN PUNCH ME, SO LET'S JUST TAKE THIS OUTSIDE!!

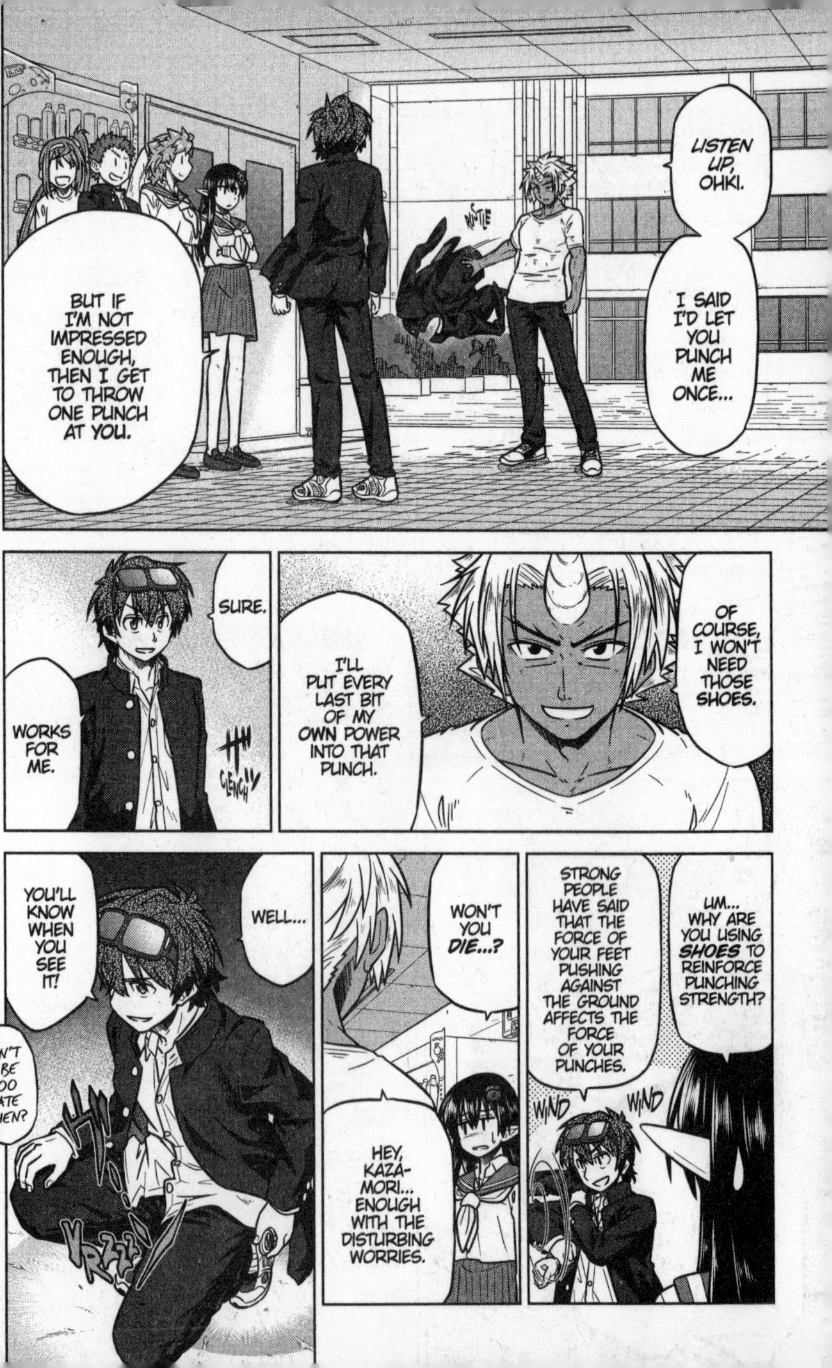
LISTEN UP, OHKI.
I SAID I'D LET YOU PUNCH ME ONCE...
RUSTLE
BUT IF I'M NOT IMPRESSED ENOUGH, THEN I GET TO THROW ONE PUNCH AT YOU.
OF COURSE, I WON'T NEED THOSE SHOES.
I'LL PUT EVERY LAST BIT OF MY OWN POWER INTO THAT PUNCH.
SURE.
WORKS FOR ME.
CLENCH
UM... WHY ARE YOU USING SHOES TO REINFORCE PUNCHING STRENGTH?
STRONG PEOPLE HAVE SAID THAT THE FORCE OF YOUR FEET PUSHING AGAINST THE GROUND AFFECTS THE FORCE OF YOUR PUNCHES.
WIND
WIND
WON'T YOU *DIE...?*
HEY, KAZAMORI... ENOUGH WITH THE DISTURBING WORRIES.
WELL...
YOU'LL KNOW WHEN YOU SEE IT!
WON'T IT BE TOO LATE THEN?

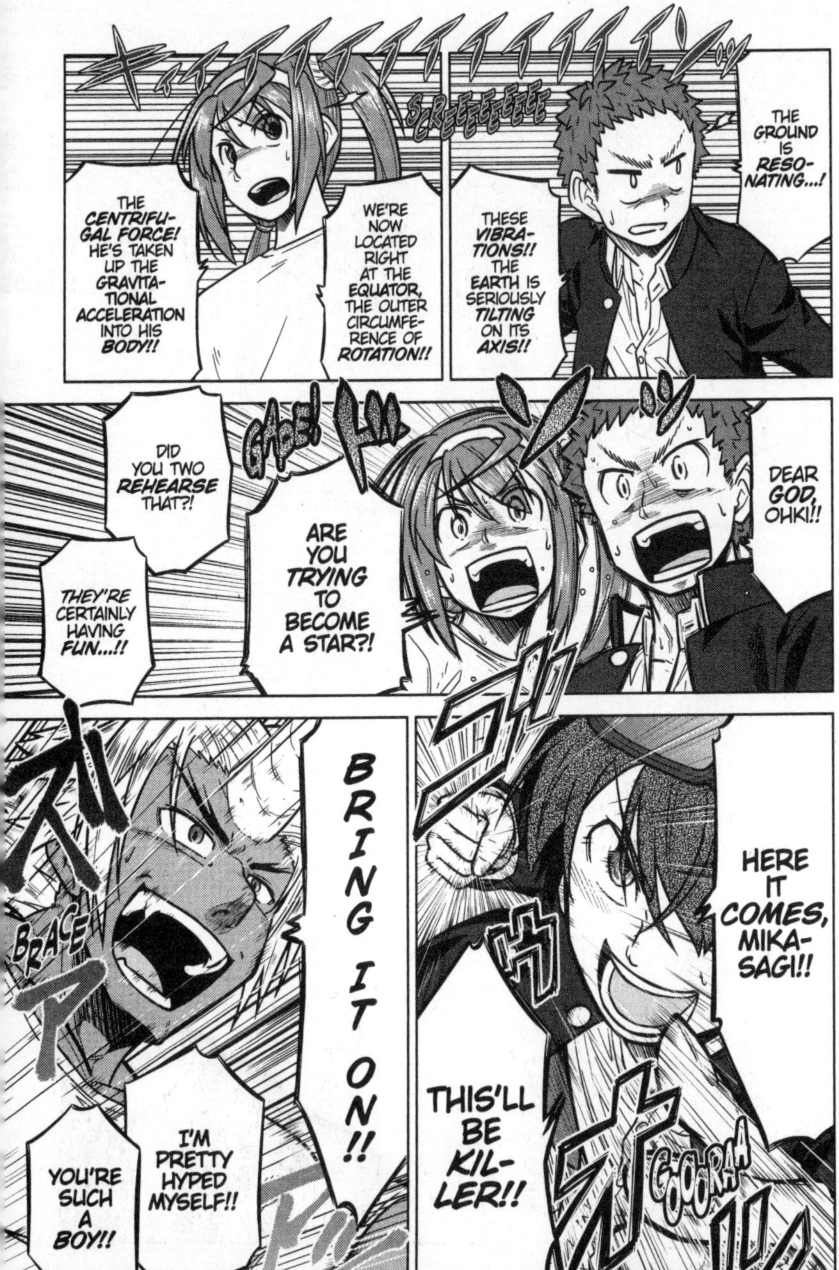
SCREEEEEEEE
THE GROUND IS RESO-NATING...!
THESE VIBRA-TIONS!! THE EARTH IS SERIOUSLY TILTING ON ITS AXIS!!
WE'RE NOW LOCATED RIGHT AT THE EQUATOR, THE OUTER CIRCUMFE-RENCE OF ROTATION!!
THE CENTRIFU-GAL FORCE! HE'S TAKEN UP THE GRAVITA-TIONAL ACCELERATION INTO HIS BODY!!
DEAR GOD, OHKI!!
ARE YOU TRYING TO BECOME A STAR?!
DID YOU TWO REHEARSE THAT?!
THEY'RE CERTAINLY HAVING FUN...!!
HERE IT COMES, MIKA-SAGI!!
THIS'LL BE KIL-LER!!
GOOORAH
BRING IT ON!!
BRACE
I'M PRETTY HYPED MYSELF!!
YOU'RE SUCH A BOY!!

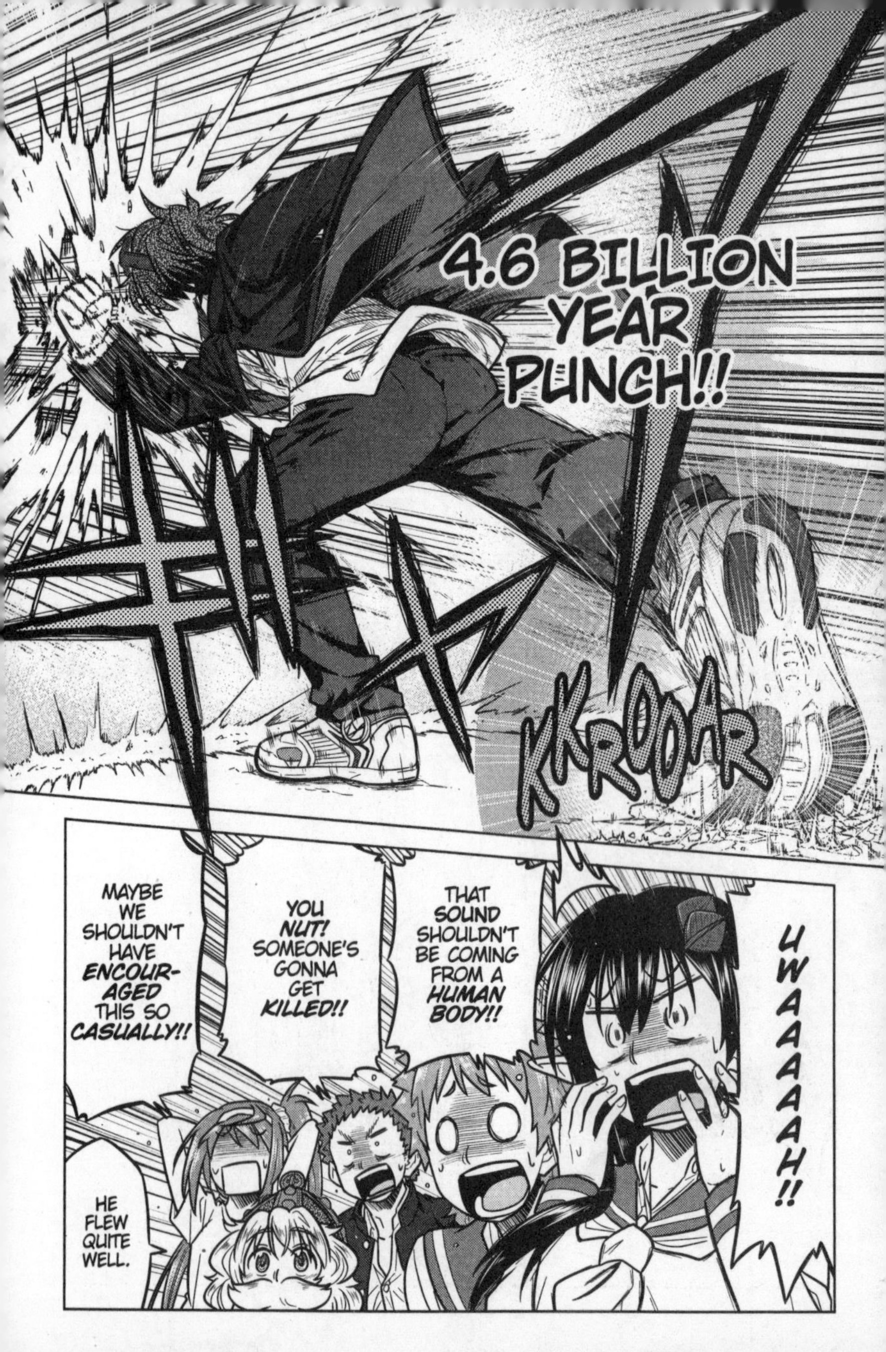
4.6 BILLION YEAR PUNCH!!
KKROOAR
UWAAAAAAAH!!
THAT SOUND SHOULDN'T BE COMING FROM A HUMAN BODY!!
YOU NUT! SOMEONE'S GONNA GET KILLED!!
MAYBE WE SHOULDN'T HAVE ENCOURAGED THIS SO CASUALLY!!
HE FLEW QUITE WELL.

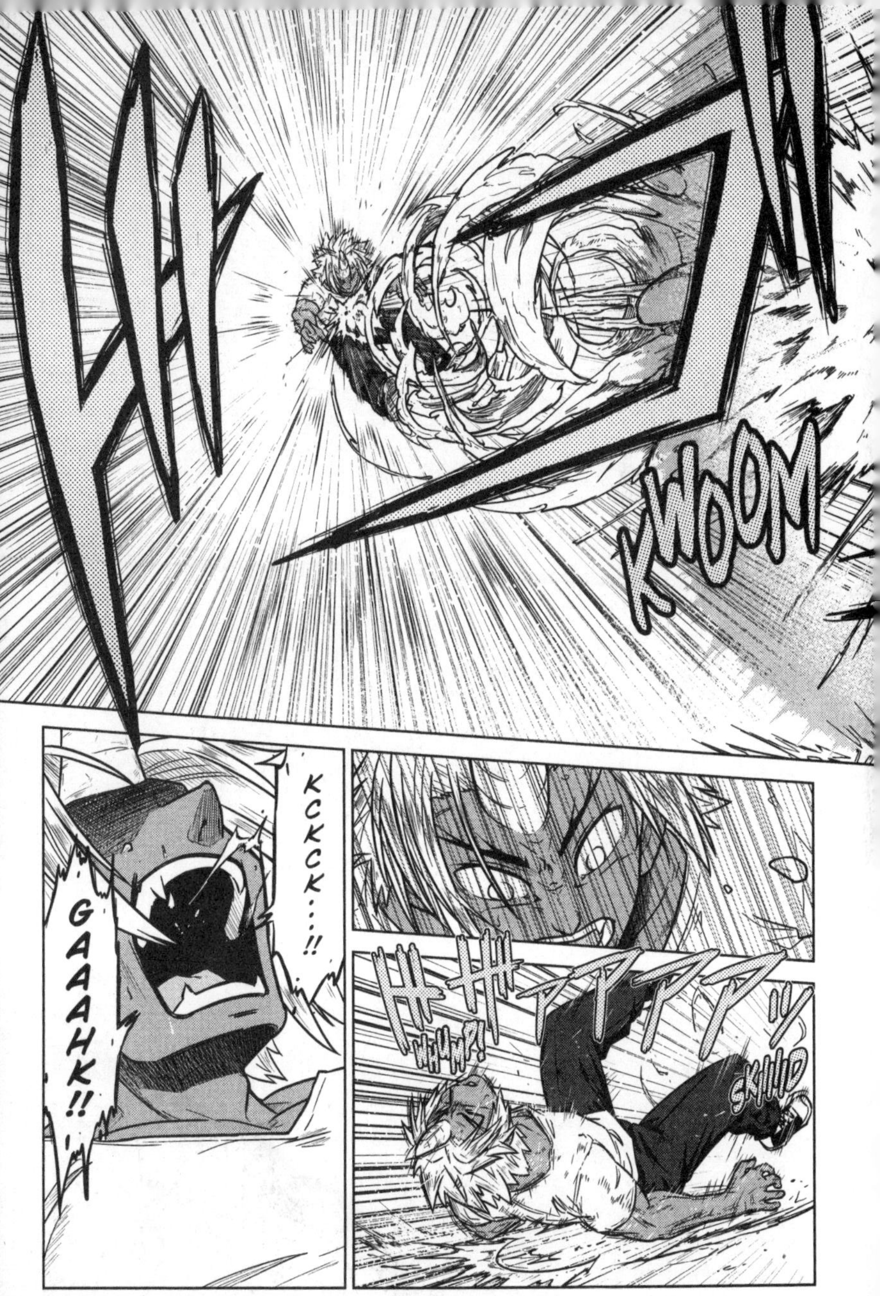
KWOOM
WHUMP!
SKIIID
KCKCK...!!
GAAAAHK!!

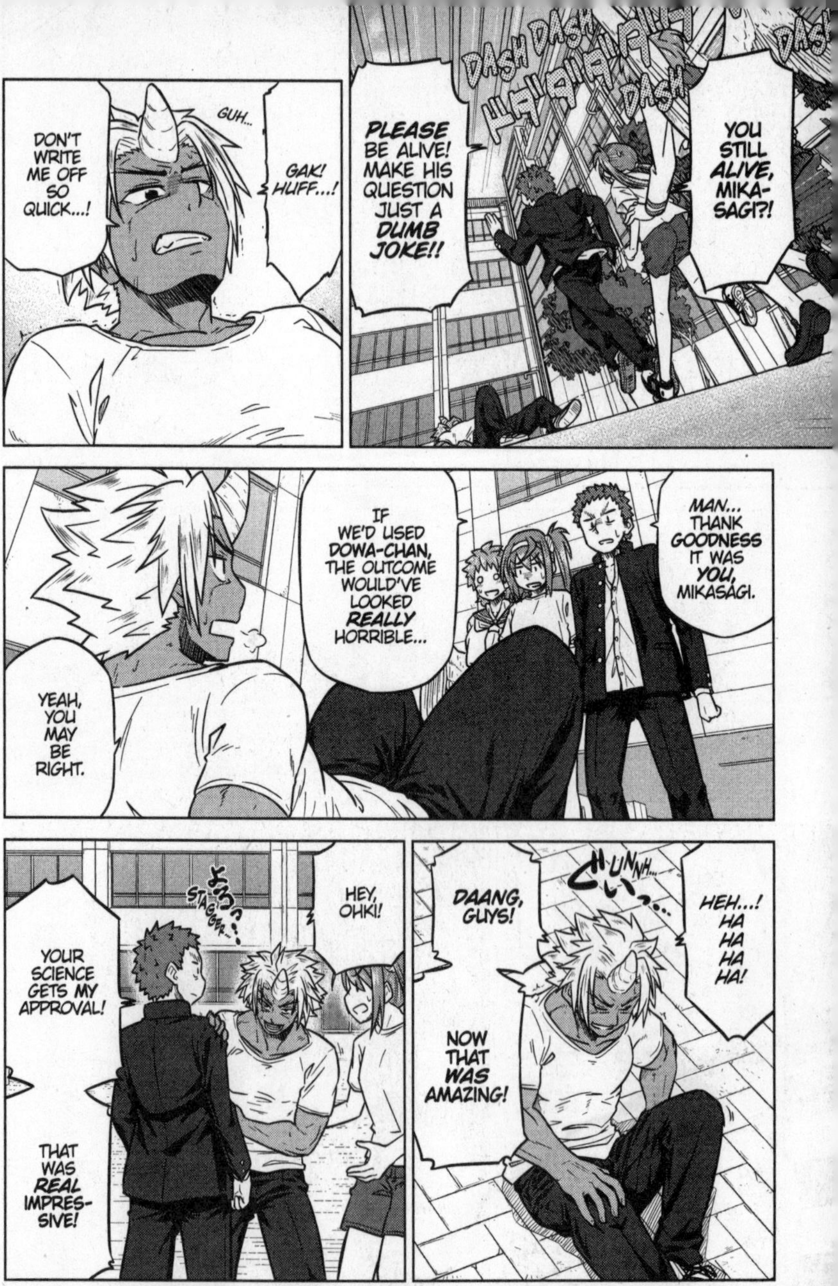
DASH DASH
DASH
DASH
YOU STILL ALIVE, MIKASAGI?!
PLEASE BE ALIVE! MAKE HIS QUESTION JUST A DUMB JOKE!!
GAK! HUFF...!
GUH...
DON'T WRITE ME OFF SO QUICK...!
MAN... THANK GOODNESS IT WAS YOU, MIKASAGI.
IF WE'D USED DOWA-CHAN, THE OUTCOME WOULD'VE LOOKED REALLY HORRIBLE...
YEAH, YOU MAY BE RIGHT.
HEH...! HA HA HA HA!
CHUNNH...
DAANG, GUYS!
NOW THAT WAS AMAZING!
HEY, OHKI!
STAGGER...
YOUR SCIENCE GETS MY APPROVAL!
THAT WAS REAL IMPRESSIVE!

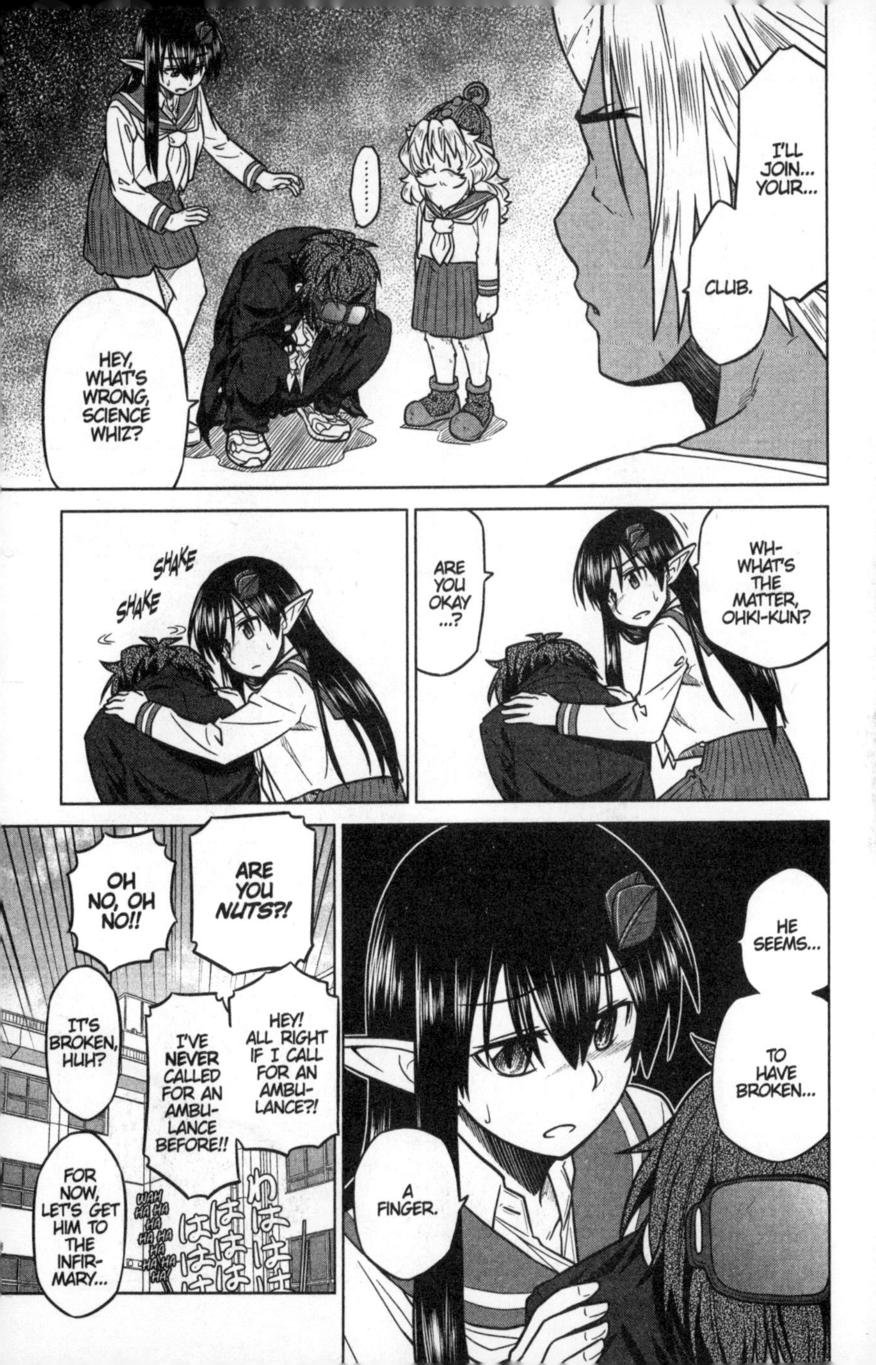
I'LL JOIN... YOUR...
CLUB.
......
HEY, WHAT'S WRONG, SCIENCE WHIZ?
WH- WHAT'S THE MATTER, OHKI-KUN?
ARE YOU OKAY ...?
SHAKE
SHAKE
HE SEEMS...
TO HAVE BROKEN...
A FINGER.
ARE YOU NUTS?!
OH NO, OH NO!!
HEY! ALL RIGHT IF I CALL FOR AN AMBULANCE?!
I'VE NEVER CALLED FOR AN AMBULANCE BEFORE!!
IT'S BROKEN, HUH?
WAH HA HA HA HA HA HA HA HA HA!
FOR NOW, LET'S GET HIM TO THE INFIRMARY...

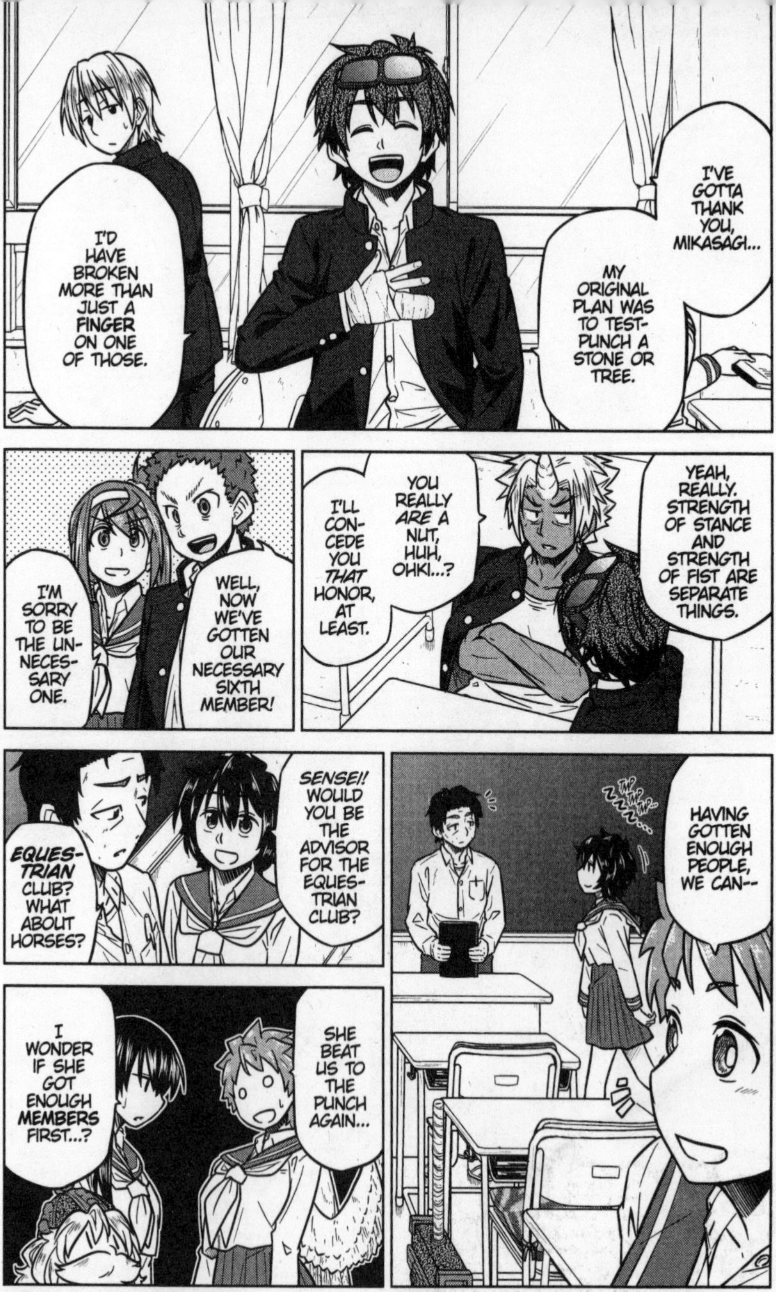
I'VE GOTTA THANK YOU, MIKASAGI...
MY ORIGINAL PLAN WAS TO TEST-PUNCH A STONE OR TREE.
I'D HAVE BROKEN MORE THAN JUST A FINGER ON ONE OF THOSE.
YEAH, REALLY. STRENGTH OF STANCE AND STRENGTH OF FIST ARE SEPARATE THINGS.
YOU REALLY *ARE* A NUT, HUH, OHKI...?
I'LL CONCEDE YOU *THAT* HONOR, AT LEAST.
WELL, NOW WE'VE GOTTEN OUR NECESSARY SIXTH MEMBER!
I'M SORRY TO BE THE UNNECESSARY ONE.
HAVING GOTTEN ENOUGH PEOPLE, WE CAN--
THP THP THP...
SENSE!! WOULD YOU BE THE ADVISOR FOR THE EQUESTRIAN CLUB?
EQUESTRIAN CLUB? WHAT ABOUT HORSES?
SHE BEAT US TO THE PUNCH AGAIN...
I WONDER IF SHE GOT ENOUGH MEMBERS FIRST...?

Species Domain Vol. 1 / End

Species
スピーシーズドメイン
Domain

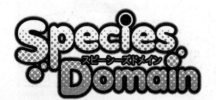

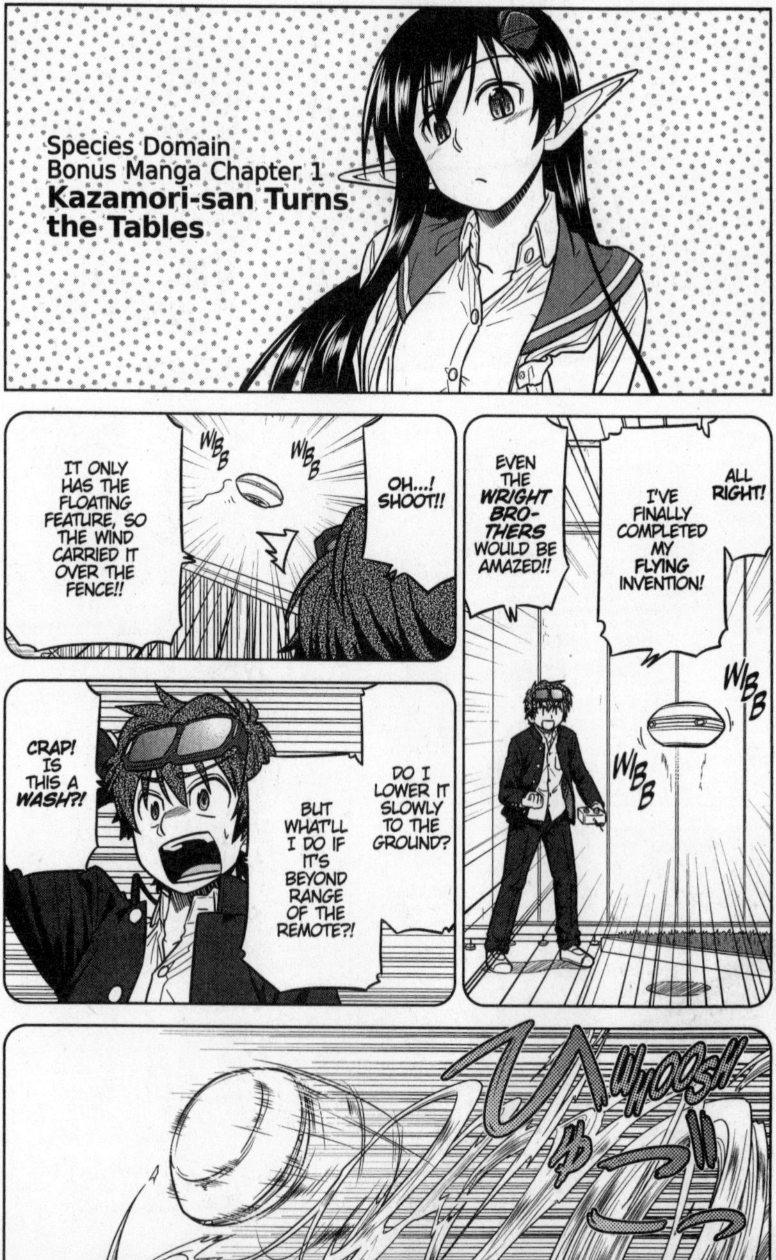
Species Domain
Bonus Manga Chapter 1
Kazamori-san Turns the Tables
ALL RIGHT!
I'VE FINALLY COMPLETED MY FLYING INVENTION!
EVEN THE WRIGHT BROTHERS WOULD BE AMAZED!!
WIBB
WIBB
OH...! SHOOT!!
WIBB
WIBB
IT ONLY HAS THE FLOATING FEATURE, SO THE WIND CARRIED IT OVER THE FENCE!!
DO I LOWER IT SLOWLY TO THE GROUND?
BUT WHAT'LL I DO IF IT'S BEYOND RANGE OF THE REMOTE?!
CRAP! IS THIS A WASH?!
WHOOSH!!

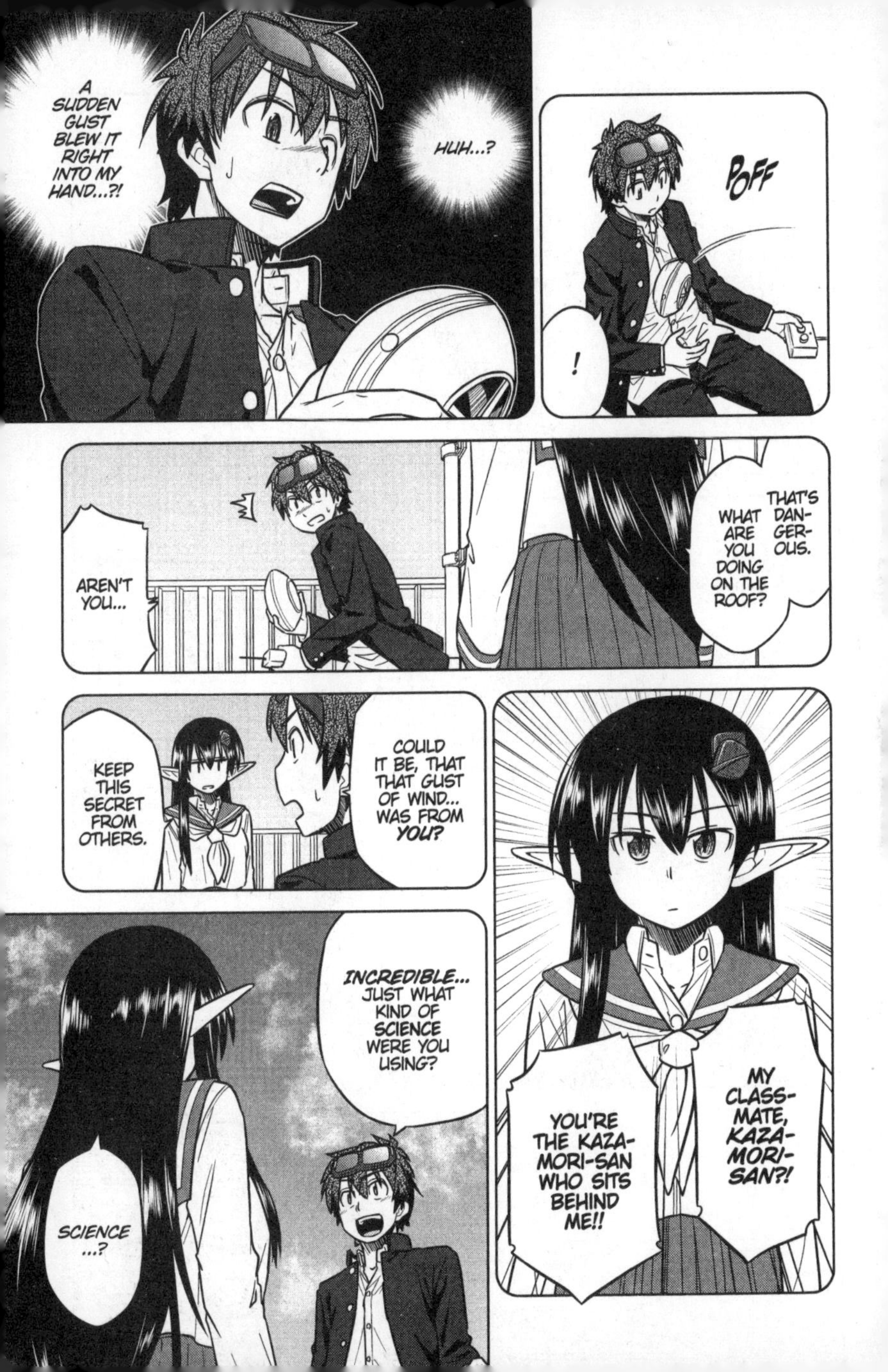
POFF
!
HUH...?
A SUDDEN GUST BLEW IT RIGHT INTO MY HAND...?!
THAT'S DANGEROUS.
WHAT ARE YOU DOING ON THE ROOF?
AREN'T YOU...
MY CLASSMATE, KAZAMORI-SAN?!
YOU'RE THE KAZAMORI-SAN WHO SITS BEHIND ME!!
COULD IT BE, THAT THAT GUST OF WIND... WAS FROM *YOU?*
KEEP THIS SECRET FROM OTHERS.
INCREDIBLE... JUST WHAT KIND OF SCIENCE WERE YOU USING?
SCIENCE...?

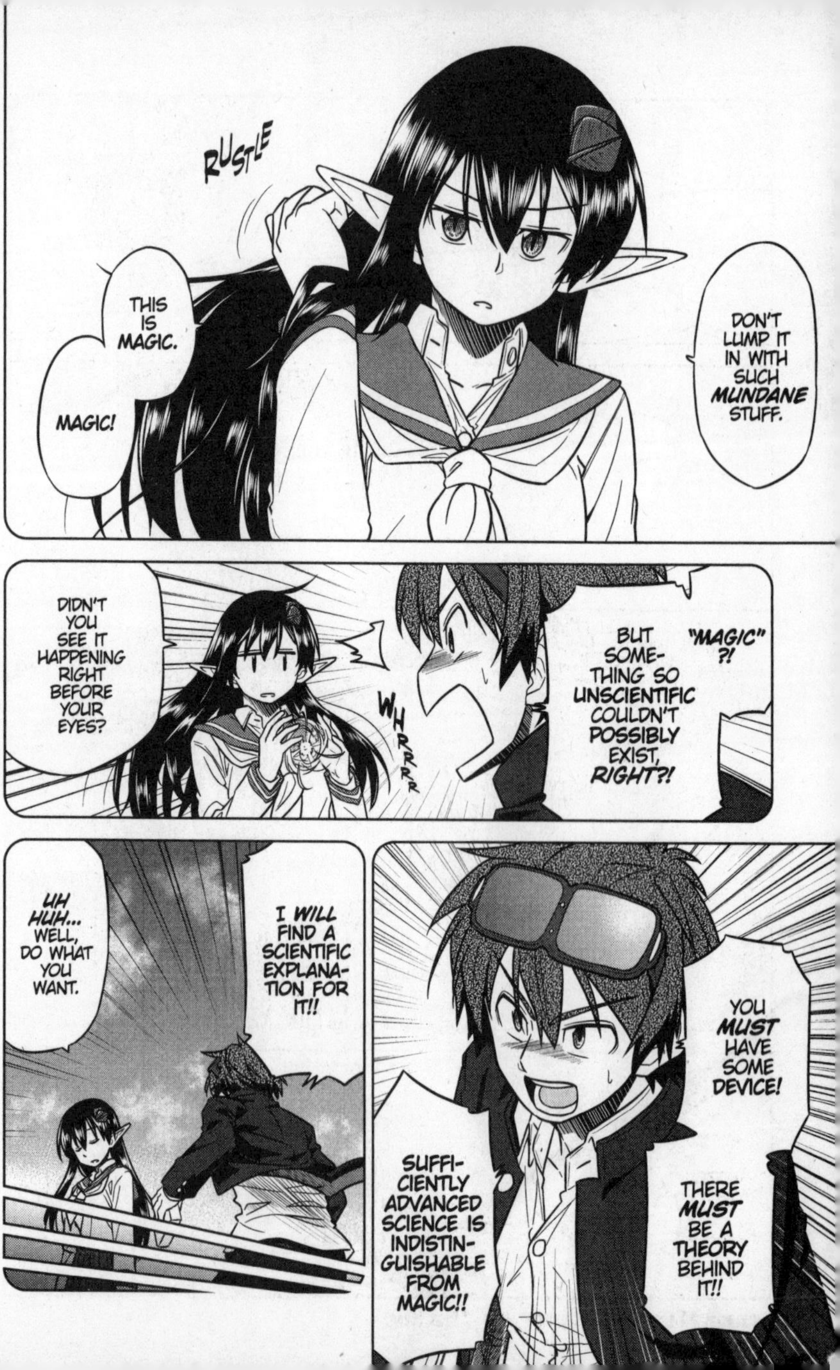
DON'T LUMP IT IN WITH SUCH MUNDANE STUFF.
RUSTLE
THIS IS MAGIC.
MAGIC!
"MAGIC" ?!
BUT SOME-THING SO UNSCIENTIFIC COULDN'T POSSIBLY EXIST, RIGHT?!
WHRRRR
DIDN'T YOU SEE IT HAPPENING RIGHT BEFORE YOUR EYES?
YOU MUST HAVE SOME DEVICE!
THERE MUST BE A THEORY BEHIND IT!!
SUFFI-CIENTLY ADVANCED SCIENCE IS INDISTIN-GUISHABLE FROM MAGIC!!
I WILL FIND A SCIENTIFIC EXPLANA-TION FOR IT!!
UH HUH... WELL, DO WHAT YOU WANT.

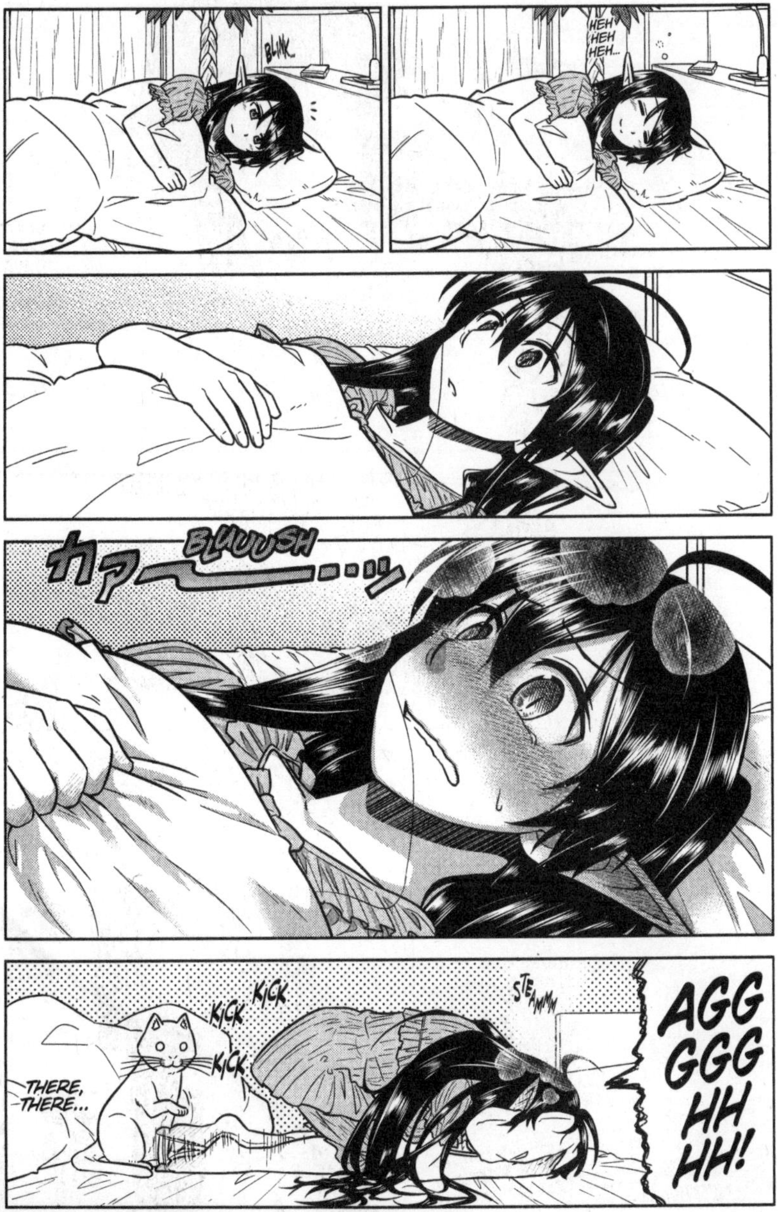
HEH HEH HEH...
BLINK...
カァ〜…ッ
BLUUUSH
AGG GGG HH HH!
STEAMMM
KICK
KICK
KICK
THERE, THERE...

Bonus Manga: Chapter 1 • The End

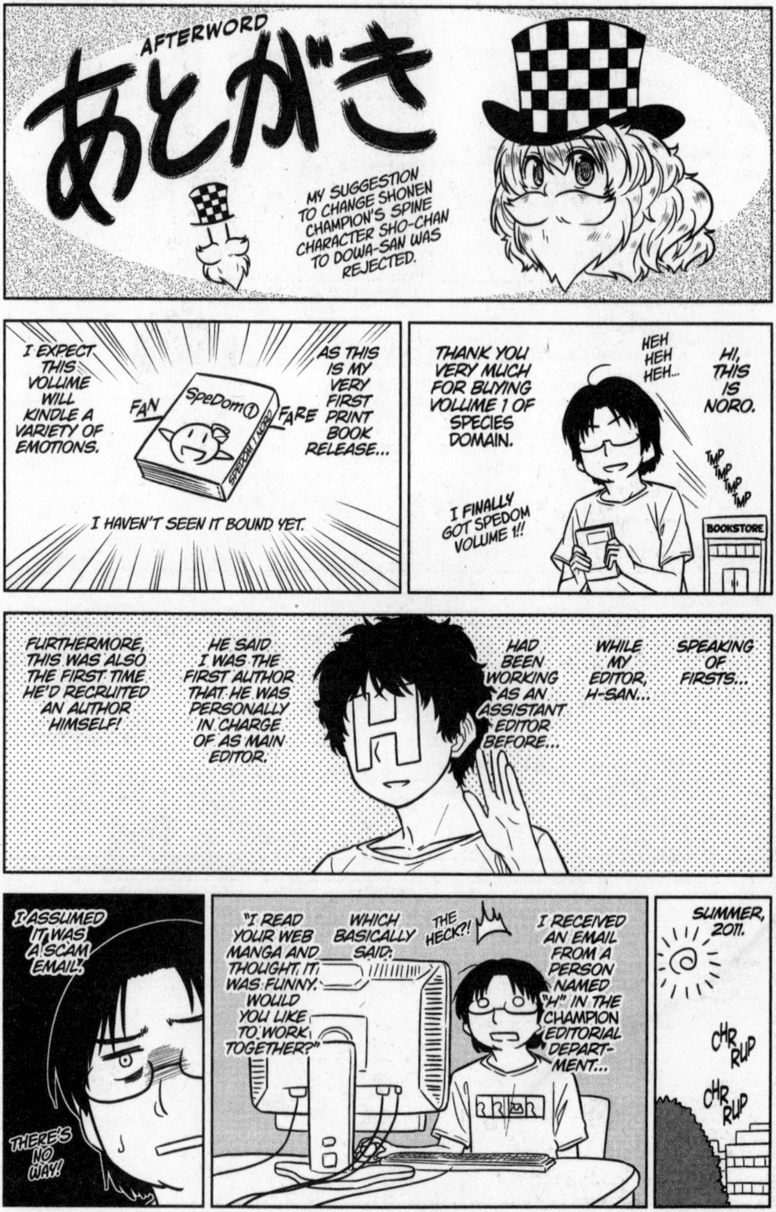
AFTERWORD
あとがき
MY SUGGESTION TO CHANGE SHONEN CHAMPION'S SPINE CHARACTER SHO-CHAN TO DOWA-SAN WAS REJECTED.
HI, THIS IS NORO.
HEH HEH HEH...
THANK YOU VERY MUCH FOR BUYING VOLUME 1 OF SPECIES DOMAIN.
TMP TMP TMP TMP
I FINALLY GOT SPEDOM VOLUME 1!!
BOOKSTORE
AS THIS IS MY VERY FIRST PRINT BOOK RELEASE...
FARE
SpeDom 1
SPEDOM 1 NORO
FAN
I EXPECT THIS VOLUME WILL KINDLE A VARIETY OF EMOTIONS.
I HAVEN'T SEEN IT BOUND YET.
SPEAKING OF FIRSTS...
WHILE MY EDITOR, H-SAN...
HAD BEEN WORKING AS AN ASSISTANT EDITOR BEFORE...
HE SAID I WAS THE FIRST AUTHOR THAT HE WAS PERSONALLY IN CHARGE OF AS MAIN EDITOR.
FURTHERMORE, THIS WAS ALSO THE FIRST TIME HE'D RECRUITED AN AUTHOR HIMSELF!
SUMMER, 2011.
CHR RUP
CHR RUP
I RECEIVED AN EMAIL FROM A PERSON NAMED "H" IN THE CHAMPION EDITORIAL DEPART-MENT...
THE HECK?!
WHICH BASICALLY SAID:
"I READ YOUR WEB MANGA AND THOUGHT IT WAS FUNNY. WOULD YOU LIKE TO WORK TOGETHER?"
I ASSUMED IT WAS A SCAM EMAIL.
THERE'S NO WAY!

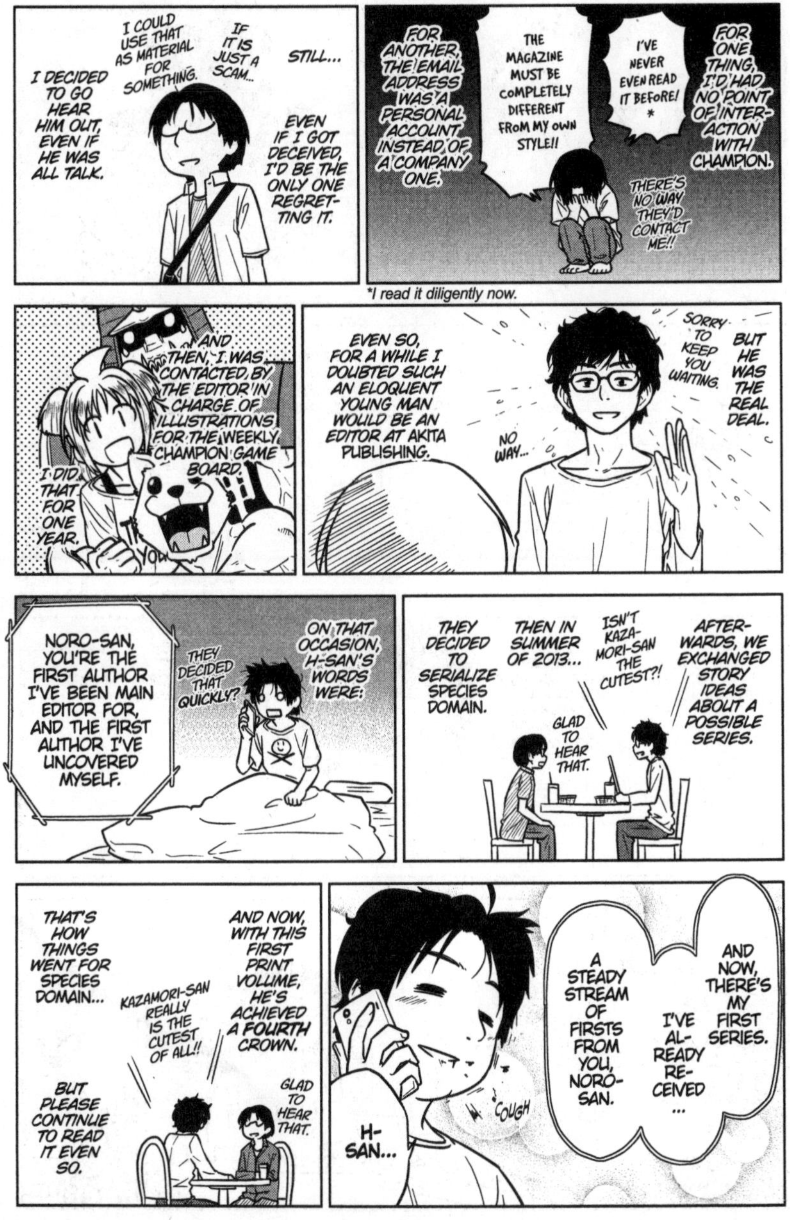
FOR ONE THING, I'D HAD NO POINT OF INTERACTION WITH CHAMPION.
I'VE NEVER EVEN READ IT BEFORE! *
THE MAGAZINE MUST BE COMPLETELY DIFFERENT FROM MY OWN STYLE!!
FOR ANOTHER, THE EMAIL ADDRESS WAS A PERSONAL ACCOUNT INSTEAD OF A COMPANY ONE.
THERE'S NO WAY THEY'D CONTACT ME!!
STILL...
IF IT IS JUST A SCAM...
I COULD USE THAT AS MATERIAL FOR SOMETHING.
I DECIDED TO GO HEAR HIM OUT, EVEN IF HE WAS ALL TALK.
EVEN IF I GOT DECEIVED, I'D BE THE ONLY ONE REGRETTING IT.
*I read it diligently now.
BUT HE WAS THE REAL DEAL.
SORRY TO KEEP YOU WAITING.
EVEN SO, FOR A WHILE I DOUBTED SUCH AN ELOQUENT YOUNG MAN WOULD BE AN EDITOR AT AKITA PUBLISHING.
NO WAY...
AND THEN, I WAS CONTACTED BY THE EDITOR IN CHARGE OF ILLUSTRATIONS FOR THE WEEKLY CHAMPION GAME BOARD.
I DID THAT FOR ONE YEAR.
AFTERWARDS, WE EXCHANGED STORY IDEAS ABOUT A POSSIBLE SERIES.
ISN'T KAZAMORI-SAN THE CUTEST?!
THEN IN SUMMER OF 2013...
THEY DECIDED TO SERIALIZE SPECIES DOMAIN.
GLAD TO HEAR THAT.
ON THAT OCCASION, H-SAN'S WORDS WERE:
THEY DECIDED THAT QUICKLY?
NORO-SAN, YOU'RE THE FIRST AUTHOR I'VE BEEN MAIN EDITOR FOR, AND THE FIRST AUTHOR I'VE UNCOVERED MYSELF.
AND NOW, THERE'S MY FIRST SERIES.
I'VE ALREADY RECEIVED...
A STEADY STREAM OF FIRSTS FROM YOU, NORO-SAN.
H-SAN...
COUGH
AND NOW, WITH THIS FIRST PRINT VOLUME, HE'S ACHIEVED A FOURTH CROWN.
KAZAMORI-SAN REALLY IS THE CUTEST OF ALL!!
THAT'S HOW THINGS WENT FOR SPECIES DOMAIN...
GLAD TO HEAR THAT.
BUT PLEASE CONTINUE TO READ IT EVEN SO.

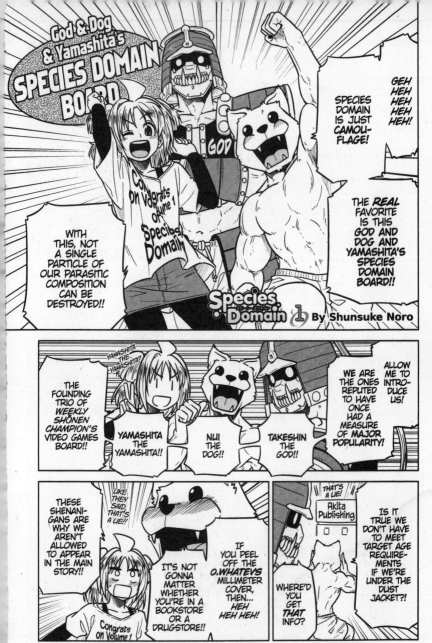

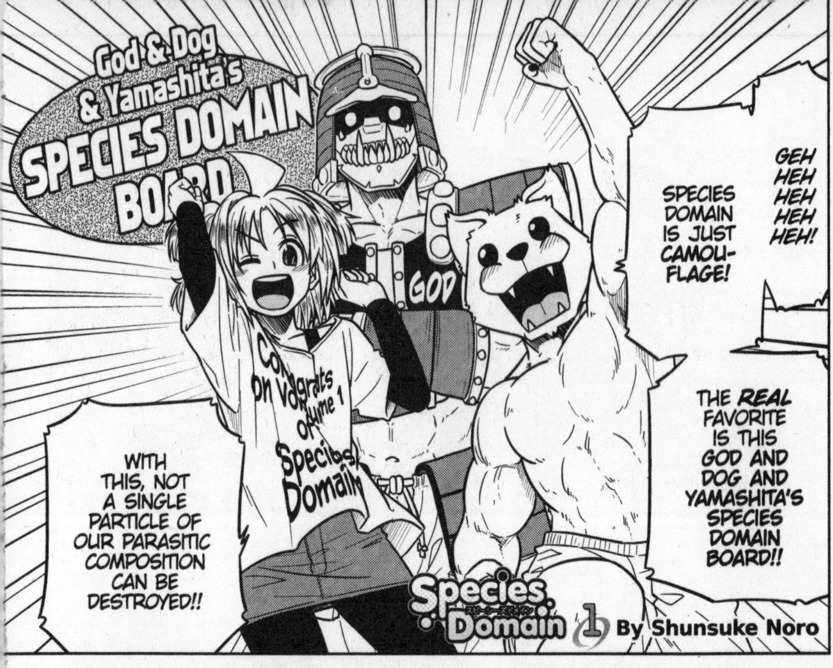
God & Dog & Yamashita's
SPECIES DOMAIN BOARD
GEH HEH HEH HEH HEH!
SPECIES DOMAIN IS JUST CAMOUFLAGE!
GOD
THE *REAL* FAVORITE IS THIS GOD AND DOG AND YAMASHITA'S SPECIES DOMAIN BOARD!!
Congrats on Volume 1 of Species Domain
WITH THIS, NOT A SINGLE PARTICLE OF OUR PARASITIC COMPOSITION CAN BE DESTROYED!!
Species Domain 1 By Shunsuke Noro

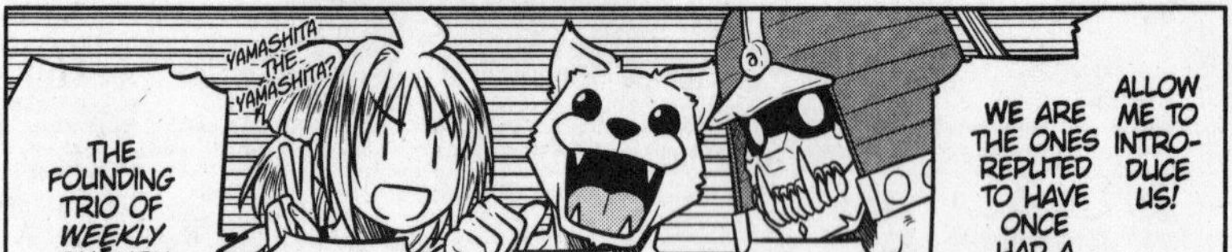
ALLOW ME TO INTRODUCE US!
WE ARE THE ONES REPUTED TO HAVE ONCE HAD A MEASURE OF MAJOR POPULARITY!
TAKESHIN THE GOD!!
NUI THE DOG!!
YAMASHITA THE YAMASHITA?!
YAMASHITA THE YAMASHITA!!
THE FOUNDING TRIO OF *WEEKLY SHŌNEN CHAMPION*'S VIDEO GAMES BOARD!!

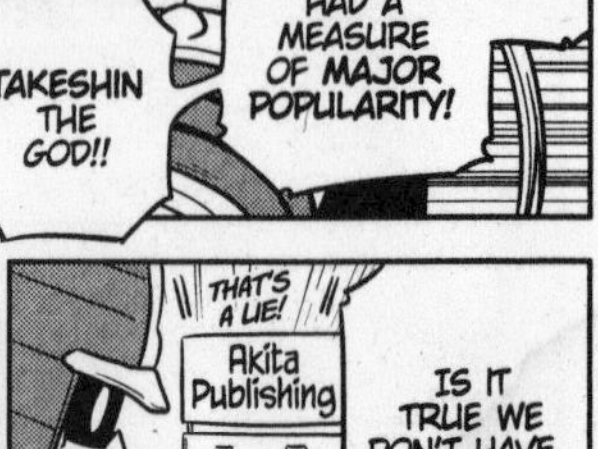
THAT'S A LIE!
Akita Publishing
IS IT TRUE WE DON'T HAVE TO MEET TARGET AGE REQUIREMENTS IF WE'RE UNDER THE DUST JACKET?!
WHERE'D YOU GET *THAT* INFO?

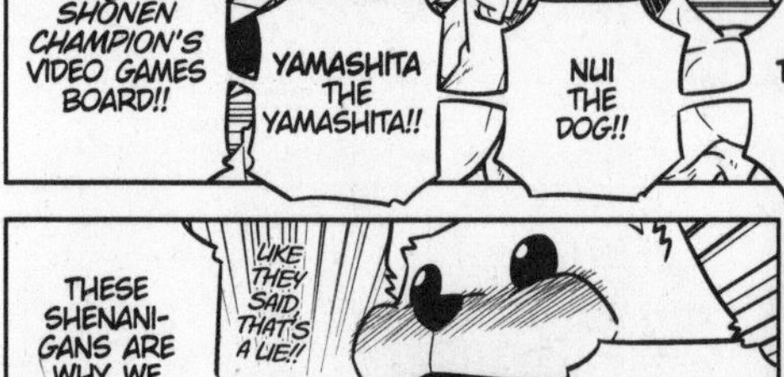
LIKE THEY SAID THAT'S A LIE!!
THESE SHENANIGANS ARE WHY WE AREN'T ALLOWED TO APPEAR IN THE MAIN STORY!!
IF YOU PEEL OFF THE *0.WHATEVS* MILLIMETER COVER, THEN... *HEH HEH HEH!*
IT'S NOT GONNA MATTER WHETHER YOU'RE IN A BOOKSTORE OR A DRUGSTORE!!
Congrats on Volume 1

※ Make sure none of your relatives strip off the dust jack...er, flip to the back of the book.